Kings &

THE TIMES

Queens
of the British Isles

Thomas Cussans

Times Books
An imprint of HarperCollins*Publishers*
1 London Bridge Street
London SE1 9GF

The HarperCollins website address is
www.harpercollins.co.uk

First published by Times Books 2002
This edition published in 2015

The Times is a registered trademark of Times Newspapers
Limited, a subsidiary of News International plc

Copyright © Times Books Ltd 2002, 2004
Edited and designed by D & N Publishing,
Marlborough, Wiltshire

British Library Cataloguing in Publication Data:
A catalogue record is available from the British Library

Printed and bound in China

ISBN: 978-0-00-795007-2

The Times Kings and Queens
of the British Isles
Edited by Thomas Cussans

Maps conceived and compiled by:
András Bereznay

HarperCollins*Publishers*:

Editoral Direction:
Philip Parker

Editorial and Picture Research:
Ceire Clark

Cartographic and Design Direction:
Direction: Martin Brown
Cartography: András Bereznay

D&N Publishing

Editorial and Design Direction:
David Goodfellow

Editorial:
Elizabeth Mallard-Shaw

Design:
Shane O'Dwyer

Proof-reading:
Michael Jones

Index:
Chris Howes

Additional Cartography:
Cosmographics, Watford, England

The publishers would also like to thank Janet Larkin
(Department of Coins & Medals, The British
Museum), Colin Brown, The Bank of Ireland Group,
Old Royal Naval College, Roxburghe Estates

CONTENTS

6 *Contents*

INTRODUCTION

*T*HE AIM OF THIS BOOK IS TO ANSWER A SERIES OF simple questions of the sort that an interested reader might want to ask about the kings and queens of Britain. Who were they? When did they rule? What was noteworthy – or not – about their reigns? What, to the extent that this can be known, were they like as individuals? At the same time, the book attempts to explain in straightforward terms the changing nature of monarchy. Why were there monarchs in the first place? How did monarchy as an institution evolve? How did today's limited, constitutional monarchy come about? It is not a specialist work; it is aimed at the general reader, although the bibliography should help readers in search of more detailed information.

The reasons for believing this a worthwhile exercise are clear-cut. First, the histories of Britain's kings and queens are interesting in themselves. Whether sordid or heroic, indolent or industrious, foolish or far-sighted, each ruler, by virtue of their office, tells us a great deal not just about themselves but about their times. The tragedy of the poor mad Henry VI in the 15th century is no less absorbing than that of the triumphs of the greatest of the Plantagenet kings, Henry II, three centuries earlier.

Second, it is impossible to understand Britain without also understanding at least the outlines of its monarchy. It is no exaggeration to claim that Britain has been defined by monarchy. The shortlived republican experiment of the Commonwealth between 1649 and 1660 aside, the monarchy as an institution has been the foundation of political life in the British Isles for over 1,500 years. Today, Elizabeth II can trace descent from Egbert, the 9th-century king of Wessex. Other than that of Denmark, no other European royal family can lay claim to anything like the same continuity.

The nature of today's monarchy may be very different from that of its medieval counterparts, its actual powers long since given up to Parliament. But it retains a key feature in common with its precursors as the ultimate guarantor of the nation's political legitimacy and stability. Republicans may take the view that the monarchy is anachronistic and a barrier to reform. Yet it is precisely the political stability of Britain that has made it one of the most dependably democratic and conspicuously free countries in the world; it is this political stability that the monarchy underpins. It is no trivial matter.

Almost inevitably, the balance of the coverage of individual rulers is canted in favour of England. This is a reflection of political reality: at least since the emergence of Anglo-Saxon Wessex in the 9th century, England, as it subsequently became, has been the dominant power in the British Isles. Wales, permanently threatened by an expansive England, whether Anglo-Saxon, Norman or Plantagenet, only briefly developed as a separate kingdom until its hold on independence was extinguished by Edward I's remorseless conquest at the end of the 13th century. Ireland, too, despite a marked cultural and religious vibrancy from as early as the 4th century, was always politically fragmented. The Norman takeover of the island after 1169 brought an effective end to Ireland's own kingships, a point rammed home in 1541 when Henry VIII imperiously proclaimed himself King of Ireland.

Even in Scotland, which could claim a continuous existence as an independent kingdom from the 9th century until its formal union with England in 1707, its kings were almost permanently in thrall to their English neighbours. That said, between the deaths of Elizabeth I in 1603 and Anne in 1714, the Stuart kings and queens of Scotland were also – albeit if only by dynastic accident – the rulers of England, the 11 years of the Commonwealth apart. Stuart rule also conveniently highlights a little-remarked fact of English and later British monarchy: that it was scarcely ever English. England as a coherent political entity may have emerged in the reign of Alfred (871–899), but it was ruled by a native Anglo-Saxon dynasty (itself originally Germanic) for less than 180 years. Even this was not continuous. Between 1016 and 1042, Cnut, a Dane, and his sons were kings of England.

Between the Norman Conquest in 1066 and the overthrow of Richard II in 1399, every king of England was clearly and unambiguously French. If it is stretching a point to claim that the Lancastrian and Yorkist kings who followed were French in the same way – time alone had made them English – their dynastic French origins are undeniable.

The following dynasty, the Tudors, who ruled for 118 years, was Welsh, while the Stuarts, who ruled England for 101 years, were Scottish. Thereafter, the Hanoverians, who came to the throne in 1714 and whose direct descendants, the Windsors, remain Britain's ruling family 288 years later, were German. In the 1,131 years since Alfred became king of England, there have been only 169 years when the monarchy has been unambiguously English.

None of this detracts from the unique influence the throne has had not just on the history of England but on that of Britain as a whole. It is a remarkable story, one whose interest only deepens on closer inspection. I hope this modest attempt to sketch its highlights will provoke some readers to look at it more closely.

THOMAS CUSSANS, *London, July 2002*

MYTHS AND ORIGINS

In his *History of the Kings of Britain*, completed probably in 1139, the Welsh cleric Geoffrey of Monmouth traced an unbroken line of 76 British kings who ruled between about 1100 BC and the first arrival of the Romans under Julius Caesar in 55 BC. All, according to Geoffrey, were descended from a Trojan, Brutus, who was the great-grandson of Aeneas and from whom Britain took its name. Among them were Llud, after whom London was named, and Leir, the original of Shakespeare's Lear.

Despite his claims to have based his genealogy on "a certain very ancient book", every one of these pre-Roman kings is fictitious. Geoffrey conjured them into being through an ingenious combination of recycled legend and his own invention.

Similar myths, in this case the product of the Celtic bardic oral tradition, chart the origins of Ireland's high kings. Between the reign of Slaigne the Firbolg (literally "bog man") and AD 1, Ireland was said to have been ruled by 107 high kings, 89 of them called Milesian (or "Son of Mil"). Another myth maintains that the name Scotland is derived from Scota, daughter of the Pharaoh Cingris, who married an early Irish traveller to Egypt. Moses, it is claimed, healed their infant son Goidel, who in turn gave his name to the Gaels.

Such myths are not confined to remote prehistory. Almost all the Anglo-Saxon kings of England claimed descent from the Norse god, Woden. With the coming of Christianity, their origins were often extended even further.

Alfred the Great's contemporary biographer, Bishop Asser, traced Alfred's ancestry, via Noah and Methuselah, to Adam himself.

All countries lay claim to foundation myths. In Europe, most stem from similar pagan, Hebrew, classical and later Christian sources. In most cases, however, these myths are all that is known. This is certainly so of Britain, none of whose pre-Roman rulers is documented. Though the archaeological record highlights the existence of Celtic tribal leaders, a number possibly with pretensions to kingship, individually they are lost in impenetrable obscurity.

It was only as a result of the conquest of Britain by the literate Romans that the first documentary evidence of Britain's rulers is available. Cassivellaunus, leader of the Catuvellauni, enjoys the unique status of being the first Briton whose name is known. Even so, the record is never more than partial. In addition, it is presented in exclusively Roman terms. All the names of tribes and rulers that have come down to us are known only in their Latin forms. The Celtic originals are a matter for arcane speculation at best.

With the slow disintegration of Roman Britain from the early 5th century, the documentary record disappears again. Later histories, often of shadowy, semi-mythical figures, are all that remain. This was the age of the "proud tyrant" Vortigern, who precipitated the Anglo-Saxon takeover of England by recruiting the Saxon mercenaries Hengest and Horsa in his wars against rival Britons. It was also the age of King Arthur, perhaps a local Welsh ruler, certainly not the heroic figure of later legend.

By the early 7th century, however, the picture becomes clearer. And it was then that "kingship" in the sense understood today began, fitfully, to develop. The most important influence in this was Germanic. The word "king" itself, from *cyning* or *kuning*, is of Germanic origin, imported by the Anglo-Saxons who, in the wake of Hengest and Horsa, migrated across the North Sea to the east coasts of Britain. Over the next 150 to 200 years, as they drove the native Britons into the mountainous western extremities of the country – Devon and Cornwall, Wales and southwest Scotland – dozens of Anglo-Saxon kingdoms were created.

If the broad chronology of these events can be reconstructed with some certainty, very little is known of the early rulers themselves. In some cases, only their names have survived; in others, not even that: the existence of many kings can only be inferred. The same is true even of some kingdoms. Of the presumed kingdom of the Middle Saxons (or Middlesex), so named

because it lay between the South Saxons (of Sussex), the West Saxons (of Wessex) and the East Saxons (of Essex), not a single documentary source exists.

This was a world of near permanent instability, dominated by warrior aristocracies, in which the fate of kingdoms was almost entirely dependent on the often transient achievements of their rulers. As kings rose, their kingdoms rose with them; as they fell, their kingdoms fell too.

Nonetheless, a new idea was taking shape: that the right to rule depended as much on legitimacy as on pure force. Whatever their actual route to the throne, rulers increasingly sought to justify their kingship by reference to a higher right, generally an hereditary claim, however bogus, or "designation" by their predecessor.

It was a process crucially reinforced by the spread of Christianity. By encouraging literacy and promoting ideals of Roman law, the Catholic Church introduced the notion of an external authority vested in the person of the king himself. Kings came to be seen as divinely appointed, uniquely equipped to interpret God's will.

In practice, Anglo-Saxon kingship was still an uncertain and brutal business, above all in the permanently vexed matter of succession. That said, the stages by which a chaotic patchwork of competing statelets had given way by the 7th century to just a handful of much larger if still rival kingdoms was the product of – and further stimulus to – the development of a new form of government: kingship.

BRITAIN: THE ROMAN CONQUEST

CELTIC BRITAIN WAS SUCKED INTO ROME'S ORBIT WELL BEFORE ITS FORMAL CONQUEST AFTER AD 43. FROM AT LEAST 100 BC, EXISTING TRADING LINKS ACROSS THE CHANNEL WERE SUPPLEMENTED BY GROWING ECONOMIC AND POLITICAL CONTACTS WITH ROME. ALL THE EVIDENCE SUGGESTS THE PRESENCE OF AN INCREASINGLY SOPHISTICATED SOCIETY, ESPECIALLY IN SOUTHERN BRITAIN.

For all his ringing assertion that he came, saw and conquered, Julius Caesar's (above left) two invasions of Britain were military disasters. Politically, however, they were hugely successful, and went far to reinforce Caesar's position as Rome's pre-eminent general. As important, they planted in Roman minds the idea of a future conquest of Britain.

From its beachhead in Kent, Rome's 40-year conquest of Britain was carried through with relentless efficiency (map left). By AD 83, the Romans had entirely subdued England and Wales and penetrated far into Scotland. The effects of the Roman take-over were uneven, however. Over much of Wales and almost all of Scotland, Romanization was never more than skin-deep: the Celtic roots of both regions, never eradicated, resurfaced, contributing significantly to the instability of the late-Roman period.

Advising against Emperor Claudius's projected invasion of Britain in AD 43, the geographer Strabo pointed out that "local chieftains have made virtually the whole island a Roman possession". Strictly speaking, this was not true: most of the north and west of Britain and all of Ireland remained outside Roman influence. Nonetheless, his point was well made. Even before Julius Caesar's two abortive invasions of Britain in 55 and 54 BC, mutually lucrative trading links were drawing central and southern Britain into the wider Roman world. As Strabo implied, the chief beneficiaries in Britain were its rulers, avid consumers of Roman luxury goods.

There were probably 20 major Celtic tribes in Britain at the time. Much of what is known of them – and almost everything about their rulers – comes from Roman sources. According to Julius Caesar, the leading tribe, ruled by Cassivellaunus, or Caswallawn, were the Catuvellauni, based to the north of what became London. Among other important southern powers were the Trinovantes in modern-day Essex, the Cantiaci (in Kent), the Regnenses (in Sussex) and the Atrebates (in Hampshire). To the north, the dominant power were the Brigantes, who headed a loose confederation of sub-

THE ROMAN CONQUEST

▨	Roman territory by 54 BC
→	Caesar's campaign, 54 BC
ICENI	Celtic tribes c. AD 43
▪▪▪▪	Limit of Roman conquest by AD 43
⌐¬	Roman client kingdoms in c. AD 40–50, with details
▨	Limit of Roman conquest by AD 83
⧄	Approximate extent of Boudicca's revolt AD 60–61
—	Northern frontier of the Roman Empire from AD 105
⧄	Temporarily added to Roman Empire, 142–85

(Right) *The benefits of embracing Roman rule could be considerable. Even so, few went as far as Togidubnus, king of the Regnenses, who in effect turned himself into a Roman, styling himself Tiberius Claudius Cogidumnus and building himself a magnificent Roman palace at Fishbourne outside Chichester, complete with intricate mosaic floors.*

55–54BC	c. AD *10*	43	47	50	60
Julius Caesar's failed invasions	*Cunobelinus, king of the Trinovantes and Catuvellauni, allied to Rome*	*Claudius launches renewed invasion*	*Southeast England (to the Humber) under Roman control*	*Caratacus captured*	*Druids on Anglesey defeated; revolt of Iceni under Boudicca*

tribes. Further north still were the Caledonii, the most numerous tribe in what would become Scotland.

It was Cassivellaunus who spear-headed the resistance to Julius Caesar. But this is not to suggest that the Celts were in any sense united against the Roman invaders. They had little sense of a wider Celtic identity, and intertribal rivalry was a permanent fact of life. In fact, there is a strong probability that Caesar was invited to Britain by tribes resentful of Cassivellaunus's aggressive expansionism and who saw an alliance with Rome as the best means of reasserting their local rule. It is known for example that Caesar was accompanied on his first invasion by Commius, the king of the Atrebates,

Close on a century followed before the Romans attempted to conquer Britain again. This time, the invasion was mounted with overwhelming force, upwards of 50,000 men. Resistance was sporadic. Most rulers chose co-operation rather than confrontation, only too happy to become client-kings of Rome. The Iceni under Prasutagus, the Brigantes under Queen Cartimandua, and the Regnenses under Togidubnus, all committed themselves to Roman rule. Even the king of distant Orkney is said to have acknowledged Roman supremacy.

Those who did resist were ruthlessly pursued. Caratacus, the son of Cunobelinus (see box), was driven progressively further west until, finally defeated in AD 50, he fled north to the Brigantes where Queen Cartimandua promptly handed him over to her new allies. In AD 60 the Iceni, led by

their formidable queen, Boudicca, rose almost as one, laying waste to Colchester and St Albans before moving on London. In the ensuing battles, 70,000 – the vast majority of them Britons – are said to have been slain. The Roman response was remorseless. Boudicca and her army were utterly destroyed.

As the Romans under Julius Agricola pushed their rule north and west, the remaining resistance was gradually crushed in campaigns that took place between AD 77 and 84. They climaxed in the Highlands of Scotland at Mons Graupius, where the Caledonii were defeated. Scotland may never have been fully incorporated into the Roman Empire and Roman rule in Wales and large parts of northern England never have penetrated very deeply, but Britain had been brought definitively within the Roman world.

Among the most striking evidence for Britain's economic links with Rome in the 1st century BC was the appearance of coins. As well as highlighting the increasing economic sophistication sparked by contact with Rome, they are uniquely revealing about Celtic kings and tribes. The first British monarch to appear on a coin (above right), minted in about 10 BC, was Tasciovan, successor to Cassivellaunus as the king of the Catuvellauni. Twenty years later, his successor, Cunobelinus, produced a series of gold coins bearing not only his name but the inscription AUGUSTUS DIVUS, the "Divine Augustus" being the Emperor Augustus, with whom the Catuvellauni were clearly allied. A further 20 years later, his coins (below) were marked simply CUNOBELINUS REX or CUN CAMU (a reference to the tribe's name), equally strong evidence of a break with Rome and the assertion of his own kingship. A number of other Celtic rulers, Volisios of the Coritani and Bodvoc of the Dobunni, for example, are known only through surviving coins.

Cunobelinus

Cunobelinus, king of the Trinovantes from AD 1 and of the Catuvellauni from AD 10, both of whom he conquered by force, ranks high as one of the great mythical figures of the immediate pre-Roman age. He figures strongly in Geoffrey of Monmouth's always unreliable History of the Kings of Britain, apparently influenced in this instance by the Roman writer Suetonius, who called Cunobelinus "Rex Britannorum". This he certainly wasn't, for all that he was the most powerful ruler of his day. The Tudor author Raphael Holinshead glamorized Cunobelinus further, claiming that he was brought up in Rome, "and there made knight by Augustus Caesar, vnder whome he serued in the warres, and was in such fauour with him, that he was at libertie to pay his tribute or not…". Whatever the inaccuracies of this account, they were the stimulus for Shakespeare's play Cymbeline in which he is described as the king of Britain. Cunobelinus's sons Togodumnus and Caratacus were in the forefront of resistance to the invasion in AD 43. Caratacus was paraded in chains through Rome after his capture in AD 50, his dignity impressing the emperor so much that he was pardoned and allowed to live in Rome until his death. Togodumnus was killed in battle against the Romans, possibly in Hampshire, soon after Claudius's invasion.

68	71	77–84	85	122	142
Southwest England and central Wales under Roman control	Uprising of Brigantes under Venutius crushed	Campaigns of Julius Agricola subdue Wales, northern England and southern and eastern Scotland	Progressive evacuation of southern Scotland (to 105)	Hadrian's Wall begun	Progressive reoccupation of southern Scotland (to 163); Antonine Wall begun

THE FIRST ANGLO-SAXON KINGDOMS

Gold purse lid discovered at Sutton Hoo (above). The level of craftsmanship of many of the objects discovered at Sutton Hoo transformed understanding of the Anglo-Saxon kingdoms.

THE DEPARTURE OF THE LAST ROMAN LEGIONS IN 407 PLUNGED BRITAIN INTO CHAOS. THERE WERE RENEWED INVASIONS FROM SCOTLAND, WHILE IN ENGLAND AND WALES RESURGENT CELTIC LEADERS STRUGGLED WITH THOSE TRYING TO MAINTAIN A SEMBLANCE OF ROMAN ORDER. INTO THIS VOLATILE MIX A NEW ELEMENT WAS ADDED AS GERMANIC PEOPLES MIGRATED ACROSS THE NORTH SEA TO BRITAIN.

The exact process by which the chaos of the immediate post-Roman period gave way to a Germanic Anglo-Saxon England can be reconstructed only tentatively. That said, it is clear that by about the mid-6th century a series of more or less stable Anglo-Saxon kingdoms were taking root across England.

The arrival of the Anglo-Saxons was just one part of the general westward migration of peoples into the former territories of the West Roman Empire. But it was also a response to the unfolding chaos in Britain itself, in which Celts fought Celts, Romano-Britons fought Romano-Britons and each fought the other. Among those struggling for supremacy was the Welshman Coel Hen, immortalized much later as "Old King Cole", who was possibly a Roman commander. Another such Roman commander-turned-warlord was Vitalinus, known variously as the Vawrtighern or Vortigern, the "Supreme Leader".

Sutton Hoo

The excavation in 1939 of a ship burial at Sutton Hoo, at the head of the river Deben, transformed understanding of Anglo-Saxon England. Not only did the burial accord closely with the description of a royal funeral in Beowulf – "Rime-crusted and ready to sail, a royal vessel with curved prow lay in harbour. They set down their dear king amidships, close by the mast" – but it revealed a treasure hoard of astonishing richness, by far the most extensive and important archaeological discovery of the period ever made. The sumptuousness of the objects makes it clear that this was the resting place of a king: among the candidates, Raedwald, king of East Anglia and listed by Bede as the fourth Bretwalda, is favourite. The magnificent armour, not least the king's helmet (right), with its bronze, silver and gold overlays, underline his warrior status. Objects such as the gold purse lid, with stone, garnet and glass inlays, display exquisite craftsmanship. Equally intriguing in what was clearly a pagan burial was the presence of two spoons, one bearing the name Paul, the other Saul. The Christian reference is clear – as is the fact that early 7th-century Anglo-Saxon England was a world straddling a pagan past and a Christian future.

449 In this year Mauricius and Valentinian obtained the kingdom and reigned seven years. In their days, Hengest and Horsa, invited by Vortigern, King of the Britons, came to Britain at a place called Ypwines fleot at first to help the Britons, but later they fought against them. They then sent to Angeln, ordered [them] to send more aid and to be told of the worthlessness of the Britons and of the excellence of the land. They then sent them more aid. These men came from three nations of Germany: from the old Saxons, from the Angles, and from the Jutes.

The Anglo-Saxon Chronicle

It was Vortigern who at some point around 430 may have recruited the Saxon mercenaries Hengest and Horsa to help repulse the Picts. Having arrived, Hengest and his followers simply stayed, establishing a kingdom in Kent. At much the same time, other Germanic settlers were arriving – the Angles on the east coast, the "South Saxons" along the Channel. They, too, began to establish their own territories, which in time became kingdoms. The net result was a gradual northward and eastward infiltration of Germanic rule into England.

The process was by no means certain or clear-cut. The Germanic settlements were piece-meal and uncoordinated, and the newcomers were

c.430	477	c.500	597	c.616	617	c.625	664
Saxon mercenaries Hengest and Horsa recruited by Vortigern	Reputed landing of Aelle, first king of Sussex, on south coast	Saxons defeated at Mount Badon	Christian mission under St Augustine, sent by Pope Gregory, lands in Kent	Northumbria united under Edwin	Conversion of Edwin to Christianity	Burial of King Raedwald at Sutton Hoo	Synod of Whitby accepts Roman authority in matters of Church doctrine

The arrival of the Anglo-Saxons drove the native Celts of Britain westwards and northwards (map left), *beginning a cultural divide that persists today.*

THE FIRST ANGLO-SAXON KINGDOMS, TO C.AD 600

- Roman Empire c. 450
- Approximate Anglo-Saxon homeland
- Presumed direction of Anglo-Saxon emigration to Britain, c.5th–6th centuries
- Frankish Empire, 532
- Approximate limit of Anglo-Saxon control, late 5th century
- United as Northumbria, 604
- Approxiate western limit of Anglo-Saxon control, late 6th century
- Added to Northumbria under Ethelfred and Edwin, by 632
- Mercian expansion under Penda
- To Mercia 628: sub-kingdom of Hwicce from mid-7th century
- Approximate northern limit of expansion of Northumbria under Oswald, 642

often as hostile to each other as they were to the Britons, a rivalry that would persist well into the 9th century. Furthermore, native resistance, however sporadic, could be effective. A major reverse was suffered by the Anglo-Saxons in about 500 at the battle of Mount Badon, later claimed to have been won by the elusive if not wholly mythical figure of King Arthur (see box). Nonetheless, by the end of the 6th century, Anglo-Saxon kingdoms were established across the whole of England, Cornwall apart.

Seven kingdoms – the so-called "Heptarchy" – are traditionally identified. Three were clustered in the

King Arthur

Even if it is now generally accepted that Arthur was a real figure, possibly a Welsh prince who fought against the Anglo-Saxons in the late 5th and early 6th centuries, few rulers have loomed larger in popular imagination on more meagre evidence. The earliest reference to him dates from over 400 years after his presumed lifetime. The 12th-century writer Geoffrey of Monmouth was the man most responsible for launching the cult of Arthur, conflating a series of legends to produce an extraordinary story in which, having conquered the Anglo-Saxons, Arthur subdued Scotland and Gaul. "Britain," wrote Geoffrey, "had reached such a standard of sophistication that it excelled all other kingdoms in its general affluence, the richness of its decorations and the courteous behaviour of its inhabitants." Arthur then defeated the Roman emperor before having to return hurriedly to Britain to deal with the traitor Mordred. It was an improbable epic that later writers — seeing in Arthur the epitome of medieval, above all French, chivalry — embroidered even further. Sir Thomas Malory's 15th-century work, Le Morte D'Arthur, *remains the best-known example.*

southeast: Sussex, Kent and Essex. To the west was Wessex. The Midlands were dominated by the kingdoms of East Anglia and Mercia, which abutted the patchwork of Celtic territories in Wales and included the sub-kingdoms of Lindsey, Hwicce and

655	from 716	731	from 756	780	787	825	829
King Penda of Mercia defeated and killed by Northumbrians under Oswy at Battle of Winwaed	Mercian supremacy under Aethelbald begins	Bede's Ecclesiastical History of England completed	Mercian supremacy extended under Offa	Offa begins the construction of his defensive barrier between Mercia and Wales	First Viking raid, on south coast	King Egbert of Wessex breaks Mercian supremacy at Battle of Ellendun	Northumbria acknowledges supremacy of Wessex

The 30,000-line epic Anglo-Saxon poem, Beowulf *(left), which dates from between the 7th and the 10th centuries, is among the most vivid contemporary records of the occupations and conduct of Anglo-Saxon kings. Long assumed to be at least partly fantasy, the discovery of the Sutton Hoo treasure strongly suggests that the poem may be accurately rooted in reality.*

Northumbrian expansion in the 7th century brought it into conflict with its British, Pictish and Gaelic neighbours to the north as well as with Anglo-Saxon Mercia to the south (map below). Subsequent Mercian expansion was at the cost of further conflict with its increasingly powerful southern Anglo-Saxon neighbour, Wessex.

Magonsaete. To the north was Northumbria, literally the kingdom "north of the Humber", which was an amalgam of two earlier kingdoms, Bernicia and Deira.

In very general terms, the subsequent development of these kingdoms was that of the domination – under a succession of powerful rulers and through a maze of confused power-struggles – of three of these kingdoms: Northumbria and Mercia in the 7th century, Mercia by itself in the 8th century, and Wessex in the 9th. Under Edwin (d. 633), Oswald (d. 642) and Oswy (d. 670), Northumbria not only extended

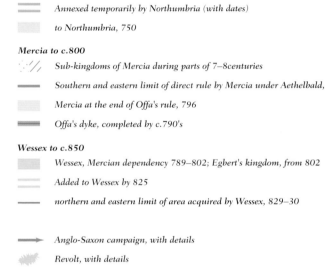

IN SEARCH OF ANGLO-SAXON UNITY
c.650–850

Northumbria to c.750

- Northumbria under Oswiu, 657
- Annexed temporarily by Northumbria (with dates)
- to Northumbria, 750

Mercia to c.800

- Sub-kingdoms of Mercia during parts of 7–8 centuries
- Southern and eastern limit of direct rule by Mercia under Aethelbald,
- Mercia at the end of Offa's rule, 796
- Offa's dyke, completed by c.790's

Wessex to c.850

- Wessex, Mercian dependency 789–802; Egbert's kingdom, from 802
- Added to Wessex by 825
- northern and eastern limit of area acquired by Wessex, 829–30

- Anglo-Saxon campaign, with details
- Revolt, with details
- ✕ Battles

its domination deep into Scotland and westwards to Wales, it also subdued Mercia, whose first great king and warlord, Penda, was defeated and killed by Oswy in 655. Northumbrian power began to wane after 685 with the defeat and death of its then king, Aegfrith, at the hands at the Picts. Mercian power reached its apex under Offa, who from the mid-780s was effectively exercising hegemony over most of Anglo-Saxon England. From Offa's death, in 796, the supremacy of Wessex was established under Egbert, who extended West Saxon control into Cornwall before defeating the Mercians at the Battle of Ellendun in 825. Four years later, he received the submission of the Northumbrian king, Eanred.

This may still have been an unstable, often violent world, but it was one increasingly dominated by a more sophisticated ideal of kingship in which a single king ruled a single more or less well-defined territory. To the traditional role of the king as warrior chief a new notion was added: that of the king as dispenser of justice and source of a

We have come to the conclusion that the temples of the idols ... should on no account be destroyed. He [Augustine] is to destroy the idols, but the temples themselves are to be aspersed with holy water, altars set up, and relics enclosed in them ... In this way, we hope that people may abandon idolatry ... They are no longer to sacrifice beasts to the Devil, but they may kill them for food to the praise of God ... If the people are allowed some worldly pleasures ... they will come more readily to desire the joys of the spirit.

Instructions from Pope Gregory
the Great to Augustine on the
conversion of the Anglo-Saxons

Offa's Dyke

*I*n about 780 – in an effort both to delimit the border of his kingdom with Wales and to prevent Welsh infiltration into it – King Offa of Mercia began one of the most remarkable building projects in medieval Europe. It was a dyke, or earth barrier, running the full length of Mercia's 149-mile border with Wales. It was not an entirely original idea. A hundred years earlier, King Wat (or Wade) had undertaken the construction of a similar dyke. But Offa's was to be on an altogether different scale: 11 feet high and 22 yards wide. Given the limitations of the technology available to him, it is an extraordinary achievement, for all that some northern sections were never completed. It remains a testimony not just to the energy and determination of Offa but to the organizing ability of his kingdom. Thousands of peasants were employed over many years to create the barrier. Substantial sections survive today.

body of external wisdom to which he alone, sanctioned by his royal birth and office, had access.

Consciousness of this new role is evident at least in part in the title Bretwalda, variously translated as "Power Wielder" or "Ruler of Britain". According to the 8th-century Northumbrian monk, Bede, whose *Ecclesiastical History of England* is the most complete and reliable contemporary source for Anglo-Saxon England, the first Bretwalda was Aelle, king of Sussex, at the end of the 5th century. Bede lists a further six Bretwaldas, ending with the Northumbrian, Oswy, in the 7th century.

In reality, any such claim to rule all Britain would have been at odds with the still confused condition of the country. Nonetheless, kings such as Oswy, Offa and Egbert were slowly coming to preside over kingdoms that were increasingly better governed and prosperous and that were also capable of disposing of considerable resources. These resources were not just military might and manpower, though the building of Offa's dyke after 780 is a graphic illustration of the great extent to which such means were available to the Mercian king (see box). This was also an increasingly literate and artistically advanced society with contacts well beyond the narrow confines of Anglo-Saxon England. The Sutton Hoo treasure demonstrates levels of craftsmanship and access to precious metals and jewels that can scarcely be said to be the products of a "primitive" society. A similarly vivid amalgam of pagan and Christian forms is represented by the Lindisfarne Gospels, produced from 698 onwards at the Northumbrian monastery of Lindisfarne and incontestably among the great works of early-medieval European art.

The Lindisfarne Gospels highlight a further essential feature of Anglo-Saxon England: that it had become Christian, the result of a two-pronged missionary push southwards from Scotland by Irish missionaries, and northwards, after 597, on the initiative of Pope Gregory the Great. Though England's pagan roots would occasionally resurface, by 664 and the Synod of Whitby (called by Oswy to determine the supremacy of Roman or Irish Christian practice), Christianity was accepted by the great mass of the Anglo-Saxon population.

The Christian conquest of Britain was significant less for doctrinal reasons than because it encouraged literacy – a fundamental requirement of good government – and brought the Anglo-Saxons into contact with a wider European world that was itself rediscovering the essentials of stable government. But like the Anglo-Saxons themselves, Christianity was to be threatened by a new and terrible threat: the Vikings.

Offa was amongst the first Anglo-Saxon monarchs to mint silver coins. The lettering on this coin (above) is characteristically elegant and clear. Though otherwise obscure, the early 9th-century East Anglian king, Athelstan, seems to have been the first monarch to produce coins describing himself as REX ANG, or King of the English. (below).

The magnificent objects of the kind unearthed at Sutton Hoo were not the only manifestation of the creative energies of Anglo-Saxon England. From the late 7th century, at the remote Northumbrian monastery of Lindisfarne (founded by St Aidan, a monk from the Irish monastery at Iona in Scotland), an exceptional series of illustrated books were produced. Collectively known as the Lindisfarne Gospels, *they are uniquely revealing of the profound spirituality and learning that infused these early northern outposts of the Church (left). Though many of the same swirling, spiralling motifs seen at Sutton Hoo are used, here they are unambiguously pressed into the service of the Christian Church. It is likely that the books were meant for the shrine of the mystic St Cuthbert on the even more remote island of Farne.*

WALES TO 1284

THE COLLAPSE OF ROMAN RULE SPARKED A RESURGENCE OF NATIVE CELTIC KINGDOMS ACROSS BRITAIN, ABOVE ALL IN AREAS SUCH AS WALES THAT HAD BEEN ONLY LIGHTLY ROMANIZED. YET MUCH SUBSEQUENT WELSH HISTORY WAS ONE OF INTERNAL DIVISION AND OF SUBJUGATION BY ITS LARGER ENGLISH NEIGHBOUR. DESPITE A SUCCESSION OF STRONG LEADERS, BY 1284 WALES HAD FALLEN UNDER PERMANENT ENGLISH CONTROL.

The 10th-century Welsh king Hywel Dda (above) held sway over a kingdom even greater in extent than that of his 9th-century predecessor Rhodri Mawr. His rule encompassed Deheubarth, Gwynedd and Powys. He sought to impose stronger central control and in 945 codified the Welsh laws.

No less than Anglo-Saxon England, Wales between the 5th and 9th centuries saw the growth of a shifting mosaic of competing states ruled by a rapidly changing cast of kings and sub-kings, clan and tribal leaders. Though the external difficulties facing these territories were often formidable – Irish settlers, Viking raiders and, above all, the expansionist Anglo-Saxons to the east – by the 10th century four dominant kingdoms had emerged: Gwent and Deheubarth in the south, and Gwynedd and Powys in the north. Wales seemed poised to develop as a centralized, unitary state.

In the event, this apparently nascent statehood proved stillborn. Critically, the Welsh never developed the more sophisticated mechanisms of government that underpinned Anglo-Saxon and Norman England. In addition, while providing strong local identities, Welsh tribal origins worked against the formation of an overarching national identity.

The country was also handicapped by geography. There was little to distinguish the south from neighbouring England – in many places the two merged seamlessly. The mountainous north, by contrast, had always been something of a land apart, with little more in common with south Wales than with its English neighbours. Crucially, north–south communication was exceptionally difficult.

Welsh law provided a further inhibiting factor. Until its repeal in the 13th century, partible inheritance – by which a king's holdings had to be divided among all his sons – made dynastic consolidation all but impossible. It is no accident that the achievements of strong rulers were rarely sustained in the following generation.

That said, Welsh disunity and, ultimately, domination by England were never a foregone conclusion. In 633, for example, Cadwallon, the ruler of Gwynedd, aided by Penda, king of Mercia, inflicted a devastating defeat on the great Northumbrian king, Edwin. Had Cadwallon brought Northumbria into his own kingdom, he would have made himself the greatest ruler in Britain. Instead, he spent the next year laying waste to Northumbria until he was killed in further fighting with the Northumbrians.

Welsh hopes revived in the 9th century under Rhodri Mawr, "the Great", who united Gwynedd, Powys and the smaller kingdom of Seisyllwg, in the process triumphing in a series of near simultaneous campaigns against the Danes and the Anglo-Saxons. But his gains were frittered away with his death in 878.

A more lasting contribution was made in the 10th century by Hywel Dda, "the Good". By 942, his rule covered Deheubarth, Gwynedd and Powys. Hywel recognized early that Wales was best served by co-operation with the Anglo-Saxons. The price was high, however. In 918 Hywel secured peace for Wales by acknowledging Edward the Elder, king of Wessex, as his feudal master. As a result, all subsequent English monarchs would claim the overlordship of Wales, a claim they would back up with force whenever they were strong enough. Nonetheless, Hywel had understood a central truth: that England was strong because it was well governed. His own attempts to introduce more efficient government to Wales focused on a far-sighted revision of the country's myriad local laws in 945. Significantly,

The Marcher Lordships

The creation of the Marcher lordships by William the Conqueror had a profound impact on Wales. William's goal was to isolate the potentially troublesome Welsh by allocating the Anglo-Welsh border to a number of his key nobles, William Fitz Osbern, Roger Montgomery and Hugh d'Avranches, who became the earls of Hereford, Shrewsbury and Chester respectively. In turn, they were allowed to take over whatever Welsh territories they could grab and administer them in any way they saw fit. Though the Marcher lords themselves were feudal subjects of the king, their territories were not technically part of his kingdom. A series of lesser Marcher lordships were created soon afterwards. A second wave of Marcher settlement followed in the reign of William Rufus. Though unable to penetrate the mountainous north, the Normans, with the Earl of Shrewsbury to the fore, carved out huge new territories in South Wales, subjecting them to a colonial conquest that was brutal even by Norman standards. The Normans' failure to conquer northern Wales had the unintended side-effect of partitioning Wales into what became known as Marchia Walliae, the March, and Pura Wallia , "deep" or "proper" Wales.

c.440	633	c.780	844–78	918	945	1055	1063	after 1066	1093
Irish settlers expelled by Cunedda, legendary founder of Gwynedd	Northumbria laid waste by Cadwallon	Construction of Offa's Dyke begun	Hegemony of Rhodri Mawr over Wales	Hywel Dda submits to Edward the Elder	Codification of Welsh laws by Hywel Dda	Gruffydd ap Llywelyn effective sovereign of Wales	Anglo-Saxon invasion overthrows Gruffydd ap Llywelyn	Marcher Lordships established	Second wave of Marcher settlement launched

Hywel remains the only Welsh king to have issued his own coinage.

The subsequent history of independent Wales was a paradoxical mixture of internal fragmentation and English conquest – by Anglo-Saxons, Normans, Angevins and Plantagenets alike – accompanied by near simultaneous regeneration and self-assertion under a number of exceptional rulers. Ultimately, however, whatever their achievements, the kings of Wales would prove no match for the increasingly powerful rulers of medieval England.

The career of the fearsomely warlike Gruffydd ap Llywelyn is a case in point. By 1055, Gruffydd had not merely destroyed his rivals in Wales: his military grip was such that he was effectively able to oblige Edward the Confessor's England to recognize him as sole ruler of Wales. In 1057 the Anglo-Saxons duly came to terms; in turn, Gruffydd acknowledged Edward as his feudal lord. The respite was brief. A whirlwind Anglo-Saxon campaign was launched against Gruffydd in 1063 under Harold Godwine. Having destroyed Gruffydd's armies, Harold demanded that the Welsh hand over their sovereign. Rather than risk further Anglo-Saxon depredations, Gruffydd's erstwhile supporters cut off his head and sent it to Harold as a sign of their submission.

The Norman Conquest in 1066 was no less a disaster for Wales than for England. Determined to pen the Welsh into their ancestral homelands, William the Conqueror turned the Anglo-Welsh border, the "March", into a series of private principalities under the control of his most important nobles (see box). There they were free to do much as they pleased. The result was the imposition of voracious Norman rule across the eastern border of the country and all of the south.

Welsh resistance centred around Owain ap Gruffudd, king of Gwynedd (1137–70), and the long-lived Rhys ap Gruffydd (1155–97), king of

Early coins are not just a significant source of information about early British rulers, they are a certain sign of political as much as of economic stability. It remains a striking fact that, whatever the pretensions to nationhood and overlordship of a number of Welsh kings, only one, Hywel Dda in the 10th century, issued his own coins (left).

Deheubarth. Both not only reconquered substantial territories from the marcher lords but withstood major campaigns by the otherwise formidable Henry II. The resulting stalemate culminated in a rapprochement in 1163. Owain was allowed to take the title Prince of Wales at the cost of reaffirming Henry's overlordship. A further rapprochement, between Henry and Rhys, in which Henry acknowledged

Fragmented and remote, Wales never emerged as a unified state. Although strong kings such as Hywel Dda and Gruffydd ap Llywelyn did temporarily unite large parts of the country (map below), after their deaths these holdings fell away or were divided between their children. Wales was also persistently threatened by the Anglo-Saxons as well as by the Norman conquerors of Anglo-Saxon England. The means to turn its fierce local identities into an overarching state remained elusive.

WALES TO 1100

————	Frontiers of Welsh states, c. 800
	Possessions of Rhodri Mawr, 872
▭	Limit of area held by Hywel Dda, 942–50
	Possessions of Maredudd ap Owain, 999
	Possessions of Gruffydd ap Llywelyn, c. 1057
➡	Norman campaigns, 1067–94
⟍⟍	Welsh control, 1094
▬	Core area of Welsh revolt, 1094
➡	Welsh counterattack, with dates
———	Western limit of area retained by the Normans, 1100

1137	1155	1163	1165	1194	1210	1247	1267	1277–84	1301
Owain ap Gruffudd King of Gwynedd	Rhys ap Gruffydd King of Deheubarth	Owain ap Gruffudd submits to Henry II and is recognized as Prince of Wales	Attempted conquest of Wales by Henry II	Llywelyn the Great king of Gwynedd	Llywelyn Fawr declares himself Prince of Wales	Treaty of Woodstock: Llywelyn ap Gruffudd submits to Henry II	Treaty of Montgomery: Henry III recognizes Llywelyn ap Gruffudd as Prince of Wales	Edward I's conquest of Wales	Edward's heir granted title of Prince of Wales

Edward I's massive military campaigns against the Welsh were followed by a programme of castle building that amounted to the largest and most expensive construction projects in Britain since the erection of Hadrian's Wall (such as Kidwelly Castle, above). In addition to their obvious military purpose, these immense structures – "the badge of our subjection" – had a crude psychological role in that they served as permanent reminders to the Welsh of their oppression.

WALES 1100–1284

- ------- Frontiers of Welsh states, c. 1188
- Gwynedd under Llywelyn the Great, c.1212
- Brought under control of Llywelyn the Great by 1234
- → Campaigns of Llywelyn the Great (with date)
- ☐ Welsh states, vassal to England under Treaty of Woodstock, 1247
- → Campaigns of Llywelyn ap Gruffydd, 1255–57
- ⋯⋯ Frontier of Llywelyn ap Gruffydd's Welsh principality under Treaty of Montgomery, 1267
- → Edward I's campaigns 1277–78
- ⧅ Welsh states, vassal to England under Treaty of Aberconway, 1277

Wales in the 13th century, first under Llywelyn the Great, then under Llywelyn ap Gruffydd, had never seemed to be more likely to assert itself as a unified, independent state (map right). Edward I's brutal campaigns against the Welsh in 1277–8 established an English domination it has never been able to escape.

Gruffydd ap Llywelyn

Fanning the flames of inter-Welsh rivalries to ensure the country's instability was a long-standing English tactic. In 1241, for example, the Welsh king Dafydd ap Llywelyn was holding his half-brother and rival claimant to his throne, Gruffydd, prisoner. Henry III forced Dafydd to release his brother and in turn imprisoned him in the Tower of London. His aim was to make Dafydd hand over territories won during the reign of his father, Llywelyn Fawr. If he refused, Henry threatened to release Gruffydd knowing he would immediately set about the overthrow of his brother. Such was the stuff of medieval realpolitik. In the event, Henry's scheme came to nothing. Gruffydd, in trying to escape from the Tower by climbing down a knotted sheet, fell to his death (left).

King Henry [II] gathered a mighty host ... planning to carry off or destroy all the Britons [Welsh]. And against him came Owain Gwynedd and his brother and all the host of Gwynedd, and the Lord Rhys ap Gruffudd and all Deheubarth and many others ... a few picked Welshmen who knew not how to admit defeat, manfully fought against him, and many of the bravest fell on both sides. Then ... [the king's] provisions failed and he withdrew to the plains of England. And filled with rage he blinded his hostages, two sons of Owain Gwynedd and a son of the Lord Rhys and others.

Chronicle of the Princes *or* Brut y Tywysogyon, *1165*

Rhys as his "justiciar" in Deheubarth, took place in 1172. The net result, however, was that the minor Welsh princes and Norman Marcher lords alike felt themselves undermined. The last years of Rhys's reign saw a series of inconclusive campaigns against him by elements of his former Welsh followers and the Marcher lords, often in uneasy alliance.

A dramatic revival of Welsh pride occurred under Llywelyn Fawr, "the Great", who by 1212 had not only firmly established himself as Prince of Wales but had faced down an attempted English invasion by King John. As important, and in the face of substantial Welsh resistance, he also overturned the long-established principle of partible inheritance. In 1240 his son Dafydd inherited a united crown whose prospects had never been more promising.

Within 27 years they were more promising yet. Llywelyn's grandson, Llywelyn ap Gruffydd, having decisively rebuffed an attempt by Henry III of England to fragment his grandfather's gains, was reluctantly recognized by Henry as the country's sole ruler. It was the first time a single Welsh king had ruled a single Welsh state. It was also the last.

It was Llywelyn's misfortune to come up against the most implacable of England's medieval rulers, Edward I. His first invasion of the country, in 1277, reduced Wales to little more than a rump state centred on Gwynedd. His second, in 1282, exterminated it. Llywelyn himself was killed in a chance skirmish towards the end of the campaign. Had he survived, it would probably have made no difference. Under the 1284 Statute of Wales, the independent existence of Wales was formally ended.

In 1301 Edward I (above) appropriated the ancient Welsh title of Prince of Wales and bestowed it upon his 17-year-old son and heir, Edward, in the very un-Welsh setting of Lincoln. The gesture may have been deliberately contemptuous, but the eldest son of the monarch has taken the title ever since.

SCOTLAND TO c.842

LACK OF NATURAL BORDERS TO ITS SOUTH, THE ABSENCE OF ALL BUT THE MOST BASIC MECHANISMS OF CENTRAL GOVERNMENT, AND THE RIVAL AMBITIONS OF DISPARATE PEOPLES – PICTS, IRISH, BRITONS AND ANGLES – MADE THE EMERGENCE OF A UNIFIED SCOTTISH KINGDOM AN UNCERTAIN AND USUALLY VIOLENT PROCESS. BY THE 9TH CENTURY, HOWEVER, THE OUTLINES OF WHAT WOULD BECOME SCOTLAND WERE HARDENING.

Fergus Mor, traditionally the first king of Dal Riada (above), *migrated from the north of Ireland to the area around present-day Argyll around AD 498. He is said to have brought with him the Stone of Destiny upon which subsequent Scottish kings would be crowned.*

Dunadd Fort (below) *was the capital of the Irish kingdom of Dal Riada, established at the end of the 5th century around Argyll. The stone, bearing the footprint of a boar (left) and an ogham inscription (right) may have played a part in the inauguration rituals of the Dal Riadan kings.*

At the time of the collapse of Roman Britain in the early 5th century, by far the largest group in Scotland were the Picts, who may have arrived in Scotland in the middle of the first millennium BC. Divided loosely into northern and southern Picts, the Caledonii and the Maetae respectively, their territories extended over most of the Highlands and Islands. Though later king lists and other legends clearly indicate the antiquity of Pictish rule, almost nothing is known of individual Pictish rulers before the mid-6th century.

By this point the Picts had long been engaged in a power struggle with the Irish kingdom of Dal Riada, which was beginning to be established – possibly from as early as the 4th century – in what is now Argyll (from Ar-gael or "the eastern Irish"). In time, the Irish settlers would be given another name, the Scotti, from the Latin name for the Irish. It was the ultimate success of the Dal Riadans in subsuming their much larger Pictish neighbours to form a new kingdom that would in turn give Scotland its name. Hardly surprisingly, Dal Riadan–Pictish rivalry would form a key strand of early Scottish history, one that would last into the 9th century.

From about 500 they were joined by a new group, the native Celtic Britons, who began to establish kingdoms of their own in southwest Scotland much as their counterparts were establishing Celtic kingdoms elsewhere in Britain. The two most important were Rheged, which extended southwards into Cumbria, and Gododdin, to the north.

By about 600, a fourth group had arrived, the Angles, part of the great wave of Germanic settlers who were establishing themselves across eastern and central Britain. Pushing north and west from their kingdom of Bernicia, shortly to become part of the much more powerful Northumbrian kingdom, they drove the Britons before them.

The net result of this slow coming together of rival peoples was a predictable pile-up in which all four found themselves variously allied with and against each other in a state of near permanent warfare. Though Northumbrian ambitions were severely checked by the Picts at the Battle of Nechtansmere in 685, which thereafter restricted Northumbrian rule in Scotland to Lothian, the Britons fared worse. By 700, Rheged and Gododdin had been wiped from the map. They were replaced by the much smaller kingdom of Strathclyde, the most northerly outpost of Celtic rule in Britain and consistently on the defensive.

Two further factors were significant. One was the unifying impact of Christianity, specifically the Irish or Gaelic variant. The Picts had been Christians since St Columba himself had converted their king, Brude I, in 565. However tentatively, this common religious heritage would in time provide an overarching identity, one reinforced by increasing political contracts and alliances.

The other factor was the Vikings. As their raiding increased, it was the Picts who came to bear its brunt. In 839, they suffered a crushing defeat at Forteviot. It is possible that they were betrayed by a Dal Riadan prince, Kenneth Mac Alpin, who had negotiated a secret pact with the Vikings.

Kenneth was able to exploit the Picts' disarray and, by about 842, had made himself undisputed ruler of a joint Dal Riadan-Pictish kingdom. The Britons of Strathclyde and the Angles had yet to be subdued. Similarly, the Vikings were building enduring kingdoms in the Orkneys and Hebrides. But Kenneth's kingdom, which would be called Alba, was poised to form the heart of a new, much more powerful kingdom: Scotland.

Pictish Symbol Stones

The Picts are among the most mysterious of Britain's early inhabitants. Opinions are divided as to whether they pre-date the Celts or were, at least partly, a Celtic people. But as a resolutely non-literate people whose culture and language were in any case effectively obliterated after the Dal Riadan/Scottish take-over in the 9th century, much of the little that is known is inevitably hedged around with qualifications. The so-called Symbol Stones, the most tangible evidence of the Picts, if anything only deepen the mystery. These are a series of about 200 incised stone slabs, all found in the east of Scotland and most dating from between the 4th and 7th centuries. Though it is presumed that their purpose was religious, their meaning remains almost completely obscure. Their elaborate symbols, some human, some animal, many abstract, are unlike any produced elsewhere in Britain or Ireland. A number of the later stones are clearly Christian, though these, too, also use some of the same elaborate abstract forms of earlier stones.

THE FORMATION OF SCOTLAND TO c.842

- Core Dal Riada, from 5th century; lost 640
- Added from late 5th century
- → Known campaigns of Aidan (574–608)
- Approximate extent of British kingdoms c. 615
- Approximate extent of Northumbria c. 632
- Approximate extent of Northumbrian expansion under Oswald, 642
- Occupied by Northumbria, 658–85
- Unified under Brude III (672–93)
- → Attacks by Oengus macFergus, with date
- Controlled by Oengus macFergus (729–61); finally united by Mac Alpin, c.842
- To Northumbria, 750 (approximately)
- Early Viking incursions around 800

The emergence of the core of the Scottish kingdom under Kenneth Mac Alpin after 840 (map above) *was made in the face of rival Anglo-Saxon, Pictish, British and Irish Dal Riadan ambitions, all of them also subject to Viking deprivations. Even after 842, Scottish control was more apparent then real, however, largely concentrated in the Pictish heartlands around Fortriu.*

603	685	c.700	795	839	c.842
Dal Riadans under Aidan routed by Northumbrians under Athelfrith at Degastan in Borders	Northumbrian expansion into Pictland halted at Nechtansmere	Effective disappearance of British kingdoms of Rheged and Gododdin	Earliest Viking raids on Scotland	Picts crushed by Vikings at the Picts' capital, Forteviot	Dal Riada and Pictland united under Kenneth Mac Alpin

SCOTLAND *c.*842–1034

THE DESCENDANTS OF KENNETH MAC ALPIN RULED SCOTLAND FOR 176 YEARS IN AN UNBROKEN LINE OF SUCCESSION. BUT THOUGH THEY SUCCESSFULLY OVERCAME MOST PICTISH RESISTANCE, THEIR RULE WAS THREATENED BY VIKINGS, BRITONS AND ANGLES, AS WELL AS BY PERMANENT DYNASTIC FEUDING. NONETHELESS, BY 1034 THEIR KINGDOM COVERED MUCH OF PRESENT-DAY SCOTLAND.

Sarcophagus of Constatine II (below right). Constantine's more than 40-year rule (900–43) saw some of the most decisive moments in the consolidation of the newly formed Scottish kingdom. Squeezed by aggressive Viking and Anglo-Saxon assaults – and variously allied with and against both – and despite a series of defeats, notably at the hands of the Anglo-Saxons at Brunanburh in 937, Constantine managed not just to preserve the core of his kingdom but to further the Scottish claim to Strathclyde.

Kenneth Mac Alpin's kingdom of Alba – Pictavia in Gaelic – contained the kernel of a nascent Scottish state but not much more. Northumbria still held sway over Lothian; the British kingdom of Strathclyde, though shrinking, remained a threat; and the Picts, especially those in the distant north, the "men of Moray", were far from reconciled to Kenneth's takeover of the joint Scottish-Pictish throne. There was also the danger posed by the Vikings, whose kingdoms in the Western Isles, Orkney and Shetland as well as on the mainland in Caithness and Sutherland were all taking firmer shape in the 9th century. The Viking presence in Ireland was hardly less of a threat.

Scottish rule also took place against a background of persistent dynastic instability. This was the result not just of the endemic political turmoil of the period but of a curious succession arrangement whereby the crown alternated between the sons of Kenneth's own sons, Constantine I (863–7) and Aed (877–8).

Against this unpromising background, the 8th

The Stone of Destiny

As a mark of his overlordship of the Picts, Kenneth Mac Alpin was crowned in 843 at Scone, in the east of Scotland, long a royal Pictish site. Significantly, he had transported there the so-called Stone of Destiny, ever since known as the Stone of Scone. It was a key symbol of Celtic and Irish sovereignty, said to have been brought to Ireland from the Holy Land, via Egypt and Spain, long before the birth of Christ. Until Fergus, traditional founder of Dal Riada, reportedly brought it with him to Scotland in about 500, it had been at Tara where all the high kings of Ireland are claimed to have been crowned on it. Nonetheless, from the time of Kenneth onwards, the Stone of Destiny became as fundamental a mark of Scottish kingship as it had once been of Irish kingship. Every Scottish monarch, up to and including John Balliol in 1292, was crowned on the Stone. Until 1120, the ceremony took place in the open air, thereafter, it was held in Scone Abbey. After his conquest of Scotland, and as a mark of Scottish subjection, Edward I of England removed the Stone and installed it in Westminster Abbey, placing it under what became in effect the first throne of England's monarchs (picture right). Every subsequent ruler of England (and later of Britain) has since been crowned on the same throne over the Stone of Scone. Despite the absence of the Stone, Scottish rulers continued to be crowned at Scone until James II in 1434 when the ceremony was moved to Hollyrood in Edinburgh. Symbolically, in 1651, Charles II, excluded from his throne in England during the Commonwealth, was nonetheless crowned in Scotland at Scone. In 1996 the Stone was returned to Scotland.

Other than in the far north and west, effective Scottish rule had been more or less successfully established by 1034 (map below).
Yet conflict with the Anglo-Saxons to the south, which would continue well into the 16th century, as well as the presence of well-established Norse settlements to the west inevitably limited the actual political control of Scotland's rulers.

SCOTLAND 849 – 1034

- Alba, from c.842
- Widespread Norse settlement from c.800
- Subject to Viking raids, from second half of 9th century
- Added to Scotia, c. 870
- to Scotia temporarily, 890-927/937 (approximate extent)
- To Strathclyde, c. 930
- probably lost by Strathclyde after 945
- to Scotia by 962
- Subject to Scotian expansion from 973, secured 1018
- Client kingdom of Scotia from late 9th century, absorbed by 1034

and 9th centuries nonetheless saw a gradual but significant consolidation of Scotland's power and, with it, the power of her rulers. The major feature was the almost complete elimination of the Picts other than in the far north. In part, this was as much a linguistic and cultural process as a political one. The supplanting of the Pictish language by Gaelic and, later, English inevitably signalled a slow end to Pictish cultural life. But at the same time there is no question that it was principally military conquest, made possible by a kaleidoscopic series of shifting alliances and enmities – with Vikings, Britons and Anglo-Saxons alike – that ensured the elimination of most of Scotland's rivals.

It was far from a straightforward business. The Scots suffered major defeats at the hands of the Vikings in 866 and again in 871. They were to be further rebuffed by the Vikings in 914 and 918. In the same year, King Constantine II was forced to "submit" to the king of a resurgent Wessex, Edward the Elder, beginning the English claim to overlordship of Scotland. The English claim was pressed again in 934 when Athelstan mounted a punitive expedition against the Scots. The long-running Anglo–Scots rivalry had been decisively begun. Salt was rubbed in Scottish wounds in 973 when Kenneth II was obliged to promise his fealty to a new English king, Edgar.

Nonetheless, Scotland's burgeoning strength was confirmed in 899 under Donald II when Strathclyde, which included much of present-day Cumbria, became in effect a dependency of the Scottish kings. By 1018, much the same mix of conquest and coercion had been exploited by Malcolm II to confirm Scottish control over the former Northumbrian territory of Lothian. However, Malcolm's attempts to extend Scottish rule further south into Northumbria in 1031 and 1032 were firmly halted by Cnut, Danish ruler of England. Cnut not only obliged Malcolm to submit to him but definitively established English rule in Northumbria. In the process, Cumbria aside,

937 In this year King Athelstan, Lord of Nobles, dispenser of treasure to men, and his brother also, Edmund Aetheling, won by the sword's edge undying glory in the battle around Brunanburh ... There lay many a man destroyed by the spears, many a Northern warrior shot over his shield and likewise many a Scot lay weary, sated with battle.

The Anglo-Saxon Chronicle

the Anglo-Scottish border was permanently fixed.

The territorial core of Scotland may have been established but, dying in 1034 with no agreed heir, Malcolm had left a kingdom that was to be plunged into a round of dynastic turmoil.

934	937	945	973	1018	1031–2	1034
Athelstan of Wessex leads punitive raid against Scotland	Combined Irish, Celtic, Viking and Scottish army defeated by Wessex at Battle of Brunanburh	Scotland's right to Cumbria recognized by Edmund of Wessex	Kenneth II swears fealty to Edgar of Wessex; Scotland's right to Lothian recognized	Lothian annexed by Scotland	Scottish expansion into Northumbria by Malcolm II halted by Cnut	Death of Malcolm II

IRELAND TO 1183

IRELAND, NEVER PART OF THE ROMAN EMPIRE, ESCAPED THE CATASTROPHIC CONSEQUENCES THAT OVERTOOK BRITAIN WITH THE EBBING OF ROMAN RULE AFTER 410. BUT THOUGH THE COUNTRY HAD AN ENDURING TRADITION OF CELTIC KINGSHIP, IT NEVER COALESCED INTO A CENTRALIZED STATE. FROM THE 9TH CENTURY, IT FELL VICTIM TO VIKING INVADERS; IN THE 12TH, TO NORMAN CONQUERORS.

Dermot MacMurrough (above), defeated by Rory O'Connor for the High Kingship of Ireland, in 1169 turned to Henry II of England for assistance. The consequences were dramatic, if unintended by Dermot. The Normans, under the earl of Pembroke, came as conquerors, not allies, and in 1177 Prince John of England was proclaimed Lord of Ireland.

By the end of the 5th century, Ireland was the most stable territory in the British Isles. If the origins of Irish kingship can never be properly disentangled from the myths surrounding them, it is clear that by the time of the partly legendary high king Niall Noígiallachi (Niall of the Nine Hostages) in the late 4th century its broad outlines were established. Dominating it, and eulogized in Celtic bardic traditions, was the notion of the high king himself, whose traditional seat was at Tara.

In reality, early medieval Ireland was divided into as many as 150 tribal kingdoms, which by the 6th and 7th centuries were gradually hardening into five centres of power, all variously claiming overlordship: Ulster, Connaught, Meath, Leinster and Munster. Of these, the rulers of Ulster, the Uí Néills, who claimed the hereditary title of kings of Tara, were consistently the most dominant, however unlikely they may have been to have exercised overlordship in practice.

However politically fragmented, Celtic Ireland was still a fundamentally dynamic entity whose horizons were by no means restricted to its home island. From the 5th century to as late as the 10th, there were significant Irish kingdoms in many parts of western Britain – for example, in Cornwall, in Wales and, most enduringly, in Scotland. Far from hemming in the Irish, the Irish Sea was the highway that led to the creation of a wider Irish world.

It was this maritime world that the Vikings, first recorded in Ireland from the 790s, sought to exploit. Norse raiders may have founded what would become Ireland's first towns – Dublin, Waterford, Wexford and Cork among others. Similarly, Turgeis, the Norse founder of Dublin in 841, may have styled himself "King of Dublin". Nonetheless, unlike the more settled Danes in eastern England, the Norsemen in Ireland were at least as concerned to construct a trading empire across the Irish Sea as they were to establish a permanent land-based kingdom.

As the Normans would later discover, the growing political instability created by Ireland's feuding kings in any case made effective control impossible. In a familiar pattern of alliance and counter-alliance,

The divided political condition of Ireland disguised the island's fundamental dynamism at least until the arrival of the Vikings at the end of the 8th century. Thereafter, Ireland fell victim not just to internal political divisions but to the growing numbers of Viking settlers (map above). Whatever existence it may still have claimed as an independent state was ended after 1170 with the arrival of the Norman invaders sanctioned by Henry II of England.

IRELAND TO *c.*1190

▨	*Irish kingdoms in the 8th century; all nominally subject to the high kingship of Brian Boru, 1005*
⋯	*Lost by Ulaid at an earlier period*
⁄⁄⁄	*Lost by Laigin in 7th century*
▭	*Areas least affected by Viking activity, late 8th century to early 11th century*
■	*Towns established by Vikings*
→	*Norman attack*
✕	*Battle*

c.400	435	795	841	866–73	902	908
Niall Noígiallachi, legendary first high king, leads raids against Britain	St Patrick's Irish mission begun	Earliest Viking raids on Ireland	Foundation of Dublin (the "Black Pool") by Vikings	Rule of Ivar the Boneless: presides over joint Irish-Jorvik kingdom; Ireland becomes major Viking slaving centre	High King Flann Sinna forces Vikings out of Dublin (return 917)	Battle of Belach Mugna: kings of Cashel destroyed by Flann Sinna

Ireland and the Church

From perhaps even as early as the end of the 4th century – certainly from significantly before St Patrick's first mission in 435 – Ireland had benefited from the activities of a series of inspired Christian missionaries, of whom St Patrick is merely the best known. Fusing Celtic lore with Christian teaching, they sparked a distinctive and rich tradition of learning and piety that, in time, a new generation would carry to Scotland and northern England. It was in Ireland's early monasteries that the country's Celtic mythology, until then an oral tradition only, was first written down, a process that went hand in hand with an explosion of literature: poetry, history, law codes and bible studies that embraced classical, Christian and Celtic sources in equal measure. The dominant figure after Patrick was the ascetic and mystical St Columba (c.521–97), almost certainly a member of the Uí Néill. It was Columba who in the mid-6th century spearheaded the missionary drive into Scotland that resulted in the conversion of the Picts and, famously, in the foundation of the monastery at Iona in 563, which became not just a powerhouse of learning but a depository of astonishingly rich artefacts. The cross of St Martin at the monastery (left) dates from the 8th century. Equally intrepid was St Columbanus (c.543–615), who founded a series of monasteries in France and Switzerland. Despite its isolation on the fringes of the European world, Ireland played a crucial role in the early medieval European rediscovery of Christianity and scholarship.

the Norse were sucked into Ireland's turbulent power-struggles. In 902, Flann Sinna, high king from 879, even managed briefly to force them from Dublin altogether.

Whatever their maritime domination, the Norse hold on Ireland became increasingly precarious throughout the 10th century. The sacking of Dublin in 999 by Brian Boru, king of Munster, high king of Ireland (from 1002), and self-proclaimed "Emperor of the Irish" from 1005, was followed by his decisive victory over a combined Norse–Leinster army at Clontarf in 1014. The Norse kingdom of Dublin limped on until 1170, but the Viking role was increasingly peripheral.

Clontarf was important for other reasons as well. His army may have triumphed but Brian himself was killed in the battle. The consequence was a power vacuum that destabilized Ireland well into the 12th century when, in 1169, Dermot MacMurrough, overthrown by his rival, Rory O'Connor, high king from 1166 to 1183, sought help from the Plantagenet king of England, Henry II.

By 1170 a substantial Norman force, led by the earl of Pembroke, had arrived. It rapidly became clear that Pembroke saw in his role chiefly an opportunity for conquest in his own right. With the enforced submission of Rory to Henry II in 1175, independent Ireland had effectively come to an end and, with it, the high kingship.

> **The power of the Irish over the Britons was great, and they had divided Britain between them into estates ... and the Irish lived as much east of the sea as they did [to the west], and their dwellings and royal fortresses were made there. Hence is Dirid Tradui ... that is, the triple rampart of Crimthann, King of Ireland and Britain as far as the ... Channel. From this division originated the fort of the sons of Liathan in the lands of the Britons of Cornwall ... and they were in that control for a long time, even after the coming of St Patrick**

The Glossary of Cormac of Cashel, c.900

The Shrine of the Cathach (left), is one of six early Irish book shrines containing the manuscript of the Gospels known as the "Cathach" or "Battler". The original manuscript was written c.550 and was said to have been copied by St Columba before he left Ireland for Iona in 563.

PRE-CONQUEST ENGLAND 871–1066

ALFRED THE GREAT 871–99

EDWARD THE ELDER 899–924

AELFWEARD 924

ATHELSTAN 924–39

EDMUND I 939–46

EDRED 946–55

EADWIG 955–59

EDGAR 959–75

EDWARD THE MARTYR 975–78

AETHELRED II 978–1016

CNUT 1016–35

HAROLD I 1037–40

HARTHACNUT 1040–42

EDWARD THE CONFESSOR 1042–66

HAROLD II 1066

THE FIRST RECORDED VIKING RAIDS AGAINST ENGLAND, A COUNTRY WHICH BARELY EXISTED, OCCURRED IN 787. HOWEVER FIRMLY ESTABLISHED AS A WHOLE, THE PATCHWORK OF CHRISTIAN ANGLO-SAXON STATES THAT DOMINATED THE COUNTRY WERE STILL VYING WITH ONE ANOTHER FOR SUPREMACY. IN ADDITION, THEIR KINGS, WHATEVER THE RELATIVELY MORE SOPHISTICATED MECHANISMS OF GOVERNMENT THEY WERE AMASSING, STILL LOOKED BACK AT LEAST AS MUCH TO THE GERMANIC TRADITION OF KING AS WARRIOR-LEADER AND RING-GIVER AS FORWARD TO THE LATER MEDIEVAL IMAGE OF KING AS DIVINELY SANCTIONED AND IMPARTIAL FOUNT OF JUSTICE PRESIDING OVER A CLEAR-CUT NATIONAL POLITY.

Yet within about 100 years, England and a self-consciously English people had evolved. The first actively English king was ruling an actively English people.

The key figure in this transformation was the late 9th-century king of Wessex, Alfred, who withstood and then reversed the Danish assault that had seemed likely to destroy Anglo-Saxon England.

Alfred's achievements were clear and remarkable – not just in resisting the Vikings but in then creating a self-sufficient kingdom distinguished by just administration and an apparently clear sense of its own Anglo-Saxon English destiny, the whole backed by an unprecedented surge in learning and literature. The achievements of his successors over the next 75 years – Edward, Athelstan, Edred and Edgar pre-eminently – were equally striking. Not merely were the previously warring Anglo-Saxon kingdoms united under one obviously English rule, but the Danish threat, if not entirely banished, was at least contained. The creation of an English nation, whatever its Germanic origins, had become a fact.

This "golden age" of Anglo-Saxon rule remains alluring. It is easy to understand why 19th-century historians had little difficulty in identifying in it not just the "real" England but the seeds of what they saw as England's future greatness.

But in reality, even at its height Anglo-Saxon England was no less fragile than any other early medieval European kingdom. The mechanisms of its government may have been more sophisticated and more firmly embedded than most, but its kings and thus its underlying stability were always vulnerable.

Paradoxically, the strength of early medieval kingship was also a major source of its weakness. That the king occupied a uniquely powerful position inevitably meant that any kingdom was only as strong and as stable as the king himself. If this provided enormous scope for strong rulers to create or consolidate strong kingdoms, it provided just as much scope for ineffective rulers to undermine even the strongest kingdoms.

At the same time, the institution of kingship itself was compromised by the lack of agreed rules of succession. If a more or less plausible hereditary claim to rule was essential, the legitimacy of a successor was at least as dependent on his having been "designated" by the existing king as on his having an hereditary right. It was also no less important that the new king should enjoy the support of the country's leading subjects in the assembly known as the Witan ("wise men"), who at least in theory "elected" the new king; in practice this meant no more than acknowledging his right to rule after the fact of his succession. (It was only in 1216, with the death of King John, that primogeniture – the right of the eldest male heir to succeed – was generally accepted as the determining factor in the succession.)

This vagueness almost invariably ensured that disputed successions, with force of arms the ultimate deciding factor, were the norm not the exception. Even in the immediate aftermath of Alfred's reign, when Wessex and its kings had never been more apparently secure, the succession was never a foregone conclusion.

In the first half of the 11th century, England was dominated by these inherent instabilities. They would come to a head with the Norman Conquest in 1066, when the England created by Alfred and his heirs was effectively exterminated.

Between about 990 and 1016, the nightmare of total Danish conquest so well resisted by Alfred had returned, this time in redoubled strength. Aethelred II, well intentioned but weak, presided over a country that was the focus of overwhelming Danish attacks. He was able neither to defeat the Danes nor to bribe them to leave, and his kingdom sank into what in the end felt like inevitable capitulation. In 1016, with the accession of a Danish king, Cnut, England seemed to have been drawn definitively within the Scandinavian orbit. The Anglo-Saxon dream of a sturdily independent England had apparently died for good.

In fact, the Danish supremacy would prove short-lived. The accession of Edward the Confessor in 1045 seemingly signalled a return to Anglo-Saxon stability and native good government. In reality, this led to a characteristically confused succession, which opened the way for a further conquest of England by a further group of Northmen, the Normans.

If Anglo-Saxon England can be said to have been the best-governed kingdom in early medieval Europe, its sudden and total overthrow in 1066 is the clearest example not just of the inherent political turbulence of the period but of the obvious limitations of early medieval kingship. Strong kings could create strong kingdoms but they could never guarantee their subsequent survival. It is a theme that one way or the other would dominate English kingship at least until the 16th century.

VIKING INVASION AND SETTLEMENT

THE VIKING INVASIONS AND SUBSEQUENT SETTLEMENT OF THE BRITISH ISLES FROM THE END OF THE 8TH CENTURY WERE JUST ONE PART OF A LARGER, FEARSOME EXODUS OF SCANDINAVIAN WARRIORS AND CONQUERORS — EAST ACROSS THE BALTIC AND EVENTUALLY TO THE BLACK SEA, AND SOUTH ALONG THE COASTS OF WESTERN EUROPE AND FROM THERE TO THE MEDITERRANEAN.

That even a conqueror as violent as Eric Bloodaxe – twice the ruler of Jorvik (947–8 and 952–4) – understood the need for orderly government is clear from his issue of coins. This example (right) is from his second reign. His aspiration to legitimacy is underlined by his designation of himself as "Rex", while the reality of his rule is illustrated in his symbol of an unsheathed sword.

Norse ships proved astonishingly seaworthy. They were manoeuvrable, fast and tough. The largest could hold up to 200 men. One would have been terrifying; collectively, their capacity to strike terror would have been overwhelming. In 850, The Anglo-Saxon Chronicle claims a fleet of 350 ships landed in Kent. The one that brought the "Great Army" in 865 was reportedly even larger. This illustration (below) is from a 10th-century Anglo-Saxon manuscript.

THE IMPACT OF THE VIKINGS ON BRITAIN was sudden and terrible. Impelled by overcrowding in their Scandinavian homelands, the Vikings exploited to the full the ocean-going abilities of their ships, and by the end of the 9th century, Viking raids were becoming a brutal fact of life in Britain. They came in two main waves. Raiders from Norway – "Viking" meant simply "pirate" or "raider" – made their way via the Shetlands, the Orkneys and the Hebrides south to the Irish Sea. Those from Denmark generally attacked the east and south coasts of England.

Their early goals were plunder, their favoured targets the rich undefended monasteries of the Western Isles and northeast England. Lindisfarne was the first to be sacked, in 793. It was followed by Jarrow in 794 and Monkwearmouth and Iona in 795. (Iona was attacked again in 802, 806, 807 and 825.) For the pagan Vikings, these repositories of treasure were irresistible. For Christian Anglo-Saxons, such desecration and slaughter could only have been a punishment from God. Alcuin, the Northumbrian-born scholar at Charlemagne's Frankish court,

lamented after the sacking of Lindisfarne: "Behold the church of St Cuthbert, spattered with the blood of the priests of God." Where there were no such obvious targets to pillage, the Vikings extorted or simply stole money and slaves.

From about the 830s, as their fleets became larger, Viking goals began to change from outright looting to settlement. As early as about 800, the kernel of what would become the Norse earldom of Orkney had been established. Dublin was first settled by Norwegian Vikings in 841. Then, from about 850, Danish Vikings took to overwintering in Kent.

793 Here terrible portents came about over the land of Northumbria, and miserably frightened the people: there were immense flashes of lightning, and fiery dragons were seen flying in the air. A great famine immediately followed these signs: and a little after that … the raiding of the heathen men miserably devastated God's church in Lindisfarne by looting and slaughter.

The Anglo-Saxon Chronicle

The climax came in 865 when a Danish "Great Army" invaded England. In less than four years, almost the whole of Anglo-Saxon England had capitulated, Wessex aside. Viking-occupied England, the Danelaw, became an established fact.

Thereafter, Viking rule in England was dominated by two contrasting developments. One was its gradual overthrow by Wessex, which ended with the death of Eric Bloodaxe, the last Viking king of York (Jorvik), in 954. The other was a parallel confused power-struggle between Danish and Irish-based Norwegian Vikings for control of Jorvik itself, which variously sucked in the Celts of Strathclyde, the Scots and the English in a shifting series of alliances and counter-alliances, as each sought to exploit weaknesses in the other.

787	793	795	841	865	866–73	c.874	878	892	902
First recorded Viking raid on England (Portland)	Lindisfarne sacked	Earliest Viking raids on Ireland and Scotland	Foundation of Dublin (the "Black Pool") by Vikings	Invasion of East Anglia by Danish "Great Army"; conquers Northumbria (867), East Anglia (869) and Mercia (875)	Rule of Ivar the Boneless: presides over joint Irish–Jorvik kingdom; Ireland becomes major Viking slaving centre	Viking earldom of Orkney established	Danes under Guthrum defeated by King Alfred at Edington	Wessex resists renewed Danish invasions (to 897)	High King Flann Sinna forces Vikings out of Dublin (return 917)

THE VIKINGS OF THE BRITISH ISLES

Almost no part of the British Isles escaped the Vikings (map left). Once early raiding had given way to long-term settlement, their major centres were along the west coast of Scotland, the east and south coasts of Scotland, Jorvik (York), capital of a maritime trading empire centred on the Isle of Man, the East Midlands of England, the so-called Five Boroughs.

The Earldom of Orkney

Viking political control in Ireland and England may have been transient but in the 9th century a much longer-lasting Norwegian kingdom was established that extended south across northern and western Scotland to the Irish Sea: the earldom of Orkney. At its height in the 10th century it included the Shetlands, Orkneys and the Hebrides, Caithness and Sutherland on the mainland and the Isle of Man.

The impetus behind its foundation by the Norwegian king, Harald Fine-Hair, was to stamp out rogue Vikings who were using the Shetlands as a base for raids not against Britain but against Norway itself. It soon developed as the focus of the pan-Irish-Scottish-English Viking maritime empire that grew up in the 10th century and for control of which so many rival Norwegian rulers struggled.

The final Anglo-Saxon conquest of Viking York in 954, and ebbing of Viking political control in Ireland towards the end of the century, shifted the focus of Norwegian ambitions back to the Isle of Man and the Western Isles. The earldom endured until 1266 when, under the Treaty of Perth, and minus the Orkneys, it was ceded by Norway to Scotland. In 1290, the Isle of Man was annexed by Edward I of England. The Orkneys themselves remained under shared Danish/Norwegian rule until 1469. Not surprisingly, this was the only part of the British Isles where Norse dialects took root: Norn was spoken in parts of the Western Isles as late as the 18th century.

Norwegian dominance appeared to have been confirmed under the rule of Olaf Gothfrith-son, who in 939 at the age of only 21 presided over a united domain that included Viking Ireland, the Isle of Man, the kingdom of Jorvik and the previously Danish "Five Boroughs" (Leicester, Lincoln, Derby, Stamford and Nottingham). But with Olaf's early death in 941, Viking hegemony was rapidly undermined. Conquest by Wessex combined with Viking infighting – Jorvik changed hands no less than five times between 941 and 954 – led to the incorporation of Jorvik into Anglo-Saxon England.

However brief their political dominance, the Vikings' cultural impact on England was enduring. But just as important was the memory of Viking settlement, a memory that would spark renewed Danish invasions at the end of the 10th century, in turn leading to the collapse of Anglo-Saxon rule in 1016 and the establishment of a new Danish kingdom in England.

910-17	923	927	937	940	947	952	954	965	981	1014
Edward the Elder defeats Danes at Tettenhall, Wednesfield and Tempsford	Viking kings of Jorvik and kings of Northumbria, Strathclyde and Scotland swear loyalty to Edward	Conquest of Viking Jorvik by Athelstan	Battle of Brunanburh: Viking power in northern England destroyed by Athelstan	Jorvik retaken by Vikings under Olaf Gothfrithson	Eric Bloodaxe seizes Jorvik; expelled by Eadred	Eric Bloodaxe retakes Jorvik	Death of Eric Bloodaxe; Eadred retakes Jorvik	Viking Limerick sacked by king of Cashel	Viking Dublin sacked by king of Tara (and again in 999 by Brian Boru, king of Cashel)	Norse–Leinster army defeated by Brian at Clontarf; effective end of Norwegian control in Ireland

ALFRED THE GREAT 871–899

THE FRAGILE STABILITY OF ANGLO-SAXON ENGLAND WAS BRUTALLY SHATTERED BY THE DANES. BY THE TIME A DANISH "GREAT ARMY" LANDED IN EAST ANGLIA IN 865, THE NORSEMEN HAD BEEN RAIDING ACROSS THE NORTH SEA FOR ALMOST 80 YEARS. IT FELL TO ALFRED, KING OF WESSEX, TO HALT AND THEN REVERSE THE DANISH ADVANCE.

Alfred was eager not merely to introduce greater literacy to Wessex – he established a school for sons of the nobility as well as bringing scholars from many parts of Europe to England – he was anxious to translate classical and biblical texts into Anglo-Saxon so as to make them as widely accessible as possible. An important feature of The Anglo-Saxon Chronicle, *for example (below), unlike most other written works of the day, was that it was written solely in Anglo-Saxon.*

I N 867, NORTHUMBRIA FELL TO THE DANES; in 869, East Anglia was overrun. The following year, the Great Army was at Reading preparing to invade Wessex. Though the West Saxons managed at least to contain the Viking attack – in the process inflicting an important defeat on them at Ashdown in 871 – their's could be no more than a defensive campaign against a much stronger enemy that had been bolstered by the arrival of a second invading army. At much the same moment, Aethelred, king of the West Saxons, died. Though he had two young sons, it was Aethelred's younger brother, Alfred, who became king.

Alfred's reputation as the greatest of the Anglo-Saxon kings – who not only withstood the seemingly invincible Danes but decisively helped create the conditions in which a unified English kingdom could emerge – resulted in his being the only English monarch ever to be called "the Great". However, such a lofty and exceptional title belies not only the shadowy circumstances of his actual life but the relative inactivity of his early years on the throne. If his overall achievements are impossible to deny, it is clear that he was nothing if not a late developer.

For the first five years of his reign, Alfred did little more than buy off the Danes, who as a result turned their attentions to Mercia, which they conquered in 875. The respite for the West Saxons was purely temporary. Though many of the Danes then concentrated their energies on establishing permanent settlements elsewhere in England, a new force, led by Guthrum, overwhelmed the West Saxons at Chippenham in a surprise attack in January 878.

It was only now, with the fate of the last Anglo-Saxon kingdom hanging by a thread, that Alfred emerged not just as a great warrior leader but as an administrator of rare talent, possessed of an unusual combination of foresight, energy and intelligence.

Literacy in the Age of Alfred

I *n common with every British king of the period, Alfred was illiterate when he came to the throne. In fact, the ability to read and write would not be thought an essential requirement of kingship until the reign of John in the early 13th century. Alfred, however, was the exception to many rules and, at 38, he learned to read. In part, he was consciously emulating the Frankish court, which he had visited as a child on his way back from Rome (which he had visited twice) and where the effects of the great revival of learning initiated by Charlemagne in the early 9th century were still evident. Though much more modest in scale, a significant revival of learning and the arts was begun by Alfred, the first English king to see how learning could be sparked by royal patronage. Among its most lasting achievements was* The Anglo-Saxon Chronicle, *a remarkable record of contemporary events that would continue until the 12th century. In part, Alfred was also driven by the realization that wisdom and knowledge were essential elements of just kingship. Among a people still only hesitantly emerging from their origins as Germanic warrior tribes whose kings and tribal leaders could enforce laws only by recourse to custom and the strength of their own arms, the idea that justice was dependent on learning (in the king's subjects as well as in the king himself) was of revolutionary importance.*

853	854–5	865	868	871	876
Four-year-old Alfred sent to Rome	*Second visit to Rome*	*Invasion of Danish "Great Army", led by Halfdan and Ivar the Boneless*	*Marriage of Alfred to Mercian princess, Eahlswith*	*Hit-and-run campaigns by Aethelred and Alfred climax in West Saxon victory at Ashdown. Death of Aethelred; Alfred proclaimed king*	*New Danish attacks, led by Guthrum, on Wessex*

Alfred's crushing victory over the Danes at Edington in 878 may have provided a respite for Wessex – crucially buying time to allow the construction of fortified towns along the key strategic areas of the Channel coast and the Thames – but the Viking threat remained persistent (map left). To a large extent, containment was the best Alfred could hope for, as the renewed Danish attacks after 892 made clear. Alfred may appear on contemporary coins as Rex Anglorum (King of the English), but the whole of the north and east of the country remained under Danish control while relations with Anglo-Saxon Mercia always demanded the utmost tact.

WESSEX UNDER ALFRED THE GREAT 871–99

Wessex under Alfred the Great, 871

under Danish control by 871 (overrun by Great Army since 865)

→ attack of the Great Army on Wessex, 871

→ attack of the Great Army on Wessex, 875–8 (with date)

┈┈➤ other Danish attacks on Wessex, 878

English Mercia liberated by Alfred from Danish control by 886 (dependency of Wessex)

Welsh principalities, vassals of Alfred from 878–81

→ Danish campaigns 892–6 (with date)

✕ battle

⚑ principal burghs fortified by Alfred

➤ attacks by Alfred with date

As important, Alfred built on the new stability of Wessex to overhaul its law codes. Royal justice, as impartially administered as the inherent instabilities of the period would allow, became a hallmark of Alfred's reign and, in time, of Anglo-Saxon England as a whole. Of equal importance, whatever the latent rivalries simmering beneath the surface of Wessex-Mercian relations, Alfred also began to be widely recognized as the king of "all the English people not under the subjection of the Danes". Whatever the pretensions of the 6th to early 9th-century *bretwaldas* to be "kings of Britain", Alfred's unique achievement was as the first English king who could legitimately claim to rule over, in his own phrase, the *Angelcynn* ("the English folk").

Forced into hiding in the marshes of Athelney in Somerset he devised the strategy to defeat the Danes.

In May 878, he inflicted a defeat on the Danes at Edington that was so complete he was able to force Guthrum to accept Christian baptism as well as to withdraw east of a line running from London to Chester, in the process bringing Mercia definitively under West Saxon control. Alfred then immediately set about strengthening the defences of Wessex: he reorganized the *fyrd*, the Anglo-Saxon army, so that troops were always available to defend the kingdom; he built a new navy of 60-oared ships; and he constructed a series of fortified towns or *burhs*. These *burhs* rapidly developed into important economic centres, in turn sparking an economic revival.

Alfred's success in bringing stability to Wessex in a period of otherwise near-permanent turbulence is highlighted in the Alfred Jewel (left). Craftsmanship of this order demanded not just a sustained period of peace but access to expensive materials: gold and enamels. At the same time, the staring eyes of the king-like figure symbolize the all-seeing wisdom that the king came to epitomize. An inscription on the reverse reads: Aelfred mec heht gewyrcan (Alfred had me made).

878	879	c.880	886	887	892	899
Alfred defeated at Chippenham; regroups to defeat Danes in May at Edington; begins reorganization of West Saxon defences	Mercia brought under West Saxon control	Alfred begins to recruit scholars	Alfred proclaimed "King of all the English"	Alfred begins to learn to read	Wessex resists renewed Danish invasions (to 897)	Death of Alfred

THE HEIRS OF ALFRED 899–975

IN ENSURING THE SURVIVAL OF WESSEX AGAINST THE DANISH THREAT, KING ALFRED HAD LAID THE FOUNDATIONS OF A NASCENT ENGLISH KINGSHIP. BUT IT FELL TO HIS HEIRS TO CONSOLIDATE HIS ACHIEVEMENTS. IN 60 YEARS THEY NOT ONLY DOUBLED THE SIZE OF THE KINGDOM, BUT EXTENDED ROYAL POWER TO AN EXTENT UNPARALLELED IN EUROPE.

Building on his father's, Alfred the Great's, legacy, Edward the Elder (899–924) – picture left – helped to consolidate and expand the territories of the newly formed kingdom of Wessex.

The extension of Wessex rule was as rapid as it was dramatic (map below). By 975, for the first time since the Roman withdrawal in 410, England was effectively under the control of a single power. Yet whatever their successes, the Anglo-Saxon kings remained vulnerable.

WHATEVER THE ADMINISTRATIVE AND military successes of Alfred, early 10th-century Wessex faced a number of pressing dangers. Though dynastic marriage had made Mercia an ally, the long-standing rivalry with Northumbria had scarcely diminished. At the same time, there was the permanent prospect of further invasion from the great swathe of Viking-held territory that stretched from East Anglia to the Lake District.

THE EXPANSION OF WESSEX 899–975

- *Wessex under Edward the Elder and dependent Mercia under his sister Aethelfled, 899*
- *Frontier of Wessex and Mercia, to 911*
- *Independent Mercia, 911–18 and 957–59*
- *Under Danish rule, 899*
- *Limit of conquest by Edward the Elder by 916*
- *Conquered by Edward the Elder by 924*
- *Forts built by Edward the Elder and Aethelfled*
- *Campaigns of Athelstan in 927 and 934*
- *Conquered by Athelstan by 939*
- *kingdom of York under Norwegian king of Dublin, Olaf Gothfrithsson, at its greatest extent, 941*
- *Further area of Norse settlement by early 10th century*
- *Borders of Wessex by 954*
- *States partly acknowledging overlordship of Wessex in 10th century*
- *The "Five Boroughs"*   **911** *Date of annexation by Edward the Elder*
- *Important Danish campaigns, with date*

But in fact most of the period saw sustained expansion by the kings of Wessex, chiefly by Edward the Elder and his son Athelstan. Decisive victories by Edward over the East Anglian Danes in 910 and 911 were followed by an equally crushing victory at Tempsford in 917. Military success on this scale made the incorporation of Mercia into Wessex the following year something of a formality. At the same time, the Danish kingdoms of East Anglia and the Five Boroughs were also added. Edward then set about reinforcing his northern borders, which by 920 had been set at the Humber.

Edward's rapid conquests ensured the primacy of Wessex not just in England but across much of Britain. In 918 the Welsh rulers of Gwynnedd and Dyfed had already taken oaths of loyalty to Edward. They were followed in 923 by the rulers of the Viking Kingdom of York and the kings of Northumbria, Strathclyde and Scotland, all of whom acknowledged Edward as their "father and lord". It was a crucial moment. The notion of a centralized kingdom under a single royal authority was taking shape.

899	910–17	918	919	920	923
Accession of Edward the Elder	*Edward the Elder defeats Danes at Tettenhall, Wednesfield and Tempsford*	*Mercia incorporated into Wessex. Welsh princes swear loyalty to Edward*	*Danish East Anglia incorporated into Wessex*	*Northern border of Wessex established at Humber*	*Viking kings of York and kings of Northumbria, Strathclyde and Scotland swear loyalty to Edward*

One of Edgar's (959–75) – picture left – most significant achievements was the reform of England's counties, which helped to make the exercise of royal power more effective in an age of turmoil and unrest.

EDWARD THE ELDER 899–924

(BORN 870) SON OF ALFRED
First of the great consolidators of Alfred's legacy who enormously extended the territories under the rule of Wessex and its military strength.

AELFWEARD

17 JULY 924–2 AUGUST 924

(BORN 899) SON OF EDWARD THE ELDER
Little is known about the shadowy Aelfweard but a reign of only 16 days suggests his death is unlikely to have been natural or accidental.

ATHELSTAN 924–39

(BORN 895) SON OF EDWARD THE ELDER
Another of the great conquering kings of Wessex who not only further extended the kingdom's borders but greatly enhanced the prestige of the monarchy.

EDMUND I 939–46

(BORN 921) SON OF EDWARD THE ELDER
Presided over the only serious setback to Wessex hegemony in the period, the successful re-taking of York and invasion of Mercia by Olaf Gothfrithson in 940. Olaf's death the following year allowed

Edmund to recover most of the lost territories. He was murdered by a follower in 946 after an argument.

EADRED 946–55

(BORN 924) SON OF EDWARD THE ELDER
Continued the re-conquest of the north after Edmund's death, leading a successful campaign against Eric Bloodaxe, who had seized York, in 947. Erik re-took the throne in 952 but his death in 954 allowed Wessex to re-establish its control over the region.

EADWIG 955–59

(BORN 942) SON OF EDMUND I
A four-year reign notable for intrigue and incompetence, which threatened to destroy Wessex's hard-won control of Mercia and Northumbria.

EDGAR 959–75

(BORN 943) SON OF EDMUND I
Saw the consolidation of Wessex's gains over the previous 60 years. Numerous reforms and firm rule made his reign the high-water mark of Wessex domination. His nickname, the "Peaceful", was testimony to his strength, not his weakness.

The dominance of Wessex was reinforced by Edward's successor, Athelstan, who in 927 extended its borders again when he drove the Danes from York. In 934, he demonstrated the military superiority of Wessex even more dramatically, leading a combined land and naval force into Scotland. Three years later, he decisively repulsed a Scottish–Danish attempt to re-take York at the battle of Brunanburh.

The apogee of Wessex power was reached under Edgar, who came to the throne in 959. In an age of almost permanent unrest, the degree of control exercised by Edgar was exceptional. If he was the beneficiary of the military success of his predecessors, it was nonetheless a measure of his intelligent rule that he recognized that peace with his still potentially dangerous Danish subjects, for example, was best preserved by allowing them considerable autonomy.

But Edgar's most important legacy was his continuation of the administrative reforms introduced by Alfred. By his death, Wessex was the most stable and, in many respects, best governed kingdom in Christendom. Among Edgar's most significant achievements was the reorganization of England's counties – they remained essentially unchanged until 1974 – which made the exercise of royal power all the more effective. He also overhauled the coinage, authorizing new mints and, in 973, a new currency. The Witan, or royal council, also continued to grow in influence (see box).

As important, Edgar set in train a series of monastic reforms, important not just because they helped fuel a lavish artistic revival but because, in encouraging the monasteries to reform, Edgar made clear that they did so only because he permitted it. Military might may have made possible the spread of Wessex, but the view was growing that the authority of England's kings ultimately stemmed from their role as Christ's vicar on earth.

The Witan

*I*f in no sense a parliament-in-the-making, the Witan, or royal council, was nonetheless fundamental to the growing stability of Anglo-Saxon England. Though its precise role, like its membership, was vague – it met only when summoned by the king, for example – it nonetheless acted as a valuable source of advice and counsel to the monarch, even if it was always subject to him. Its two major responsibilities were to "elect" the king, which in practice meant confirming his right to the throne after the fact rather than in any sense choosing him in the first place, and to give assent to royal measures. Again, this in no way implied a veto over the king's decisions.

On the other hand, it did provide an additional layer of legitimacy. It was this reinforcement of the rule of law that was the Witan's most lasting significance. It may have taken conquest to establish Anglo-Saxon rule, but once in place Anglo-Saxon kingship was deeply concerned to bolster its position by the spread of royal law. That the king, supported by the Witan, should increasingly come to be regarded as the sole source of authority was a development of lasting importance.

Edgar's reign saw an important reform of the coinage, with new currency being introduced in 973. This silver penny (left) was minted in Shrewsbury by the moneyer Hildic.

927	937	940	947	954	959	973
Conquest of York by Athelstan	Battle of Brunanburh: Viking power in York destroyed by Athelstan	York re-taken by Vikings under Olaf Gothfrithson; Mercia invaded	Eric Bloodaxe seizes York; expelled by Edred	Death of Eric Bloodaxe; Edred re-takes York	Accession of Edgar leads to further consolidation of Wessex rule and administrative reforms	Ceremonial double coronation of Edgar (at Bath and Chester); Edgar receives homage of eight "British kings"

KING

AETHELRED II

BORN: *c.*968
ACCEDED: March 978;
crowned April 978,
Kingston-upon-Thames

King of the English

THE HEIRS OF ALFRED: AETHELRED II 978–1016

AETHELRED II HAS LONG BEEN WRITTEN OFF AS ONE OF THE MOST DISASTROUS OF ENGLISH KINGS. IN 978 HE INHERITED AN ANGLO-SAXON KINGDOM THAT WAS PROSPEROUS, UNIFIED AND EXCEPTIONALLY WELL GOVERNED. BY THE TIME OF HIS DEATH IN 1016 HE HAD LOST IT ALL. YET, WHATEVER HIS OWN FAILINGS, IT WAS ULTIMATELY A WAVE OF RENEWED AND IRRESISTIBLE DANISH ATTACKS THAT UNDERMINED HIS RULE.

In 991 a raiding party of Danes made their headquarters on Northey Island. The English general Byrhtnoth blocked the narrow entrance to the causeway (above), but the Danes over-whelmed the defenders. This defeat at the Battle of Maldon led to the first payment of Danegeld.

Anglo-Saxon Administration

Aethelred's reign contained a number of enduring ironies. Though he was without question the least successful of Alfred's principal successors, he was, by some way, the longest reigning. Similarly, despite the increasing chaos caused by the Danish raids, the administrative efficiency of Anglo-Saxon England, crucially important in extending the range of royal authority, was significantly strengthened under Aethelred. Among the most important developments was the creation of new representatives of the king in each shire. These representatives were called bailiffs or "reeves", from which the term "shire-reeve", later sheriff, came. It was the sheriff's task to implement royal decisions in each shire and to preside over the new shire courts, where royal pronouncements and decisions were announced. The sheriffs were also instrumental in the much more efficient tax system that developed under Aethelred. This itself was more than just an administrative convenience but the direct consequence of having to raise huge extra taxes across the country to meet the payments of Danegeld. In a further irony, in the reign of Cnut, this greatly improved tax system was used not to buy the Danes off but to meet the costs of a new Danish standing army in England.

P re-eminently, Aethelred was a victim of circumstances. Even his nickname "Unraed" – meaning not "unready" but "bad counsel", a pun on Aethelred, meaning "noble counsel" – suggests a rule that seems to have been consistently at the mercy of events. In many ways, his kingship was blighted from the beginning.

Aethelred came to the throne, aged only 10, when his elder brother, Edward – himself just 16 but already king for three years – was murdered by Aethelred's supporters while visiting Edward. However much an innocent bystander, Aethelred never quite shook off the stain of implication in the murder of his brother, who within a matter of years was being venerated by Aethelred's opponents as "Edward the Martyr".

Even after his majority, Aethelred remained the victim of Anglo-Saxon power politics, unable either to cow his senior subjects or to win their trust. But his overriding weakness was military. No great general, he had the overwhelming misfortune to rule England at exactly the moment that a resurgent Denmark was not merely determined to regain its lost territories in England but had the clear military capacity to do so.

From the early 980s, under two formidable Danish kings – Harold Bluetooth and, after 988, his equally fearsome son, Sweyn – a series of Danish invasions were launched against England. Early Danish successes climaxed in 991 in a devastating Anglo-Saxon defeat at Maldon in Essex. Danish attacks followed throughout the decade. With each Danish victory, Aethelred progressively lost the support of his most powerful nobles, who were increasingly dismayed by his inability to defend the kingdom.

Aethelred's response was logical but flawed. If he was unable to defeat the Danes, he could surely buy them off. For almost 20 years, he paid increasingly large sums to the Danes in an attempt to halt their depredations. Called "Danegeld", these payments became a central feature of Aethelred's rule. Rich though it was, Anglo-Saxon England risked being bled dry within a matter of years. The Danes predictably came back for more.

c.980	982	991	997	1002	1003–5
Renewed Danish raids under Harold Bluetooth	*London sacked by Danes*	*Anglo-Saxon defeat at Battle of Maldon heralds further Viking invasions (994, 997, 1002) – Danegeld payments begin. Anglo-Saxon–Norman anti-Danish alliance formed*	*Wantage Law Code: major revision of Anglo-Saxon laws by Aethelred*	*Massacre of all Danes in England ordered*	*Major Danish reprisals against England led by Sweyn*

991 This year was Ipswich plundered: and very soon afterwards was Ealdorman Byrhtnoth slain at Maldon. In this same year it was resolved that tribute should be given, for the first time, to the Danes, for the great terror they occasioned by the sea-coast. That was first £10,000. The first who advised this measure was Archbishop Siric.

The Anglo-Saxon Chronicle

Anglo-Saxon successes in containing and then rolling back the Vikings depredations were dramatically undone in the reign of Aethelred II (map right). For over 30 years after 980, Anglo-Saxon England was subjected to a series of devastating Danish attacks that left only the northwest untouched. With the accession of Cnut in 1016, the Viking triumph was complete.

Fatefully, Aethelred also tried to outflank the Danes by allying himself with the French dukedom of Normandy, an alliance strengthened in 1001 with his marriage to Emma, daughter of the Duke of Normandy. Though he could scarcely have known it, the consequences of his diplomatic marriage would later open the way to an even greater disaster.

He committed a much more immediate and avoidable blunder in 1002, however, when, determined to assert his authority, he ordered the massacre of all the Danes in England. His scheme had the triple disadvantage of being barbaric, unenforceable and of provoking Sweyn yet further. A decade of devastating Danish invasions was unleashed in which much of the north of England, swayed partly by its Danish population but above all by its eagerness to see an end to the conflict, threw itself behind Sweyn. By late 1013, Oxford, Winchester and London had also fallen and Aethelred had fled to Normandy.

The denouement followed swiftly. By 1014, Aethelred was back in England confronting Sweyn's successor, Cnut. To his existing military incapacity, he now had an additional handicap in the shape of his son, Edmund "Ironside", who had defied his father by taking control of the remaining Anglo-Saxon forces in the north. What was left of the king's royal authority was undermined further.

In the event, it hardly mattered. In early 1016, Aethelred suddenly died. In October, Cnut inflicted an overwhelming defeat on Edmund. Within a month, Edmund, too, was dead and Cnut was king.

The Welsh states were also subject of Viking attacks coming from Man and Ireland, 980-999

On Sweyn's death in 1014, Cnut withdrew the Danish forces

Aethelred's flight to Normandy, 1013

WARS WITH THE DANES, 980–1016

- *Early Danish attacks*
- *Area attacked by Sweyn and Olaf Tryggvason, 994*
- *Danish campaigns, 997–1001*
- *Areas attacked by Sweyn, 1003–6*
- *Thorkell the Tall's campaigns, 1009–10*
- *Area attacked by Sweyn, 1011–12*
- *Sweyn's campaign, 1013*
- *Approximate limit of Cnut's campaign/s, 1015–16*
- *Awarded to Edmund "Ironside" under Treaty of Olney, 1016*
- *Other areas possibly forming part of Edmund's kingdom*
- ✗ *Battles*

This coin of Aethelred II (left) shows the king bare-headed and was minted in London by the moneyer Leofnoth.

1006–7	1009	1012	1013	1014	1015	1016
Further Danish invasion bought off by payment of £30,000	*Renewed Danish invasions under Thorkell the Tall*	*Thorkell's troops murder Alphege, the Archbishop of Canterbury*	*Sweyn leads army of conquest against England; gains immediate Northumbrian submission; Aethelred flees to Normandy*	*Danish army led by Cnut after death of Sweyn; Aethelred leads renewed attack against Cnut*	*Further Danish invasion of England under Cnut; Edmund "Ironside" heads English forces in the north*	*Death of Aethelred; Cnut defeats Edmund at Ashingdon (Oct.) and under Treaty of Olney restricts Edmund's rule to Wessex. Death of Edmund (Nov.)*

CORONATION RITES

THE GROWING POWER OF ANGLO-SAXON KINGSHIP IN THE 10TH CENTURY WAS CRUCIALLY REFLECTED IN A MORE ELABORATE FORM OF EXPLICITLY CHRISTIAN CORONATION. THIS CONFIRMED NOT JUST THE SECULAR POWER OF THE KING BUT HIS STATUS AS THE LORD'S ANOINTED. IN UNDERLINING THAT THE KING WAS NOT AS OTHER MEN, THE CORONATION IN TURN REINFORCED HIS AUTHORITY.

If a formal ceremony of inauguration had been a part of the ritual whereby a new ruler was proclaimed since perhaps as early as the 6th century, it was only with the coronation of Egfrith of Mercia in 787 that the outlines of the ceremony as it would subsequently evolve first seem to have emerged. The details of Egfrith's coronation may be known only vaguely, but it is clear that the ceremony held an important new religious dimension.

In fact, this religious element had an obvious political goal: to reinforce Egfrith's legitimacy, a fact clearly seen in Egfrith's being crowned during the lifetime of his father, Offa. Anxious to secure an orderly succession for his son, Offa arranged that the papal legates then visiting the country anoint Egfrith as king. In subsequently being able to proclaim himself as divinely sanctioned, Egfrith's eventual right to his father's throne was significantly strengthened.

By the coronation of Edgar in 973, itself apparently influenced by that of the German emperor, Otto the Great, in 952, the ceremony had taken on essentially the same form and significance it retains today as a solemn, public confirmation of the new monarch's divine right to the throne and of his responsibilities. It is striking that Edgar's coronation was the first at which the anthem used in every subsequent coronation, "Zadok the Priest and Nathan the Prophet" was sung; it is best known in Handel's arrangement of it, composed for the coronation of George II in 1727.

The ceremony itself was divided into five principal elements. First, the recognition, in which the new monarch was presented to the congregation by the presiding cleric, from the coronation of Henry II in 1154 always the Archbishop of Canterbury. It was followed by the oath, in which the monarch swore to safeguard his people and the church, to uphold justice and to be merciful. Then followed the most sacred moment of the ceremony, one which confirmed the king's semi–divine status: the anointing of the monarch with holy oil. (It was precisely the religious character of the anointing that made Elizabeth II in 1953 reluctant to have this part of the ceremony televised).

The monarch was then handed the regalia, essentially symbols of the secular character of kingship: a ring; sword, symbol of his protection of his kingdom; and the crown itself, sceptre and rod, the whole standing for "the glory, virtue, equity and justice reposing in an anointed king". Finally, now crowned and as a mark of his status at the head of the feudal chain, the monarch received the homage of his leading subjects. (Until the coronation of William IV in 1831, there was then also generally a banquet at which the king's champion offered to take on any rival claimant to the throne. William IV discontinued the practise as the conspicuous luxury of his predecessor, George IV's, banquet had been thought so excessive).

Anointed and proclaimed in this way "by the grace of God", a form of words used by every monarch since William Rufus in 1087, normally with as much magnificence as could be mustered, the legitimacy of the new monarch's rule was emphatically established and the principal of hereditary succession reinforced. Needless to say, where the succession was disputed, the sooner the coronation was held, the sooner the legitimacy of the new rule could be asserted. It is no coincidence that in 1066 Harold II, whose succession was among the most disputed in medieval England, was crowned only the day after the death of Edward the Confessor.

In much the same way, in 1170 Henry II had his eldest son, also Henry, the "Young King", crowned king of England, the clearest possible indication that it was the Young King who would succeed Henry in England while his other lands, in France and Ireland, were to be divided among his three younger sons. Further, at least until the succession of Edward I in

The coronation of Henry IV in 1399, taken from the late-15th century Froissart's Chronicles (below). This was the first occasion where holy oil was used for the anointing. For Henry, who had deposed his predecessor Richard II just two weeks previously, the coronation, with its near-sacerdotal aura was a prime opportunity to display to his subjects God's blessing on his succession to the throne.

The Royal Regalia

*T*he royal regalia, assembled over several hundred years, and including a number of pieces, a crown and several sceptres among them, dating from the reign of Edward the Confessor, were melted down or sold on the orders of Parliament after the execution of Charles I in 1649. The motive was partly the need to raise cash. But it was also a deliberate attempt to destroy for good the most symbolic of objects representing the monarchy. With the Restoration of Charles II in 1660, it was decided in an act of equally deliberate symbolism that the entire regalia should be re-created as precisely as possible. In fact, one item had survived, the 12th-century anointing spoon. All the rest, however, triumphantly used for the first time at Charles's coronation in 1661, was entirely new. Importantly, within years it was being widely assumed that the reconstituted regalia were the original items, a state of affairs the monarchy itself was keen to promote. The first printed guide to the collection, published in 1710, described the centre-piece of the collection, the so-called St Edward's Crown as "The Imperial Crown, which all the Kings of England have been Crown'd with, ever since Edward the Confessor's Time".

1172, by which point the automatic right of the eldest son to the throne had become established, in an important sense the reign of a medieval king began only with his coronation. The sooner it could be held, the sooner his reign could be properly said to have begun.

Similarly, whatever his rather shrill claims to have been designated his heir by Edward the Confessor, William I, Norman or not, deliberately retained the Anglo-Saxon form of the ceremony, the better to emphasise the continuity (non-existent in fact) of his reign with that of Edward's. In very much the same way, the coronation of Henry IV in 1399 after the overthrow of Richard II was not only deliberately magnificent, it was also the first occasion in which the anointing was done with holy oil said to have been given to Thomas Becket by the Virgin Mary. Having usurped the throne, it was essential for Henry IV to legitimize his rule by every means available to him.

Until the consecration of Westminster Abbey in 1065, most Anglo-Saxon monarchs were crowned at what appropriately came to be called Kingston, on the Wessex-Mercia border. Thereafter, beginning with Harold II, every English and later British king other than the uncrowned Edward V in the 15th century and Edward VIII in the 20th century, was crowned at Westminster Abbey. From the coronation of Edward II in 1308, the monarch has always been crowned on the throne constructed by Edward I and incorporating the Stone of Scone, appropriated by Edward I in 1296, on which the kings of Scotland had traditionally been crowned (though not anointed, a practise begun only with the coronation of David II in 1331 after papal recognition of the independence of Scotland was granted).

St Edward's crown is replaced by the lighter Imperial State Crown (above) for the closing procession of the coronation service. It is worn by the Sovereign on leaving Westminster Abbey after the coronation ceremony. This crown was originally made for Queen Victoria in 1838 and was used at the coronations of Edward VII and George V. It was remade with similar stones for George VI in 1937 and is set with 2,868 diamonds, 17 sapphires, 11 emeralds, five rubies and 273 pearls.

The 12th-century anointing spoon (above left), is the only item of the royal regalia to survive the destruction of the original regalia in 1649. It is used to anoint the new monarch with holy oil; this conscious use of Christian symbolism reinforces the legitimacy and status of the newly-crowned monarch.

The coronation of King George VI and Queen Elizabeth at Westminster Abbey (12th May, 1937, left). A comparison with the coronation of Henry IV in 1399 (far left) shows how many elements of the ceremony and the sense of sacred ritual have remained intact over the centuries.

KING CNUT
BORN: *c*.995
ACCEDED: November
1016; crowned January
1017, London

*King of England, King of
Denmark (from 1018)
and King of Norway
(from 1028)*

THE DANISH KINGDOM OF ENGLAND: CNUT AND HIS SONS

CNUT WAS AMONG THE GREATEST KINGS OF HIS DAY, RULER OF A POWERFUL NORTH EUROPEAN MARITIME EMPIRE THAT INCLUDED DENMARK, NORWAY AND PARTS OF SWEDEN AS WELL AS ENGLAND. YET HIS RULE DEMONSTRATES THE TRANSIENT AND PERSONAL NATURE OF EARLY MEDIEVAL KINGSHIP. HIS EMPIRE DISINTEGRATED WITH HIS DEATH AND, WITHIN SEVEN YEARS, ENGLAND WAS ONCE MORE UNDER ANGLO-SAXON RULE.

CNUT'S TAKEOVER OF ENGLAND IN 1016 WAS A conquest in every sense. Vigorous, determined and harsh (if not unduly so by the standards of the time), the new Viking king was quick to assert his authority. His principal Anglo-Saxon rivals, including Edmund Ironside's brother Eadric (and probably his eldest son, Edwy) as well as the earls of Mercia and East Anglia, were summarily executed. Edmund's other son, Edward, was exiled, reputedly to Novgorod with orders to its Viking rulers that he be murdered on arrival. (In the event,

he made his way to Hungary.) At the same time, substantial numbers of Cnut's Danish followers were granted English lands and titles. In 1017, to underline his claim to the throne more strongly still, Cnut married Aethelred's widow, Emma.

Unlike William the Conqueror 50 years later, Cnut went no further. The large majority of the Anglo-Saxon nobility were left in place. In much the same way, the key figure of Wulfstan, Archbishop of York under Athelstan, was allowed to remain in office. As important, the mechanisms of government were left essentially undisturbed.

Cnut's motives were pragmatic. His focus was at least as much on his Scandinavian homelands as on England. Once he had inherited the Danish throne in 1018 and begun a successful ten-year conquest of Norway, a stable England was fundamental to the control of his North Sea empire. Not only would a ruler – even one as capable as Cnut – have been unable to cope with simultaneous unrest in England and Scandinavia, but a prosperous England could be used to fund his Scandinavian campaigning. It was essential that England be allowed to recover from the quarter-century of invasion and war that preceded the final

CNUT'S KINGDOMS

- Acquired by Cnut, 1016
- Acquired by Cnut, 1018
- Acquired by Cnut, 1028
- Disputed between England and Scotland; to Scotland 1018
- Added to Denmark, 1025
- —— Under Cnut's rule at the time of his death, 1035
- ······ Frontiers, 1030

Cnut's English kingdom was just a part of the most formidable maritime empire in 11th-century Europe, almost all of it acquired by force (map right). Yet, however potent and however intelligent Cnut's rule, it would not last. England, by far the richest part of the empire, had been restored to Anglo-Saxon rule by 1042.

King Cnut greets in friendship his archbishops and his diocesan bishops, and Earl Thorkell and all his earls, and all his people... And I inform you that I will be a grateful lord and a faithful observer of God's rights and just secular law ... [and] that I [will] everywhere exalt God's praises and suppress wrong and establish full security, by that power which it has pleased God to give me ... Now I thank Almighty God for his help and his mercy, that I have so settled the great dangers which were approaching us that we need fear no danger to us ...

From a proclamation to the people of England, c.1019

1014	1016	1017	1018	1018–20
Cnut marries Aelfgifu	Assumes throne of England	Marries Emma, widow of Aethelred. Creates earldoms of Wessex, East Anglia, Mercia and Northumbria	Godwine created Earl of Wessex. Cnut inherits Danish crown on death of his brother, Harold. Scots under Malcolm II invade Northumbria	Cnut in Denmark; launches conquest of Norway

Cnut's transformation from Viking warrior to Christian benefactor was among the most remarkable aspects of his reign. His piety seems to have been quite genuine and to have gone well beyond the conventional religious requirements of the time. Here, in a manuscript produced in Winchester in 1031 (left), he is shown with his queen, the formidable Emma, presenting a cross to the New Minister at Winchester. The angel placing the crown on Cnut's head makes explicit the king's divine sanction.

Cnut's Successors

However well established at the time of his death, Cnut's empire was undermined by dynastic uncertainty. Ever the Viking, Cnut had two wives at the same time: Aelfgifu, daughter of the former ealdorman of Northumbria, whom he married in 1014; and Emma, the Norman-born widow of Aethelred. After his second marriage, Aelfgifu was sent to Denmark, where she was recognized as Cnut's legitimate queen. Emma meanwhile ruled as Cnut's queen in England. Even by the standards of early medieval Europe, it was an unusual arrangement.

Aelfgifu had two sons by Cnut, Sweyn, king of Norway until his death in 1036, and Harold; Emma had one son by him, Harthacnut. Though designated his successor by Cnut, Harthacnut was in Norway when his father died in 1035. Harold, however, was in England and Harthacnut accordingly appointed him regent. Two years later, with Harthacnut still in Norway, Harold, supported by the all-powerful pirate-turned-nobleman, the rapacious Earl Godwine of Wessex, claimed the throne for himself. Emma fled to Flanders.

By the time Harthacnut returned to England in 1040 Harold was dead, possibly murdered. Just in case there should be any doubt as to who was now king, Harthacnut had Harold's body exhumed, beheaded and "cast into a marsh". His reign, every bit as oppressive as his half-brother's, ended suddenly after two years when, drinking a toast at a wedding, he died "with terrible convulsions".

Of the possible heirs, the two with the strongest claims were the new king of Norway, Magnus I, and Aethelred's and Emma's sole surviving son, Edward. Magnus, though powerful, was in Norway; Edward, by contrast, in England. He also had the support of Earl Godwine, who almost certainly believed that with Edward on the throne he, Godwine, would constitute the real authority in the kingdom. In June 1042, cowed by Godwine's usual crude mixture of threats and bribes, the Witan agreed to Edward's succession and Cnut's short-lived royal line was ended. The Anglo-Saxons had been restored.

Danish conquest. The celebrated proclamation to his leading subjects issued in about 1019 was a clear statement of intent to govern with the support of his nobles and the Church as well as to maintain order.

But Cnut introduced one major innovation that, however sensible in his terms, would in the longer run prove seriously destabilizing to Anglo-Saxon England. In 1017, he divided England into four earldoms – Northumbria, East Anglia, Mercia and Wessex. His intention was to centralize power in these regions and thereby ensure consistent government during his long spells overseas. In effect, he was acknowledging a key limitation of early medieval kingship: that the king could rule only with the support of his nobles. However, by concentrating power in the hands of just four magnates, he created power bases of sufficient strength to challenge the rule of the king himself.

Under Cnut at least any latent conflict was held firmly in check. His rule was increasingly marked not just by his personal dominance but by clear, capable government, among it legal reforms that further reinforced the country's reputation for efficient administration. At the same time, the one-time pagan Viking marauder became an enthusiastic supporter of the Church. In 1027 and 1031, he even journeyed to Rome. A 12th-century chronicler would admiringly describe Cnut's transformation "from a wild man into a most Christian king".

That he was still a warrior king, however, was obvious not just from his conquest of Norway but from the submissions he was able to force from the Scottish king, Malcolm II, and the Norse ruler of Dublin, Margad Ragnallson, in 1031. As king of Denmark, Cnut's authority also extended over the earldom of Orkney. By his death in 1035, Cnut was unquestionably the most powerful ruler in northern Europe.

St Andrew's church (right) at Ashingdon in Kent was founded by Cnut c.1020 after the battle of Ashingdon (1016), "for the souls of the men who were slain".

KING EDWARD THE CONFESSOR
BORN: *c.*1005
ACCEDED: June 1042;
crowned April 1043,
Winchester

King of England

EDWARD THE CONFESSOR 1042–66

FEW ENGLISH KINGS CAME TO THE THRONE BY A MORE CIRCUITOUS ROUTE THAN EDWARD THE CONFESSOR. NONE LEFT A MORE UNCERTAIN OR DAMAGING DYNASTIC DISPUTE. EDWARD'S CLAIMS TO BE KING WERE ENTIRELY LEGITIMATE, HIS REIGN AT LEAST AVERAGELY COMPETENT. BUT LIKE HIS FATHER, AETHELRED, EDWARD WAS TRAPPED IN CIRCUMSTANCES FROM WHICH HE WAS LARGELY UNABLE TO ESCAPE.

The Cult of the Confessor

Despite being universally known as "the Confessor" the evidence for Edward's piety is thin and mostly dates from after his reign. As a young man, he seems to have been typically dissolute. Even in his early years as king his fondness for hunting was considerably more obvious than any latent holiness. Yet almost from the moment of his death Edward was being venerated as a miracle worker and healer of the sick. In 1161, the cult reached a climax when Edward was canonized. The cult of the Confessor seems to have been created partly through nostalgia for a lost Anglo-Saxon past and partly through Edward's apparent simplicity of dress and celibacy (even if his and his queen's failure to have children was almost certainly just because they were unable to). But overwhelmingly, he was remembered as the builder of a great abbey church just outside London, the West Minster of St Peter. Its original construction was fired as much by Edward's desire to establish a new centre of royal authority, preferably one that echoed the great Norman churches being built on the other side of the Channel, as to glorify God. It was consecrated in 1065, just in time for Edward to be buried there. By the time Henry III rebuilt the Abbey in the 13th century, Edward's cult was unchallenged and Henry constructed a new, impressively lavish tomb for the last of the 15 English kings to be made a saint.

IN 1014, AGED ONLY NINE, EDWARD AND HIS brother Alfred had been sent to Normandy for safe keeping from what looked like the increasing probability of a Viking conquest of England. There they were brought up. Whatever its own Viking origins and political turbulence, early 11th-century Normandy deeply coloured Edward's outlook. It is clear that for Edward, England took on the appearance of an alien land.

Nonetheless, the dynastic uncertainties caused by the death of Cnut in 1035 raised the prospect that either Alfred or Edward could reclaim the throne of England. In 1036, both returned to England. Alfred made his way to Earl Godwine's semi-court in Guildford. There, Godwine, crime boss as much as nobleman, ritually submitted to Alfred and then arranged his murder.

In the circumstances, Edward's subsequent distrust of Godwine was hardly surprising. More surprising is that in 1041 Edward allowed himself to be persuaded to return to England again by the new king, Harthacnut. Once in England, Edward was the obvious candidate to succeed Harthacnut after the latter's sudden death in 1042, not least in order to forestall a rival Scandinavian claim by Magnus I of Norway.

The first years of Edward's reign were dominated by a struggle for supremacy between him and Godwine. The latter struck an early blow when he manoeuvred Edward into marrying his daughter, Edith, raising the prospect of a future Godwine claim to the throne. But in 1051, in what must have seemed his apotheosis, Edward succeeded in banishing Godwine. Within a year, however, having mounted almost an invasion of England, Godwine was back stronger than ever.

Godwine's personal triumph was shortlived: he died the following year. But his dynasty seemed assured. By 1055, his sons Harold, Tostig and Gyrth

The Bayeux Tapestry is the single most vivid and compelling pictorial account of the Norman Conquest. The scene here (left) is divided in two. The upper panel shows the death of Edward the Confessor, who reaches out his hand to Harold, designating him his successor. In the lower scene, the body of the dead king is prepared for burial.

Edward the Confessor's rule was dogged by the rival ambitions of his leading subjects, Earl Godwine and his sons, Harold, Tostig and Gyrth, pre-eminently, from whose rapacity the beleaguered king was largely unable to escape (map left). Of greater significance was the damaging succession dispute left by the increasingly feeble king. In less than a year, Anglo-Saxon England was violently overthrown.

ENGLAND UNDER EDWARD THE CONFESSOR

	Harold's earldom, 1056
	Ralph's earldom, 1056
	Leofric's earldom, 1056
	Tostig's earldom, 1056
	Aelfgar's earldom, 1056
	Temporary Welsh conquests, 1057–62
	Harold's campaigns against Gruffydd ap Llywelyn, with dates
	Revolt, with details
	Advance of anti-Tostig rebels, supported by Edwin, 1065
	Frontiers of the earldoms, 1066, with name of earls

The shrine of Edward the Confessor (above) in Westminster Abbey was built by Henry III in the 13th century when the cult of the Confessor was at its peak.

were respectively the earls of Wessex, Northumbria and East Anglia. Their dominance was reaffirmed in 1063 when Harold and Tostig routed the hitherto invincible Welsh king Gruffydd ap Llywelyn. However secure on his throne, Edward seemed to have been comprehensively outplayed.

The difficulty facing Edward was not just humiliation but rather the succession. His marriage to Edith, often claimed never to have been consummated, had left him with no heir. Given his Norman sympathies, as well as his need to outflank the Godwines, it is credible that he should have nominated his cousin William, duke of Normandy, as his successor – as William steadfastly maintained. If so, he later seems to have changed his mind. In 1056, he arranged for Edmund Ironside's son, another Edward, banished as a baby by Cnut in 1016, to return to England. He would have made a credible successor had he not died the following year.

William meanwhile had never forgotten his designation as successor. At any rate in his own mind, he dramatically strengthened his claim in 1064 when

he secured – or so he asserted – a promise from Harold Godwine, who was in Normandy on a mission that remains mysterious, to support his succession. Nonetheless, within a day of Edward's death in January 1066 it was Harold who was hurriedly crowned. His hereditary right may have been non-existent, but as the man on the spot and in the absence of an obvious native heir his candidature was compelling. When he heard the news, William "… became as a man enraged".

1052 There took up Earl Godwine his burthen, and cleared himself there before his lord King Edward, and before all the nation; proving that he was innocent of the crime laid to his charge, and to his son Harold and all his children. And the king gave the earl and his children, and all the men who were with him, his full friendship, and the full earldom, and all that he possessed before.

The Anglo-Saxon Chronicle

HAROLD II 1066

KING

HAROLD II

BORN: *c.*1022
ACCEDED: January 5
1066; crowned
January 6 1066,
Westminster Abbey

King of England

HAROLD II WAS KING FOR LESS THAN A YEAR, YET HIS RULE WAS AMONG THE MOST DRAMATIC AND FATEFUL OF ANY RULER OF ENGLAND. IT WAS DOMINATED BY HIS DISPUTED SUCCESSION. HAROLD HARDRADA IN NORWAY, AND WILLIAM, DUKE OF NORMANDY, BOTH BELIEVED THEIR CLAIMS WERE SUPERIOR AND BOTH MOUNTED INVASIONS TO SUPPORT THEM.

Harold and William

Central to William the Conqueror's claim to the English throne was not just that Edward had designated him his heir in 1051 but that Edward had sent Harold Godwine to France to confirm the fact in 1064. It seems unlikely that Harold, whose own designs on the throne were clear, would have been prepared to act so obviously against his own interests in this way. On the other hand, there is no question but that he did go to France and that once there swore to uphold William's claim. The scene is vividly portrayed in the Bayeux Tapestry (below).

Though it was commissioned by a Norman (William's half-brother, Bishop Odo) and was in general a faithful reflection of the post-Conquest Norman view, the tapestry was actually produced by English embroiderers. So far as Harold's oath is concerned, they seem to have slipped in a particularly subtle contradiction of the official Norman line. The scene immediately following Harold's oath-taking shows Harold and his party leaving the Norman court. The implication is clear: that Harold was William's prisoner and the oath the price of his freedom.

It is possible that Harold went to France not on Edward's initiative but his own to propose that he would support William in his struggles against the king of France if William would support Harold's claim to the English throne. If so, it was a disastrous misjudgement. Nothing would deflect William from his absolute conviction that the throne of England was his by right. Further, having extracted the oath from Harold, he would – and did – do everything in his power to see it honoured.

ONLY ONE OF THE FOUR CANDIDATES FOR THE English throne in 1066 had a clear hereditary right: Edgar the Atheling (or prince), the great-grandson of Aethelred the Unready. Neither Harold nor the Norwegian king, Hardrada, had any hereditary claim; duke William in Normandy had only the most tenuous – through his great-aunt, Emma, second wife of King Cnut.

Nonetheless, for the majority of England's leading subjects, Harold was always the most likely choice. The threatened invasions by William and Hardrada made it essential that the country had a strong king to defend it. As its leading native subject and the country's most outstanding general, Harold had obvious advantages. The Atheling, by contrast, as an untried 14-year-old, had none of Harold's political or military strengths. It seems clear, too, that Harold had been lobbying for the throne for some years, building up substantial support. He also seems to have secured the ailing King Edward's designation as his successor. At any rate, that he was crowned the day after Edward's death in a ceremony that immediately followed the old king's funeral strongly suggests the culmination of a careful, long-term strategy.

The rival claims of Hardrada and duke William both rested on their assertions that they (or, in the case of Hardrada, his predecessor, Magnus) had been designated successors by Harthacnut and Edward the Confessor respectively. Both were prepared to use force to back their claims. William in particular, before and after his successful invasion, consistently stressed the legitimacy of his right to the throne, damning Harold as a perjurer and usurper.

There was in fact a further threat to Harold, his brother Tostig. As earl of Northumbria, Tostig had acquired a reputation as an incompetent tyrant, harrying his subjects while simultaneously unable to stop border raids by Malcolm III of Scotland. The previous autumn, Harold had arranged for Tostig's replacement by Morcar, brother of the earl of Mercia. Harold may have acquired a valuable new ally in Morcar but he had made an unforgiving enemy in Tostig.

The first months of Harold's reign were almost entirely given over to strengthening his defences.

1053	1063	1064	1065	
Harold Godwine becomes earl of Wessex	*Defeat of Gruffydd ap Llywelyn in Wales confirms Harold as pre-eminent military leader in England*	*Harold journeys to Normandy; forced to uphold William's claim to English throne*	*(Nov.) Harold masterminds overthrow of his brother Tostig as earl of Northumbria and his replacement by Morcar*	*Jan. 5: Death of Edward the Confessor Jan. 6: Coronation of Harold II May: Failed landings by Tostig on south and east coasts of England July: Major Saxon forces and fleet readied to withstand expected Norman landing*

1066 This year died King Edward, and Harold the earl succeeded to the kingdom, and held it for forty weeks and one day. And this year came William, and won England. And in this year Canterbury was burned. And this year appeared a comet on the fourteenth before the kalends of May.

The Anglo-Saxon Chronicle

Harold himself took charge of those in the south, where the threat posed by William was judged the more imminent. Morcar was given responsibility for the north. Their strength seemed amply demonstrated by the ease with which Harold, then Morcar, withstood attempted landings by Tostig, who, with support from the Low Countries, had assembled a fleet of sorts. Rebuffed, Tostig continued north, to Scotland.

By early September, with no sign of either William or Hardrada, Harold was forced to stand down his defences and allow his men to return home. On the 19th, he learned that Tostig and Hardrada had mounted a joint invasion and were laying waste the north. In an epic of improvised organization and fortitude, Harold hastily regathered as many of his troops as he could and set out for Northumbria.

There, outside York, he annihilated Tostig and Hardrada. Three days later, 250 miles to the south, William's fleet landed. Harold set off on a further exhausting whirlwind march back the way he had come. Rather than re-group and pick off the Normans during the winter, Harold threw his depleted forces into action immediately.

The battle, fought near Hastings on October 14th, lasted all day. By evening, his army was overwhelmed and the Godwine family wiped out: Harold and his two remaining brothers, Gyrth and Leofwine, were among the dead. The Anglo-Saxon supremacy established by Alfred had been definitively ended. A decisive new chapter in the history of England and its kings had begun.

THE INVASIONS OF ENGLAND, 1066

- → Harold's campaigns
- → Harald Hardrada's campaigns
- → Tostig's campaigns
- → William's campaigns
- ✕ Anglo-Saxon victory
- ✕ Anglo-Saxon defeat

However well organized, not even Anglo-Saxon England could hope to defeat near simultaneous invasions at opposite ends of the country (map right). Had Harold not thrown his men against the Normans the moment he arrived back from York, in all probability, hemmed in by Harold and far from home, they could have been picked off with relative ease. As it was, Norman victory was just the start of a four-year campaign to pacify the country.

Harold, famously, was killed when he was shot in the eye towards the end of the Battle of Hastings (left). Despite their sapping 450-mile march to and from York, the Saxons had come close to holding off the Normans, whose repeated cavalry charges failed to break their defensive line. But a series of feigned Norman retreats then fatally drew elements of the Saxons away from their strong defensive position. Those that remained, Harold among them, became progressively more vulnerable to further Norman charges and the Normans' archers.

ENGLAND: THE NORMANS 1066–1154

WILLIAM THE CONQUEROR
1066–87

HENRY I 1100–35

WILLIAM RUFUS 1087–1100

STEPHEN 1135–54

A SERIES OF INTERLOCKING THEMES DOMINATED ENGLAND IN THE AFTERMATH OF THE NORMAN CONQUEST IN 1066. BY FAR THE MOST OBVIOUS WAS THE WHOLESALE OVERTHROW OF ENGLAND'S ANGLO-SAXON RULING ELITE – NOT JUST ITS RULING FAMILY AND LEADING MAGNATES BUT PRACTICALLY EVERY LANDOWNER, LARGE AND SMALL, AS WELL AS ALMOST EVERY CHURCHMAN OF NOTE. ALL WERE REPLACED BY FOLLOWERS OF THE NEW KING, WILLIAM. THE MAJORITY OF THE NEWCOMERS WERE NORMAN BUT THERE WERE SUBSTANTIAL NUMBERS OF WILLIAM'S BRETON AND FLEMISH ALLIES AMONG THEM, TOO.

This displacement was begun and sustained by force. Along with significant areas of Scotland and Wales, England was placed under an occupying army that subjected it to a remorseless rule of conquest. All attempts at revolt were peremptorily crushed. The massive programme of castle-building begun by William was a permanent and visible mark of English subjection and Norman overlordship. The takeover of Anglo-Saxon England by the Normans was a root-and-branch operation. By any standard, it was hugely traumatic.

A number of consequences flowed from these central facts. One was that the position of the king himself was greatly strengthened. Having conquered and subdued England, in effect the country became William's personal property, to be disposed of as he thought fit. In practice this meant sharing the spoils among his French followers, whose principal motive for joining William's invasion had been precisely the prospect of enriching themselves in this way. But since it was directly to the king that they owed their new titles and huge estates – which could at any time revert to him – the king was placed at the heart of the burgeoning enterprise of conquest that was Norman England. Significantly, just a year before his death in 1087, William was able to insist that all his landholders, major and minor, swear an oath of personal loyalty to him. This was feudalism redrafted.

The king's position was further strengthened by continuing improvements in the efficiency of royal government. The Normans had a strong base on which to build. Anglo-Saxon government had been the most sophisticated in western Europe. When allied to the conquerors' own brand of absolute rule, it significantly expanded the reach of royal authority. The most celebrated example of this was the compilation of the Domesday Book, undertaken on the orders of William in 1086. Detailed information of this kind had simply never been available before. It is no exaggeration to claim that in the exercise of royal power Norman England saw something of a revolution-in-the-making.

Nonetheless, no king could rule without his leading subjects. If the most effective way to ensure their loyalty and support was by rewarding them lavishly, this also raised the risk that a coalition of disaffected magnates could muster sufficient strength to challenge the king. Needless to say, under strong rulers this was relatively less likely to happen. William himself and his two immediate successors, William Rufus and Henry I, were formidable personalities and practised manipulators of the subtle crudities of early medieval power politics.

By contrast, Stephen (Henry I's nephew), who came to the throne in 1135, found himself almost permanently at the mercy of these inherent instabilities. He was helped by the fact that the forces ranged against him, however powerful, were often as much at odds with each other as with him. Nonetheless, the pattern of baronial revolt and civil war that developed during his reign would become a recurring feature of English medieval history.

At stake of course was the crown itself. To a large extent, this was nothing new. Succession disputes and the ambitions of over-mighty subjects had been consistently destabilizing elements in Anglo-Saxon England. What was new now, however, was not just the shameless aggression the Normans brought to their family feuding but that their relentless struggles had acquired a wider, continental dimension. Put simply, the prize had been dramatically increased. Now, it was not merely the crown of England that was up for grabs but the dukedom of Normandy. The political fates of both had become inextricably intertwined.

A curious tension resulted, one that reflected the unusual imbalance in the status of England and Normandy. In part, this was the inevitable consequence of Normandy's geographical position. In an age of uncertain and slow communications, the effective exercise of cross-Channel power would test even the most dynamic of England's French kings. But the essential problem was more complicated still. By any objective measure, England was significantly more powerful than Normandy: it was substantially larger, very much richer, and considerably better governed. In short, it was a hugely valuable prize. In conquering England so unequivocally, William had achieved an extraordinary success. Furthermore, imbalance and tension were heightened by William's exceptional position: while he was only the duke of the conquering Normandy, he was the king of the subjugated England.

For William and his successors, Normandy remained the priority. This is partly explained by the natural inclination to give precedence to the mother-country over the colony: in most Normans' reckoning, Normandy would always count for more than England. More particularly, however, it was a reflection of the relative vulnerability of Normandy. In making Normandy the most powerful dukedom in France, William had made enemies of his neighbours. These included not just Brittany, Flanders and Anjou, but the kings of France, to whom William was at least nominally subject. But no French king could easily accept the presence of such a threateningly strong subject. Reducing the power of Normandy consequently became a central goal of French royal policy. The result, predictably, was near permanent conflict.

England in effect had not just become an offshoot of a much smaller power but a pawn in its native power struggles. In drawing it into the political orbit of France, William the Conqueror decisively and irreversibly altered the course of history.

WILLIAM THE CONQUEROR 1066–1087

BORN: 1028
ACCEDED: December
1066; crowned
December 25 1066,
Westminster Abbey
❦ ❦ ❦
*Duke of Normandy,
Count of Maine,
King of England*

Unlike even Harold's most formidable professional soldiers, the huscarls, William's knights went into battle on horseback. The Normans are said to have brought up to 6,000 horses with them. At Hastings, their military superiority would eventually prove decisive. The illustration (below) from the Bayeux Tapestry shows William just before the battle.

BORN A BASTARD, AND INHERITING THE DUKEDOM OF NORMANDY AT ONLY SEVEN, THE ODDS AGAINST WILLIAM'S SURVIVAL IN THE VIOLENT WORLD OF 11TH-CENTURY FRANCE WERE LONG. YET IN LITTLE MORE THAN 30 YEARS HE NOT ONLY MADE NORMANDY THE STRONGEST DUKEDOM IN FRANCE BUT CONQUERED ANGLO-SAXON ENGLAND. BY ANY MEASURE, HIS ACHIEVEMENTS WERE EXCEPTIONAL.

OF THE 4,000 LAND-OWNING THEGNS (OR nobles) in England in 1066, only two were left by 1087. The whole of the rest of England had been divided among just 200 Norman and other French magnates. The Anglo-Saxon Church had been similarly purged. There was only one English bishop still in office when William died in 1087. As remarkable, this takeover of an England whose population approached two million had been achieved by no more than about 10,000 men.

Guillaume I le Bâtard, as the French know William, was among the most relentlessly single-minded and successful rulers of early medieval Europe. His conquest of England was not just daringly conceived but precisely planned and executed. Taking on a well-organized opponent fighting on home soil was a hugely ambitious undertaking. To have any chance of success, William needed the support not just of his nobles in Normandy but of a disparate collection of allies in Brittany and Flanders. Before he could assemble his forces, William was forced into a complex round of diplomatic manoeuvres, which included winning papal backing, that were hardly less demanding than the invasion itself.

Even so, had it not been for the simultaneous invasion of northern England by the Norwegians under Harold Hardrada, which left Harold II in

Castle Building

The Norman Conquest was begun and maintained by force of arms. It was in every sense a military occupation by an alien power for whom war and conquest were central facts of life, justifications for almost any atrocity – provided they were successful. It was only appropriate that the most obvious visible expressions of this martial obsession were the castles the Normans built the length and breadth of the country. As the Bayeux Tapestry relates, almost the first thing William did on arriving in England was to build a castle, at Hastings itself (picture below). Thus established, the pattern of

Norman occupation scarcely deviated. As they arrived in a new location, so they would throw up a castle which could later be rebuilt on a larger scale in stone. The practical use of these castles was obvious: a secure base from which to dominate the surrounding town or countryside. In time they evolved as much into administrative centres as purely military ones but their prime function as the focus of Norman power never changed.

1035	1047	1051	1062	1064	1066	1067	1068
Normandy inherited by William	*William defeats his cousin Guy de Brionne to consolidate his hold on Normandy*	*William visits Edward the Confessor and is promised throne of England*	*William conquers County of Maine*	*Harold Godwine reputedly swears to uphold William's claim to English throne*	*Jan: Death of Edward the Confessor and accession of Harold Godwine (Harold II) summer: William assembles invasion fleet. Sept. 28: William lands at Pevensey. Oct. 14: Harold defeated at Battle of Hastings. Dec.: London submits: William crowned*	*William returns to France (Feb.–Dec.); revolt by Welsh under Edric the Wild*	*Landings in southwest by Harold II's sons: William besieges and sacks Exeter. Revolts in Northumbria under Edwin and Morcar*

ENGLAND

⟶ The Norman Conquest, to Dec. 1066

Early Anglo-Saxon revolts, with details

⇢ William's campaigns, 1068

Anglo-Saxon revolts, 1069

⟶ Danish campaign in alliance with Anglo-Saxon rebels, 1069

⟶ William's campaigns, 1069

Later risings, with details

⟶ Later Danish interventions, with details

⟶ Campaigns against Scotland, with details

Secured by Normans in Wales by 1086

Welsh kingdom, reduced to status of dependency

Owing homage to William

⚑ Castles built following the Norman conquest, to 1086

FRANCE

William's holdings at the outset of his campaign to conquer England

Under Norman rule, contested by Anjou

Revolt, with details

Disputed with king of France

⟶ William's campaigns in France, with date

William the Conqueror's subjection of England was made in the face of numerous revolts, large and small, against his rule as well as further Danish attempts to seize the country (map left). It was a relentless and brutal process carried out with extraordinary single-mindedness and played out against the background of William's continuing campaigns to assert the position of Normandy in France.

### Map labels

SCOTLAND

ABERNETHY

William, 1072

FALKIRK • EDINBURGH

William's son, Robert, 1080

BAMBURGH

In support of Edgar the Aetheling, 1069; later in alliance with Sweyn of Denmark

GATESHEAD NEWCASTLE

1069 ✗ *Outbreak of discontentment with local governance, 1080*

DURHAM

WHITBY

RICHMOND SCARBOROUGH

NORTHALLERTON

KINGDOM OF MAN

IRISH KINGDOMS

In support of Edgar the Aetheling, 1067

1069 ✗ YORK SKIPSEA

PENWORTHAM PONTEFRACT

1075

King Sweyn, 1070

DEGANWY

ABERLLEINIOG RHUDDLAN LINCOLN

CAERNARVON BANGOR CHESTER

Hereward, 1070–1; supported by Danes, joined by Morcar

Inspired by Danish intervention, allied to Edric, 1069

WELSH KINGDOMS

STAFFORD TUTBURY NOTTINGHAM

MONTGOMERY SHREWSBURY 1069 ✗

STANTON HOLGATE DUDLEY NORWICH

RICHARD'S CASTLE PETERBOROUGH

WIGMORE WARWICK ELY EYE

EARDISLEY AILEY WORCESTER HUNTINGDON

CLIFFORD HEREFORD NORTHAMPTON CAMBRIDGE

Edric the Wild, 1067; Earl Roger joined by Earls Ralf and Waltheof, 1075

EWIAS HAROLD BUCKINGHAM IPSWICH

MONMOUTH BISHOP'S STORTFORD COLCHESTER

Harold's sons, 1068

CAERLEON GLOUCESTER BERKHAMSTED

OXFORD HERTFORD RAYLEIGH

CHEPSTOW WALLINGFORD LONDON *Count Eustace of Boulogne, 1067*

BRISTOL READING SOUTHWARK ROCHESTER

WINDSOR CANTERBURY

DUNSTER DOVER

SALISBURY

Inspired by Danish intervention, 1069

MONTACUTE WINCHESTER LEWES 1066 ROMNEY

New Forest ARUNDEL HASTINGS CALAIS

BRAMBER PEVENSEY

Exeter Townspeople, 1068

CORFE CARISBROOKE FLANDERS

TREMATON

ENGLAND

PONTHIEU

Gerberoi 1078 ✗

ROUEN

1078 MANTES VEXIN

DIVES

NORMANDY PARIS

1073

DOL 1076

BRITTANY MAINE

RENNES *Supported by Anjou, 1069; Norman rule reaffirmed, 1073*

ANJOU

The White Tower at the Tower of London (above) was just one of the 70 castles built by William the Conqueror in his vast kingdom.

Timeline

1069	1070	1071	1072	1078	1079	1080	1085	1086	1087
Revolt in Maine forces William to return to France. York captured by Edgar the Aetheling and Sweyn II of Denmark (Sept.), recaptured by William (Dec.); Northumbria laid waste by William (to 1070)	Norman-born Lanfranc of Bec appointed Archbishop of Canterbury	Uprising in East Anglia suppressed	Malcolm III of Scotland forced to submit to William at Abernethy	Tower of London begun. Robert, William's son, supported by Philip I of France, leads revolt in Normandy	Robert defeated at Battle of Gerberoi. New Forest made exclusive royal hunting preserve	Robert leads punitive campaign against Malcolm III	Threatened invasion of England by Cnut IV of Denmark. Domesday survey ordered	First draft of Domesday Book presented to William	William dies besieging Mantes

William's minting of coins followed a long-established pattern in stamping royal authority on his new kingdom. Interestingly, as with coins issued in the reign of his son William Rufus, he is named not as WILLIAM REX but PILLELM REX (above). The runic form of the letter W was P. The Conqueror's Scandinavian roots had not been entirely forgotten.

England facing equally dangerous enemies at opposite ends of his kingdom, it is unlikely that William's cross-Channel assault would have succeeded. As it was, William was able to land unopposed in southern England before facing an English army that, in less than a month, had endured two forced marches of more than 200 miles each and a major battle.

With Harold defeated, William moved quickly to consolidate his victory. He marched his troops through southeast England in a formidable demonstration of his military superiority during which the key cities of Canterbury and Winchester both capitulated. Realizing the futility of continued resistance, the earls of East Anglia and Northumbria, Edwin and Morcar, submitted, as did Edgar the Aetheling, grandson of Edmund Ironside, who had briefly been proclaimed king by the Witan. By December, William had taken London. On Christmas Day he was crowned at Westminster Abbey.

Within two months William was back in France. There is some evidence to suggest that he may have felt that England, having apparently been brought to heel, could now be left to take care of itself. If so, he was wrong. By the following December, when William returned, he was facing revolts on almost every side. Over the next four years, he systematically crushed them all. As important, William began the extension of Norman authority into Scotland and Wales. Neither was conquered but both were forced to acknowledge the reality of Norman power.

The challenges to his rule came from various quarters: there were spontaneous outbursts of local protest, notably in East Anglia and the north; more sustained attempts at his overthrow, chiefly by Harold's sons in the southwest; opportunistic Welsh and Scottish attempts to extend their rule into England; and a substantial Danish attempt at conquest of the whole of England by Sweyn II. That these challenges were piecemeal made their suppression relatively more easy. That they sprang up without warning across almost the whole country taxed even the implacable William.

His response was brutal and absolute. In 1068, revolts in the southwest were summarily put down. In the winter of 1069–70, huge areas of Northumbria, where Sweyn's invading Danes had been enthusiastically welcomed, were effectively obliterated. Villages and towns were destroyed in their hundreds; thousands of people were slaughtered. By the summer of 1071 the uprisings in East Anglia had been similarly eradicated. To contain the Welsh, William authorized the creation of the Marcher lordships along the borders of Wales where a handful of his most powerful supporters were effectively allowed to rule as they pleased, carving out huge territories for themselves. In 1072, Malcolm III of Scotland was forced to submit to William. Everywhere, Anglo-Saxon lands were expropriated and given to the king's French followers.

Almost everywhere castles were built, no less than 78 in William's reign. These were the focus of Norman rule, heavily garrisoned and easily defended strong points from which punitive military raiding parties could be sent almost at will. Simple earth-and-wood constructions at first, they were later rebuilt in stone as time and means allowed.

The Domesday Book

Domesday Book – so called because there was no appeal against it – was the most detailed land survey made in the whole of medieval Europe. It consisted of two immense volumes that not merely listed every landowner in England but gave a precise account of their worth. According to the 12th-century chronicler Orderic Vitalis, "… so very narrowly did he [William] have it investigated that there was no single hide [landholding] nor indeed was one ox or one cow or one pig left out that was not put down in his record." Even more remarkably, it also listed every pre-Conquest landowner, comparing the value of their properties before 1066 with those in 1086, when the survey was made. If it is clear that pre-Conquest Anglo-Saxon records were the basis on which the survey was compiled, Domesday Book thus also provides a vivid record of just how completely the Anglo-Saxon landowning class had been expunged by the Normans. William's motive in ordering the survey was to be able to tax his subjects more efficiently. If he knew in detail what they were worth, they would have no choice but to meet his demands. Ironically, though William was presented with a first draft on August 1 1086, he was personally able to make almost no use of it. Almost immediately, he returned to France, never to return to England.

Hunting: A Royal Pastime

Hunting was a central preoccupation of England's kings well before the Norman Conquest. But under the Normans it became royalty's pre-eminent leisure activity. William created no fewer than 22 hunting preserves, among them Cranborne Chase and Poorstock in Dorset. A typical example is the New Forest in Hampshire, so called because its "afforestation" in 1087 saw much of its ancient woodland removed in order to create a more favourable hunting ground. Some 22 Saxon villages were razed to create it. All hunting preserves were subject to what was known as the "Forest Laws", a new category of law introduced by the king and outside the Common Law. Under the Forest Laws, only the king or his nominees were allowed to hunt the "venison" – red and fallow deer, roe, and wild pig. The grazing of other animals was outlawed. Under his successor, William Rufus, the Forest Laws were made harsher still. Anyone found guilty of "disturbing" the deer would be blinded. Those found guilty of shooting deer would have their hands amputated. If convicted of killing a deer, the penalty was death. In the words of The Anglo-Saxon Chronicle, "The rich complained, the poor lamented; but he [William] was so hard he set their hate at naught."

Every major town and city had one, as did key strategic points such as Dover and Rochester in the south and the New Castle in the north.

Though Malcolm III continued to probe across the England's northern borders, notably in 1079, and the new king of Denmark, Cnut IV, had still not relinquished the Danish claim to the English throne, the Norman subjection of England was a fact by 1072.

During the last 15 years of William's rule, a pattern emerged that in various forms would characterize the reigns of most of England's French kings until into the 13th century. However important their position as kings of England, their real ambitions remained centred on France. England, once secured, tended to be seen largely as a means of financing further French campaigns. In William's case, these were directed not just against his neighbours – the counts of Anjou and Flanders and the French king, Philip I – but against his eldest son, Robert.

Since as early as 1066, Robert had been recognized – at least in Normandy – as his father's heir. Typically, however, William refused to allow him any real power and, by 1078, Robert was actively conspiring with the French king to overthrow his father. Though reconciled within two years – in 1080, William brought Robert with him to England, where he led a further campaign against Malcolm III – Robert's treachery began a round of dynastic infighting to secure the succession to William's second son, William Rufus.

William's final visit to England was in 1085, when he returned with a huge army intended to resist a Danish invasion under Cnut IV. Though the Danish threat petered out with the murder of Cnut, the difficulty of raising taxes in England to pay for his army persuaded William of the need for more accurate information on his English subjects and their holdings. The result was the compilation of the Domesday Book, the most extensive record of its kind in medieval Europe. Though it might have been made possible only as a result of the earlier Anglo-Saxon records on which it was partly based, it nonetheless remains a remarkable achievement wholly characteristic of the exceptional thoroughness of William's reign.

... For I did not attain that high honour by hereditary right but wrested it from the perjured King Harold in a desperate battle, with much effusion of blood, and it was by the slaughter and banishment of his adherents that I subjugated England to my rule. I have persecuted its native inhabitants beyond all reason. Whether noble or commons I have cruelly oppressed them: many I have unjustly disinherited ... Having therefore made my way to the throne of that kingdom by so many crimes I dare not leave it to anyone but God alone.

Deathbed confession of William the Conqueror according to Orderic Vitalis, from The Ecclesiastical History of England and Normandy, *early 12th century*

William died in Normandy in September 1087 while embarked upon yet another round of punitive campaigning against Philip I, who was again being supported by Robert. Almost at once, a damaging dynastic dispute broke out between William's sons for control of the Conqueror's Anglo-Norman legacy. It would prove to be no more than the forerunner of many such draining conflicts.

Monarchy in the Age of Feudalism

FROM ABOUT 1000 ONWARDS, FEUDALISM WAS THE CORNERSTONE OF WEST EUROPEAN POLITICAL ORGANIZATION, A KEY ELEMENT IN THE PRACTICAL AS WELL AS THEORETICAL EXERCISE OF ROYAL AUTHORITY. DEVELOPED IN DIRECT RESPONSE TO THE DIFFICULTIES OF EXERCISING STRONG CENTRAL GOVERNMENT IN AN AGE OF PERSISTENT TURBULENCE, IT SUBSTANTIALLY REINFORCED THE REACH OF MEDIEVAL KINGSHIP.

THE BASIC PREMISE UNDERPINNING FEUDALISM WAS simple: a ruler would delegate authority over a given region (or "fief") to his followers (or "vassals") in return for a promise to support him politically, financially and, above all, militarily. The promise was sealed by a personal act of homage made by the vassal in which the vassal swore to bear "fealty" (or fidelity) to his lord. In turn, the lord promised to defend his vassal. This in effect was a contract that specified the rights and obligations of each party. Senior vassals were in turn expected to "subinfeudate" by extracting similar oaths of loyalty from their subjects, chiefly knights.

John Balliol, king of Scotland paying homage to the English king, Edward I, in 1292 (above). Positioned at the top of the hierarchy as the king's vassal, Balliol would then be expected to extract similar oaths from his own subjects. That a king could submit himself as the vassal of another monarch was a distinctive feature of the feudal system, but it inevitably caused tensions; when, in 1295, Balliol finally rebelled against the impositions of his feudal overlord, he was arrested and imprisoned in the Tower of London.

The result was a chain of relationships that descended vertically from the king and bound together all his leading subjects, the "feudal class". The feudal class consisted of nobles, knights, and monastic and secular clergy. It did not include women, children or the peasantry, all of whom were effectively the property of their lord and were in any case excluded on the ground that the surrender of freedom implied in the act of homage could only be made by a freeman.

Feudalism first emerged, haphazardly, in France after the break-up of the Carolingian empire in the 9th century. The immediate impetus was to fend off incursions by the Vikings through military alliances, under the French crown, between otherwise rival French territories. With time, however, the leading French nobles, all of whom claimed descent from Charlemagne and thus considered themselves at least the equal of the king and certainly sovereign in their own lands, became progressively less willing to acknowledge the French kings as their full feudal lords. Most recognized the king as superior, or "suzerain", but refused to do homage or to render military service except when it was obviously in their own interests.

Nonetheless, it was essentially this French feudal system that William the Conqueror, himself a vassal of the French king, brought with him to England in 1066. Having crushed the native aristocracy, William also had the advantage of being able to impose feudalism wholesale. For a brief period, feudalism in post-Conquest England probably represented the purest form it ever attained. In essence, claiming that he held England "of no one but God", William was able to divide the country among his principal vassals, ecclesiastical as well as secular. As the king's men, these vassals then subdivided it among their own vassals and administered it on his behalf.

In constructing these chains of mutual self-interest – the nobles received substantial territories while the king was assured of valuable allies bound to him by a personal oath of loyalty – the scope of royal power was considerably extended. There were, however, significant risks for rulers. Providing military assistance in the form of men and arms may have been a fundamental requirement of vassals, but it also meant that the most powerful vassals possessed military assets that could rival or even outstrip the king's.

On the other hand, what the king had given he could also take away. Investing a vassal with a fief meant that the lord was in effect co-owner of the fief, not that he had relinquished his rights to it. In practice, however, the most powerful rebellious vassals could be dispossessed only by a major military action. In much the same way a coalition of vassals, when driven by common interest to act together, could challenge the authority of even the most powerful kings. In essence, it was precisely this kind of co-ordinated opposition by his barons that in 1215 obliged King John to agree, under Magna Carta, to their demands for greater feudal "liberties". Retaining the loyalty of their senior vassals was a prime preoccupation of all medieval kings.

The position of ecclesiastical vassals was also a persistent source of difficulty. Since most senior churchmen were members of royal or noble families, and since the Church itself enjoyed such substantial feudal rights, the king's appointment of leading churchmen was every bit as politically sensitive as that of leading barons. But by the 12th century, senior Church figures were actively disputing that kings, anointed by God or not, could enforce feudal rights over the Church. At heart, this was a conflict between the temporal authority of the king and the spiritual authority of the Church. In general, the political strength or otherwise of individual rulers usually settled such disputes. But fundamentally this was an inherent conflict that was irreconcilable in feudal terms, one whose tensions ebbed and flowed throughout the Middle Ages.

Nonetheless, for the most part feudalism provided clear advantages for kings in financial as well as military terms. All vassals were obliged to provide their lord with financial help for particular projects, which in practice almost always meant financing wars. Similarly, though fiefs were normally hereditary, an heir could generally expect to inherit only on payment of a cash sum to his lord. This payment was known as a "relief" and was set at £5 for a knight, £100 for a baron. If the vassal died without an heir, the fief reverted permanently, or "escheated", to the king. By the same token, the widow of a vassal automatically found herself the king's property. If she was still marriageable, and the fief was valuable, the king gained an important asset to be bartered for the highest possible price.

Feudalism was a response to weak central authority; by the same token, strong central authority progressively rendered it redundant. With the emergence of powerful, territorially defined states by the 15th and 16th centuries, the system gradually withered. In England, it had effectively come to an end by Henry VIII's reign, although the notion of the contract that lay at its heart had by then been assimilated into English Common Law. Feudal tenures themselves were legally abolished in 1660.

A knight swears the oath of allegiance to William the Conqueror (left). The fact that William was in turn a vassal to the French king caused significant complications in his relations to the French crown. That the Angevin kings held England in their own right, whilst possessing extensive lands in France as vassals of the French king, and later, indeed, claiming the French throne itself, created a still more complex situation.

An ecclesiastical magnate does homage to his temporal lord (above). Although owing spiritual obedience only to the Pope, bishops and archbishops who held land often did so as the vassal of the king or another powerful lord. This contradiction frequently caused problems in relations between the Papacy and European monarchs; in 1103 the Pope threatened to excommunicate Henry I of England over the king's refusal to accept the Papacy's right to appoint clergy.

WILLIAM II 1087–1100

BORN: *c.*1060
ACCEDED: September 9
1087; crowned
September 26 1087,
Westminster Abbey

King of England

*William II from an early
13th-century manuscript
by Matthew Paris (above).
For early medieval
monarchs to be depicted
holding a church, as
William is here, was a
conventional recognition
of their piety and support
for the Church. William
did, it is true, endow the
abbey founded by his
father at Battle in thanks
for his victory over the
Anglo-Saxons in 1066.
But England can surely
never have had a monarch
more obviously out of
sympathy with the Church
than William II – nor one
more cynical in his
attempted manipulation
of it.*

THE SUCCESSION OF WILLIAM II IN 1087 SPARKED A DAMAGING SUCCESSION DISPUTE BETWEEN HIM AND HIS INDOLENT ELDER BROTHER, ROBERT, THE NEW DUKE OF NORMANDY, FOR THEIR FATHER'S ANGLO-NORMAN TERRITORIES. THE DIFFICULTIES OF UNITING ENGLAND AND NORMANDY UNDER ONE RULE WOULD DESTABILIZE THE ENGLISH MONARCHY UNTIL THE MIDDLE OF THE NEXT CENTURY.

WILLIAM II (OR "RUFUS", A REFERENCE to his red hair and ruddy complexion) has long been considered one of England's most unappealing kings, one whose coarse, brutal and dissolute reign threatened to undermine the new Anglo-Norman world and spark civil war. In many ways, the judgement is unfair, a reflection of the prejudices of contemporary ecclesiastical, chroniclers. There is no question that William was an unprepossessing figure or that he antagonized the Church. But that he was an effective ruler who consolidated Norman rule in England is equally plain.

William II came to the throne by the simple expedient of seizing it. The general assumption was that his elder brother, Robert, would inherit England as well as Normandy. But on William the Conqueror's death in Rouen in 1087, William Rufus made his way to England, secured the Treasury in Winchester, and persuaded the Archbishop of Canterbury, Lanfranc, to crown him. It is an episode that precisely illustrates the continuing uncertainties of royal succession even in an age when the monarchy itself was firmly established. With no automatic presumption of the right of the eldest son to succeed, the crown was always likely to go to the candidate at hand if only so as to avoid the damaging effects of a long drawn-out dispute.

The problem in this case was that England and Normandy now had two, mutually hostile rulers, which posed a near-insoluble dilemma for its leading subjects. Remaining loyal to one risked losing one's position under the other. With Normandy still very much the senior partner, most, led by Bishop Odo, preferred to throw in their lot with Robert. In 1088, William faced a serious revolt by his English magnates.

William dealt with the immediate problem in typical Norman style: he banished Odo and his supporters and confiscated their English estates. The fundamental difficulty remained, however, and there followed seven years of generally inconclusive campaigning, mostly by William in Normandy. This came to an

William and the Church

WILLIAM had little time for the Church, barely bothering even with conventional pieties. For its part, the Church was shocked not just by William's licentious court but by his refusal to appoint new bishops and abbots so as to keep Church revenues for himself. When Anselm, who was to prove a persistent thorn in William's side, was appointed Archbishop of Canterbury by William in 1093, the see had been vacant for four years. But to this existing conflict was added a growing Europe-wide dispute over the primacy of monarchical authority in Church affairs. It had long been taken for granted that, as divinely anointed rulers, kings had supreme authority in spiritual as well as temporal matters. This was not only a religious matter. The Church was enormously rich: controlling its assets was a prime necessity for all rulers. Yet from the reforming papacy of Gregory VII in the mid-11th century, the view had grown that papal authority over the Church was absolute.

During William's reign, the issue was further clouded by the existence of two rival popes, the broadly pro-Gregorian Urban II in Rome and Clement III in Ravenna. Deciding which one to recognize was, for William, a simple matter of determining which was more likely to support him in his own struggles against the Church in England.

1088 In this year was the land much stirred, and filled with great treachery, so that the richest Frenchmen that were in this land would betray their lord the king, and would have his brother Robert king, who was early in Normandy … When the king understood all these things, and what treachery they were employing against him, then was he in his mind much agitated.

The Anglo-Saxon Chronicle

1087	1088	1090	1091	1092	1093	1094
Accession of William	*William crushes uprising led by Bishop Odo, who with other anti-William magnates returns to Normandy*	*William leads inconclusive invasion of Normandy. Malcolm III of Scotland attempts to extend Scottish control over Northumbria*	*Degree of rapprochement reached between William and his brother Robert, duke of Normandy*	*William appoints Anselm Archbishop of Canterbury. Cumbria annexed by William; construction of Carlisle castle begun*	*Death of Malcolm III of Scotland; William engineers succession of pro-Norman Duncan*	*Attempt by William to conquer Wales is repulsed by Gruffydd ap Cynan; William authorizes further expansion of Marcher lordships*

The consolidation of Norman rule in England was vigorously continued by William Rufus (map right): The Marcher Lordships were expanded, Norman influence over its Scottish vassals reinforced. More damagingly, his reign also saw the first of a series of power-struggles – between the king and his leading magnates in England as well as between the king and his brother Robert in Normandy – that would destabilize much subsequent Norman kingship.

end in 1096, when Robert decided to join the First Crusade. To raise money for the venture, he pawned Normandy to his brother, who became regent of the duchy. Although this was clearly no more than a short-term solution – for it could be assumed that Robert would eventually return – it proved surprisingly effective for the remaining four years of William's reign. That Robert did return and, moreover, that William died childless, meant only that the succession problem had been postponed. It duly resurfaced on William's death, this time between Robert and his other brother, Henry.

The question of the succession took place against the background of two other far-reaching developments. One was William's dispute with the Church. The other was a further extension of Norman influence into Scotland and Wales. In Scotland, early disputes between William and Malcolm III of Scotland were decisively settled in William's favour in 1093 when, with Carlisle now in Norman hands, Malcolm was killed by a party of Norman knights. In the dynastic turmoil that followed, William played a leading role in the accession of Malcolm's sons, Duncan II and Edgar, both with strong Norman leanings. In Wales the Marcher lordships established by William the Conqueror were substantially expanded.

ENGLAND AND NORMANDY UNDER WILLIAM RUFUS 1087–1100

- Rebellions instigated by Odo de Bayeux on behalf of Robert in 1087, with leaders
- → William's campaigns, with dates
- Other revolts, with details
- Lost by Normans, recovered under William Rufus, 1097–9
- Annexed from Scotland, 1092
- Marcher Lordships, 1100
- Disputed with the King of France

The Death of William II

*T*he apparently accidental death of William II on August 2 1100 in the New Forest has long given rise to suspicions that he was murdered. The most commonly accepted theory is that it was no more than mischance, that William was shot by a companion, Walter Tirel, entirely by accident. On the other hand, William's brother Henry, who had designs of his own on the English throne, was with the hunting party and thus conveniently placed no more than a few hours' ride from Winchester. In any case, when William died, Henry did what William himself had done on their father's death: he made straight for Winchester, secured the royal Treasury, and then headed for London where, three days later, he was crowned by the Archbishop of London. Crucially, he had forestalled the return of his brother Robert from the Holy Land by little more than a month. Had Robert returned in time, he would surely have been able to reunite Normandy and England under his sole rule. In the matter of William's death, the case against Henry – strong though it seems – remains entirely circumstantial. It is unlikely ever to be proved one way or the other.

1095	1096	1097	1098	1099	1100
Further revolt against William by Norman magnates in Northumbria is crushed. Council of Rockingham meets to resolve disputes between Anselm and William and to decide between rival popes Urban II and Clement III	Robert pawns Normandy to William to finance his participation in First Crusade	Anselm flees to Normandy; William seizes his property	Attempted invasion of North Wales by Magnus "Barefoot", King of Norway, repulsed by marcher lords	Counties of Maine and Vexin in Normandy lost by Robert, retaken by William	Death of William in hunting accident in New Forest

HENRY I 1100–35

BORN: *c*.1068
ACCEDED: August 3
1100; crowned August 6
1100, Westminster
Abbey

King of England, Duke of Normandy (from 1106), Lord of Domfront (from 1092)

Henry (picture above) was an exceptionally able king, well able to master the seething, competing ambitions of his barons and rivals. He could also be surprisingly generous. He seems to have held genuine affection for his nephew and successor Stephen, for example, showering him with titles and lands. Yet a streak of cruelty bordering almost on savagery ran through him. In his youth, he is said to have personally thrown a rebellious merchant in Rouen from the castle battlements. As king, he authorized the blinding of two of his grandchildren who he was holding hostage.

AFTER WILLIAM THE CONQUEROR, HENRY I WAS BY SOME WAY THE MOST SUCCESSFUL OF THE NORMAN KINGS OF ENGLAND. BY A RUTHLESS COMBINATION OF FORCE AND DIPLOMACY HE OUTMANOEUVRED ALL HIS ENEMIES TO MAKE HIMSELF ABSOLUTE RULER OF ENGLAND AND NORMANDY. YET ULTIMATELY HIS REIGN, TOO, WAS CLOUDED BY A SUCCESSION DISPUTE. HIS LEGACY WAS A WASTEFUL CIVIL WAR.

AS THE YOUNGEST SON OF WILLIAM THE Conqueror (and the only one born in England), Henry had had no realistic expectations of inheriting any of his father's lands. Instead, it was assumed that he would go into the Church. As a result Henry was the only one of William's sons to receive much in the way of an education and the only Norman king who was not illiterate – hence his nickname Beauclerc, or "good writer". That his own instincts led him in quite another direction was clear not just from an abortive bid for power against both his brothers in 1091 – with the result that each viewed him with equal mistrust – but from the decisive manner in which he grabbed the throne after the death of William Rufus in August 1100.

Robert, duke of Normandy, whose own hopes of becoming King of England had long been thwarted by William, had nonetheless agreed with William that each would inherit the other's territories if the other died first and without an heir. Arriving back in Normandy just a month after William's death, and hailed on all sides for his exploits in the Holy Land, Robert's hopes of taking England from Henry were high. Instead, he found himself comprehensively outmanoeuvred.

Henry's actions on coming to the throne set the tone for most of his reign. Within six days of his coronation, he married Edith, the daughter of Malcolm III of Scotland, whose mother was directly descended from the Anglo-Saxon rulers of England. At a stroke, he had simultaneously allied himself with Scotland and proclaimed his kinship with the dispossessed Anglo-Saxon majority. He also issued a series of proclamations promising to end William's oppressive practices while simultaneously courting his leading subjects by making extravagant promises of lands and titles in return for their support. Crucially, he capped his diplomatic offensive by striking alliances with both the King of France and Count of Flanders and repairing William's break in relations with the Church by inviting the exiled Anselm to return to his office as Archbishop of Canterbury.

Thus, when Robert launched his inevitable invasion of England the following June, he had neither the military nor the diplomatic advantage he might reasonably have expected. Humiliatingly – albeit in return for £2,000 a year, under a deal brokered by Anselm – he was forced to recognize Henry's right to the English throne and acknowledge him his heir in Normandy.

Henry was far from finished. First, he dispossessed all those Normans in England who had not supported him. Then he took the fight to Robert. In 1106 he invaded Normandy, defeated Robert and imprisoned him. Robert spent the remaining 27 years of his life as Henry's prisoner.

Despite being forced on to the back foot by the Church in 1107 when, threatened with excommunication, he was obliged to concede the Church's superior authority in "investing" new bishops and abbots, in almost every respect bar one, the rest of his reign as unchallenged ruler in Normandy and England was strikingly successful. His solitary failure was his inability to produce an heir. Henry had two legitimate sons, William and Richard, but they were both drowned when the *White Ship*,

1120 This year were reconciled the King of England and the King of France; and after their reconciliation all the King Henry's own men accorded with him in Normandy … And on this expedition were drowned the King's two sons William and Richard, and Richard, Earl of Chester, and Ottuel his brother, and very many of the King's household, stewards, and chamberlains, and butlers, and men of various abodes; and with them a countless multitude of very incomparable folk besides. Sore was their death to their friends in a twofold respect: one that they so suddenly lost this life; the other, that few of their bodies were found anywhere afterwards.

The Anglo-Saxon Chronicle

The White Ship

I t is one of the great ironies of English monarchical history that Henry I had no surviving legitimate male heirs at the end of his reign. Henry in fact fathered 29 children, more than any other king of England or Britain. Unfortunately all but four were illegitimate and of them only one, Matilda, survived into full adulthood. The deaths of the teenage William and Richard, Henry's two legitimate male heirs, in 1120 on the White Ship – which was run on to a rock outside Barfleur by its supposedly drunken crew – threw all Henry's careful plans for his succession into disarray. Though Henry made his barons accept Matilda as his heir in 1126, most did so with extreme reluctance. Her marriage in 1128 to the 14-year-old count Geoffrey of Anjou provoked further suspicion. Henry had meant to bind Anjou, a traditional enemy of Normandy, within his diplomatic web. But to many Normans, it looked like no more than an opportunity for Anjou to reassert its claims to Normandy. They were proved right. By 1135, Henry and Geoffrey were at war. It was a further irony that it was one of Henry's illegitimate sons, Robert Fitzroy, earl of Gloucester, who was the mainstay of Matilda's campaign to make herself queen after Henry's death, a campaign that produced a vicious and brutal 15-year civil war in the reign of Henry's eventual successor, his nephew Stephen of Blois.

ENGLAND AND NORMANDY UNDER HENRY I, 1100–1135

- → Robert Curthouse's abortive invasion, 1101
- ⚑ Strongholds of Robert de Bellême seized by Henry
- → Henry's campaign against Robert de Bellême, 1102
- ▭ Surrendered to Henry I by Robert Curthouse, 1104
- → Henry I's campaigns against Robert Curthose, 1106
- ▬ Allied to Henry I, 1104-06
- ▬ Allies of the King of France, 1111–13, 1116–19
- ▬ Controlled by Anjou, periodically under Henry's influence
- ▬ Marcher Lordships, 1100
- ▬ New Marcher Lordships by 1100
- ▬ Brought under royal control by Henry I
- 🗲 Revolts, with details

Henry I's active brand of brutal kingship was strikingly successful in England and Normandy. Revolts in both countries were smartly suppressed (map right). As important, the threat posed by his elder brother, Robert, duke of Normandy, was put down equally effectively. Henry I did more than just consolidate the Norman hold on England: he actively redrafted the powers of medieval kingship.

taking them from Normandy to England, sank in November 1120. Henry's wife Edith (who had become known as Matilda) had died in 1118; in 1126, after a hurriedly arranged second marriage had failed to produce a new son, Henry designated his daughter, Matilda, his heir. In an age when female rights to any throne were viewed with deep suspicion, it was a move fraught with risk. When, in 1135, Henry famously died from a "surfeit of lampreys", a new round in England's long-running Norman succession crises was duly begun.

A saddened Henry I (left) after the death of his two sons in an accident in 1120 (see box). As Henry failed to produce another legitimate male heir, the accident represented the worst disaster of his reign.

1119	1120	1121	1126	1127	1135
Louis VI of France forced to recognize Henry as duke of Normandy	Henry's two heirs, William and Richard, drowned on the White Ship	Henry remarries, to Adeliza, daughter of the count of Louvain	Henry nominates Matilda as his heir and forces his barons to swear an oath accepting her	Matilda remarries, to Geoffrey (count of Anjou from 1129)	Geoffrey and Henry at war over Normandy

STEPHEN 1135–54

BORN: *c.*1097
ACCEDED: December 22
1135; deposed April 7
1141; restored Novem-
ber 1 1141; crowned
December 26 1135,
Westminster Abbey

❦ ❦ ❦

*King of England, Count
of Mortain
(to 1115), Count of
Boulogne (from c.1125)*

*Stephen (above) seems to
have had genuine religious
feelings. He established two
substantial religious
foundations, the abbeys of
Furness, in Lancashire, and
Faversham, in Kent,
where, with his wife
Matilda, he was buried.*

HOWEVER AGGRESSIVELY ESTABLISHED AND MAINTAINED, NORMAN ENGLAND HAD BEEN PERSISTENTLY UNDERMINED BY DYNASTIC FEUDING SINCE THE DEATH OF WILLIAM THE CONQUEROR. WITH THE ACCESSION OF STEPHEN IN 1135, THE INFIGHTING SPILLED OVER INTO OUTRIGHT CIVIL WAR. THE RESULT WAS NOT JUST 15 YEARS OF NEAR ANARCHY BUT THE EVENTUAL OVERTHROW OF THE CONQUEROR'S FAMILY

Stephen's right to the throne of England on the death of the domineering Henry I was no more or less than that of his predecessors. As the grandson of William the Conqueror, his heredi-tary claim was at least credible. Moreover, by instantly making his way to England from France on the death of Henry, he ensured that he was the man on the spot. To these advantages he added geniality – far from a usual quality in England's Norman kings – and, crucially, his sex. By contrast, his principal contender for the throne was not only still in France when Stephen was crowned but she was a woman.

Matilda, Henry's daughter – designated his heir fully nine years before he died – was unusually unapp-ealing, imperious, vain and cruel. These were not in themselves qualities that would have disqualified her from the throne, but combined with her sex they made her a less credible candidate than her cousin Stephen. As important, she was now also married to Geoffrey, the count of Anjou, whose designs on Normandy were clear – and as such an obvious threat to the French lands of England's leading Norman subjects. She was, however, determined to gain what she saw as her rightful throne in England.

Matilda brought her own brand of implacable vindictiveness to the resulting conflict; the insecure Stephen, by turns unpredictably magnanimous or harsh, nonetheless had the greater resources available

Stephen and Kingship

The contemporary chronicler William of Malmesbury wrote of Stephen: "by his good nature and the way he jested and enjoyed himself even in the company of his inferiors, Stephen earned an affection that can hardly be imagined." Stephen in fact was almost entirely unlike his Norman predecessors: kind where they were cruel, forgiving where they were vengeful, irresolute where they were absolute. Above all, he was persistently unable to master his barons. When he indulged them, they only saw him as a weakling; when he attempted to punish them, he only guaranteed their enmity. He had managed to contain and defeat Matilda, but this was largely because as king he could ultimately offer greater inducements to his senior subjects than she could. But perhaps the most damning verdict on this well-intentioned man was not just the chaos that engulfed England during his reign but his loss of Normandy in 1144 to the voracious Geoffrey of Anjou. However brutal, the Anglo-Norman empire had never been less than brashly self-assertive. Under Stephen, it came close to disintegration. As the 12th-century chronicler Gervase of Canterbury noted: "It was the king's custom to start many endeavours with vigour, but to bring few to a praiseworthy end."

1137 ... for every rich man built his castles, which they held against him [Stephen]: and they filled the land full of castles. They cruelly oppressed the wretched men of the land with castle-works; and when the castles were made, they filled them with devils and evil men. Then took they those whom they supposed to have any goods, both by night and by day, labouring men and women, and threw them into prison for their gold and silver, and inflicted on them unutterable tortures, for never were any martyrs so tortured as they were ... This lasted nineteen years while Stephen was king; and it grew continually worse and worse ... never did the country endure greater misery

The Anglo-Saxon Chronicle

1137	1138	1139	1140	1141
Robert of Gloucester, half-brother of the rival claimant to the English throne, Matilda, accompanies Stephen on a punitive expedition to Normandy against Matilda's husband, Geoffrey of Anjou	*David I of Scotland, seeking to extend his territories in the north of England, defeated by Stephen at Battle of the Standard. Robert renounces his oath of allegiance to Stephen; Stephen strips him of his lands and titles. Stephen alienates his brother, Henry, by refusing to make him Archbishop of Canterbury*	*Stephen arrests three of his senior bishops and administrators – the bishops of Salisbury, Lincoln and Exeter – accusing them of plotting to support Matilda. Robert and Matilda's invasion lands at Arundel (Sept.); they set up a rival court in the West Country*	*Stephen faces a separate rebellion in Lincoln by Ranulf, earl of Chester, who enlists the aid of Robert and Matilda*	*Stephen defeated at Lincoln and deposed and imprisoned (Feb.). Matilda declares herself Queen and moves to London; alienating her supporters, she is forced to retreat to Oxford. Robert captured by followers of Stephen (Sept.); Matilda is forced to exchange Stephen for Robert; Stephen restored (Nov.)*

to the king of England. Neither displayed much in the way of decisive generalship. Both also attempted to win the shifting, self-interested loyalties of the Norman barons, alternately bribing and oppressing them as their respective fortunes waxed and waned.

The result was a civil war in every sense – destructive, divisive and brutal. As with all such conflicts, it took on a pointless logic of its own in which neither side could give way. Predictably, it ravaged large areas of the country. Equally predictably, it also undermined its political security. The consequences were felt less in England than in Normandy, which by 1144 had been taken over by Matilda's husband, Geoffrey of Anjou. The Norman legacy so tenaciously defended by Henry I had been lost for good by the Conqueror's immediate family. Nonetheless, large areas of England suffered more than their fair share of brutal and arbitrary devastation as each side sought to assert itself and settle scores with its rivals.

By 1141, with Stephen the prisoner of her half-brother and chief ally Robert Fitzroy, the earl of Gloucester, Matilda could briefly claim to have triumphed. But her combination of haughtiness and political ineptitude rapidly turned a dominant position into a losing one. Few would-be monarchs have played such a strong hand so badly. She suffered a further setback in September that year when Robert himself was captured and Matilda was forced to exchange Stephen for him. By Christmas Stephen was again firmly in the driving seat.

By 1148, Stephen had effectively seen off Matilda but his victory was pyrrhic at best. With the unexpected death of his son, Eustace, in August that year he was in no position to resist the insistent claims of Matilda's French son, the hyperactive Henry Plantagenet. In November 1153 Stephen acknowledged Henry as his heir. A year later he was dead. A new and even more aggressive French dynasty had inherited the throne of England.

*For Stephen and the Anglo-Norman barony, the loss of Normandy in 1144 to Matilda's husband, the count of Anjou, was almost as serious as the ravages of the civil war sparked by Matilda's claim to the throne (**map right**). The elaborate cross-Channel empire so tenaciously defended by Henry I was unravelling at the seams .*

STEPHEN 1135–1154

→ *Stephen's movements*
🍂 *Rebellions*
▨ *Marcher Lordships, 1135*
▨ *to Scotland, 1036*
▨ *to Scotland, 1039*
✚ *Bishoprics where Stephen took preventive action against bishops plotting against him, 1139*
→ *Matilda's movements*
▨ *Approximate eastern limit of area in England generally held by Matilda's supporters*
⌂ *Castles besieged by Stephen in 1039 (only Malmesbury taken)*
○ *Seized by Stephen, 1042*
▢ *Area ravaged by Geoffrey de Mandeville, 1143–4*
---- *Eastern limit of area of England held by Henry Plantagenet at Treaty of Wallingford, 1153*

SCOTLAND

KINGDOM OF THE ISLES *(to Norway)*

(to Norway)

IRISH KINGDOMS

NORTHUMBERLAND

David I of Scotland

CUMBRIA

The Standard 1138

CHESTER

† LINCOLN
✕ 1141

SHREWSBURY

E N G L A N D

1136

RAMSEY ● † ELY

● CAMBRIDGE

English held area reduced to Pembroke Castle and environs by end of Stephen's reign

W A L E S

HEREFORD

PEMBROKE

GLOUCESTER ● RADCOT ● BAMPTON
CIRENCESTER ○○○ ● OXFORD
MALMESBURY ○ ● Cricklade 1147
✕✕✕ WALLINGFORD
BRISTOL ● *1141* Faringdon 1145
TROWBRIDGE ● MARLBOROUGH LONDON ●
DEVIZES *1135* CANTERBURY

DUNSTER ● *1141*
Wilton 1143 ✕ SALISBURY DOVER ●
WINCHESTER *1141*
Matilda under escort provided by Stephen, 1139 ARUNDEL ● BOULOGNE ●

1136 EXETER
WAREHAM ●
CORFE *1139*

Failed attempt to secure Normandy, 1137

Anarchy from 1137; Conquered by Count of Anjou, Matilda's husband, 1141/45; Governed on behalf of their son, Henry

NORMANDY

1142	1144	1145	1147	1148	1149	1153
Matilda besieged in Oxford; escapes to Abingdon	Geoffrey of Anjou gains control of Normandy	Matilda defeated by Stephen at Battle of Faringdon	Death of Robert	Matilda gives up her struggle and leaves for France	Half-hearted attempts by Matilda's son Henry to overthrow Stephen	Henry, already duke of Normandy, inherits Aquitaine on his marriage to Eleanor of Aquitaine; mounts further invasion of England. Death of Stephen's son and heir, Eustace (Aug.). Stephen acknowledges Henry as his heir under Treaty of Wallingford (Nov.)

SCOTLAND: FROM DUNKELD TO BRUCE 1034–1329

DUNCAN I 1034–40

MACBETH MACFINLAY 1040–57

LULACH 1057–58

MALCOLM III "CANMORE" 1058–93

DONALD III BÁN 1093–94 AND 1094–97

DUNCAN II 1094

EDGAR 1097–1107

ALEXANDER I 1107–24

DAVID I 1124–53

MALCOLM IV 1153–65

WILLIAM I THE LION 1165–1214

ALEXANDER II 1214–49

ALEXANDER III 1249–86

MARGARET 1286–90

JOHN BALLIOL 1292–96

ROBERT I THE BRUCE 1306–29

THE TERRITORIAL CORE OF A VIABLE SCOTLAND MAY HAVE BEEN ESTABLISHED AT THE DEATH OF MALCOLM II IN 1034, BUT IN REALITY MID-11TH-CENTURY SCOTLAND WAS JUST ONE AMONG A NUMBER OF COMPETING POLITIES IN THE REGION. THESE WERE TERRITORIES, ECONOMICALLY BACKWARD AND POLITICALLY IMMATURE, THAT EXISTED ON THE REMOTE MARGINS OF EUROPE. SCOTTISH KINGSHIP ITSELF WAS STILL AN ESSENTIALLY TRIBAL, OFTEN BRUTAL BUSINESS.

By 1290, however, though Scotland was still only in the second rank of western European polities, its independence and identity had been firmly established, its political institutions substantially strengthened and its territorial extent greatly increased. England aside, the chief threats to its continued existence — whether Irish, Norwegian or the disparate band of semi-independent barons and local rulers in the western isles – had all been forced to acknowledge Scottish supremacy. An independent Scottish kingdom had become a clear reality.

The key element in this transformation was Scottish kingship itself. By virtue both of the continuity provided by an unbroken line of royal succession between 1097 and 1290 and, from the 12th century, a deliberate if gradual extension of royal authority, Scotland's kings increasingly defined and shaped the emerging nation. To some extent, this was a matter of luck, above all in the appearance of a number of exceptionally able, long-lived rulers. Chiefly, however, it was a reflection of the transformation of medieval kingship occurring elsewhere in Europe. The rapid growth of feudal royal authority epitomized by Henry II in England found a ready echo in Scotland.

That said, the process was rarely clear-cut. Even during the reigns of the most dominant of these kings – David I and Malcolm IV in the 12th century, Alexander III in the 13th – there were clear limits to the reach of royal power. Rebellion on the part of disaffected barons was a recurrent problem, not least after the 12th-century influx of Anglo-Normans in the service of the crown that created serious disputes with the native aristocracy. Scotland's kings also had to contend with a shifting series of power bases, from which were mounted more or less serious challenges to their rule; these lay in the far north and west of the mainland as well as in the Norwegian-ruled Isle of Man and Western Isles.

Above all, Scotland was overshadowed by its stronger and often hostile neighbour, England. For substantial periods, Scotland was effectively no more than a client of England. Even after the border between Scotland and England had been more or less permanently fixed on the Solway-Tweed line in 1157, border clashes were a regular feature. And at the end of the 13th century, Edward I came close to ripping apart for good the still vulnerable Scottish polity.

It was precisely these aggressive Norman and Plantagenet kings, however, who provided the direct stimulus for the transformation of Scottish kingship. From the reign of Edgar onwards, Scotland's kings actively modelled themselves on their counterparts in England. In part, this emulation was almost a form of new Norman conquest. A number of Scottish kings, most notably David I, had been brought up in England under Norman protection. Importing the new style of French kingship was natural to them: it was a central element of a world they were intimately familiar with. But in part it was also a matter of necessity, a realization, however slow, that Scotland could only hope to keep England at bay by imitating the institutions that had made it strong.

The most obvious indication was the spread of feudalism, and through it the extension of royal power. By tying their nobles to them in direct chains of loyalty and service, Scottish kings in the 12th and 13th centuries substantially increased their own authority. The process was necessarily slow. Where William the Conqueror had been able to impose feudalism wholesale on England by the simple fact of conquest, in Scotland it could only be introduced piecemeal, often in the face of considerable resistance.

Alongside feudalism came the development of more effective forms of government, again on the Anglo-Norman model. David I was once more the key early figure. Not only was his court reorganized – with a steward, chamberlain, chancellor and constable – as an exact, if smaller version of Henry I's in England, he introduced Scotland's first counties, each with a sheriff to administer royal justice. The position of Scotland and its rulers was also significantly improved by the forging of closer links with the papacy, then at the height of its prestige.

As royal authority grew, so successive kings were able to extend their rule over larger areas. Moray, Caithness and Galloway were all brought under the actual rather than nominal rule of the crown. Crucially, in 1266 Norway was forced to surrender the western isles to Scotland.

The succession, in 1153, 1249 and 1286, of under-age rulers went undisputed, but in 1290 Scotland's dynastic luck ran out with the death of the uncrowned seven-year-old child-queen, Margaret, the "Maid of Norway". With no obvious successor left, the kingdom was suddenly vulnerable to the formidably rapacious Edward I of England. Whatever Scotland's new institutional stability, a new and bloodier chapter in Anglo-Scottish relations was begun.

THE HOUSE OF DUNKELD 1034–1153

THERE WERE SIX SUCCESSIONS TO THE THRONE OF SCOTLAND BETWEEN 1040 AND 1097. EVERY ONE OF THESE KINGS WAS EITHER MURDERED OR OVERTHROWN. BETWEEN 1097 AND 1290, BY CONTRAST, THE SUCCESSION OF NOT ONE OF THE COUNTRY'S SUBSEQUENT EIGHT RULERS WAS DISPUTED. THIS SIMPLE STATISTIC SPEAKS VOLUMES FOR THE GROWING POLITICAL MATURITY OF THE SCOTTISH MONARCHY.

Duncan II's reign in 1094 may have been brief, but from it dates the oldest surviving Scottish charter (above), a grant of land to the monks of Durham, then under Scottish rule. It is a distinct sign of the slowly growing sophistication of royal administration.

In becoming the first Scottish king to issue his own coins (above right), David initiated something of an economic revolution, one paralleled by his sponsorship of a number of trading communities, or "burghs", among them Berwick, Edinburgh, Stirling and Jedburgh. They not only transformed Scotland's economic life, opening valuable trading links across the North Sea, they were important sources of revenue for the king.

Double portrait of David I and his grandson, Malcolm IV (right), from the charter for Kelso Abbey, 1159. The biblical connotations in this rare portrait, produced shortly after David's death, are obvious. It is clearly intended that the old king should be seen as a reincarnation of the Old Testament King David, his youthful successor as a second King Solomon. The figures sit within the initial letter "M" of the charter.

T HE ACCESSION IN 1034 OF DUNCAN I, grandson of Malcolm II, brought the House of Dunkeld to the throne of Scotland. Its name came from Duncan's father, the Abbot of Dunkeld. Much of Duncan's six-year reign was spent campaigning against Thorfinn, earl of Orkney, and Macbeth Macfinlay, *mormaer* (ruler) of Moray, a rival claimant as king of Scots. Such feuding was hardly unusual. There is no historical reason why Shakespeare should later have portrayed Duncan as particularly wronged and Macbeth as particularly scheming, even though in 1040 Macbeth overthrew Duncan, seized the crown, and drove Duncan's sons into exile in England.

By the standards of the day, Macbeth's rule was not just stable, it was long-lived. And though it included considerable campaigning against the Norse in the north, Macbeth was secure enough to make a pilgrimage to Rome in 1050, evidence of Scotland's increasing integration with the wider European world.

For the rest of the 11th century, Scotland's fate was closely bound with events in England. To begin with, this took the form of English support for Duncan I's two exiled sons, Malcolm and Donald Bán. In 1054, Edward the Confessor ordered a successful invasion of Scotland in which Macbeth was overthrown. The following year, after a brief and confused rule by Lulach (Macbeth's stepson), Malcolm III "Canmore" ("big head") became king of Scots.

Though Malcolm's relations with Anglo-Saxon England were generally good, in 1066 he was nonetheless an eager participant in the failed invasion of England launched by the Norwegians and King Harold's disaffected brother, Tostig. The consequences for Scotland of the subsequent successful Norman takeover of England were momentous.

That Malcolm was now also sheltering Edgar, the remaining Anglo-Saxon claimant to England's throne, made Norman aggression all the more likely. Yet at the same time Norman influence over the Scottish ruling house was rapidly growing. In 1072, not only was Malcolm forced to become William's vassal, his eldest son, Duncan, was given as a hostage to William. Brought up in a Norman court, Duncan became a keen proponent of Norman ways. The struggle between the pro- and anti-Norman factions within Scotland would become a dominant theme in the development of Scotland's monarchy well into the next century.

In 1093, the murder of Malcolm III himself by the Norman earl of Northumbria provoked a fierce anti-Norman backlash which brought Malcolm's brother, Donald III Bán, to the throne. Within a year, he had been ousted by a Norman-backed invasion led by the strongly pro-Norman Duncan. A year later, Donald Bán had taken the throne back.

In 1097, a second Norman-sponsored invasion led by another of Malcolm's sons, Edgar, proved decisive. Donald Bán was captured and murdered. Edgar brought Scotland firmly within the Norman orbit, a process continued by his brothers and successors, Alexander I and David I. In part, this was a matter of the assertion of Norman and later Angevin overlordship. Equally important, however, it was a conscious attempt to remodel the Scottish monarchy on Anglo-French lines. Scotland could never hope to rival England, but by imitating its newly powerful kings it could go far towards assuring an independent and increasingly secure identity.

1040	1054	1057	1058	1061	1066	1068	1070	1072	1079	1091
Duncan I killed by Macbeth at Pitgaveny; Duncan's sons Malcolm and Donald Bán forced into exile in England	Macbeth defeated by Earl Siward of Northumbria and Duncan's son, Malcolm at Dunsinnan	Macbeth killed by Malcolm at Lumphanan; his stepson, Lulach, becomes king of Scots	Lulach killed; accession of Malcolm III	Northumbria raided by Malcolm III	Attempted conquest of England by Malcolm and allies Hardrada of Norway and Tostig defeated by Harold II	Edgar the Aetheling taken in by Malcolm III, who marries his sister Margaret	Malcolm III raids Northumbria seeking to pre-empt Norman conquest of Scotland	Malcolm III submits to William the Conqueror at Abernethy after retaliatory Norman invasion of Scotland	Another invasion of Northumbria by Malcolm III provokes further Norman retaliatory action	Final invasion of Northumbria by Malcolm III leads to further Scottish submission to Norman king of England, William Rufus

Scotland, 1034–1153

By the death of David I in 1153, the reach of a Scottish kingship actively modelling itself on its Norman and Plantagenet neighbours in England had been greatly increased. The west coast may still not have been brought under Scotland's kings but their authority, as well as their relations with England, had been transformed (map below).

Duncan I 1034–40
(born c.1010) Grandson of Malcolm II

Last king of Strathclyde and first ruler of the House of Dunkeld. Attempts to extend his rule into the far north saw repeated clashes with Thorfinn, earl of Orkney, and Macbeth, ruler of Moray. Also unsuccessfully attempted to consolidate Scottish rule in Northumbria. Defeated and killed by Macbeth at Pitgaveny.

Macbeth Macfinlay 1040–57
(born c.1005) Mormaer (ruler) of Moray from 1032

(Moray's rulers were longtime rivals of the Mac Alpin kings of Scotland). Though unable to subdue the Norse in Caithness and Sutherland, his rule was otherwise stable until, in 1054, Duncan's eldest son, Malcolm, supported by Siward, earl of Northumbria, defeated him at Dunsinnan. In 1057, he was killed by Malcolm at Lumphanan.

Lulach 1057–8
(born c.1032) Stepson of Macbeth

Last mormaer of Moray to become King of Scots, Macbeth ruled for less than a year before the future Malcolm III, already effective ruler of southern Scotland, killed him at Essie.

Malcolm III "Canmore" 1058–93
(born c.1031) Son of Duncan I

Last of the fearsomely warlike warrior-kings of old. His first marriage, to Ingibiorg, daughter of the Earl of Orkney, cemented relations with the Norse and allowed him to concentrate on the attempted conquest of Northumbria, which he repeatedly raided. William the Conqueror and his son William Rufus permanently worsted him, however, extracting oaths of allegiance in 1072 and 1092 (when Cumbria was also lost).

Donald III Bán 1093–4 and 1094–7
(born c.1032) Son of Duncan I

Brother of Malcolm III. Came to the throne after Malcolm's murder by the Normans. Fierce opponent of the growing Norman influence in Scotland. Ousted by Malcolm's eldest son, Duncan, with the support of William Rufus. Within months, Duncan himself had been murdered and Donald restored. A second Norman-backed invasion in 1097, led by another of Malcolm's sons, Edgar, saw the final defeat of Donald.

Duncan II 1094
(born c.1060) Son of Malcolm III

Though initially a beneficiary of Norman support, he was obliged by fierce anti-Norman feeling within Scotland to dismiss all the Anglo-Normans from his court. Suddenly vulnerable, he was powerless to resist Donald III. His reign was chaotic and brief.

Edgar 1097–1107
(born c.1074) Son of Malcolm III

Capable and competent; restored stability to the crown. Strongly subservient to Norman England, however, with whom relations were accordingly peaceful. The first Scottish king to imitate the English practice of sealed writs to enforce his will.

Alexander I 1107–24
(born c.1077) Son of Malcolm III

Marriage to one of Henry I's many bastard daughters, Sybilla, cemented relations with England (as well as confirming Scotland's vassal status), allowing Alexander to launch successful campaigns against still strongly anti-Norman Moray, and to initiate basic reforms in government.

David I 1124–53
(born c.1084) Son of Malcolm III

The dominant figure in Scottish 12th-century history, author of the "Davidian revolution". He almost single-handedly initiated the transformation of Scottish kingship, substantially increasing its authority and prestige, principally through the imposition of feudalism, a process supported by the introduction of large numbers of Anglo-Norman families. Successful subjugation of Moray from 1130 was matched by numerous administrative reforms and remarkable patronage of the Church. If unable to overcome Norman military superiority, he nonetheless helped to carve a distinctive and increasingly admired Scottish identity.

1093	1094	1097	1107	1124	1127	1128	1130	1136	1138	1149
Malcolm III murdered on orders of Robert de Mowbray, earl of Northumbria; his brother Donald Bán succeeds	Donald Bán briefly overthrown by Malcolm's son, Duncan II, then restored after death of Duncan	William Rufus sponsors invasion of Scotland by Malcolm III's son, Edgar; Donald Bán overthrown and Edgar accedes	Accession of Alexander I; initiates minor reforms	Accession of David; beginning of major programme of reforms	David I swears to uphold right of Henry I's daughter, Matilda, to throne of England (and again in 1133)	Holyrood Abbey founded by David I	Moray annexed for crown by David I	David I supports Matilda's claim to England after accession of Stephen (1135) by invading Cumbria.	Further invasion of Northumbria crushed by Stephen at Battle of the Standard	David I agrees to support claim of Matilda's son, Henry of Anjou, to English throne in return for right to retain Cumbria and Northumbria

THE HOUSE OF DUNKELD 1153–1296

THE NORMANIZING POLICIES OF DAVID I WERE CONTINUED BY HIS SUCCESSORS IN THE 12TH AND 13TH CENTURIES, CONSIDERABLY INCREASING SCOTTISH ROYAL AUTHORITY AS WELL AS THE TERRITORY UNDER ITS CONTROL. YET THROUGHOUT THE PERIOD SCOTLAND'S KINGS ALSO HAD TO CONTEND WITH A SERIES OF VERY MUCH MORE POWERFUL ENGLISH KINGS. SCOTTISH AMBITIONS ALWAYS HAD TO CONFRONT THE REALITY OF SUPERIOR ENGLISH ARMS.

Alexander II's imperial self-projection as ruler of a largely peaceful, united Scotland is underlined in his image on his seal (right), majestically enthroned, sword and sceptre in hand. Though no less determined to increase his prestige than his predecessors, he was adept at balancing the competing ambitions of his nobles, Anglo-Norman and native alike.

John Balliol (below), his crown and sceptre symbolically broken. As has rightly been said, the humiliation of Balliol by Edward I was "a calculated exercise in demoralization". In 1293, summoned to Westminster by Edward I, John was treated almost as an object of ridicule by the English king. Disowned by his Scottish magnates and systematically abused and then overthrown by Edward, his eventual imprisonment in the Tower must have come almost as a relief to him.

THE UNDISPUTED ACCESSION OF THE 11-year-old Malcolm IV, David I's grandson, in 1153 may have demonstrated a new political stability in Scotland but it also left the country vulnerable. The most obvious threat came from Henry II, king of England from 1154. Despite having promised David I in 1149 that he would allow Scotland to retain Northumbria and Cumbria if David would support his claim to the English throne, in 1157 Henry imperiously informed Malcolm that he was taking them back. Though the Anglo-Scottish border would not be formally fixed on the line of the Tweed and Solway until the Treaty of York in 1237, and Malcolm and his immediate successors would make repeated attempts to regain northern England, in effect Scotland's southern limit had been permanently established.

The other danger came from those magnates, above all in the still strongly Gaelic and Norse west and north – Ross, Argyll, Moray and Galloway – who were alarmed at the continuing influx of Anglo-Normans into Scotland, and at David's determination to extend feudalism. Resistance centred on Somerled, so-called king of the Isles, who in the name of the king of Norway ruled a large, if vaguely defined area embracing much of western Scotland. Somerled's unsuccessful attempt to unseat Malcolm in 1164 led not just to his own death but brought Argyll and Galloway under increasing royal control.

The twin themes of conflict with England and the extension of royal authority, in the face of baronial and Norwegian resistance, into the north and west of Scotland persisted through the long reigns of Malcolm's successors, William the Lion and Alexander II. In 1174, with Henry II preoccupied with the attempt by his sons to overthrow him, William attempted to retake Northumbria. It was a humiliating fiasco. Under the subsequent Treaty of Falaise, William was forced to become Henry's vassal, English troops were garrisoned in Scotland (at Scottish expense), and the Church of Scotland was made subject to that of England.

Though Richard the Lionheart reversed the treaty in 1189 in return for a payment of 10,000 marks, his successor, John, was determined to reassert English overlordship. In 1212, in a further humiliating setback for the now ageing William, the Scottish king was obliged to confirm John as his lord and surrender his daughters for John to marry off (the elder in theory to John's heir). Hardly surprisingly, William's son, Alexander, who acceded in 1214, enthusiastically supported the English barons who forced Magna Carta on John in 1215. In a similar spirit of rebellion, Alexander also threw his weight behind the French claimant to the English throne, Prince Louis.

John's sudden death in 1216 and the accession of Henry III transformed Anglo-Scottish relations. The mood of co-operation, symbolized by Alexander's marriage in 1221 to Henry III's sister, Joan, allowed him and his son, Alexander III, to devote themselves to the extension of royal authority over western Scotland, a process which climaxed in 1266 with the Treaty of Perth, under which Norway surrendered the western isles to Scotland.

Through a mixture of pragmatism and military success, Alexander III had brought renewed stability to Scotland. However, the death in 1290 of his successor, his seven-year-old Norwegian-born granddaughter, Margaret, en route to Scotland, opened the way for Edward I to reassert English overlordship. In 1292, he in effect appointed a new king, John Balliol, whom he lost no time in humiliating. In 1296, in flat contradiction of earlier promises, Edward began the conquest of Scotland.

THE ARMIS OF THE BALLIOVN

1157	1160–4	1163	1174	1187	1189	1196	1209–12	1215
Henry II forces Malcolm IV to accept English control of Northumbria and Cumbria; Malcolm becomes Henry's vassal	Galloway and Argyll subdued by Malcolm IV; rebellion by Somerled, Lord of Argyll, crushed (1164)	Malcolm IV forced to renew his homage to Henry II	William the Lion invades northern England; captured by Henry II and made his vassal (Treaty of Falaise)	Revolts against William in Galloway put down	The "Quitclaim of Canterbury": Richard I cancels the Treaty of Falaise	Successful campaign by William against Norse earl of Orkney	Invasions of Scotland by King John lead to restoration of English overlordship	Alexander II supports Magna Carta and does homage to Prince Louis of France in attempt to aid the overthrow of John

Whatever the vicissitudes of its relations with Henry II and John, by the death of Alexander III in 1286 the authority of the Scottish crown had been extended well into the far north and west and a series of challenges to its rule dealt with (map below). In much the same way, the Anglo-Scottish border had also been more or less permanently fixed, albeit it very much in the former's favour.

SCOTLAND 1153–1286

- Scottish control, 1153
- Effective Scottish control established by c.1164
- to England, 1157
- Personally held by Scottish kings, 1150–1296
- Taken by Somerled, Lord of Argyll, by 1158
- Other areas possibly controlled by Somerled, by 1158
- Acquired by Scotland in 2nd half of 12th century
- Towns occupied by English garrisons, 1174 (with dates of return to Scottish control)
- To Scotland under Treaty of Perth, 1266
- Campaigns to secure the north
- William's campaign, 1174
- Other Scottish campaigns
- Campaign of King John of England, 1216
- Campaign of King Haakon IV of Norway, 1263
- Revolts
- Frontier, 1237

MALCOLM IV (BORN 1142)
1153–65
GRANDSON OF DAVID I
Consistently outflanked by Henry II, whose vassal he became, Malcolm was nonetheless successful in extending his authority into much of the west. The high point of his reign was the defeat of Somerled's rebellion in 1164. He was an ardent feudalizer and generous patron of the Church.

WILLIAM I THE LION (BORN 1143)
1153–1214
GRANDSON OF DAVID I
Longest-reigning king of medieval Scotland. Continued the extension of royal authority into western Scotland, successfully putting down a number of challenges to his rule; launched many administrative initiatives. Thwarted by Henry II, however, whose overlordship of Scotland was complete, and by his son, John, who treated William with close to contempt.

ALEXANDER II (BORN 1198)
1214–49
SON OF WILLIAM I
Early years of his reign dominated by attempts to regain Northumbria, which involved marching a Scottish army as far as Dover to do homage to Prince Louis of France. Thereafter reached a new accord with England, which included the new permanent southern border of Scotland on the Solway–Tweed line in 1237. Also made further progress in extending royal authority to the west.

ALEXANDER III (BORN 1241)
1249–86
SON OF ALEXANDER II
Despite inevitable difficulties in his early years – he was only eight when he came to the throne – Alexander's reign was solidly prosperous. Good relations with England allowed him to push forward the conquest of the western isles, which, under the Treaty of Perth, became Scottish in 1266. His death in a riding accident plunged Scotland into crisis

MARGARET (BORN 1283)
1286–90
GRANDDAUGHTER OF ALEXANDER III
The Maid of Norway never set foot in her kingdom: daughter of the king of Norway, she died in the Orkneys, at only seven, on her way to Scotland. Her death, at just seven years old, allowed Edward I – who had welcomed her accession, proposing a marriage with his son – to stake his claim on Scotland.

JOHN BALLIOL (BORN c.1250)
1292–6
One among several possible candidates for the throne after Margaret's death, Balliol rapidly became no more than a pawn of Edward I, whose vassal he was. Captured by Edward in 1296, "Toom Tabard" as he was known, meaning "empty coat", possibly a reference to Edward's symbolic removal of his royal arms from his surcoat, was sent to the Tower of London. In 1299 he was released, under papal protection, and ended his days in France, where he died in 1313. His son, Edward, later bid for the Scottish throne, backed by Edward III of England.

1221	1237	1249	1251	1263	1266	1286	1290	1291	1296
Anglo-Scottish relations stabilized with marriage of Alexander II to sister of Henry III	Anglo-Scottish border fixed on Solway–Tweed line under Treaty of York	Death of Alexander II on further campaign against Western Isles	Marriage of Alexander III to Margaret, daughter of Henry III	Attempt by King Haakon of Norway to reassert Norwegian supremacy over Western Isles	Western Isles ceded to Scotland by Norway under Treaty of Perth	Death of Alexander III; three-year-old Margaret becomes queen	Edward I guarantees independence of Scotland under Treaty of Birgham. Death of Margaret	Edward I asserts overlordship of Scotland and approves choice of John Balliol as new king (1292)	John Balliol deposed by Edward I; conquest of Scotland launched

ROBERT I THE BRUCE 1306–29

EDWARD I'S SYSTEMATIC ATTEMPTS TO BRING SCOTLAND PERMANENTLY UNDER ENGLISH RULE CAME CLOSE TO EXTERMINATING THE KINGDOM PAINSTAKINGLY ESTABLISHED BY DAVID I AND HIS SUCCESSORS. YET BY 1328, ENGLAND WAS FORCED TO RECOGNIZE SCOTLAND'S INDEPENDENT EXISTENCE UNDER A SINGLE RULER, ROBERT I, THE BRUCE. ROBERT REINVIGORATED A SCOTTISH SENSE OF IDENTITY THAT ENDURES TODAY.

BORN: July 11 1274,
Turberry
ACCEDED: March 25
1306; crowned March
27 1306, Scone Abbey

King of Scotland

The achievements of Robert
(above), *not just in resisting
the Plantagenets but in
rekindling Scottish
independence, were
remarkable. That Scotland
survived as an independent
kingdom was almost
entirely thanks to him.*

THE INTERMITTENT CONFLICT BETWEEN England and Scotland was raised to new heights of savagery by Edward I's remorseless campaigns to subdue Scotland after 1296. In the face of Edward's overwhelming military superiority, Scotland's nobles had been forced to acknowledge a new English overlordship by 1304, under the "king's peace". The very public execution the following year of William Wallace, whose guerrilla campaigns had briefly threatened English supremacy, underlined Edward's apparently complete triumph.

Hopes of a Scottish revival were made all the more distant by infighting between the nobles. Prominent among the competing factions were the Comyns, consistent opponents of the English, and the Bruces, who had been prime candidates for the Scottish crown eventually awarded to John Balliol in 1292. In 1306, Robert Bruce, Earl of Carrick, brutally murdered his rival, John Comyn, in Greyfriars Abbey, Dumfries, and had himself crowned king. Yet the prospect of Robert posing any serious threat to English control of Scotland seemed remote at best. Almost immediately, he was defeated by an English army at Methven and forced into exile in the Western Isles.

The problems facing Robert were twofold: to triumph in what had effectively become a Scottish civil war; and only then, as he gathered strength, to overthrow the English. A long and brutal campaign of attrition and raiding followed, in which further Scottish rivals were eliminated and English strongholds in Scotland, as well as in northern England, were attacked. By 1314, Robert who was ably supported by his brother Edward, had established his control over all but southeast Scotland.

The death of Edward I in 1307 may not have reduced the scale of the Plantagenet war machine, but his successor, the impetuous and pleasure-loving Edward II, had none of his father's remorseless genius in deploying it. In 1314, with Robert threatening the great English fortress at Stirling, Edward II, determined to destroy him for good, led a massive army into Scotland. It was ignominiously routed at Bannockburn outside Stirling.

English defeat at Bannockburn may have confirmed Robert's position as king of Scotland, but it did nothing to lessen Anglo-Scottish hostility. The following years saw repeated cross-border attacks

The English defeat at Bannockburn (right) *may partly have been the result of complacent generalship, but it was nonetheless a startling overturn of what had been a consistently superior English army. The Plantagenets were far from finished, but they could no longer count on automatic Scottish military inferiority.*

Robert Bruce, 1306–1329

- Possessions of Edward I at start of reign, 1272
- Conquered by Edward I, by 1282
- Under direct English occupation, early 14th century
- Seats of Church dignitaries who supported Robert's coronation
- Presumed movement of Robert, March 1306 to May 1307
- Presumed movement of Robert, May 1307 to end 1308
- Edward II's campaigns, with date
- Approximate area of Bruces' campaigns, 1315–18
- Claimed by Edward Bruce in terms of his election as High King in 1316
- Robert and Edward Bruces' campaign 1317
- Subject to frequent Scottish raids to 1328
- Robert's campaigns, 1311-28
- Battle won by Robert, with date
- Battle lost by Robert, with date
- Frontier

Huge areas of northern England and southern Scotland were laid low by the struggles for supremacy between the Plantagenet kings, Edward I and Edward II, and the Scots (map right). *The devastation was increased by no less bitter conflicts between Robert Bruce and his rivals for the Scottish throne: the Comyns, the MacDougalls and the Earl of Ross. Once established as sole king of Scotland, and after having defeated the English at Bannockburn, Robert carried the struggle to Ireland. If unsuccessful in driving the English from Ireland, Robert at least partly diverted their attention from their attempts to retake Scotland.*

ORKNEY ISLANDS (to Norway)

In all this fighting the Scots were so divided that often father was with the Scots and his son with the English or one brother was with the Scots and another with the English, or even one individual was first on one side and then on the other.

The Lanercost chronicler, *1311–12*

FRANCE

by both sides devastating large areas of northern England and southern Scotland alike. Bannockburn also prompted an ambitious attempt by Robert in 1315 to outflank the English by making common cause with the Irish. The campaign, mostly led by Edward Bruce, was a failure, provoking only a bitter and futile three-year civil war and bringing misery to large areas of Ireland.

Much more significant, however, was what came to be called the Declaration of Arbroath, signed by Scotland's leading nobles in 1320, with the apparent encouragement of Robert, and amounting, in effect, to a potent assertion of Scotland's right to independent nationhood. Crucially, it made provision for the legal overthrow of Robert if ever he should surrender Scotland to the English. Scottish self-identity has rarely been more convincingly stated.

In 1328, following the deposition of Edward II, England finally renounced all claims to Scotland under the Treaty of Edinburgh. It was to prove no more than a temporary lull. The death of Robert the following year from leprosy, and accession to the English throne of the vastly more able Edward III the year after opened another, bitter chapter in Anglo-Scottish hostility.

1327	1328	1329
Edward II deposed	Treaty of Edinburgh and Northampton England recognizes Scottish independence	Death of Robert the Bruce

The Declaration of Arbroath, 1320

[If Robert] should give up what he has begun and agree to make us and our kingdom subject to the king of England or the English we should exert ourselves at once to drive him out as our enemy and a subverter of his own rights as well as ours, and make some other man who was well able to defend us our king; for as long as but a hundred of us remain alive never will we, on any condition, be brought under English rule. It is in truth not for glory nor riches nor honour that we are fighting but for freedom – and for that alone which no honest man gives up but with life itself.

THE AULD ALLIANCE, 1295–1560

BY THE END OF THE 13TH CENTURY, THE INTERMITTENT CONFLICT BETWEEN THE KINGS OF FRANCE AND ENGLAND WAS JOINED BY A NEW STRUGGLE, BETWEEN ENGLAND AND SCOTLAND. THE NET RESULT WAS THE FORGING OF THE SO-CALLED "AULD ALLIANCE" BETWEEN SCOTLAND AND FRANCE AGAINST THEIR COMMON AND, IN TIME, TRADITIONAL ENEMY, ENGLAND. IT PROVED EXCEPTIONALLY ENDURING, LASTING FULLY 265 YEARS.

THE DYNASTIC TURMOIL CAUSED BY THE DEATH OF THE seven-year-old Scottish queen, Margaret, presented Edward I of England with an all-but-irresistible opportunity to assert his overlordship. By 1295, it was clear that Edward was set on the total subjection of Scotland.

In response, the Council of Twelve, a self-appointed group of nobles and leading churchmen who effectively took over the government of Scotland, looked for allies wherever they could find them. With France and England themselves close to war after the French king, Philippe IV, had declared the English province of Gascony forfeit in 1293, alliance with France carried clear benefits. In October 1295, a Scottish embassy to Philippe agreed the Treaty of Paris.

As with most subsequent renewals of what became the Auld Alliance, the treaty was more favourable to the French than to the Scots. The French were required to do no more than continue their existing struggles with Edward in Gascony, while the burden of any outright military conflict between England and Scotland was to be borne entirely by the Scots. Nonetheless, Scotland, remote and impoverished as it was, was now formally allied to the greatest power in continental Europe. Even if more symbolic than actual, the benefits inherent in the alliance mattered.

In the short term, however, the treaty proved no protection against Edward I, whose whirlwind four-month invasion of 1296 all but exterminated Scotland as an independent kingdom. Worse still, peace between England and France in 1299, followed in 1303 by a treaty "of perpetual peace and friendship", allowed Edward to devote even more of his formidable military energies against the Scots. Scotland owed its eventual survival to Robert the Bruce and the military blundering of Edward II rather than to its French alliance.

When Robert the Bruce and Charles IV of France renewed the alliance in 1326, the motive was more precautionary than immediate: neither seemed to have much to fear from the English. But this changed rapidly after 1330, when Edward III set out to complete the conquest of Scotland and to reassert his authority in France. For the first time the Franco-Scottish alliance had been given real urgency. The prospects for both kingdoms were far from promising, however.

In 1346, Edward overwhelmed the French at Crécy. Two months later, David II of Scotland was captured in an abortive Scottish invasion of northern England. Not only did his enforced 11-year absence as Edward's prisoner increase the already bitter internal power struggles in Scotland, it led David to attempt to reach an accommodation with Edward III as the price of his freedom. Even after his release in 1357, David spent much of the remainder of his reign actively seeking ways to further English interests in Scotland.

Even with the accession in 1371 of the actively pro-French Robert II, who set in motion an immediate renewal of the alliance, the benefits to Scotland were mixed. In 1385, for example, plans for a simultaneous Franco-Scottish invasion of England – including the despatch, for the first time, of a small French force to Scotland – ended farcically when the French invasion

A double portrait of James V and his French wife, Mary of Guise (above). The couple married in 1538, after the death of James's first wife Madeleine, daughter of François I of France. Although in the 1530s, relations between England and France were reasonably stable, by 1542 they had worsened again and Scotland was inexorably drawn into the conflict. A rout of the Scottish army at Solway Moss in November ensued and soon after James died.

failed to materialize. The tone of the deteriorating Franco-Scottish relations was summed up by the French chronicler Jean Froissart, who "wished the king of France would make a truce with the English for two or three years and then march to Scotland and utterly destroy it".

Mutual regard, however, had never been the impetus behind the Auld Alliance. It was necessity that had driven France and Scotland together, just as it was necessity – specifically the imperative of resisting the aggressive new Lancastrian kings of England – that kept it alive in the early 15th century, in important respects the high point of the Auld Alliance.

Just as much as Scotland, early 15th-century France was gripped by dynastic dispute. Weakened by internal division and confronting a palpably superior opponent in Henry V, France came close to total surrender to the English. In 1418, the Dauphin (later Charles VII) called on his Scottish allies for help. Between 1419 and 1424, perhaps as many as 15,000 Scottish troops were sent to France.

This was a formidable force. It was not uniformly successful, however. A major victory over the English at Baugé in 1421 was followed by equally disastrous defeats at Cravant in 1423 – prompting the Dauphin to comment: "only Scots, Spaniards and other foreigners … and who are no great loss [were killed]" – and Verneuil in 1424. But if it was the death of Henry V in 1422 and the improbable apparition of Joan of Arc to rally the French armies in 1428 that were ultimately the keys to revived French success, the importance of these Scottish "armées de mer" as evi-

dence of Scottish commitment to its French ally was indubitable.

Through the rest of the 15th century, though the alliance was formally renewed four times, the eventual French triumph in the Hundred Years War, combined with the dynastic turmoil within England sparked by the Wars of the Roses, greatly reduced the English threat, rendering the Auld Alliance increasingly obsolete. The marriage in 1502 of Henry VIII's sister Margaret to James IV of Scotland, and the signing of a Treaty of Perpetual Peace between England and Scotland seemed finally to have ended the Franco-Scottish alliance for good.

Its dramatic revival in 1512, when it was formally renewed (as it was again in 1517 and 1548), was the result chiefly of Henry VIII's extravagant attempts to conquer France and Scotland. Both soon fizzled out, but Scotland nonetheless suffered most, when James IV, along with most of his nobles, was killed at Flodden in 1513. Yet again dynastic turmoil loomed.

Periodic Anglo-French and Anglo-Scottish conflict continued throughout Henry VIII's reign, but the certainties that had driven the Auld Alliance were disappearing. With the rise of the Hapsburg Empire, the balance of power in Europe as a whole was changing: in essence; Scotland was becoming more marginal. At the same time, the Reformation was adding a religious dimension to European conflicts. To begin with, the survival of Catholicism in Scotland tended to reinforce its links with Catholic France. But as Protestantism gained ground in Scotland, so a growing body of Scottish opinion favoured closer links with Protestant England.

With the exile of Mary, Queen of Scots, to England in 1568, the political and dynastic prospects for Scotland and its new king, James VI, were transformed. James was heir to the Protestant English throne as well as king of Scotland, and both his own and Scotland's best interests were clearly served by forging new and stronger links with England. Anglo-Scottish distrust might endure but the Auld Alliance itself had clearly outlived its usefulness.

ous auez bien ouy recordez de treues entreles anglois z les~

The siege of Berwick in 1333 (left). Edward III of England invaded Scotland in 1333 in support of Edward Balliol (the son of John Balliol). After a comprehensive defeat of the Scottish forces at Halidon Hill, David II was forced to flee to France, where he spent the next eight years, even though he was formally restored to the Scottish throne in 1336. Despite his sojourn at the French court, David became a resolutely pro-English king – a fact perhaps not unrelated to the huge sum of 100,000 marks he had to pay to Edward III under the Treaty of Berwick (1357).

ENGLAND: THE ANGEVINS AND PLANTAGENETS 1154–1399

HENRY II 1154–89	*EDWARD I 1272–1307*
RICHARD I 1189–99	*EDWARD II 1307–27*
JOHN 1199–1216	*EDWARD III 1327–77*
HENRY III 1216–72	*RICHARD II 1377–99*

IN THE 12TH AND 13TH CENTURIES, KINGSHIP ACROSS MUCH OF WESTERN EUROPE WENT THROUGH A PROCESS OF CONSOLIDATION AMOUNTING ALMOST TO A REVOLUTION. THIS WAS THE HIGH POINT OF MEDIEVAL ROYAL RULE. MONARCHICAL AUTHORITY IN A NUMBER OF COUNTRIES – SPAIN, FRANCE AND ENGLAND PRE-EMINENTLY – WAS SUBSTANTIALLY EXPANDED. SO TOO, AT LEAST PARTLY BY EXTENSION, WERE THE MECHANISMS OF GOVERNMENT, WHICH BECAME MORE POWERFUL, BETTER INFORMED AND SIGNIFICANTLY MORE EFFICIENT.

As Europe recovered from the centuries of disruption following the collapse of Roman power and the Muslim, Magyar and Viking invasions of the 8th to 10th centuries, the reach of its rulers increased. But this development was also a reflection of increasingly sophisticated ideas about the nature of royal rule and the rule of law. Though never wholly reconciled, these drew on Roman, Germanic and Christian traditions to create a theoretical ideal which justified and sustained medieval kingship and which placed the king, from whom all authority flowed, at the absolute heart of government. In England one crucial development was the acceptance after 1216 of royal succession through the king's eldest male heir. The damaging succession disputes of the pre- and post-Conquest age largely became a thing of the past.

In reality, theory and practice were rarely complementary. All medieval kings had to contend with a variety of checks to their authority: the ambitions of their leading magnates, the successful control of whom was a permanent preoccupation of all rulers; conflicts with the Church over supremacy in spiritual authority; wars with rival rulers; and the inevitable vicissitudes of strict dynastic succession, in which strong kings were frequently followed by weak or under-age ones. Nonetheless, that royal authority was being strengthened was undeniable.

In England, this period coincided with the country's single most successful royal dynasty, the Plantagenets, whose 331-year rule remains by far the longest of any English ruling house. Plantagenet rule divides broadly into three phases. The first was that of the Angevins – so-called because they were originally counts of Anjou in France – which lasted from the accession of Henry II in 1154 to the death of his last son, John, in 1216. The second phase ran from the accession of John's nine-year-old son, Henry III, in 1216 to the deposition of Henry's great-great-great-great-grandson, Richard II, in 1399. The third, which if only by virtue of the longevity of the Plantagenets more properly belongs in another chapter (*see* p.98), lasted from the usurpation of Henry IV to the overthrow of Richard III by Henry Tudor in 1485.

But there is a further reason for separating the final phase of Plantagenet rule from the earlier two: whereas the Plantagenet rulers after 1399 can justifiably be considered the first actively English kings of England since 1066, those before 1399 were just as clearly French – in culture, in speech, and in their dynastic and political instincts. No less than the Normans (whom they ousted in France as well as in England), the Angevin kings were at least as concerned to maintain their French lands and titles as to hold onto England. Their persistent wars with the French crown make most sense not so much as a conflict between two rival national polities – England and France – but as a continuation of a domestic conflict between the kings of France and their leading subjects. The kings of England, by virtue of their French lands and titles, were merely one among a number of such subjects, albeit often the most powerful. It is a precise reflection of Angevin priorities that Henry spent about a third of his reign in England, while his son Richard I spent only six months of his ten-year reign there. Both were buried in France.

The catastrophic loss by John of the great majority of his French lands by 1214 naturally led to a greater focus on English affairs. By incurring the wrath of his heavily taxed barons, most of whose own lands in France were also lost, it also indirectly gave rise to two of the most far-reaching developments of the period: Magna Carta and the growth of Parliament. Paradoxically, these tended more to reinforce royal authority than to dilute it. Provided the king was seen to be acting legally, Parliament in particular effectively became a bastion of kingship, an additional layer of royal legitimacy. But if the notion that Parliament in itself could constitute a higher authority than the king would have to wait until the 17th century, its first development under the Plantagenets was nonetheless of central importance.

Denied access to their traditional homelands in France, the more aggressive of the Plantagenets turned their attentions to the conquest of their British neighbours. The creation of an English "empire" in Britain is among the most enduring Plantagenet legacies. Henry II began the process, above all in Ireland, the invasion of which he authorized in 1167. But the key figure was Edward I, whose overwhelming conquest of Wales at the end of the 13th century saw the Plantagenet war-machine deployed at its most merciless. His no less ambitious but ultimately unsuccessful assaults on Scotland, however, served largely only to ensure continued tension between England and Scotland as well as to cement the Auld Alliance between Scotland and France.

That France nevertheless remained a prime focus of Plantagenet ambitions was emphatically underlined in the 14th century by Edward III, who launched a sustained attempt to re-establish Plantagenet supremacy there, beginning what later came to be called the Hundred Years War. In 1340, Edward went so far as to claim the French crown. On purely hereditary grounds, his claim was at least as good as that of the reigning French king, Philippe VI.

Whatever the temporary successes of Edward III and his son, the Black Prince, in France, it was clear nonetheless that the Plantagenets were gradually losing their French identity. By the time of the deposition and murder of the absolutist Richard II by his cousin Henry Bolingbroke in 1399, they had become as fully English as their subjects.

HENRY II 1154–89

KING HENRY II
BORN: March 5 1133,
Le Mans
ACCEDED: October 25
1154; crowned
December 19 1154,
Westminster Abbey

*DUKE OF NORMANDY
(FROM 1150),
COUNT OF ANJOU,
TOURAINE AND MAINE
(FROM 1151),
DUKE OF AQUITAINE
(FROM 1152),
KING OF ENGLAND*

HENRY II TRANSFORMED KINGSHIP IN ENGLAND. FOR OVER 30 YEARS HE HELD TOGETHER THE LARGEST EMPIRE IN WESTERN EUROPE THROUGH SHEER FORCE OF PERSONALITY. MOST OF HIS FRENCH HOLDINGS MAY HAVE BEEN LOST WITHIN 15 YEARS OF HIS DEATH, BUT ENGLAND, REINFORCED BY THE ADMINISTRATIVE AND INSTITUTIONAL UNITY HE HELPED TO CREATE, ENDURED NOT JUST INTACT BUT GREATLY STRENGTHENED.

HENRY II'S HUGE TERRITORIAL HOLDINGS made him by far the most powerful and richest ruler in western Europe. Anjou, Maine, Touraine and Normandy were his by inheritance; the vast sweep of Aquitaine, the hereditary lands of his wife Eleanor, came to him by marriage. Brittany, his other major French holding, became Henry's by diplomatic conquest in 1166, Ireland was his by outright conquest after 1167.

Henry's claim to the throne of England was much less clear cut than his Norman predecessors', if scarcely worse. His mother, Matilda, may have been unable to wrest the throne from her cousin Stephen (*see* pp. 56–7), but she could claim at least partial vindication in 1153 when Stephen confirmed Henry as his successor after the 20-year-old had mounted what in effect was an invasion of England. Henry's accession the following year was the first undisputed succession to the English crown since Harold II's in 1066.

Henry's immediate priority in 1154 was not just to repair the civil strife of Stephen's reign but to create sufficient stability in England to allow him to turn his attentions to France. In doing so, his distinctive brand of energetic kingship became immediately clear, above all his determination to stamp his authority everywhere. Within two years, Henry had overseen the destruction of scores of unlicensed castles, ending almost at a stroke the numerous local tyrannies that had flourished in Stephen's reign. At the same time, he secured the homage of Malcolm IV of Scotland and Owain Gwynedd in Wales.

Henry also set in train legal reforms that would decisively reduce the influence of local, baronial courts in favour of royal courts presided over by his own

Henry and Eleanor

On the face of it, the marriage of Henry Plantagenet and Eleanor of Aquitaine in May 1152 was just another arranged diplomatic marriage, albeit one in which the stakes were higher – and the personalities very much larger – than most. Henry was 18, Eleanor was 30. Until eight weeks earlier, Eleanor had also been queen of France, married to Louis VII, who had divorced her on the ground that they were too closely related. In reality, the marriage had been ended for a much

Fresco, reputedly showing Eleanor, from the Chapel of St Redegone, Chinon.

more prosaic reason: Eleanor had not produced an heir. Under the terms of the divorce, all Eleanor's hereditary lands in Aquitaine were returned to her and she was free to remarry – but only if she received the king's permission. This she signally failed to do.

With Aquitaine thus added to Henry's existing lands of Anjou, Maine and Normandy, Louis found himself confronting the kind of extended power base that the terms of the divorce had been expressly designed to avoid. As king, Louis might have been expected to set about the immediate reduction of his over-mighty vassal. In practice, he was powerless.

Against the odds, Eleanor and Henry seem to have been attracted to each other, perhaps as a result of the heady power they now disposed of. By about 1163, however, it was clear that they were drawing apart, with the ageing Eleanor never able to compete with Henry's string of much younger mistresses. Eleanor withdrew to her court in Poitiers, which she made the most glamorous chivalric centre in France. Here, more and more embittered by her estrangement from Henry, she raised her children and plotted his downfall.

In 1173 Eleanor actively encouraged the revolt against Henry by his sons Richard and Geoffrey, who were jealous of the preferential treatment handed out to their older brother, Henry. Henry II, now in his prime, easily crushed the rebellion. Eleanor was shipped to England, where she spent the next ten years under arrest. The young Henry's death (from dysentery) in 1183 brought about a rapprochement of sorts between the king and his queen. Eleanor was allowed to return to France, where she immediately began to encourage her remaining sons to mount a further revolt. She had her final, bitter revenge in 1189 when her favourite, Richard, allied to the new king of France, Philippe II, forced a humiliating defeat on her husband.

Eleanor died in 1204, aged 82, the wife of two kings and the mother of two more. She was buried next to Henry at Fontevrault on the Loire.

1142	1147	1149	1150	1151	1152	1153
First visit by Henry, as nine-year-old, to England	*Unsuccessfully attempts to continue the struggle of his mother, Matilda, against King Stephen*	*Third visit to England; knighted by David I of Scotland*	*Created duke of Normandy*	*Death of Geoffrey of Anjou; Henry becomes count of Anjou and Maine*	*Marries Eleanor of Aquitaine, more than ten years his senior; becomes duke of Aquitaine*	*Invades England (Jan.); Stephen forced to designate Henry his successor under Treaty of Wallingford (Dec.)*

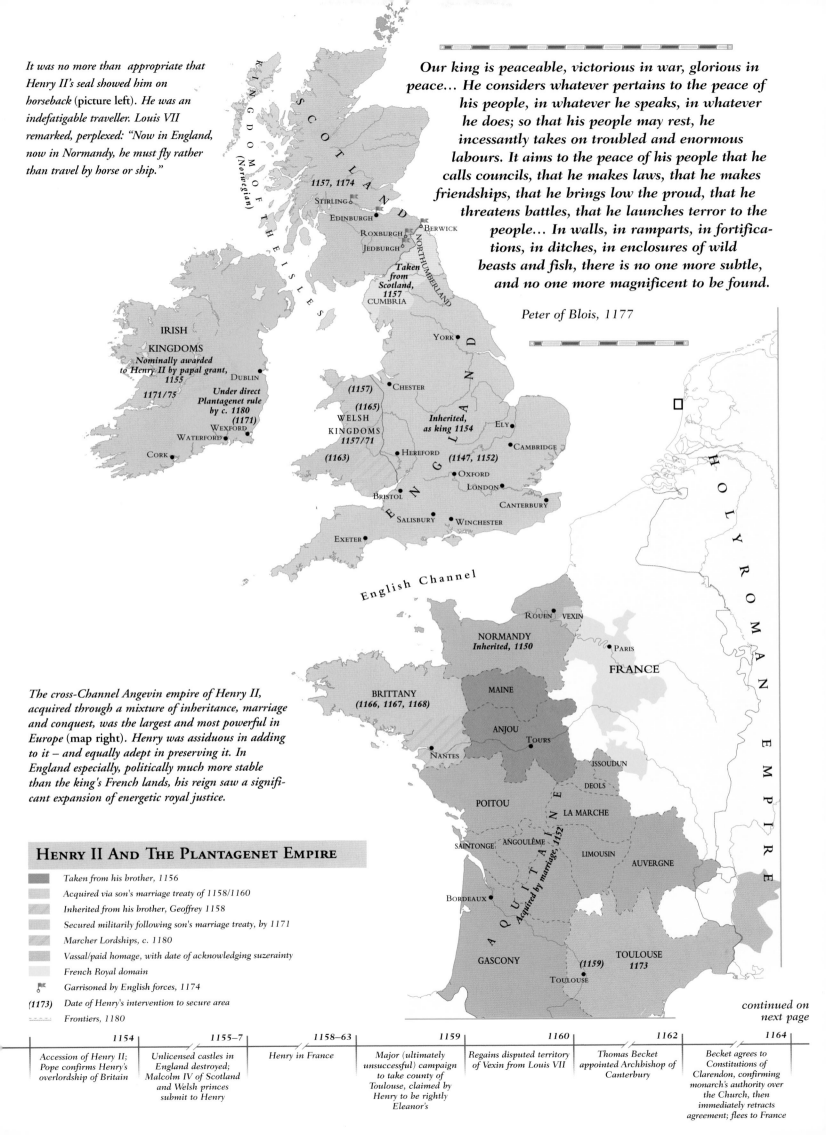

It was no more than appropriate that Henry II's seal showed him on horseback (picture left). He was an indefatigable traveller. Louis VII remarked, perplexed: "Now in England, now in Normandy, he must fly rather than travel by horse or ship."

Our king is peaceable, victorious in war, glorious in peace... He considers whatever pertains to the peace of his people, in whatever he speaks, in whatever he does; so that his people may rest, he incessantly takes on troubled and enormous labours. It aims to the peace of his people that he calls councils, that he makes laws, that he makes friendships, that he brings low the proud, that he threatens battles, that he launches terror to the people... In walls, in ramparts, in fortifications, in ditches, in enclosures of wild beasts and fish, there is no one more subtle, and no one more magnificent to be found.

Peter of Blois, 1177

KINGDOM OF THE ISLES

KINGDOM OF (Norwegian)

SCOTLAND

1157, 1174

STIRLING
EDINBURGH
ROXBURGH
JEDBURGH
BERWICK

NORTHUMBERLAND

Taken from Scotland, 1157
CUMBRIA

YORK

IRISH KINGDOMS
Nominally awarded to Henry II by papal grant, 1155
1171/75

Under direct Plantagenet rule by c. 1180
(1171)

DUBLIN

(1157)
(1165)
WELSH KINGDOMS
1157/71
(1163)

CHESTER

Inherited, as king 1154

ELY

CAMBRIDGE

HEREFORD

(1147, 1152)

OXFORD

LONDON

WEXFORD
WATERFORD
CORK

BRISTOL

SALISBURY
WINCHESTER

CANTERBURY

EXETER

ENGLAND

HOLY ROMAN EMPIRE

English Channel

The cross-Channel Angevin empire of Henry II, acquired through a mixture of inheritance, marriage and conquest, was the largest and most powerful in Europe (map right). Henry was assiduous in adding to it – and equally adept in preserving it. In England especially, politically much more stable than the king's French lands, his reign saw a significant expansion of energetic royal justice.

ROUEN VEXIN

NORMANDY
Inherited, 1150

PARIS

FRANCE

BRITTANY
(1166, 1167, 1168)

MAINE

ANJOU
TOURS

NANTES

ISSOUDUN

DEOLS

POITOU

LA MARCHE

SAINTONGE
ANGOULÊME
LIMOUSIN

AUVERGNE

BORDEAUX

AQUITAINE
Acquired by marriage, 1152

GASCONY

(1159)

TOULOUSE
1173

TOULOUSE

HENRY II AND THE PLANTAGENET EMPIRE

- Taken from his brother, 1156
- Acquired via son's marriage treaty of 1158/1160
- Inherited from his brother, Geoffrey 1158
- Secured militarily following son's marriage treaty, by 1171
- Marcher Lordships, c. 1180
- Vassal/paid homage, with date of acknowledging suzerainty
- French Royal domain
- Garrisoned by English forces, 1174
- (1173) Date of Henry's intervention to secure area
- - - - - Frontiers, 1180

continued on next page

1154	1155-7	1158-63	1159	1160	1162	1164
Accession of Henry II; Pope confirms Henry's overlordship of Britain	Unlicensed castles in England destroyed; Malcolm IV of Scotland and Welsh princes submit to Henry	Henry in France	Major (ultimately unsuccessful) campaign to take county of Toulouse, claimed by Henry to be rightly Eleanor's	Regains disputed territory of Vexin from Louis VII	Thomas Becket appointed Archbishop of Canterbury	Becket agrees to Constitutions of Clarendon, confirming monarch's authority over the Church, then immediately retracts agreement; flees to France

Dividing Henry II's immense empires among his four sons would prove harder than acquiring it in the first place. Actively encouraged by his wife, Eleanor, and the new king of France, Philippe II, his sons mounted a series of attempts not just to oust their father but to increase their own inheritances (map below). Only at the very end did the ageing Henry succumb.

HENRY II AND HIS SONS

- Henry II's possessions, 1169
- Vassals of Henry II, 1174
- Granted by Pope to Henry II, 1155; conquered/vassalized by 1175; assigned to John, 1177
- Assigned by Henry II in 1169 as the inheritance of Henry
- Assigned by Henry II in 1169 as the inheritance of Geoffrey
- Assigned by Henry II in 1169 as the inheritance of Richard
- Expected to go to Henry II's son, John, under 1173 marriage treaty with count of Maurienne
- Reassigned to John by Henry II under treaty with count of Maurienne, 1173
- Promised to foreign rulers by Henry in exchange for help against his father, 1173 (with beneficiaries)
- Henry II's foreign foes during hostilities
- Revolts, 1173, 1174
- → Campaigns against Henry II, with details
- ┄►Movement of William of Scotland in captivity, 1174
- → Campaigns of Henry II
- Area of Richard's activities during 1189 revolt
- Frontiers, 1180

officials, who were increasingly dispatched across the country on what became an almost endless series of circuits. In the process, as has been said, the impartial application of justice gradually became "an obligation of the king's state". The Common Law – law "common" to the realm as a whole and available to all freemen – was among Henry's most enduring legacies. With other innovations such as 12-man

juries, it made the application of royal law much more consistent, a process reflected in the codification of legal practice in works such as the *Treatise on the Laws and Customs of England* by Henry's chief legal officer, or justiciar, Ranulph Glanville.

With England secured, Henry was free to concentrate on France. His aim never deviated: to prevent the French king, his nominal overlord but in reality

continued from previous page

1166–70	1166	1167	1170	1171	1172	1173
Henry in France	Brittany taken over by Henry. Grand jury system established by Assizes of Clarendon and of Northampton (1176)	Further campaign launched against Wales. Initial Anglo-Norman invasion of Ireland launched	Henry's eldest son (also Henry), the "Young King", crowned king-designate; Becket returns to England in protest and is murdered at Canterbury (Dec.)	Henry leads renewed invasion of Ireland	Second coronation of the Young King, who is also created duke of Normandy and count of Anjou, prompts revolt against Henry, encouraged by Eleanor	William I of Scotland supports revolt against Henry by invading England; captured and forced to pay homage to Henry in Normandy

much the weaker, from taking any of his territory, while at the same adding to his own whenever possible. In 1157, Henry attacked Toulouse, claiming it was rightfully part of Eleanor's inheritance. For once, Henry came off second best when Louis VII sent an army to support his brother-in-law, the Count of Toulouse. Toulouse remained a persistent point of contention between Henry and the French crown for the rest of his reign.

Henry had his revenge within less than two years when, in return for Henry's support in a disputed papal election, Pope Alexander III agreed to the immediate marriage of Louis's daughter Margaret to Henry's eldest son (also called Henry). As the two monarchs had themselves agreed the marriage, with Louis promising the long-disputed Vexin territory to Henry as part of Margaret's dowry, the Pope's agreement may, on the face of it, have seemed of only incidental importance. In practice, however, with Margaret only three and Henry only five, Louis could have assumed the marriage would not take place for several years. An immediate marriage, by contrast, meant the equally immediate surrender of the Vexin or the incurring of serious papal displeasure. For Henry, it was a diplomatic masterstroke, for Louis, something close to humiliation.

Henry used a combination of diplomacy and conquest to secure Brittany, which he had claimed since the death in 1158 in Lower Brittany of his brother Geoffrey, count of Nantes. The duke of Brittany, Conan, was also earl of Richmond in England and thus Henry's vassal. Henry, backing his claim with an implied threat of invasion, gradually obliged Conan to acknowledge his overlordship in Brittany. By 1166, Henry had taken over the dukedom.

Henry faced two further major challenges. The first – in England – from Thomas Becket, he saw off with minimum fuss (see box). The second, from his own family, would eventually prove too much even for this most indefatigable of rulers. Ensuring a valid line of succession was a priority for all medieval kings. With four surviving sons, Henry might have been thought to have accomplished this triumphantly. Henry, the "Young King", was to inherit Anjou, Normandy and England; Richard, Aquitaine; Geoffrey, Brittany; and John, the youngest, Ireland. Being Plantagenets, however, they were unwilling to wait for their father's death before taking over their inheritance. Each was also deeply suspicious of the others.

Henry crushed a major rebellion, which Eleanor actively encouraged, by Richard and Geoffrey in 1173. The subsequent deaths of the younger Henry and Geoffrey in 1183 and 1186 merely encouraged the two remaining sons to press all the harder, not least once they had won the support of the new French king, Philippe II, whose determination to do

Thomas Becket

Stained glass of Becket and Henry from Trinity Chapel, Canterbury.

Worldly, cynical and power-hungry, Henry II and his Chancellor, Thomas Becket, seemed an ideal match. In appointing Becket Archbishop of Canterbury in 1162, Henry could justifiably have expected to gain a valuable ally in the continuing Europe-wide conflict with the Pope over who had ultimate spiritual supremacy. This was more than a matter of doctrinal nicety. Papal claims to spiritual authority directly threatened the status of Europe's monarchs, who were actively asserting their authority in all spheres, religious as much as secular.

It is almost impossible to judge the extent to which Becket's subsequent refusal to support Henry was a matter of genuine religious principle or a stubborn refusal, born of pride, to kowtow. Becket remains an enigmatic mix of show-off and saint, infuriating and inspirational by turns. A major falling-out between Henry and Becket in 1164, after which Becket took himself off to self-righteous exile in France and Henry confiscated his holdings in England, was followed by a partial reconciliation in 1170. On his return to Canterbury the same year, Becket was then murdered in his own cathedral by four French knights apparently carrying out Henry's largely rhetorical plea: "Will no one rid me of this turbulent priest?" If there is little doubt that Henry personally mourned the death of Becket, there is equally little question that, in the longer term, his own authority was scarcely even dented, for all that Becket was canonized in record time. For Henry, it was always the exercise of power that counted.

down Henry equalled their own. In July 1189, Henry at last met his match when, faced by the combined forces of Richard and Philippe II, he was forced to accept their humiliating terms. However undignified the end, it was at least brief. Within two days, Henry was dead.

Henry, part warrior-king, part bookworm, was a remarkable figure. He faced threats on all sides – from the Church, from the kings of France, from an assortment of French magnates, from the Scots and Welsh, from his barons in England, and, finally, from his sons. Through a mixture of bluster, cunning, charm and brutality he repelled them all before, exhausted, he fell victim to the dynastic manoeuvrings of his own family. In his terms, his reign was ultimately a failure. In almost every other respect, it was a resounding success.

Effigy of Henry II from his tomb at Fontevrault Abbey on the Loire (below). A request from Queen Victoria that the bodies of Henry II and Richard I (also buried here) be returned to England for reburial was turned down by the French on the grounds that both were French.

1174	1175	1177	1180	1183	1186	1189
Eleanor placed under house arrest	Irish kings of Leinster and Meath acknowledge Henry's overlordship	Henry's youngest son, John, made lord of Ireland	Death of Louis VII; succeeded by Philippe II Augustus	Death of the Young King; abdication of Rory O'Connor, last high king of Ireland	Death of Geoffrey	Richard and Philippe II join forces to invade Normandy; Henry forced to accept Treaty of Azay-le-Rideau; dies two days later

THE EVOLUTION OF THE ROYAL COURT

THE MOST VIVID EARLY DESCRIPTION OF MEDIEVAL COURT LIFE IS THAT PROVIDED BY THE 8TH-CENTURY ANGLO-SAXON EPIC POEM, *Beowulf.* THOUGH THE SOCIETY IT DESCRIBES – OF AN "ILLUSTRIOUS PRINCE AND GIVER OF GOLD RINGS" FEASTING WITH HIS FOLLOWERS – WOULD CHANGE, MANY OF ITS ESSENTIAL FEATURES ENDURED WELL INTO THE 13TH CENTURY.

D URING THIS PERIOD, TWO CENTRAL FACTORS STAND out. One was the primacy of the king, and of his court or household, in the government of the realm. The other was that the king and his court were permanently on the move.

The household had a dual function. It was domestic, in the sense of providing the king with the necessities of daily life. And it was also administrative, the epicentre of government, the whole presided over by the monarch himself. The earliest surviving factual account of a medieval royal household, the *Constitutio domus regis*, describes Henry I's court in detail. It is probable that the households of the Anglo-Saxon kings as early as the 9th century were fundamentally the same, if smaller.

Henry I's core household was at least 100 strong. Senior officials, mostly drawn from leading magnates and churchmen, included the chamberlain and the treasurer. They were jointly responsible for the royal chamber, where the king slept and ate (other than on special occasions), and the Treasury, a part of which travelled with the court and was kept in the king's chamber. Some chamberlains were clerics; most were laymen. Until the 1340s, the treasurer was always a cleric. The same was true of the chancellor, who was head of the royal chapel as well as being in charge of the royal scribes, themselves clerics (or "clerks"). The chancellor was also responsible for the king's seal, used to authenticate documents issued by the king. It was usual for a chancellor to be rewarded with a bishopric at the end of his term of office.

Among the exclusively domestic staff, the most important were the "sewers" or stewards, also called "cupbearers", who supervised the king's hall and household staff. Among these were the cooks and the butler, who occupied an important ceremonial position as well as being responsible for the supply of wine. Lesser members of staff included grooms, carters, packhorse drivers, tent-keepers, the bearer of the king's bed and launderers.

Significantly, the largest single department was the hunting staff. It included hornblowers, keepers of greyhounds, keepers of the royal pack, a leader and a feeder of the hounds, huntsmen of the "trained pack", a keeper of small hounds, wolfhunters, a series of archers and 20 sergeants.

The court was also the centre of the king's army, which was administered by the constables and marshals and consisted of household knights and often large numbers of infantry, the "household men" or *familiares*. This was in effect a permanent standing army, available for immediate deployment at moments of crisis. It could be rapidly expanded to deal with longer-lasting conflicts.

To this more or less permanent household were added sundry hangers-on, petitioners, merchants, nobles, justices, sheriffs and foreign dignitaries, some visiting on official business, many simply anxious to garner royal favour.

There were a small number of permanent royal palaces. Those at Yeavering in Northumberland and Cheddar in Somerset, the latter still being used as late as the reign of King John, were Anglo-Saxon. Both bear a marked resemblance to Heorot, the great "mead hall" described in Beowulf. They were imposing wooden halls – that at Yeavering was 90 by 18 feet – with simple window openings and a central fire. Though "golden tapestries" were hung to mark important occasions, permanent furniture was sparse: plain tables and benches. It was here that most of the household slept. The later Norman palaces at Winchester, Windsor, Westminster and the Tower of London itself, though larger and built of stone, would scarcely have been more comfortable. As late as the 12th century, glass windows remained an

As demonstrations of knightly prowess, tournaments were popular throughout the Middle Ages (above). *Banned in the reign of Henry II, who feared the large numbers of knights who congregated to them, they were restored by Richard I. Tournaments continued to be popular into the 16th century.*

almost unimaginable luxury. Among the goods lost by King John in 1216, when a number of his baggage carts were lost during an attempted crossing of the Wash, was his set of portable glass windows.

Though Westminster began to emerge as a permanent centre of government during the reign of Henry I, what most distinguished the medieval court was its constant travelling. In an age of difficult communication, the effectiveness of any ruler depended on his being able to make his presence felt personally. And as the court revolved around the king, the court travelled, too.

From 1069, with large areas of England in open revolt, William the Conqueror found himself permanently on the move from one end of his realm to the other. The same was true of Stephen in his civil war against Matilda. Henry I, with an even larger cross-Channel realm to administer, was another incessant traveller. In 1170, for example, despite spending almost two months seriously ill in Normandy, he still covered more than

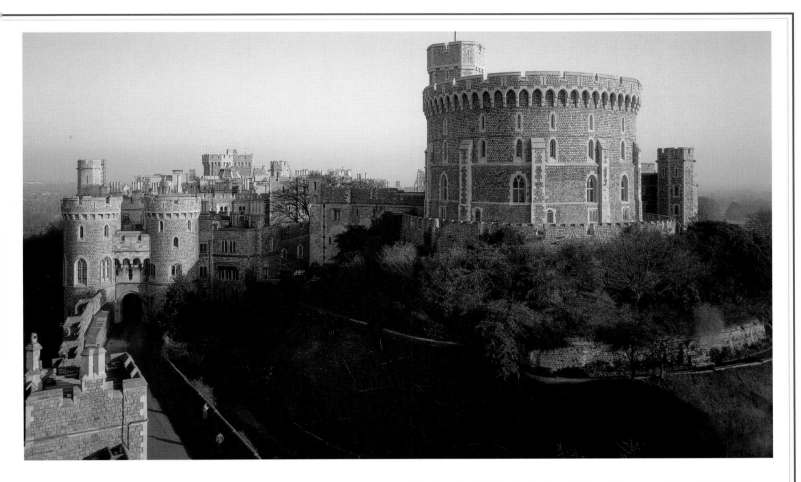

If the king has said he will remain in one place for a day, he is sure to upset all the arrangements by departing early in the morning. And you see the men dashing around as if they were mad, beating packhorses, running carts into another, in short giving a lively imitation of Hell … I hardly dare say it but I believe in truth he took delight in seeing what a fix we were in. After wandering some three or four miles in an unknown wood and often in the dark we thought ourselves lucky if we stumbled upon some filthy hovel.

Peter of Blois, on Henry II's court

2,000 miles. In the course of his reign, he crossed the Channel 28 times. As the sinking of the *White Ship* in 1120 and the loss of John's baggage carts almost 100 years later underlined, the risks could be considerable.

If the logistics involved in moving the court were formidable, the consequences for those on whom the court descended could be severe. A monk from Canterbury described the calamitous impact of William Rufus's itinerant court: "Those who attended his court made a practice of plundering and destroying everything; they laid waste all the territory through which they passed. Consequently, when it became known that the king was coming everyone fled to the woods." When it was announced that Edward I would spend Easter at Nottingham, the local people were assured that the king would leave as rapidly as he had arrived.

The Dukes of York, Gloucester and Ireland dine with Richard II (above) from the 15th-century Chronique d'Angleterre. *The importance of the king's inner circle of favourites was increased by the growing size and sophistication of the court; the Richard de Vere, Duke of Ireland, became so influential that Parliament dismissed him and the Lords Appellant seized power from Richard III.*

RICHARD I 1189–99

THE CHIVALRIC IMAGE OF RICHARD I "COEUR DE LION" (LIONHEART) AS THE JUST, CHRISTIAN WARRIOR-KING PAR EXCELLENCE HAS ALWAYS BEEN ALLURING. IN REALITY, WHATEVER HIS KNIGHTLY PROWESS AND MILITARY ABILITY, AS KING OF ENGLAND HE WAS A DISTANT FIGURE. IT IS TESTIMONY TO THE GOOD GOVERNMENT ESTABLISHED BY HENRY II THAT HIS PROLONGED ABSENCES HAD SUCH LITTLE EFFECT.

BORN: September 8 1157, Oxford
ACCEDED: July 6 1189; crowned September 2 1189, Westminster Abbey

DUKE OF NORMANDY AND DUKE OF AQUITAINE (FROM 1172), KING OF ENGLAND

THE RELATIVE INSIGNIFICANCE OF ENGLAND in the wider Angevin world was unambiguously underlined by the reign of Richard I. The new king regarded England, which was inherently more stable and much more easily defended than his French realms, chiefly as a means of financing his foreign ventures, above all his passionate determination to "take the Cross". He had been raised on a diet of knightly virtue by his mother, Eleanor, who had herself made the arduous journey to the Holy Land with her first husband, Louis VII; tall, flamboyant and blue-eyed, Richard had little difficulty in seeing himself as the *preux chevalier* personified. In July 1190, exactly a year after coming to the throne and having spent less than four months in England, he left France for the Holy Land on the Third Crusade.

Self-regarding he may have been, but Richard understood the realities of Angevin power politics. As his overthrow (in tandem with Philippe II of France) of his father Henry II in 1189 made clear, Richard's capacity for naked self-advancement was fully the equal of his military talents. He was under no illusion that his inevitably lengthy absence in the Holy Land placed his realms at risk.

His precautions proved inadequate. Rightly seeing his younger brother John as the chief threat to his rule in England, Richard extracted a promise from John, whom he lavishly rewarded with lands and titles, that he would stay out of England until Richard's planned return three years later. Meanwhile, the Bishop of Ely, William Longchamp, was entrusted with the realm's government. Neither scheme worked. Longchamp alienated many leading barons, who naturally gravi-

Richard and the Third Crusade

War defined Richard. His departure for the Holy Land in 1190 was a crusade in every sense. But as a contemporary recorded: "As the earth shudders at the absence of the sun, so the face of the kingdom was changed by the departure of the king."

Measured against its stated objective of liberating Jerusalem, which had been captured by Saladin in 1187, the Third Crusade, led jointly by Richard I and Philippe II of France, was a failure. Furthermore, Richard and Philippe fell out even before they got to the Holy Land. Wintering in Sicily, they argued over Richard's continuing refusal to honour his promise to marry Philippe's sister, Alice. When Eleanor arrived with an alternative bride, Berengaria of Navarre, Philippe took offence. In high dudgeon, he sailed ahead on his own.

En route to the Holy Land, Richard captured Cyprus after its Greek ruler had come close to seizing the ship carrying Alice and Berengaria. The island would prove a crucial advance base for later crusaders. Richard celebrated the victory by marrying Berengaria.

Richard and Philippe were partly reconciled once Richard had arrived in the Holy Land in June 1191. Together they took Acre, whose Christian besiegers had themselves become besieged by Saladin. Richard was in his element. When Saladin delayed his payment of the ransom for the 2,700 prisoners taken by Richard, Richard had them executed. The victory was somewhat marred by Philippe's decision to return home early and by a bitter squabble between Richard and Duke Leopold of Austria over the division of the spoils.

From Acre, Richard made his way south to Jaffa and from there inland towards Jerusalem. The city proved impregnable, however. In September, realizing the futility of continuing the effort, Richard and Saladin came to terms. Richard sailed for home.

The value or otherwise of the Crusades have long been questioned. Compared to some of the more obviously catastrophic of the Crusades, Richard's effort was a success. Certainly, it confirmed his reputation as a great Christian warrior. But for the king of England to spend so long away from his kingdom smacked of a reckless disregard for the realities of political power.

1173	1189	1190	1191
With his brother Geoffrey, Richard rebels against his father, Henry II	*Allies with Philippe II of France to defeat Henry II. Makes first visit to England (Sept.–Dec.) for coronation and to raise finance for Crusade*	*Leaves France (July) and, with Philippe II, leads Third Crusade to Holy Land*	*Reaches Holy Land (June) and takes Acre. John illegally takes over government of England*

Richard's possessions and dependencies, 1189
Other Christian states, 1189
Muslim states, 1189
Assigned by Richard to John, 1189
Taken by Richard by storm
Secured by Richard for Christendom by treaty, 1192
Richard's movements to and from the Holy land
Richard's fleet
Richard's movement in captivity
Other movements of Richard, with dates
Theatre of war between Richard and Philippe II, 1194-8
Battle
Frontier of the Holy Roman Empire
Frontiers, 1189

SCOTLAND
IRELAND
SWEDEN
DENMARK
ENGLAND
Fief of the Holy Roman Empire 1194-8
LONDON
POMERANIA
POLISH STATES
PORTSMOUTH
SANDWICH
12 May 1194
13 August 1189
12 December 1189
13 March 1194
BARFLEUR
NORMANDY
CHÂTEAU GAILLARD
BRITTANY
WÜRZBURG
KINGDOM OF BOHEMIA
Gisors 1198
WORMS
SPEYER
HOLY
KINGDOM OF GERMANY
PARIS
FRANCE
ERDBERG
1193
VIENNA
CHINON
Tours 1190
VÉZELAY
ROMAN
AQUITAINE
KINGDOM OF BURGUNDY
HUNGARY
EMPIRE
LEON
NAVARRE
GASCONY
PORTUGAL
CASTILE
ARAGON
KINGDOM OF ITALY
MARSEILLES
SERBIA
BULGARIA
CONSTANTINOPLE
ROME
PAPAL STATE
BYZANTINE
RUM
ARMENIAN RULERS
EMPIRE
KINGDOM OF SICILY
MESSINA
ANTIOCH
Captured by Richard, 1191
CYPRUS
TRIPOLI
E M P I R E   O F   T H E   A L M O H A D S
M e d i t e r r a n e a n   S e a
ACRE
1192
Arsuf 1191
Jaffa 1191
JERUSALEM
E M P I R E   O F   A Y Y U B I D S

tated to John as a rival source of authority. For his part, John rapidly broke his word, made his way to England, and set himself up as king in all but name. Longchamp fled to Normandy.

Richard fared little better in France. Though his chief and most obvious French rival, Philippe II, had accompanied Richard to the Holy Land, the two quarrelled when Richard – who may have been homosexual – prevaricated over his marriage to Philippe's sister, Alice, to whom he had been engaged for 20 years. Returning early, Philippe launched a major assault against Normandy.

On his way home in 1192, Richard was captured by another former ally in the Holy Land, Duke Leopold of Austria, and ransomed for 150,000 marks (the equivalent of 34 tonnes of gold). By now, a much more able administrator, the new Chief Justiciar, Hubert Walter, had replaced Longchamp. It was Walter who was mainly responsible for raising the enormous ransom – almost the only direct impact Richard had on his kingdom. All his

subjects had to pay. Among the drastic measures was the requisitioning of the entire Cistercian wool crop. Once freed, in 1194 Richard paid his second (and last) visit to England, spending a mere two months there.

The remaining five years of Richard's reign were spent in France, campaigning to regain the territories lost to Philippe II. With the help of John, magnanimously pardoned for his attempted take-over of England, Richard repeatedly demonstrated his military ability. By the time he died, shot in the shoulder besieging the castle of Chalus in the Limousin, he had restored and strengthened all his French inheritance.

As a king, warfare was Richard I's only real talent. The niceties of administration bored him. Even more seriously, he failed in the elementary precaution of leaving an heir. In consequence, it was the unscrupulous John who inherited his throne. The great Angevin inheritance so painstakingly preserved by Henry II would not endure for long.

Whatever King John's difficulties with his barons in England, his reign was dominated by his catastrophic loss of the vast majority of Henry II's Plantagenet empire in France (map above). Disastrous in itself, it also enormously strengthened the hitherto much weaker kings of France, making its recapture all the harder. The contrast with Henry II's subtle stewardship could hardly have been greater.

1192	1193	1194	1194–99	1196
Two attempts to take Jerusalem (Jan. and June) rebuffed by Saladin; Richard and Saladin conclude truce (Sept.); while returning home, captured by Duke Leopold of Austria (Dec.)	*Hubert Walter appointed Archbishop of Canterbury and Chief Justiciar in place of William Longchamp*	*Richard ransomed and freed; makes second visit to England (Mar.–May)*	*French territories lost to Philippe II reconquered*	*Château Gaillard, Richard's most imposing fortress, built overlooking Seine*

JOHN 1199–1216

KING JOHN

BORN: December 24 1167, Oxford
ACCEDED: April 6 1199; crowned May 27 1199, Westminster Abbey

LORD OF IRELAND (FROM 1177), COUNT OF MORTAIN (FROM 1189), DUKE OF NORMANDY (1199–1203), KING OF ENGLAND

THE RUTHLESS DYNASTIC SELF-SEEKING OF HENRY II'S SONS REACHED ITS APOGEE IN JOHN. THE REIGN OF THIS SUSPICIOUS, VIOLENT AND UNPRINCIPLED MAN WAS DOMINATED BY SHORT-TERM ATTEMPTS TO GAIN WHATEVER IMMEDIATE ADVANTAGE SEEMED MOST OBVIOUSLY AT HAND. THE RESULT WAS THE LOSS OF ALMOST ALL THE ANGEVIN LANDS IN FRANCE, AND, IN ENGLAND, BARONIAL REVOLT THAT CULMINATED IN MAGNA CARTA.

MOST OF JOHN'S LIFE WAS SPENT IN A fevered pursuit of power. The start was unpromising. As the youngest son, John was not due to inherit any of the immense Angevin realms, hence his nickname "Lackland". Richard's subsequent refusal to transfer his original inheritance, Aquitaine, to John when he, Richard, became heir to England, Normandy and Anjou in 1183 sparked the first armed clash between the brothers. Two years later, Henry sent John to rule in Ireland. John's four-month visit, in which he alienated almost everyone, was a disaster from first to last. Typically, he repaid his father by joining the revolt by Richard and Philippe II against the ageing king in 1189.

John's prospects immediately improved. To keep his brother out of England during his absence in the Holy Land, Richard, now king, gave John a series of vast estates in England and France. He also allowed him to marry the daughter of the Earl of Gloucester. John, however, wanted more.

Breaking his word, he set himself up in England and fomented resistance to Richard's nominee as ruler in his absence, William Longchamp. When Richard, at long range, managed to force him out again, John joined forces with Philippe II of France to plot Richard's overthrow. The conspirators were given added impetus in 1192 with the news of Richard's imprisonment in Austria. Normandy was invaded and John declared himself king of England.

Even in the context of Plantagenet family politics, Richard's subsequent pardon of John after his release seems surprising. However, John now rejoined forces with his brother against his former ally, and over the next five years he proved a more than competent military commander as together they retook all the lands lost to Philippe. John's reward was his designation as heir to all Richard's realm.

Within five years of his accession, John had lost almost all his French inheritance. John's problem was not just Philippe II but his nephew, Arthur, Duke of Brittany, whose claim to Richard's French territories was at least as good as his own. Arthur formed a natural rallying point for those French barons reluctant to accept John as their lord. In 1202, John compounded their resentment by capturing and murdering the 12-year-old Arthur, whose body

Magna Carta

Magna Carta, or "Great Charter", signed by a reluctant John in June 1215, has traditionally been seen as the cornerstone of English liberty, the first step in the development of English constitutional government. The actual impetus behind it was very different. After the defeat at Bouvines the year before, England's magnates were determined to assert themselves by rolling back the feudal privileges that the Angevins had been assiduously amassing. Nonetheless, by placing the king within a legal framework – by saying in effect that the law existed independently of the king and was more than whatever he declared it to be – the issuing of the Charter represented a key moment. For his part, John agreed to it simply to buy time. He had no intention of implementing the Charter. But when he died the following year, his heir, Henry III, was only nine. Immediately on his accession, the Charter was re-issued, as it was again in 1217 and 1225. In 1297, even as powerful a king as Edward I was forced to agree to a further confirmation of the Charter. Although the position of the king within the state was still absolute, Magna Carta had begun – however tentatively – the process by which the rule of law was to become supreme.

1177	1183	1185	1191	1193	1194	1200	1202	1203
John made Lord of Ireland by Henry II	Richard's refusal to transfer Aquitaine to John leads to armed conflict between the brothers	Visits Ireland (for four months), earning deep distrust on all sides	Journeys to England and conspires against Richard's regent, William Longchamp	Conspires with Philippe II to overthrow the imprisoned Richard; declares himself king of England	Pardoned by Richard, whom he joins in combating Philippe II in France	Divorces Isabella of Gloucester; marries Isabella of Angoulême, incurring wrath of her fiancé, Hugh de Lusignan	Refuses to pay homage to Philippe II, who formally dispossesses John of his French territories; war ensues	Murders his nephew, Arthur, duke of Brittany, in Normandy; retreats to England (Dec.)

Whatever King John's difficulties with his barons in England, his reign was dominated by his catastrophic loss of the vast majority of Henry II's Plantagenet empire in France (map right). Disastrous in itself, it also enormously strengthened the hitherto much weaker kings of France, making its recapture all the harder. The contrast with Henry II's subtle stewardship could hardly have been greater.

Map labels and legend:

JOHN 1189–1216

- Plantagenet possessions and dependencies, 1199
- John's movements, 1199
- Area where Barons swore allegiance to Eleanor; transferred by her to John
- Area where Barons swore allegiance to Arthur; secured by John by 1202
- English losses under treaty of Le Goulet, 1200
- Revolts against John in France
- French and Breton campaigns in Normandy, 1204
- Remained English in France by end of 1204
- Remaining English strongholds in areas lost otherwise (date indicates surrender)
- John's campaigns, with date
- English-held in Ireland and Wales at end of John's rule
- English vassals, 1216
- Campaign of rebel barons, 1215
- Southern limit of largely rebel-held area
- Prince Louis's landing, 1216
- Area of Prince Louis's activity in 1216
- ✕ Battles

Map place names and annotations:

SCOTLAND — Kingdom of the Isles (Norwegian) — BERWICK — NORHAM — William of Scotland did homage, 1212 — NEWCASTLE — CARLISLE Captured by Scots, 1216 — North Sea — THIRSK — YORK — BEVERLEY — MELTON — IRISH KINGDOMS — CARRICKFERGUS — DUBLIN — LIMERICK — WEXFORD — WATERFORD — GWYNEDD AND SMALLER WELSH STATES — 1211 — CHESTER — LAXTON — NOTTINGHAM — LEICESTER — STAMFORD — NORWICH — NORTHAMPTON — BEDFORD — CAMBRIDGE — HEREFORD — ST. ALBANS — LONDON — COLCHESTER — PEMBROKE — BRISTOL — WINDSOR — RUNNYMEDE — STAINES — ROCHESTER — CANTERBURY — DOVER — John signed Magna Carta, 1215 — WINCHESTER — PORTSMOUTH — EXETER — Damme 1213 — FLANDERS — Bouvines 1214 — HOLY ROMAN EMPIRE — 1213 — English Channel — ARQUES — John murdered Arthur, 1203 — ROUEN — (1204) CHÂTEAU GAILLARD — LE GOULET — PARIS — NORMANDY — FALAISE — DOL — MAINE — In response to Arthur's murder, 1203 — BRITTANY — Barons deserted John, 1203 — FRANCE — La Roche-aux-Moines 1214 — ANGERS — ANJOU — (1204) TOURS — CHINON (1205) — LOCHES (1205) — ISSOUDUN — NANTES — 1206, 1214 — 1214 — Mirebeau 1202 Arthur taken captive — PARTHENAY — POITIERS — DEOLS — LA MARCHE — NIORT — POITOU — LA ROCHELLE — 1201 — 1214 — LIMOGES — SAINTONGE — ANGOULÊME — 1207 — LIMOUSIN — AUVERGNE — MONTAUBAN — BORDEAUX — LA RÉOLE — AQUITAINE — GASCONY — TOULOUSE — LEON — CASTILE — NAVARRE — ARAGON

Photograph caption:

Effigy of John on his tomb at Worcester Cathedral (left). John has always had his defenders, who point not just to his close interest in the daily business of government but, in equally marked contrast to his brother Richard, to his obvious fondness for England. John specifically made clear that he wanted to be buried in England.

---

he flung into the Seine. The coalition raised against John proved over-whelming. In 1203, he retreated to England. By 1205, Normandy and Anjou had been lost.

John's overriding priority was to retake his French lands. But only a massive and hugely expensive military operation could achieve this. Given the vastly increased level of taxation needed to sustain it, almost all of which fell on his English subjects, it was clear that John's English barons would support him only as long as he was successful in France. When the defeat at Bouvines in July 1214 signalled the final

collapse of John's French hopes, it inevitably prompted a baronial revolt. John had not just lost his French lands, he was on the verge of losing England.

His agreement to Magna Carta (see box) in 1215 eased the immediate pressure, but the underlying problems were as acute as ever. His sudden death 16 months later in the midst of near full-scale civil war was about the best way out he could hope for.

1206	1207	1211	1212	1213	1214	1215	1216
All Angevin territories north of the Loire lost to Philippe II	John refuses to appoint Langton Archbishop of Canterbury. Papal interdict of England (1208) and John's excommunication (1209) follow	Successful Welsh campaign against Llywelyn the Great	Pope declares John no longer legal king of England	Restores relations with papacy by making England a papal fief; renews campaign to regain French realms	Final Angevin defeat in France by Philippe II at Bouvines (July)	John forced to agree to Magna Carta	Rebel barons declare Louis king of England; Louis invades and takes Tower of London (May); John loses crown jewels crossing the Wash (Oct.)

HENRY III 1216–72

HENRY III'S REIGN WAS A PARADOXICAL ONE. GENERALLY REGARDED AS ONE OF ENGLAND'S MOST INEFFECTUAL KINGS, HE REMAINS ITS LONGEST-REIGNING MONARCH. THOUGH NO LESS AUTOCRATIC THAN HIS PREDECESSORS, HIS REIGN SAW CRUCIAL DEVELOPMENTS IN WHAT WOULD BECOME EVENTUALLY DEVELOP INTO PARLIAMENT. ESSENTIALLY PACIFIC IN OUTLOOK, HE NONETHELESS PROVOKED A CIVIL WAR THAT THREATENED TO OVERTURN THE PLANTAGENETS.

KING HENRY III

BORN: October 1 1207, Winchester
ACCEDED: October 18 1216; crowned Gloucester October 28 1216, (and again Westminster Abbey, May 17 1220)

☙ ☙ ☙ ☙ ☙ ☙

DUKE OF NORMANDY (UNTIL 1259), AND AQUITAINE, KING OF ENGLAND

Henry III has enduring claims to be regarded as one of the few English monarchs with a genuine interest in the arts. He sparked a wide-ranging artistic revolution in England, above all in Gothic church architecture. His greatest project was the rebuilding of Westminster Abbey, a 36-year undertaking that cost the huge sum of £46,000. The first portrait of an English monarch shows Henry directing the building of another new cathedral at St Albans (below).

ENRY'S REIGN BEGAN IN CRISIS. THE NEW king was only nine. In addition, many of his barons still supported the claims of Louis, son of Philippe II, to the English Crown. There was also the continuing problem of how to regain the huge French territories lost in John's reign. That these immediate crises were successfully overcome was largely due to what, for the period, was the unusually untroubled regency of Henry's early reign, competently presided over first by William Marshall, latterly by Hubert de Burgh.

Rapid victories by Marshall over Louis in 1217 summarily ended the lingering civil war. Though relations with some barons remained tense, for the immediate future they rarely spilled over into outright opposition – even if the relative weakness of Henry's position obliged him to approve two reissues of Magna Carta, in 1217 and 1225. More serious was the swift conquest of Poitou in 1224 by Louis, now king of France. Of the once-vast Angevin French lands, only Gascony was left.

Nonetheless by the time the 19-year-old Henry assumed personal control of England in 1227 his kingdom was largely stable, its mechanisms of royal government secure and efficient.

Henry's personal qualities – good and bad – were evident from the start. Though every bit as certain of the absolute nature of monarchy as his Plantagenet forebears, he had none of their relentless, martial energy. To the extent that his sedentary, self-indulgent kingship encouraged the development of more centralized government, above all at Westminster, Henry was in tune with his times. At the same time, however, it made him a singularly ineffective military leader. All his attempts at conquest, whether in Wales (in 1228, 1231 and 1232) or in France (in 1228, 1230 and 1242), ended in failure. Eventually, under the Treaty of Paris of 1259, and in return for confirmation of the Plantagenet rule in Gascony, Henry was forced to renounce all his claims to Normandy, Anjou and Poitou.

But Henry's most obvious failing, as with many medieval kings, was an inability to control his leading subjects. Simmering resentments over Henry's extravagant building projects were increased by Henry's high-handed promotion of his wife's Provençal relations and his own French-born stepbrothers over the interests of native-born magnates. They came to a climax in 1254 when, without consulting his barons, Henry agreed to finance a hugely expensive papal campaign to conquer Sicily.

By any measure, it was an exceptionally illjudged move. In 1258, cowed by his charismatic brother-in-law, Simon de Montfort (*see* box), Henry was forced to agree to the Provisions of Oxford. In effect, he surrendered control of his realm to a council of barons. In 13th-century Europe, this was a breathtakingly radical step. Even as half-hearted a ruler as

> *... [Henry] acknowledged the truth of the accusations ... and humbled himself declaring that he had too often been beguiled by evil counsel and ... made a solemn oath at the shrine of St Edward that he would fully and properly amend his old errors and show favour and kindness to his native-born subjects.*
>
> Matthew Paris Chronica Majora, on Henry III's promise in 1258 to limit royal power

---

1217	1219	1224	1227	1229	1232	1234	1236	1238	1242
Treaty of Lambeth: French dauphin, Louis, renounces claims to England after defeats at Lincoln and Sandwich	Death of regent, William Marshall; Hubert de Burgh appointed regent	Poitou lost to Louis IX of France	Henry III begins personal rule	French-born Simon de Montfort arrives in England, claiming earldom of Leicester	Hubert de Burgh dismissed; Peter des Roches, appointed in his place, encourages Henry to ignore advice of his principal barons	Rebellion by Richard Marshall forces Henry to expel Peter des Roches and other Poitevins in England	Henry's marriage to Eleanor of Provence begins influx of position-seeking Provençals	de Montfort consolidates position in England by secret marriage to Eleanor, Henry's sister	Unsuccessful attempt to retake Poitou

The full consequences of the loss of the whole of the northern Plantagenet French empire by John had to wait until the Treaty of Paris in 1259. In confirming the supremacy of the French crown in France, it at least normalized Anglo-French relations and allowed a period of stability. It did nothing to stabilize Henry II's relations with his barons in England, however, where full-scale civil war had broken out by 1263 (map left).

HENRY III 1216–1272

- Plantagenet possessions and dependencies, 1216
- Territory mostly controlled by Prince Louis, April 1217
- Plantagenet territories in Ireland and Wales, 1247
- → Henry's campaign, 1230
- → Henry's campaign, 1242
- Plantagenet claim abandoned under Treaty of Paris, 1259
- Transferred to Plantagenet control under Treaty of Paris
- To be transferred later to Plantagenet control under Treaty of Paris
- Welsh vassals of England under Treaty of Woodstock, 1247
- Principality of Wales under the Treaty of Montgomery, 1267
- Area of activity of rebellious barons, 1263
- → Richard of Cornwall's movements, 1263
- → Edward's movements, 1263–4
- → Henry's movements, 1263–4
- → Simon de Montfort's movements, 1263–4
- ✕ Battles
- Frontiers, 1272

Simon de Montfort 1208–65

Simon de Montfort is generally remembered as the greatest medieval champion of native-born English liberties, a worthy opponent of despotic royal power. As prime instigator of the Provisions of Oxford and the rowdy parliaments that followed, he is also celebrated as an early champion of Parliament itself. Yet not only was he just as much a foreign-born place seeker as those French favourites of Henry III he successfully expelled, his whole career was largely spent in the accumulation of the power and position he violently attacked in others. Personally abstemious and deeply pious, he nonetheless travelled with a retinue of lavishly attired knights that put to shame anything that Henry himself could muster. Yet whatever these inconsistencies and the hint of self-righteous fanaticism that surrounded him, his commitment to the pursuit of liberty was undoubtedly genuine – even if it can be hard to disentangle from his sense of his own self-worth and greater glory.

De Montfort was hacked to death at the Battle of Evesham. Afterwards, his hands and feet were cut off and his genitals draped on his face.

Henry III was stung to respond. Inevitably, civil war followed.

A crushing victory by de Montfort at Lewes in 1264 not only saw Henry and his heir, Edward, taken prisoner, but effectively confirmed the increasingly regal de Montfort as ruler of England. Henry became king in no more than name. That in the end the radicals were defeated, at the Battle of Evesham in 1265, owed little to Henry and almost everything to Edward, whose military prowess was in marked contrast to his father's petulant impotence.

Royal authority may have been re-established but ever-clearer limits to its scope had been set. Even as aggressive a king as Edward I would have to acknowledge the growing importance of Parliament.

1245	1248	1252	1254	1258	1259	1261	1263	1264	1265
Reconstruction of Westminster Abbey begun by Henry	de Montfort appointed governor of Gascony	de Montfort arraigned for alleged misrule in Gascony; provokes early feud with Henry	Henry agrees to finance papal campaign to conquer Sicily; provokes widespread baronial resentment	The Provisions of Oxford: Henry forced to agree to appointment of magnate-dominated council to co-rule England	Treaty of Paris confirms Plantagenet loss of Normandy, Anjou and Poitou	Backed by pope, Henry renounces Provisions of Oxford	Armed campaign begun by de Montfort against Henry	de Montfort triumphs at Battle of Lewes: Henry and his heir, Edward, are captured	de Montfort overthrown and killed at Battle of Evesham; royal authority restored

THE KING-IN-PARLIAMENT

THE DEVELOPMENT OF REPRESENTATIVE INSTITUTIONS OF GOVERNMENT OCCURRED FITFULLY. WELL INTO THE 17TH CENTURY, POLITICAL POWER REMAINED FIRMLY IN THE MONARCH'S HANDS. YET AS EARLY AS THE 13TH CENTURY, PARLIAMENT OF A KIND WAS BEGINNING TO EMERGE. THOUGH VERY MUCH A TOOL OF ROYAL GOVERNMENT AND ALMOST ENTIRELY SUBORDINATE TO THE MONARCH, IT WOULD PROVE IMPOSSIBLE TO IGNORE.

FROM THE VERY EARLIEST DAYS OF EUROPEAN KINGSHIP, no king could hope to rule without the support of his leading subjects. Ultimate authority may have been vested in the monarch, but disposing of it in the face of baronial opposition was an impossibility. Whether semi-formal, as in the Anglo-Saxon Witan, or more informal, councils of leading subjects naturally formed around the king to advise, on occasion to restrain, and, more extremely, to overthrow him. Even rulers as absolute as William the Conqueror and Henry II found themselves circumscribed in this way. It is no exaggeration to claim that managing their magnates was the central preoccupation of medieval rulers.

As the mechanisms of government developed, the role of the king's advisors increased. There was a paradox here. The aim of feudal kingship was to reinforce the king's authority at the expense of his subjects. But effective rule demanded further layers of government, in turn increasing the role of the king's advisors and officers.

Complementary to this development, and beginning in earnest in the reign of Henry II, was the spreading acceptance of law. Writing in the 12th century, John of Salisbury asserted: "Between a tyrant and a prince there is this single or chief difference, that the latter obeys the law and rules the people by its dictates, accounting himself as but their servant." Arguments of this kind were in no sense intended to limit royal authority. John of Salisbury went on to make the point that: "… the prince is the public power, and a kind of likeness on earth of the divine majesty," adding for good measure," …[the king's] will is to have the form of a judgement."

Of course, power of this kind could be abused. King John, for example, determined to imitate the authority of his father, repeatedly crossed the border between strong, effective kingship and what to his barons was quite clearly tyranny. Their response was to force him to agree to Magna Carta. Its purpose, bitterly resisted by John, was to guarantee the liberties of the barons by putting limits on the arbitrary exercise of feudal power. But crucially it reinforced the belief that an external body of law existed – "the law and custom of the realm" – above and beyond the person of the king and within which he had to operate. As important, it also introduced the idea that the barons spoke for "the community of the whole land".

An even more far-reaching step was taken in the reign of John's son, Henry III. Again, the immediate cause was baronial discontent which, as in John's reign, spilled into civil war. The key figure was Simon de Montfort who through the Provisions of Oxford of 1258 effectively made the king subject to what was now widely called Parliament (from the French *parlement*, meaning "discourse" or "consultation"). In 1265, with Henry III his prisoner, de Montfort went further still, calling a Parliament that consisted of 120 clerics, 23 barons, two knights from every shire and two burgesses from every borough.

Simon de Montfort may have been astonishingly radical but he was not operating in a vacuum. Increasingly sophisticated theories on the nature of representative forms of government were being developed in many parts of Europe. No less a figure than Henry Bracton, one of the king's own judges, put forward the view: "For the king, since he is the minister and vicar of God on earth, can do nothing save what he can do *de jure* [by right] … nor is that anything rashly put forward of his own free will, but what has been rightly decided with the counsel of his magnates, deliberation and consultation having been had thereon, the king giving it *auctoritas* [authority]."

If de Montfort's death during the royalist revival led by the future Edward I meant that his more extreme proto-republicanism came to nothing, his legacy in general would prove impossible to ignore. That said, though Edward I may be the king most generally credited with the consolidation of Parliament at the heart of government, Edward's motives were never less than pragmatic. For one thing, co-operation with his leading subjects was always likely to prove a more successful basis for effective rule than opposition. Equally important was the growing belief that taxation, which naturally affected all the property-owning classes, could be approved only by "the community of the realm", meaning Parliament. In 1295, in the so-called Model Parliament, Edward was forced to concede that: "No tallage [tax] or aid shall be laid or levied by us or our heirs in our realm without the good will and assent of the archbishops, bishops, earls, barons, knights, burgesses and other freemen of our realm."

The system of government that evolved is sometimes called "the king in parliament", a name that accurately reflected the primacy of the monarch. As has been said, Parliament in this sense remained essentially "an instrument of government at the king's disposal". For example, Parliament could be called only by the king, who could also dismiss it at any time. Even when the Commons – the knights of the shires and the burgesses – became a permanent feature after 1336, its members had no legal immunity. Criticism of the king could lead to imprisonment or worse. And, unlike the Lords, the Commons had no voice outside Parliament.

However, that its influence was increasing is undeniable. To some extent this was a reflection of the continuing expense of the Hundred Years War and consequent persistent need for taxation. Parliament met almost every year during the Hundred Years War, for example, but only about once every three years thereafter until Henry VIII's massive legislative programmes of the 1530s. Yet it is also highly significant that those behind the overthrow of Edward II in 1327 and of Richard II in 1399 felt it necessary to secure parliamentary authority, however obviously rigged, to legitimize their actions. By the same token, again if only as a smokescreen for their own ambitions, the lords appellants, who removed most effective power from Richard II, did so by recourse to parliamentary censure of him in the so-called Merciless Parliament of 1387.

Importantly however, and Simon de Montfort's brief experiment notwithstanding, any suggestion that Parliament might itself be sovereign and enjoy an authority greater than the monarch's was an idea that surfaced only in 1641. In every sense, it was to prove revolutionary.

Edward I presiding over Parliament, probably in 1298 (above). The subordination of Parliament to Edward I is made clear in this 16th-century image. Lords, clerics and commons are all shown flanking the English king, as are the rulers of Scotland and Wales, over both of whom Edward claimed lordship. In the centre are the law officers, sitting on bales of wool, symbols of the nation's prime export and wealth, and forerunners of the Woolsack, the official seat of the Lord Chancellor today. Two clerks are making a record of the proceedings.

EDWARD I 1272–1307

KING EDWARD I
BORN: June 17 1239,
Westminster
ACCEDED: November 16
1272; crowned August
19 1274,
Westminster Abbey

*EARL OF CHESTER AND
DUKE OF GASCONY
(FROM 1254),
KING OF ENGLAND,
WALES (FROM 1284),
MAN (FROM 1294),
SCOTLAND (FROM 1296),
LORD OF IRELAND*

EDWARD I, NAMED AFTER EDWARD THE CONFESSOR, HAD THE FIRST EXPRESSLY ENGLISH NAME OF ANY KING OF ENGLAND SINCE THE NORMAN CONQUEST. IT WAS ALL HE HAD IN COMMON WITH HIS UNWORLDLY ANGLO-SAXON PREDECESSOR. NO KING OF ENGLAND, WILLIAM THE CONQUEROR ASIDE, DEVOTED HIMSELF QUITE SO REMORSELESSLY TO MILITARY CONQUEST.

THE REIGNS OF EDWARD I'S TWO IMMEDIATE predecessors, his grandfather John and father, Henry III, made clear the difficulties facing weak kings in an age of absolute monarchy. Edward I, by contrast, bestrode his kingdom. He didn't just act the part, he looked it. At an imposing six-foot two, he was almost a giant by 13th-century standards – hence his far from derogatory nickname, "Longshanks".

His military talents were evident from the start. He distinguished himself in 1259, when he played a central role in Henry III's hesitant campaigns against the Welsh under Llywelyn ap Gruffydd; and more importantly, he did it again in 1265 when, seizing the leadership of the royalist cause from his hapless father, he routed Simon de Montfort's forces at the Battle of Evesham. He won further plaudits crusading in the Holy Land between 1270 and 1272, winning a notable victory at Haifa. He came to the throne at the age of 33, mature, confident and expectant.

Edward was always more than just a warrior-king par excellence. He had fully absorbed the lessons of his grandfather's and father's reigns and understood the importance of not alienating his leading subjects. It is no accident that the role of Parliament, above all in approving new taxation, increased greatly during Edward's reign, as did its membership, which from 1290 included the knights of the shire as well as leading magnates. Though never more than an instrument of royal authority, its growing standing was to prove hugely significant.

Edward was never slow to discipline his magnates, however. Much of the early part of his reign was spent rooting out corruption among them as well as among his own royal officials. He was particularly severe on those who claimed rights and territories "from time immemorial", which was now precisely defined as dating from before the reign of Richard I. Henceforward, any such vague assertions had to be backed by clear written proof. The avalanche of legislation and legal codifications that this and similar exercises gave rise to led 19th-century historians to dub Edward "the English Justinian". In fact, Edward was very much less interested in abstract notions of justice for its own sake than in extending his authority and revenues, a goal attainable only by efficient administration. Not for nothing was Edward dubbed *le Roi Coveytous*. Nonetheless, energetic, forthright kingship on this dynamic scale went a long way in extending the rule of law in England.

Yet it is mainly for his conquests that Edward I is rightly remembered, specifically his attempts to extend Plantagenet hegemony over the whole of Britain to create, in effect, the first English empire. On the whole, he was less successful in France. Though no less French in origin and instinct than any of his Plantagenet predecessors – French was his mother tongue; Edward's English was never better than adequate – in the face of an expansionist French monarchy he was never able to do much

The Expulsion of the Jews

In 1290, Edward I authorized the expulsion of all England's 3,000 Jews. Anti-Semitism had long been rife across Christian Europe. By 1218, all Jews in England were required to wear two distinctive yellow stripes on their clothes. Although Jewish communities were generally distrusted, most were tolerated as ready sources of finance. In 1275, however, Edward forbade them from money-lending. Characteristically, Edward's action was entirely pragmatic. Most Jews had already been exhausted as potential money-lenders. Further, Edward had Italian bankers standing by to advance him money to continue his extravagant castle-building in Wales. Above all, however, Edward was concerned to keep the support not just of his magnates but of the Church. The expulsion of the Jews would, he knew, be hugely popular – as indeed it proved to be. For Edward, it was a small price to pay to win the support of parliament.

Llywelyn ap Gruffydd's Welsh principality under Treaty of Montgomery, 1267

Edward's campaign, 1276–77

Remaining Welsh areas - English vassals under Treaty of Aberconway, 1277

Core area of revolt, March 1282

Approximate limit of area affected by the revolt by June 1282

English campaign, 1282–83

Area affected by revolt of Rhys ap Maredudd, 1287

Area affected by Welsh revolt, 1294–95

Edward's campaign, 1295

The most obvious consequence of the loss of the bulk of their French lands was to re-focus Plantagenet ambitions in Britain. By any measure, Edward I's conquest of Wales after 1277 (map right) was a savagely brutal affair. That in 1282–3 following the revolt by Daffydd Llywelyn was even more so. The string of castles built by Edward I was a permanent mark of Plantagenet overlordship.

Castles holding out for Edward I during 1294–5 revolt

The tongue of man can scarcely recount the evil deeds committed by the Welsh against our progenitors ... but God wishing as it seems to put an end to these evil proceedings has, after the prince had been slain, destined Daffydd as the last survivor of the family of traitors ... to be the king's prisoner after he had been captured by men of his own race.

Edward I on the execution of Llywelyn ap Gruffydd's brother, Daffydd, 1285

more than hold on to his existing territories in Gascony. That Gascony was important to Edward is clear not merely from the fact that it was Gascony he visited first on his way back from the Holy Land after his accession (having first paid homage to the new French king, Philippe III, for his Gascon territories), but from the fact that he returned there for no less than three years in 1286. When he left in 1289 it was as the last Plantagenet king to hold court in Bordeaux.

Edward's initial moves into Wales, in 1277, were intended less to conquer the principality than to reassert his authority over it as an English fief. The growing strength of Llywelyn ap Gruffydd, whom Henry III had reluctantly recognized as Prince of Wales in 1267, had given rise to a state of near anarchy in the Welsh marches. Further, Llywelyn was now repeatedly refusing to pay homage to Edward.

Whereas most medieval monarchs rushed to be crowned so as to be able to assert their authority as soon as possible, Edward I's coronation (left) took place almost two years after his accession. In Sicily when news of Henry III's death was received, Edward's subsequent stately progress back to England, via Paris and Gascony, was a measure of his confidence in the security of his throne.

1277	1282–3	1284	1286	1286–9
Defeats Llywelyn ap Gruffydd, stripping him of many of his lands and compelling him to do homage	*Second invasion of Wales leads to complete conquest and death of Llywelyn ap Gruffydd*	*Statute of Wales reorganizes Wales on English model; Edward's heir declared Prince of Wales*	*Death of Alexander III prompts succession crisis in Scotland and allows Edward to assert overlordship*	*Edward visits Gascony*

continued on next page

Though never more than conventionally pious, the briskly efficient Edward enjoyed generally harmonious relations with his leading churchmen, as he did with the majority of his leading subjects. Here (above), sword in hand, he consults with bishops.

In a swift and exceptionally well-organized campaign, Edward's huge army cut off Llywelyn's forces. In view of what was to follow, the subsequent settlement was relatively mild. Though Llywelyn, who in 1278 finally performed homage to Edward, lost most of his southern territories, he was allowed to continue as Prince of Wales over Gwynedd.

When five years later Llywelyn's brother, Daffydd, led an uprising against the marches, Edward's response was savagely different. This time, his goal was nothing less than the annexation of Wales. Though the campaign dragged on into 1283, Llywelyn's death in November 1282 effectively signalled the end of Welsh resistance. Daffydd himself was captured and gruesomely executed as a traitor.

The subjection of Wales, brutal even by the standards of the time, was achieved and sustained by a massive occupying army based in the grimly imposing fortresses that Edward constructed across Wales. Under the Statute of Wales of 1284, it was also given legal force. Wales was divided into new shires on the English model with English officials brought in to administer them. Welsh humiliation was made complete the same year when Llywelyn's title, Prince of Wales, was appropriated by the king and bestowed on Edward's son, the future Edward II.

The expression of Edward's ambitions in Scotland were, to begin with, restricted to diplomacy. The accession of the three-year-old Margaret, the "Maid of Norway", to the Scottish throne after the sudden death of Alexander III in 1286 prompted Edward to propose marriage between his heir, Edward, and Margaret. However reluctantly accepted by the Scots, the eventual union of the Scottish and English crowns would then naturally have followed. Margaret's death in 1290 not only put paid to such dynastic ambitions but sparked a further succession crisis in Scotland. Even now, however, Edward, though asserting his overlordship of Scotland, acted as no more than arbiter in the choice of the new sovereign, John Balliol, in 1292.

The Eleanor Crosses

Edward's image as a ruthless warmonger is entirely belied by his relationship with his first wife, Eleanor, the Infanta of Castile (whose name, corrupted in English to "Elephant and Castle", is commemorated in the London district and many inns of the same name). Their marriage, in 1254, was conventionally diplomatic, intended to secure an important ally on the southern border of Gascony. Edward was 15, Eleanor 13. They had 15 children, nine of whom died. Remarkably, rather than the mutual loathing such marriages normally produced, Eleanor and Edward seem to have been genuinely fond of one another.

On her death, Edward wrote: "My harp is turned to mourning, in life I loved her dearly, nor can I cease to love her in death." As remarkable were the 12 stone crosses that were erected by Edward to mark the stopping points of her funeral cortège from Harby in Nottinghamshire, where she died, to Westminster Abbey, where she was buried. Three survive today, at Hardingstone and Geddington (right) in Northamptonshire and at Waltham Cross in Essex (far right). The most famous, at Charing Cross, is not the original cross but a replica put up in 1863.

Almost as surprising was that Edward's second marriage, in 1299, to Margaret, sister of Philippe IV of France, which was again arranged to cement a diplomatic alliance, was equally happy. Edward was 60, Margaret 20.

continued from previous page

1290	1292	1293	1294	1295
Death of first wife, Eleanor. Expulsion of Jews. Treaty of Birgham agrees marriage of Edward's son to new child queen of Scotland, Margaret; Edward agrees to respect "rights and liberties" of Scotland.	John Balliol confirmed by Edward as new king of Scotland	Escalating tensions with Philippe IV of France leads Philippe to declare Gascony forfeit	Revolt in Wales delays Edward's plans for French campaign	Scotland and France formally ally against England

It is an exceptional testimony to the sense of nation-hood fostered by Scotland's kings from the 12th century onward that, however overwhelming the forces directed against it by Edward I, the war-like Plantagenet was never able to conquer the country (map right). He would, however, guarantee contin-ued Anglo-Scottish hostility until well into the 16th century.

EDWARD I's SCOTTISH CAMPAIGNS, 1296–1307

- ▬▬ Area affected by Edward I's 1291 campaign
- ➜ Edward's campaign, 1296
- ➜ Edward's campaign, 1298
- ➜ Edward's campaign, 1300
- ➜ Edward's campaign, 1301-02
- ▓▓ Area affected by Edward's 1303–4 campaign
- 🌿 Revolt, with details

But now, buoyed by his success in Wales, it is clear that conquest rather than control was beginning to dominate Edward's ambitions. Though Balliol remained as defiant as his weakened circumstances allowed, by 1295 Edward had reduced him to scarcely more than a cipher. The Scottish response, to seek an alliance with France (*see* pp.66–7), was treated by Edward as tantamount to a decla-ration of war. In March 1296 he mustered an army of 25,000. Reaching Berwick, he slaughtered almost the whole population of 11,000. By July, the campaign was over. Edward declared himself king of Scotland and returned to England with the Stone of Destiny, the single most potent symbol of Scottish independence.

Ultimately, whatever his overwhelming military and financial superiority, Edward failed in Scotland, brought up short by the upsurge of patriotic leadership supplied first by William Wallace and more lastingly by Robert the Bruce (*see* pp.64–5). Further terrifying campaigns in 1298, 1300, 1301–2, 1303–4 and 1307, and the stationing of large permanent English garrisons across much of Scotland, highlight the extent of Edward's obsessional determination to subjugate his northern neighbours. But the bloodshed succeeded only in poisoning Anglo-Scottish relations for sev-eral centuries. Appropriately, Edward died near Carlisle leading another vengeful campaign against Scotland in 1307.

Like Henry II, Edward I imposed strong rule in an age that demanded it. But also like Henry, he was unable to guarantee it from beyond the grave. With-in years, his heir, Edward II, supine, vacillating and indolent, came close to bringing the whole mag-nificent edifice of Edwardian Plantagenet kingship crashing to the ground.

CAITHNESS
WESTERN ISLES
ROSS
ELGIN
INVERNESS
Andrew of Moray, 1297
ABERDEEN
SCOTLAND
MONCSA
DUNKELD
DUNDEE
PERTH
ST ANDREWS
Stirling 1297
Falkirk 1298
EDINBURGH
Dunbar 1297
GLASGOW
Roslin 1303
BERWICK
ROXBURGH
William Wallace, 1297
JEDBURGH
AYR
Robert Bruce, 1297
DUMFRIES
LIBERTY OF TYNEDALE
Held by Scottish kings to 1296
CARLISLE
ENGLAND
IRELAND
(to England)
ISLE OF MAN
Plantagenet-held from 1290

Though otherwise peaceful, relations between Edward and his French counterparts deteriorated after 1293. The following year, Edward renounced his homage to the French king. In 1295, parts of northern Gascony were overrun by the French. As his designs on Scotland took firmer shape, such cross-Channel distractions proved increasingly troublesome. Nonetheless, in 1297 Edward went to France where, with papal intervention, his lordship of Gascony was confirmed. In return, Edward renewed his homage to Philippe IV (left).

1296	1297	1298	1299	1300–7	1306
Edward invades Scotland; strips Balliol of crown and incarcerates him in Tower of London	William Wallace leads Scottish resistance; defeats English at Stirling Bridge. Edward travels to France to secure Gascony from further French attacks	Wallace crushed by Edward at Battle of Falkirk	Peace treaty between England and France sealed by marriage between Edward and Margaret, sister of Philippe IV	Sustained efforts by Edward to conquer Scotland	Scottish resistance led by Robert Bruce, who is crowned King of Scotland

EDWARD II 1307–27

KING
EDWARD II
BORN: April 25 1284,
Caernarvon Castle
ACCEDED: July 8 1307;
crowned February 25
1308, Westminster
Abbey

PRINCE OF WALES
(DECLARED 1284,
INVESTED 1301),
DUKE OF AQUITAINE
(FROM 1306),
KING OF ENGLAND
AND SCOTLAND,
LORD OF IRELAND

WHETHER IT WAS BECAUSE HE WAS COWED INTO PETULANT REBELLIOUSNESS BY HIS OVERBEARING FATHER OR BECAUSE HE WAS SIMPLY TEMPERAMENTALLY INCAPABLE OF KINGSHIP, EDWARD II WAS MEDIEVAL ENGLAND'S MOST INEPT KING. AN EASY PREY TO PLACE-SEEKERS AND THE NAKED AMBITIONS OF HIS MOST CYNICAL MAGNATES, HE PROVOKED FIRST A CIVIL WAR AND THEN THE MOST SERIOUS CONSTITUTIONAL CRISIS ENGLAND HAD KNOWN.

EDWARD II INHERITED A THRONE AS SECURE as any in medieval Europe and a government that, if indebted, was efficient and centralized. Tall, dashing and intelligent, his advantages were obvious. From the start, however, he seemed determined to antagonize his leading subjects and to fritter away his inheritance in juvenile pleasure-seeking.

Even before his father's death his friendship with Piers Gaveston, the son of a Gascon knight, was raising eyebrows. But if swapping clothes and mocking court ceremonial may have been just acceptable in a teenage heir to the throne, in a king of England it was little short of scandalous. Worse, within weeks of his accession, Edward made Gaveston earl of Cornwall, a title normally reserved for the king's eldest son. When Edward went to France to collect his bride, Isabella, he left Gaveston as

Despite persistent rumours of his homosexuality, Edward II and Isabella's marriage (above) seems to have been relatively happy in its early days. But no wife of an English king treated her husband with the same degree of contemptuous loathing as Isabella treated Edward after 1325. Edward memorably called her the "she-wolf of France".

Edward II's attempts to subdue Scotland (map left) were a pale shadow of his father's. His most ambitious attempt, in 1314, ended with ignominious defeat at Bannockburn, despite a huge numerical advantage. To all intents and purposes, the battle confirmed Scottish independence under Robert the Bruce. Later incursions into Scotland by Edward II were equally futile.

EDWARD II IN SCOTLAND 1307–22

→	*Edward's campaign, 1307*
→	*Edward's campaign, 1310*
┅⯈	*Gaveston's campaign, 1310*
▨	*Area affected by Edward's 1311 campaign*
→	*Edward's campaign, 1314*
→	*Edward's campaign, 1322*
→	*Scottish campaign, 1322*
▨	*Area subjected to Scottish campaigns during Edward's rule*

1307	1308	1310	1311	1312	1313	1314	1318
Gaveston made regent in England during Edward's visit to France to collect his bride, Isabella.	Gaveston briefly banished; created Regent of Ireland	Edward forced to agree to council of 28 barons, the Lords Ordainers, headed by the earl of Lancaster; Gaveston banished permanently	Return of Gaveston; immediately reinstated as his favourite by Edward	Gaveston arrested and executed by Lancaster	Despensers begin rise to favour; Hugh the Younger made chamberlain	Edward's forces overwhelmed by Scots under Robert the Bruce at Battle of Bannockburn	Partial reconciliation engineered between Edward and Lancaster by the earl of Pembroke

regent. When, in 1308, Edward was prevailed upon to banish Gaveston, he did so by making him Regent of Ireland.

Had Edward shown any talent for administration or conquest, such fecklessness might have been tolerated. As it was, his distaste for the day-to-day business of kingship allied to high-handed disdain for his magnates provoked only outrage. In 1310, goaded into action by the earl of Lancaster, Edward was forced to banish Gaveston again and to agree to a council of barons, the Lords Ordainers, led by Lancaster, who in effect took over the government. Gaveston was not to be denied, however. In 1311 he turned up again. It proved his undoing. He was arrested by Lancaster and executed.

Much of the rest of Edward's troubled reign saw an increasingly lawless power struggle between Lancaster and Edward's new favourites, the Marcher lords Hugh le Despenser and his son, Hugh the Younger. Showered with gifts and titles by Edward, they built up a huge powerbase in Wales. For Edward, the advantages were clear: the Despensers could be used to counterbalance Lancaster's grip on government. The other Marcher lords, however, greeted their rapid rise with growing alarm.

These sorry, often sordid rivalries were played out against the background of Edward's devastating defeat by Robert the Bruce at Bannockburn in 1314 (*see* p. 64), which was his only serious attempt to continue his father's Scottish campaigns. Forced into humiliating retreat, Edward thereafter effectively abandoned the north of England to Scottish raiding.

In 1321, a coalition between Lancaster and the most powerful of the other marchers, Roger Mortimer, forced Edward to banish the Despensers. For the only time in his reign, Edward was roused into action. A rapid campaign in 1322 led to the imprisonment of Mortimer and the overthrow of Lancaster, who was duly executed. With the Despensers restored, Edward's triumph seemed complete.

In fact, it did no more than to herald his own overthrow, this time at the hands of his wife, Isabella, who had joined forces in France with Mortimer, soon to be her lover, after he had escaped from the Tower of London. Their trump card was their possession of Edward's heir. In 1326, having raised a mercenary army in Flanders, they invaded England. Edward's fall was swift. In January 1327, held prisoner by Isabella and Mortimer, he was forced to abdicate in favour of his son. The following September, Mortimer had him gruesomely murdered.

After Lancaster had been executed by Edward in 1322, the king forbade the corpse to be cut down for two years. When Isabella and Mortimer executed Hugh le Despenser in 1326 (above), they ordered that he be hanged, then, while still alive, his intestines be cut out and burned in front of him. He was then to be beheaded.

Edward was buried two months after his death at Gloucester Abbey. Both Isabella and Mortimer attended the ceremony. Edward III subsequently had this tomb effigy (below) made as an act of atonement.

The execution of Edward II

Edward's deposition and death at the hands of Isabella and Mortimer was the most blatant act of self-advancement in England before the overthrow of Richard II at the end of the 14th century. There was no legal mechanism whereby an anointed king could be deposed. Edward had already reluctantly handed over his great seal, allowing Parliament to issue writs in his name. But Parliament could not meet without the king. The solution was to force the king to abdicate by threatening to disinherit his heir, the future Edward III, in favour of Mortimer. This the pathetically tearful Edward finally agreed to. A hastily summoned Parliament at Kenilworth, where Edward was held, then formally declared Edward III king.

Afterwards, fearful that opposition to the new regime would form around the deposed monarch, Isabella and Mortimer murdered him. Having transferred him to Berkeley Castle, they first tried to starve Edward to death so as to leave no visible evidence of his fate. Impatient at Edward's lingering refusal to die, Mortimer ordered that he be killed by inserting a red-hot poker into his rectum.

1321	1322	1323	1324	1325	1326	1327
Lancaster and Mortimer force Edward to exile Despensers	Edward leads punitive campaign against Lancaster and Mortimer; Lancaster beheaded, Mortimer imprisoned; Despensers recalled; Lords Ordainers dissolved under the Statute of York. Edward continues to Scotland before being routed	Peace treaty agreed with Robert the Bruce	Mortimer escapes from Tower of London and flees to France. Isabella stripped of her estates	Isabella sent to France (March) to smooth worsening relations with French over Gascony; joined (September) by her son, Edward, whom she refuses to return to England	Isabella and Mortimer banished by Charles IV of France after their open liaison causes scandal; they recruit mercenary army in Hainault and invade England: Despensers overthrown, Edward captured	Edward forced to abdicate; Parliament recognizes Edward III as king. Edward II murdered

EDWARD III 1327–77

EDWARD III
BORN: November 13
1312, Windsor Castle
ACCEDED: January 25
1327; crowned
February 1 1327,
Westminster Abbey

*EARL OF CHESTER (FROM
1312), DUKE OF
AQUITAINE, COUNT
OF PONTHIEU AND MON-
TREUIL (FROM 1325),
LORD OF
IRELAND, KING OF
FRANCE (FROM 1340),
KING OF ENGLAND*

EDWARD III NOT ONLY HEALED THE CIVIL STRIFE OF HIS FATHER'S REIGN, HE LAUNCHED A SERIES OF TRIUMPHANT CAMPAIGNS AGAINST SCOTLAND AND FRANCE THAT MADE HIM THE MOST FÊTED WARRIOR IN CHRISTENDOM. HIS COURT WAS THE MOST GLAMOROUS IN EUROPE. YET HE DIED LONELY AND EMBITTERED, HIS EARLIER FRENCH GAINS LOST, HIS HEIR ALREADY DEAD.

EDWARD III WAS ONLY 14 WHEN HE CAME to the throne, an unwitting participant in the overthrow and murder of his father by Edward's mother and her lover, Roger Mortimer. Though king, the youthful Edward III was in reality no more than a cipher for his mother and Mortimer.

The Black Prince 1330–76

Edward III's eldest son, also called Edward, became something of a symbol of Edward's expansionist kingdom at its most militarily successful. "The comfort of England" as he was known, or more commonly, after the colour of his armour, the Black Prince, seemed to have inherited all his father's most noble virtues, chief among them his military ardour. To the French he was a "bon capiteine et un féroce pillard". Much of his life was spent in Gascony, where he was Lord Lieutenant. Though he was the third Prince of Wales, he never visited it.

He led a number of notable English victories against the French, above all at Poitiers, in 1356, when Jean II was captured. Yet the escalating cost of these campaigns could only be financed by punitive taxation in Gascony, sparking resentment that would continue to grow.

He died in 1376, a year before his father, from a debilitating ear infection picked up in Castile, where the fighting had spilled over from Gascony. His ten-year-old son, Richard de Bordeaux, became Richard II the following year.

The tomb of the Black Prince in Canterbury Cathedral.

But within three years, the hallmarks of his decisive kingship became clear.

In 1330 Edward had Mortimer arrested, tried in Parliament for treason and executed. Isabella, the king's mother, was treated more leniently: she was allowed to see out her days in Norfolk, albeit in greatly reduced circumstances.

The challenges now facing Edward were two-fold: the continuing conflicts with Scotland and France and the repair of relations with his leading subjects. He set about both tasks with gusto and intelligence.

His prime tactic in healing the bitter divisions of his father's reign was to co-opt his barons into a genuinely common national enterprise in which for the first time the monarchy became properly consultative in Parliament. Inevitably, this involved Edward in surrendering an element of executive authority, though as an anointed king Parliament was always answerable to, and derived its authority from, him. In any case, Edward's attitude towards Parliament was really no more than prudence demanded. The huge and growing expense of his foreign wars meant a comparable increase in taxation, which only Parliament could approve. Edward literally could not afford to alienate Parliament.

Edward's adroitness in his relations with his magnates also found an echo in his love of chivalry and courtly display. This was far from empty showmanship. Splendour on this scale not only enhanced the dignity of the monarchy but made the glamour of Edward's court and the lavishness of its entertainments a focus for all his barons, binding king and subjects in a sumptuous pseudo-Arthurian chivalric code. Much of this – the Order of the Garter, begun by Edward in 1348 (*see* box) or the elaborate single-combat tournaments he favoured – also had the crucial benefit of underpinning Edward's military ambitions. By making his magnates "co-partners in peace and war", Edward ensured that they had a stake in military success, enabling them to share the glory and plunder of foreign conquest. At least to begin with, there was no shortage of either.

It was perhaps part of Edward's genius to present his wars with Scotland and France as ennobling. In reality, both were brutal, seemingly endless affairs in

1327	1328	1329	1330	1331	1332	1333	1334
Edward leads retaliatory raid against Scots. Isabella unsuccessfully claims throne of France for Edward after death of Charles IV	Treaty of Northampton, agreed by Isabella and Mortimer, confirms Scottish independence	Philippe VI threatens Gascony; Edward does homage to him for it. Death of Robert the Bruce, accession of David II	Edward assumes full authority after arrest and execution of Mortimer and enforced retirement of Isabella	Edward renews homage to Philippe VI	Edward sponsors seizure of Scottish throne by Edward Balliol	Edward reinforces Balliol's position in Scotland when he defeats anti-Balliol patriots at Halidon Hill	Balliol transfers southern Scotland to the English and acknowledges English overlordship of remainder; David II flees to ally France

> Since, therefore, the kingdom of France has by divine disposition
> devolved upon us by the clearest right owing to the death of
> Charles of noted memory ... and the Lord Philip of Valois,
> son of the king's uncle and thus further removed from the royal
> blood, ... has intruded himself by force into the kingdom while
> we were of tender years, and holds that kingdom against God
> and justice, ... we have recognized our right to the kingdom ...
> resolving ... to cast out the usurper when the opportunity
> shall seem most propitious.
>
> Edward III's assertion of his French kingship, March 1340

THE HUNDRED YEARS WAR I, 1337–77

Plantagenet possessions in France at the outbreak of the war
Edward III's campaign, 1339
Edward III's campaign, 1340
Edward III's campaign, 1342
Edward III's campaign, 1346
Edward III's campaign, 1359-60
The Black Prince's campaigns
Other English campaigns
French campaigns
Acquired by the English under Treaty of Brétigny, 1360
Frontiers, 1377

Edward III made England's monarchy strong
and respected again. Whatever the disappoint-
ments of his old age, the tyranny and chaos of
his father's reign became a thing of the past.
Here he invests his son, the Black Prince, as
Prince of Aquitaine in 1362 (above).

which no side could deliver a decisive
blow. Nonetheless, at least until 1360,
Edward could justifiably claim the
upper hand in both.

In 1328, Edward had been obliged by
his mother and Mortimer to sign the
Treaty of Northampton, guaranteeing
Scottish independence. It was not an
agreement Edward intended to honour.
The death of Robert the Bruce in 1329
and accession of the five-year-old David
II provided his opportunity.

In 1332, meaning to revive the overlordship of Scotland established by
Edward I in the reign of John Balliol,
Edward backed an attempt by Balliol's
son, Edward, to seize the throne.

However dramatic Edward III's initial successes in France, above all the crushing
victory at Crécy in 1346 and the Black Prince's similarly overwhelming victory at
Poitiers in 1356 (map above), it never seemed quite enough. Plantagenet control may
have been restored over much of the southwest by 1360, but with neither side ever able
to summon sufficient means for a decisive victory stalemate thereafter became the norm.

1335–8	1336	1337	1338	1340	1341	1343
Regular campaigns launched against Scotland to shore up Balliol	French fleet assembled for invasion of England	Edward III claims French crown; Philippe invades Gascony: effective start of Hundred Years War	Walton Ordinances put Edward's finances on firmer footing. Edward launches first, inconclusive attack on France	Edward III declares himself King of France. Destroys French fleet at Sluys	David II returns to Scotland; begins active campaigns against England in support of France	Truce agreed with France

continued on next page

The first major engagement of the Hundred Years War was fought in June 1340 at Sluys on the coast of Flanders, where Philippe IV had gathered a fleet of over 200 ships (above). The English victory was absolute. The numbers of French dead were such, it was claimed, that the fish could have learned French. Much more important, Sluys dissuaded the French from attempting any further large-scale invasion of England. Henceforth, the Hundred Years War would be fought in France.

The Most Noble Order of the Garter

The distinctive star of the Order, with motto and garter surrounding the red cross of St George.

E dward's love of ever-more elaborate chivalric ritual was epitomized by his foundation in August 1348 of the Most Noble Order of the Garter, the oldest and most prestigious chivalric order in Britain. As today, there were no more than 26 members, including Edward III himself and his eldest son. They became in effect King Arthur's imagined knights of the Round Table reborn, the king's most valued "companions-in-arms". They met, and solemnized their proceedings, in the chapel at Windsor Castle, which was rebuilt and dedicated to England's new patron saint, St George, whose heroic 3rd-century exploits had inspired English knights in the crusades.

It says something for Edward III's easy camaraderie with his fellow knights that, whatever the higher aims of the Order, its name and motto came from a slightly smutty in-joke. At a dance, the king's mistress, the countess of Salisbury, lost her garter. Gallantly, the king retrieved it with the words: "Honi soit qui mal y pense" – colloquially, "Keep your dirty thoughts to yourselves."

Though the younger Balliol's grip on Scotland was never more than tenuous and would in any case not last much beyond 1336, by 1334 he was nonetheless sufficiently well established to force the now nine-year-old David II to flee to France and to cede the whole of southern Scotland to Edward Balliol, doing homage to him for the rest.

But thereafter, though periodically sucked into the much larger Anglo-French conflict by virtue of the Auld Alliance, and despite a series of energetic Scottish campaigns by Edward in the mid-1330s, Scotland, beset by near-permanent dynastic unrest, became only a side-show in Edward's eyes. France was his real goal.

In essence, this new Anglo-French conflict, much later dubbed the Hundred Years War, was no more than a continuation of the much older one that began with the Norman Conquest. But it was given new urgency in 1328 with the death of the childless Charles IV of France. As Edward was Charles's nephew, Edward could reasonably have expected to succeed to the French throne. But his claim, put forward by his mother, was rejected by the French *Parlement*. Instead it was Charles IV's cousin, Philippe VI, who was eventually chosen as the new king of France.

Simultaneously, the long-standing French resentment at the continued Plantagenet presence in Gascony, allied to Anglo-French rivalry in Flanders (by far England's most important Continental trading partner yet coveted by France), was increasing. The situation was temporarily improved in 1329 and in 1331 when Edward travelled to France to do homage to Philippe for Gascony, the last king of England to do so. But it deteriorated in 1334 when Philippe agreed to shelter the child-king of Scotland, David II. By 1336, Philippe was assembling a fleet for an invasion of England.

The following year, Edward dramatically upped the stakes by claiming the French throne. Philippe promptly declared Gascony forfeit and invaded it. In fact, skirmishing aside – a French raid on Southampton in 1338, an inconclusive invasion of France by Edward the same year – little of consequence happened until 1340. Edward needed time to put his finances on a firm footing and to secure allies elsewhere in Europe. In March 1340, Edward formally declared himself King of France, a title retained by every English and British monarch until 1801, and added the fleur-de-lys to his arms. In June, he wiped out the French fleet at Sluys. 16,000 French soldiers and sailors died.

A temporary truce in 1343 was followed in 1346 by Edward's first major invasion of France. It was stunningly successful. Not only was the much larger

continued from previous page

1344	1345	1346	1348	1350	1355	1356	1358
Coinage reformed by Edward III	Sporadic campaigns in Flanders, Brittany and France	Major invasion of France: victory at Crécy and seizure of Calais. David II captured at Neville's Cross	Black Death strikes France and England. Order of the Garter established	David attempts to secure release by proposing that Edward's heir inherits Scottish throne	Scots raid Berwick	Edward leads renewed campaign against Scotland. Black Prince captures Jean II at Poitiers	France disrupted by widespread rioting: the "Jacquerie"

The Black Death

T he greatest convulsion of Edward III's reign was not caused by the wars with France and Scotland but by a terrible outbreak of plague, the Black Death. It struck indiscriminately. Within two years of its appearance in France, in the summer of 1348, a full third of the population of western Europe was dead. A Yorkshire monk, Thomas Burton, recorded: "The pestilence grew so strong that men and women dropped dead in the streets." In Bristol, where the plague first struck England, 45 per cent of the population died in less than a year.

The Black Death was terrifyingly indiscriminate, disrupting social and economic life for years. It could be explained only as a punishment from God.

The most immediate effect of the plague, other than to halt the fighting between England and France, was wage inflation. A greatly reduced working population could naturally now demand higher wages, a trend Edward III's Statute of Labour in 1351 attempted to halt. But the political impact was surprisingly low: no European monarch died, for example. Within six years, there was renewed fighting with Scotland; within eight years, the war with France had been resumed. However, Edward III did lose his "dearest daughter" Joan to the plague. "No fellow human being could be surprised if we were inwardly desolated by the sting of bitter death," wrote the king, "for we are human too." There were further outbreaks of plague in 1361 and 1375.

The significance of Edward III's great victory at Crécy in August 1346 (**right**) *was as much psychological as actual. As with most English victories in the Hundred Years War, it proved impossible to convert military success into sustainable political control. But the battle was important, too, in the evolution of military technology, in that the devastation wracked by Edward was primarily the result of his use of Welsh longbow-men and professional soldiers rather than a purely feudal army. Yet, however much more effective these new forces, paying them always strained Edward's resources.*

French army crushingly defeated at Crécy, Edward also took Calais, thereafter a vital English foothold in France. In October, an English army under the formidable Archbishop of York, Walter de la Zouche, captured David II, who had returned to Scotland in 1341. David would remain Edward's prisoner for 11 years as well as, once profitably ransomed by Edward, an enthusiastic promoter of English interests in Scotland.

Hostilities resumed after a further truce forced by the horrors of the Black Death (*see* box) in 1348. In 1355, Edward's eldest son, the Black Prince, rampaged through France, looting and pillaging, before inflicting yet another major defeat on France in 1356 at Poitiers in which the new French king, Jean II, was captured. Briefly, both the kings of France and Scotland were Edward's prisoners. Jean's ransom was set at the staggering sum of three million gold crowns, perhaps £700,000.

Edward could never quite make these military victories stick. Despite pouring men and money into the war, he never had enough of either. In 1360, having tried and failed to deliver the knock-blow over the winter of 1359–60, he was forced to come to terms with the French. In return for renouncing his claim to the throne, Edward's sovereignty in Gascony was acknowledged.

By 1369, the war had restarted. Thereafter, the advantage slipped tantalizingly from Edward. Rallied by their new king, Charles V, the French chipped away at Edward's gains. A series of cripplingly expensive attempts to contain the inexorable French advance came to nothing. By his death in 1377, only Calais and a narrow coastal strip in Gascony remained in Plantagenet hands. It was less than Edward had begun with.

1359–60	1361	1369	1370	1372	1373	1375	1376
Treaty of Brétigny: Edward renounces claim to French throne in return for acknow-ledgement of sovereignty of Gascony, Ponthieu and Calais	Renewed plague outbreak	French conflict restarts; Portsmouth raided. Edward's wife, Queen Philippa dies.	English defeat at Limoges	English naval defeat at La Rochelle	John of Gaunt leads long-range looting raid – chevauchée – in France	Failed campaign against France	Death of the Black Prince. Edward rebuked by "Good" Parliament

KING
RICHARD II
BORN: January 6 1367,
Bordeaux
ACCEDED: June 22 1377;
crowned July 16 1377,
Westminster Abbey

*PRINCE OF WALES,
EARL OF CORNWALL,
EARL OF CHESTER,
LORD OF IRELAND,
KING OF ENGLAND*

RICHARD II 1377–99

MEDIEVAL ABSOLUTISM REACHED ITS APOGEE WITH RICHARD II. HIS SUCCESS IN FACING DOWN THE PEASANTS' REVOLT WHEN HE WAS ONLY 14 REINFORCED HIS UNSHAKEABLE BELIEF IN HIS OWN DIVINELY APPOINTED MONARCHICAL RIGHT TO RULE. THE RESULT, INEVITABLY, WAS A PROTRACTED POWER STRUGGLE BETWEEN RICHARD AND HIS BARONS. IT ENDED WITH RICHARD'S OVERTHROW AND A NEW ROUND OF DYNASTIC TURMOIL.

Richard II was undone as much by his refusal to renew the war with France as by his belief in his right to rule absolutely. In fact, however much it went against the grain of the times, his pursuit of peace was both imaginative and shrewd. In other circumstances, he might have made a successful monarch. Here (below), gorgeously attired and apparently at the height of his power, he leaves for his second visit to Ireland, in 1399.

THE UPHEAVALS OF THE BLACK DEATH, reverses in the wars against France, continuing high levels of taxation, a smouldering anti-clericalism sparked by reformers such as John Wyclif and Edward III's slow decline into senility had combined to produce a mood akin to crisis at Richard's accession. That the new king was a child only added to the sense of foreboding. Many of the country's leading magnates in effect commanded private armies that were formed during the endless French and Scottish wars, and fears of a power struggle among them now seemed justified.

In the event, the immediate crisis passed. The key figure – as it would be for almost all of Richard's reign – was John of Gaunt, Richard's uncle and the eldest of Edward III's surviving sons. Though never a member of the council appointed to oversee the government in Richard's regency, there was little doubt that real power lay with him.

Richard's authority was immeasurably boosted in 1381 when he faced down the leaders of the Peasants' Revolt (*see* box). By any standard, the king's behaviour was exceptionally courageous. There seemed little doubt that he was a worthy heir to his most war-like Plantagenet forebears.

Despite this, the crisis ultimately proved Richard's undoing. At least to his own satisfaction, his sanction to rule as God's direct representative on earth had been demonstrated beyond question. Yet any such assumption of absolute power inevitably ran counter not just to the growing influence of Parliament, but also to the ambitions of Richard's magnates. The situation was exacerbated by Richard's championing of a series of self-seeking favourites, chief among them Michael de la Pole, the Chancellor, and Robert de Vere, appointed Regent of Ireland in 1385. In 1386, Parliament

The Peasants' Revolt

*I*n June 1381, an army of rebels from Kent and Essex, perhaps as many as 10,000 strong, converged on London, inflamed by the imposition of yet another flat rate poll tax, this time at the unprecedented rate of 1s. a head. John of Gaunt's immense palace was sacked and destroyed, the Archbishop of Canterbury, Simon of Sudbury, and the Treasurer, Robert Hales, were murdered. Richard II, only 14, twice rode out to meet them, promising to agree to their demands in full. When their leader, Wat Tyler, was cut down and killed by the Lord Mayor of London, the king defused what had suddenly became an even uglier mob, crying out: "You shall have no captain but me." Having all along professed their loyalty to their sovereign, the rebels meekly gave way.*

The promises to them were honoured only partially, however. Remaining pockets of resistance were savagely dealt with, their leaders executed. For Richard, the experience seemed not only to show that deceit worked but to confirm the unique potency of his own royal person.

1381	1383	1385	1386	1387	1388
Peasants' Revolt defused by Richard's personal intervention	Michael de la Pole made Chancellor	Richard leads inconclusive and expensive punitive expedition against Scotland	Robert de Vere made Duke of Ireland without Parliamentary consultation; Parliament enforces his dismissal; Richard reappoints him after Parliament dissolved	Lords Appellants impeach de Vere and de la Pole and force Council of Government on Richard	"Merciless Parliament" further reasserts Parliamentary authority

RICHARD II

	English-held in Ireland at start of Richard's reign, 1377
	Irish vassals of Richard II
O'NEILL	Irish chieftains knighted by Richard and accepting vassal status, 1395
	Wat Tyler's revolt, 1381
	Maximum extent of Peasants' Revolt, 1381
→	John of Gaunt's campaign, 1384
→	Richard II's campaigns,
→	Scottish campaigns, 1388
	Revolts, 1393
···→	Route of Richard in captivity
→	Henry of Bolingbroke's march on London, 1399

demanded their dismissal. Famously, Richard replied that he would not dismiss so much as a kitchen maid at its insistence. The next year, he was comprehensively outmanoeuvred. Led by a group of five senior magnates, the "Lords Appellants", Richard's inner circle was ruthlessly purged. Power passed to a "Council of Government" answerable to Parliament, itself now controlled by the Lords Appellants.

Even after Richard had declared his majority in 1389, and despite his abrasive conviction that he was "the deputy elected by the Lord", the king was still effectively circumscribed by the Lords Appellants. His response suggests a shrewdness at odds with his later image as power-mad tyrant. Richard bided his time, waiting for the moment of inevitable revenge. He also achieved two notable triumphs: in 1394 he restored at least a measure of order to an increasingly lawless Ireland; and in 1396 he negotiated a 30-year truce with France. That it lasted only 19 years was no fault of Richard's.

Richard struck against the Lords Appellants in 1397. Gloucester was murdered, Arundel executed, Warwick and Nottingham exiled for life, and Bolingbroke, John of Gaunt's son, was exiled for ten years. For the remaining two years of his reign, Richard's rule grew increasingly arbitrary and cruel. With the death of the ageing John of Gaunt in February 1399, Bolingbroke's exile was increased to life and his estates seized

It was a fatal mistake. Not even the most cowed of Richard's subjects could now feel anything but threatened. When in May Richard returned to Ireland, the way was clear for Bolingbroke's return. By September, Richard had been forced to abdicate. By October, Bolingbroke was king (Henry IV). Three months later, Richard was murdered.

Richard's self-projection as divinely sanctioned monarch is portrayed in the Wilton Diptych, *painted in the 1390s (below). It seems likely that the painting was Richard's own travelling altarpiece. Though variously interpreted, its central message of the king's closeness to God is unmistakable.*

> **You wretches, detestable on land and sea; you who seek equality with lords are unworthy to live. Rustics you were and rustics you still are: you will remain in bondage not as before but incomparably harsher. For as long as we live we will strive to suppress you, and your misery will be an example in the eyes of posterity.**
>
> Richard II to the remaining leaders of the Peasants' Revolt, June 1381.

1389	1394	1396	1397–8	1399	1400
Richard declares majority	English authority reimposed in Ireland after Richard visits it. Death of Richard's queen, Anne of Bohemia	Thirty-year truce negotiated with France	Richard breaks power of Lords Appellants	Death of John of Gaunt (Feb.); Richard increases sentence against his heir, Bolingbroke, and seizes his estates. Richard leaves for Ireland (May); Bolingbroke lands in Yorkshire (June) and raises revolt against Richard, who abdicates (Sept.)	Richard dies, almost certainly murdered by the new king, Henry IV

PROJECTIONS OF ROYALTY: *One*

FROM THE 12TH CENTURY ONWARDS, INCREASING PROSPERITY, THE GROWING SOPHISTICATION OF THE MACHINERY OF GOVERNMENT WITH THE KING FIRMLY AT ITS HEAD, AND THE EVOLUTION OF CHIVALRIC CODES CREATED THE CONDITIONS IN WHICH MONARCHY ITSELF BECAME NOT JUST GRANDER BUT ANXIOUS TO STRESS ITS GRANDEUR. PROJECTING ITS INCREASINGLY MAJESTIC NATURE WOULD BECOME A CENTRAL PREOCCUPATION OF KINGSHIP.

Richard II, portrait in Westminster Abbey, c.1390 (above).

KINGSHIP AS A DIVINELY SANCTIONED office had been a commonplace of medieval theories of monarchy at least since the coronation of the Frankish emperor Charlemagne in Rome by the Pope on Christmas Day 800. In the case of Anglo-Saxon England, the double coronation of Alfred's great-great grandson Edgar in 959 (*see* p. 33) reinforced the idea that the king, ruling by the authority of God, was as much priest as king. He may have been mortal, but he was not as other men. As the intermediary of God, his will was in effect God's will and, as such, law.

But it was the monarch's patronage of the arts that had the most lasting impact on the projection of royal authority. This took the form of increasingly sumptuous court buildings – the most startling and impressive example being the great hammerbeam roof constructed over Westminster Hall – and portraiture. The portrait of Richard II in Westminster Abbey, painted perhaps in 1395, epitomizes Richard's self-image: austere and absolute, staring hieratically amid a shimmer of gold leaf. As a symbol of royal authority, it was without equal in medieval England. Its importance also rests in its being almost the first known portrait of an English king – for all that it is as much icon as likeness.

That the actual person of the king was majestic – remote, mysterious and powerful, a presence demanding rigid and elaborate ceremony – was a development that occurred only later. The key figure was Richard II at the end of the 14th century. His self-absorbed personality, steeped in chivalric codes, took naturally to the notion that the mystique of his royal authority could be bolstered by – indeed demanded – the trappings of power and obeisance: in essence, an ever-more rigid courtly ritual centred on himself as king. It was no coincidence that Richard II was the first English king to style himself "highness". During his minority, even the most noble of his increasingly resentful subjects were allowed access to him only via his inner circle of pampered royal favourites. Later, as his belief in his own majestic person intensified, he built an immense throne from which he could look imperiously on his subjects below. If your eye ever caught his, you were obliged to look away.

Similarly overwhelming projections of royal authority would not reoccur until the 16th century. When they did, it was to even more striking effect. Both Henry VIII and Elizabeth I recognized almost instinctively that their own power – and by extension that of the state – could be enhanced by

Henry VIII by Hans Holbein the Younger, c.1536 (far left)

Elizabeth I, Armada Portrait (left).

Charles I on Horseback by Sir Anthony Van Dyck c.1637 (below).

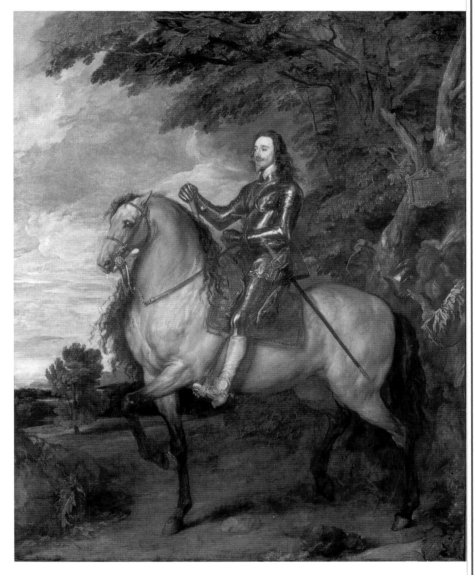

projecting themselves as figures of absolute regal authority, and that royal propaganda of this kind was an essential tool in reinforcing their rule.

In part, this was no more than a reflection of developments elsewhere. Courtly ritual everywhere in Europe was becoming more elaborate and formal. Fashions, too, had grown more ornate and extravagant. But few European monarchs embraced the trend with the uninhibited gusto of the Tudors. Holbein's 1536 portrait of Henry is of the commanding Renaissance prince par excellence, legs apart, hands on hips, regally bestriding his kingdom and his subjects alike. His daughter Elizabeth's long and exultant reign was marked by innumerable portraits of the queen, all no less concerned to bolster her royal status. The *Armada Portrait*, painted to celebrate the defeat of the Spanish Armada in 1588, is as much religious icon as triumphant state portrait: the all-seeing, all-wise Regina, a chalky-white, mask-like face surmounting a halo of lace over a pearl-strewn silk dress. Behind her, the victorious English fleet basks in placid sunshine while the galleons of the impious Spaniards are dashed against a rocky coast. The queen's right hand, meanwhile, brushes a globe, her attenuated fingers resting on the New World colony named in her honour, Virginia. The message is clear: through their growing command of the seas, England and its virgin queen were becoming a world power.

If royal portraiture had become an established means of boosting royal ideology, it nonetheless still required artists of exceptional talent to do it full justice; competition among Europe's monarchs to attract leading painters could be intense. In the 17th century, Charles I (whose taste in art was a lot more sure than his political touch) was able to retain the services of the great Flemish portraitist Anthony Van Dyck only by knighting him and giving him a generous pension. Of the many paintings Van Dyck produced of Charles and his family, his *Charles I on Horseback,* painted probably in 1637, comes closest to Charles's view of himself as an ideal, omniscient ruler. Horse and rider alike deliberately echo the 2nd-century Roman equestrian statue of the Emperor Marcus Aurelius. The stammering, five-foot-four Charles has been transformed into a commanding Christian warrior-emperor, victoriously horsed and clad in glinting armour, his boots tipped with gold spurs. Behind him is a shield bearing the inscription: *Carolus Rex Magnae Britanniae*. But if art as the servant of kingship had reached its apogee, its limitations were clear. Not even the genius of Van Dyck could preserve Charles from the executioner's block.

ENGLAND:
LANCASTER AND YORK
1399–1485

HENRY IV 1399–1413	EDWARD IV 1461–70/1471–83
HENRY V 1413–22	EDWARD V 1483
HENRY VI 1422–61/1470–71	RICHARD III 1483–85

THE ACCESSION OF THE TEN-YEAR-OLD HENRY III IN 1216 APPEARED
TO HAVE SETTLED FOR GOOD THE DAMAGING DYNASTIC DISPUTES THAT
HAD DISRUPTED THE NORMAN AND ANGEVIN KINGS. HENCEFORWARD,
THE PRINCIPLE WAS ESTABLISHED THAT THE SUCCESSION AUTOMATICALLY
PASSED TO THE KING'S ELDEST SON, REGARDLESS OF AGE. HERITABLE
MONARCHY, WITH THE LEGITIMACY AND STABILITY THIS IMPLIED,
HAD BECOME A FIXED POINT OF ROYAL GOVERNMENT.

Even the overthrow of Edward II in 1327 by his wife, Isabella, and her lover, Roger Mortimer, tended to reinforce the principle: however dubious the legality of Edward II's deposition, he was at least succeeded by his son, Edward III, for all that the boy-king's mother and Mortimer retained actual control of the government. That Edward III at 17 then subjugated Isabella and Mortimer seemed only to justify the principle of heritable kingship. The rightful king was ruling in every sense.

The overthrow of Richard II in 1399 by the new duke of Lancaster, Henry Bolingbroke, was a very different matter. The issue was not Richard's abuse of his office, albeit that even by the standards of late-medieval England Richard II had passed well beyond mere delusions of grandeur in the last two years of his reign. Rather, the problem was how Bolingbroke, now Henry IV, could justify his kingship when he was so far from being in the direct line of succession.

In effect, he could not. His was a usurpation in everything but name. A variety of mostly specious claims were put forward by Henry and his supporters. Parliamentary acclamation for the new king was also cited. But at bottom, justified or not, Bolingbroke had seized the throne and everyone knew it. That he was a vastly more just and able ruler than Richard II was not the point. The principle of hereditary monarchy underpinning the government of England had been overturned. The natural order had been set on its head.

The new king paid a heavy price. Ultimately, so would England. Lingering doubts about the legitimacy of his rule and intermittent baronial discontent punctuated his reign. He may have successfully founded a new dynasty, in the process restoring the kind of efficient government last seen in Edward III's reign, but for Henry personally the fruits of kingship were bitter.

With the accession of his son, Henry V, in 1413 all such anxieties were swept away in a blast of martial vigour when the war with France was begun again. A series of startling victories over the French (Agincourt in 1415 among them) not only dramatically increased the French territories under English control but forced the French — in the throes of a civil war of their own and ruled by the palpably insane Charles VI — to accept Henry V as heir to the French throne.

Whether Henry V's slender resources would have allowed him to rule both England and France is open to doubt. As Edward III had discovered, conquest was one thing, the establishment of stable government over the conquered territories another. But what is not in dispute is that Henry's early death from dysentery in 1422 brought not just another child-king to the throne, the nine-month-old Henry VI, but one who, in adulthood, demonstrated the disadvantages of a very different sort of hereditary principle.

Like his cousin Charles VI, Henry VI, saintly and well intentioned, suffered from a form of madness. In an age when effective government was almost entirely dependent on the personality of the king, it was a catastrophic disadvantage. Precisely as in France under Charles VI, Henry VI duly became the tool of his competing magnates. That his father's spectacular gains in France were now being lost almost as rapidly as they had been won only increased the stakes. His overthrow became a matter of time.

England itself may have become richer and more powerful but its government, personified in the feeble person of the king, was becoming scarcely more stable than during the unruly aftermath of William the Conqueror's reign.

Dynastic certainty was giving way to a naked struggle for power. This was the true legacy of Bolingbroke's *coup d'état*. It climaxed in 1461 and 1485, when England found itself in the grip of a protracted dynastic civil war. On the one hand there were the Lancastrians, supporters of Henry VI, himself a descendant of Edward III's youngest son, John of Gaunt, the duke of Lancaster. On the other were the Yorkists, descendants of Edward III's third son, the duke of York. Its poetic name, the Wars of the Roses, derives from each side's respective heraldic badge: a red rose for the Lancastrians, a white one for the Yorkists.

As with any family quarrel, logic had little to do with it. Both sides shared the same view of kingship yet believed their innate right to rule was unchallengeable. Neither was prepared to compromise. Inevitably, retaining the support of a fickle aristocracy whose own calculations were dominated by short-term advantage was a central pre-occupation. Treachery, betrayal and revenge became common currency.

The result was predictably vicious. In 1461, supported by the formidably unprincipled earl of Warwick "the kingmaker", Richard II's great-nephew, the duke of York, seized the throne as Edward IV. In 1470, he was ousted by an improbable alliance between Warwick, Henry's VI's endlessly scheming wife Margaret, and the king of France, Louis XI. The following year he triumphantly regained his throne.

His death in 1483 sparked a further round of dynastic turmoil. His heir, the 12-year-old Edward V, was abducted and probably murdered by Edward IV's brother, the duke of Gloucester, who had already declared himself Richard III. Within two years, Richard III himself was ousted by a new part-Welsh Lancastrian pretender, the obscure Henry Tudor, who became King Henry VII.

Richard III's death signalled more than just the end of the Wars of the Roses. After 331 years, Plantagenet rule in England had been brought to an end. Yet, though Tudor rule might elevate English kingship to new heights of "imperial" pretension, it, too, would prove no less vulnerable to the uncertainties of personal rule.

HENRY IV 1399–1413

KING HENRY IV
BORN: April 3 1367,
Bolingbroke Castle
ACCEDED: September 30
1399; crowned October
13 1399,
Westminster Abbey

*Earl of Derby (from
1377), Earl of
Northampton and
Hereford (from 1384),
Duke of Lancaster, Earl
of Leicester
and Earl of Lincoln
(from 1399), King of
England and France,
Lord of Ireland*

FROM THE START OF HIS REIGN, HENRY'S OVERRIDING CONCERNS WERE TO LEGITIMIZE HIS SEIZURE OF RICHARD II'S THRONE AND TO NEUTRALIZE THE INEVITABLE BARONIAL REVOLTS THAT THE USURPATION PROVOKED. HE WAS UNAMBIGUOUSLY SUCCESSFUL WITH THE LATTER. THE FORMER, HOWEVER, REMAINED TANTALIZINGLY ELUSIVE. IN THE END, THE STRAIN OF KINGSHIP DRAINED AND EXHAUSTED HIM.

HENRY IV HAD ALL THE ATTRIBUTES of a successful medieval king – decisiveness, high political intelligence and martial ardour. Dealing with mutinous barons was, if not a workaday matter, at least relatively straightforward. But squaring his conscience was altogether different. A contradiction remained at the heart of Henry's kingship, one that he could never forget: that it claimed to be hereditary when it had been acquired by force. It did not, however, inhibit the new king from pursuing those magnates who, favoured by Richard II, had most to gain from Henry's downfall. In December 1399, a plot by the earls of Huntingdon, Kent and Salisbury was easily foiled. Their execution and those of 30 other rebel barons swiftly followed. At the same time, Henry had Richard II, now plain Richard of Bordeaux, a prisoner in Pontefract Castle, murdered. The corpse of the former monarch, who seems to have been starved to death, was displayed in London The threat to Henry remained, however. It took

HENRY IV 1399–1413

Spread of the revolt, 1401
Additional areas held by Owain Glyn Dwr by 1403
Eastern limit of Owain Glyn Dwr's advance, 1404
Held further by Owain Glyn Dwr by 1405
Still held by Owain Glyn Dwr, 1410
→ Henry's campaign, with date
→ French attack/campaigns, with date
→ Henry Percy's advance, 1403
✷ Revolt, with details

Allocation of lands by 1405 Tripartite Indenture
☐ to Mortimer
☐ to Percys
— Eastern limit of land to Owain Glyn Dwr

The measure of Henry IV's success was that, in a reign of near-persistent conflict the king, increasingly troubled or not, consistently gained the upper hand. Domestic opponents, the Percys above all, were routed, the Welsh revolt under Owain Glyn Dwr, though long-lived, similarly successfully seen off (map left).

*Canst thou, O partial sleep! give thy repose
To the wet sea-boy in an hour so rude,
And in the calmest and most stillest night,
With all the appliances and means to boot,
Deny it to a king? Then, happy low, lie down
Uneasy lies the head that wears a crown.*

Shakespeare, Henry IV Part Two

1399	1400	1401	1402	1403
Revolt by dispossessed former supporters of Richard II crushed	Richard II murdered in Pontefract Castle. Inconclusive raid against Scotland led by Henry IV. Welsh revolt begins after Owain Glyn Dwr proclaims himself Prince of Wales	Henry IV becomes first English king to authorize death at the stake for religious heretics, in particular the "Lollards" (who were inspired by the reforming ideas of John Wycliffe)	Scots defeated at Homildon Hill	Percys lead major revolt against Henry and are defeated at Battle of Shrewsbury

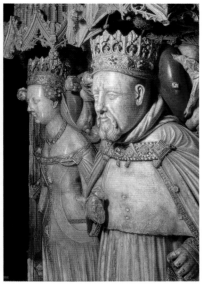

two forms. First, a widespread and long-lasting popular uprising in Wales under the leadership of Owain Glyn Dwr, who in 1400 proclaimed himself Prince of Wales (see box). Second, a concerted effort to unseat Henry by his former supporters, the ambitious and disgruntled Percy family – the earl of Northumberland, his brother the earl of Worcester, and Northumberland's son Henry (or Hotspur).

In 1403, against the background of spreading revolt in Wales, Henry defeated Hotspur and his uncle in a savage battle at Shrewsbury. Hotspur was killed, Worcester was executed. Northumberland, however, was spared, though his castles and most of his honours were stripped from him. By 1405, he had joined forces with Glyn Dwr and the disaffected Marcher Lord, Edmund Mortimer. With the support of the Archbishop of York, Richard Scrope, they concocted an ambitious plan to overthrow Henry and divide England and Wales between them. Henry had his revenge. Though Northumberland escaped to Scotland and Mortimer fled to Wales, all the other conspirators, including the archbishop, were rounded up and executed. With Northumberland's death three years later in an abortive raid on England, domestic opposition to Henry was crushed.

Henry enjoyed notable successes in other fields. His relations with Parliament were generally good. Scotland, too, posed little threat after 1402 when a major border raid, the last such until 1513, was wiped out at Homildon Hill. Then, in 1406, the 12-year-old king of Scotland, James I, en route to sanctuary in France, was captured. He remained an English prisoner for 18 years. The campaign against Wales, if expensive, was also increasingly being won. By 1409, though Glyn Dwr himself remained at large, most Welsh resistance had been broken.

Yet Henry IV's last years were ones of obvious decline compounded by persistent ill-health. To some extent, this may have been provoked by his worsening relations with his son, the future Henry V. In 1411, the king reacted angrily to suggestions that

Owain Glyn Dwr
c.1359–c.1415

O wain Glyn Dwr, better known in English as Owen Glendower, was an unlikely rebel. Solidly prosperous and with substantial estates in northeast Wales, he appeared a natural supporter of the English cause in Wales. As a follower of the Earl of Arundel, he had fought in Richard II's 1385 campaign against Scotland. But in 1400, a minor property dispute with a neighbour escalated violently. Almost at once, it ballooned into open rebellion, with Glyn Dwr – self-proclaimed Prince of Wales in September 1400 – at its head. The decade or more of guerrilla warfare that followed presented Henry IV with his most testing problem. Substantial armies, as many as 4,000 strong, had to be mustered at equally substantial expense.

Glyn Dwr's plans for Wales were nothing if not ambitious. He didn't just aim to throw out the English but, with the Percys and Mortimer, to take over England itself. Wales would be extended to the Trent and the Mersey. The Welsh Church was to take over no less than five English bishoprics. Two Welsh universities were also to be founded, one in the north, one in the south. He recruited allies in Scotland and France. He had plans to transfer allegiance from the Pope in Rome to the Pope in Avignon. Crucially, he also established a Welsh Parliament.

In the end, as so often before, the English slowly crushed the life out of the Welsh rebellion. With the fall of Harlech Castle in 1409, it was as good as over. Glyn Dwr, now a fugitive on the run and taking refuge in caves, refused to surrender. In 1415 he turned down a pardon from Henry V. No one knows where or how he died.

he abdicate in favour of him. The following year, it was put about that the young Henry was actively trying to overthrow his father, an accusation angrily denied. But more than anything, Henry seems simply to have wasted away, tormented by the memory of his overthrow and murder of a legitimate king.

1404	1405	1406	1408	1409	1411
Owain Glyn Dwr calls first Welsh Parliament	Revolt following pact between Northumberland, Mortimer and Owain Glyn Dwr put down; Archbishop of York executed. French troops sent to Wales to support Owain Glyn Dwr	James I of Scotland captured during attempted escape to France	Northumberland killed in attempted invasion of England from Scotland	Rebel Welsh forces in Harlech Castle, including Edmund Mortimer, starved into submission – signals gradual end to Welsh revolt	Split between Henry and his son over suggestions that the king should abdicate in his favour

KING HENRY V

HENRY V 1413–22

THOUGH HE HAD THE SHORTEST REIGN OF ANY ENGLISH MONARCH SINCE HAROLD IN 1066, HENRY V IS WIDELY CELEBRATED AS ENGLAND'S MOST COMPELLINGLY HEROIC KING: A VALIANT CHAMPION OF HIS COUNTRY, A BRILLIANT POLITICAL MANAGER AND AN EVEN BETTER MILITARY STRATEGIST WHOSE CONQUESTS TOOK HIM WITHIN REACH OF THE FRENCH THRONE.

BORN: September 16 1387
ACCEDED: March 20 1413; crowned April 9 1413, Westminster Abbey

Prince of Wales, Duke of Cornwall, Earl of Chester, Duke of Lancaster and Duke of Aquitaine (from 1399), King of England, King of France, and Lord of Ireland

D ESPITE THE 30-YEAR TRUCE AGREED WITH France by Richard II in 1396, the conflict had resumed by 1411. Unlike the now secure Henry IV, the hapless French king, Charles VI, ruled over an increasingly faction-ridden country that from 1407 had fallen into a state of near civil war. For the English, it was too tempting a prospect to resist. But in expeditions in 1411 and 1412, Henry IV could afford to commit only relatively modest forces. Henry V, however, was determined from the start on a much larger invasion. But to mount it, he needed finance, which meant Parliamentary approval. It is a remarkable feature of Henry V's reign that he not only secured this but, in part by extension, gained the trust and support of practically every one of his magnates.

For the first time, a general sense not just of England but of Englishness was being created. Brilliantly stage-managed by the young king, it united the whole country in a growing blaze of patriotic fervour. Henry's Norman, Angevin and earlier Plantagenet predecessors had been French kings of England struggling to hold on to or expand their traditional lands in France against their feudal superior, the king of France. Henry V, however, whatever his French origins, was indisputably an English king leading an English army against France in an outright war of conquest. It was a crucially important difference.

In the spring of 1415, Henry formally revived the claim to the French throne first put forward by Edward III. In addition, he demanded the return of all former Plantagenet lands in France. In August, having successfully put down the only baronial revolt he faced, he sailed for France with an army of 10,000. Within three months of his departure, Henry was making a triumphal return to London: in September he had stormed Harfleur; a month later, at Agincourt, he had annihilated a French army three times larger than his own.

Having seized the initiative, Henry did not intend to let it go. In August 1417, he was back in France. This time, there would be no lightning victories;

Henry V has had a consistently good press. It is no accident that Shakespeare's **Henry V** *is the centrepiece of his history cycle. Just, a devout patron of the Church, a keen enthusiast for the spread of English, a shrewd politician, a brilliant propagandist and, above all, a great conqueror, there seemed almost no limits to his attainments. This portrait* (above), *painted in about 1600, remains the best-known image of him.*

The Battle of Agincourt, 1415

English soldiers strip the armour from a French corpse at Agincourt; to the right, two others haggle over plunder.

B y any measure, Agincourt was an exceptional victory. Henry V's original plan had been to march on Paris but, with the season so far advanced and Harfleur already in English hands, the king judged it more prudent to make for Calais. Exhausted and bedraggled, the English struggled across the Somme only to be confronted by a French army outnumbering them three to one.

Henry V's generalship has never been questioned but there is no doubt that the French made his victory simpler by sending their heavy cavalry on a narrow front straight at the English bowmen, much as they had at Crécy 70 years before. The result was little more than a slaughter – 6,000 Frenchmen were killed while English losses amounted to only about 400. Henry's chaplain recorded: "No king of England ever achieved so much in so short a time and returned home with so great and glorious a triumph."

The battle may have confirmed England's military superiority but the French did not make the same mistake again. In all subsequent campaigns they prudently refused to be drawn into large set-pieces battles. Fighting on home soil inevitably gave them the advantage in the grim, attritional struggle that followed. Had Henry lived, it is possible he could have continued his triumphs. But after 1429, the English were increasingly on the defensive. The prospect of total victory, opened up by Agincourt, proved an illusion.

1414	1415	1416	1417
Lollard rising put down. Henry accepts principle that king can accept or reject bills put forward to Parliament but not amend them	*Henry breaks off negotiations with the French and demands throne (June). Revolt by earls of March and Cambridge suppressed. Sails for France (Aug.); takes Harfleur (Sept.); defeats main French army at Agincourt (Oct.); returns to London (Nov.)*	*Treaty of Canterbury agrees alliance with Holy Roman Empire. English naval victory at Harfleur*	*Henry's mother, Joan of Navarre, imprisoned on suspicion of witchcraft. Minor Scottish raids against Berwick and Roxburgh. Henry resumes Norman campaign*

THE HUNDRED YEARS WAR
1415–28

- English possessions in France, 1415
- → Henry's campaign, 1415
- → Henry's campaign, 1417-19
- → Henry's campaign, 1421-2
- Under English control by 1422
- ⚑ Dauphinist outposts surrendering, 1422-6
- Burgundian-held, 1428
- Dauphinist-held, 1428

English arms had never been more consistently successful than under Henry V (map below). To his victory at Agincourt in 1415 was added a series of attritional campaigns that by 1420 had confirmed not just the Plantagenet stranglehold over northern France and Henry's recognition as heir to the French throne but a significant expansion of English territory in the southwest.

The Treaty of Troyes, signed in May 1420, was the climax of English ambitions in France that dated back to the Norman Conquest. Here, Henry kneels before Charles VI (below). That summer, Henry took the witless French monarch with him on campaign, as he also took the king of Scotland, James I, an English prisoner since 1406. It was a startling vindication of superior English arms.

instead there would be the slow, remorseless grind of siege warfare. But with the capitulation of Normandy in 1419, Henry was in a position to dictate terms to the French. Under the Treaty of Troyes of May 1420, Henry was recognized as Regent of France and heir to Charles VI. The agreement was sealed with his marriage to Charles's daughter, Catherine. In return, Henry agreed to carry the fight to Charles's now formally disinherited son and heir, the Dauphin. In early 1421, Henry returned to England with Catherine for her coronation. Thereafter, acclaimed on all sides, the king took his queen on a royal progress around her new kingdom. It was his apotheosis.

By June, Henry had returned to France. For once, the news was less than good. In March, in a major skirmish at Baugé near the Loire, an English force under the king's brother, the duke of Clarence, had been routed by the Dauphin. Henry himself, however, pressed on.

Our mother tongue, to wit, the English tongue, hath in modern days begun to be honourably enlarged and adorned ... and our most excellent lord, King Henry V, hath procured the common idiom to be commended by the exercise of writing and [the] greater part of the Lords and Commons have begun to make their matters noted down in their mother tongue.

The London Company of Brewers

His last victory, the surrender of Meaux, came in May 1422. By now, the king was already ill, probably with dysentery. By the end of August, he was dead. His triumphs, real though they were, would prove shortlived.

HENRY VI 1422–61/1470–1

KING HENRY VI

IT IS DOUBTFUL IF ANY ENGLISH KING WAS LESS QUALIFIED FOR HIS ROLE THAN THE PIOUS, SIMPLE-MINDED HENRY VI. IN STARK CONTRAST TO HIS FATHER, HE WAS ALWAYS THE VICTIM, NEVER THE MASTER, OF EVENTS. THE RESULT WAS RAPID DESCENT INTO ANARCHY LEADING TO HIS OVERTHROW, AN UNLIKELY RESTORATION AND FINALLY HIS MURDER.

BORN: December 6 1421
ACCEDED: September 1 1422; crowned November 6 1429, Westminster Abbey, and December 16 1431, Notre Dame de Paris
DEPOSED: March 4 1461; **RESTORED:** October 3 1470; **DEPOSED:** April 11 1471

Duke of Cornwall, King of England, King of France, and Lord of Ireland

THE ACCESSION OF HENRY VI AT THE AGE OF nine months – he was the youngest-ever king of England – carried with it the inevitable risk of instability. In fact, his minority under a council headed by his uncle, the duke of Gloucester, was reasonably stable; and as he grew older, Henry himself appeared intelligent and dutiful. There seemed no reason for him not to become a capable monarch.

At much the same time, however, the initiative in the war in France was beginning to slip towards the French. In 1431, in a panicky move to shore up crumbling English rule, the ten-year-old Henry

was shipped to France for his coronation as Henri II. It was an empty gesture. Power in France was rapidly passing to Charles VI's son, who had in any case been crowned Charles VII in 1429.

English hopes of clinging on in France were ended in 1435 when its key ally, Burgundy, defected, and the inspirational English commander in France, the Duke of Bedford, died. The following year Paris fell to Charles VII. Though it took another 18 years for the final English defeat in France, the story thereafter was one of accelerating French military success.

It was against this background of mounting crisis

Henry VI's (above) misfortune was to be a man of peace in an era of perpetual war. In fact, in the face of a resurgent France, even the most active ruler might have found it difficult to hold on to England's French territories. Henry VI was simply overwhelmed by them. Nonetheless his greatest failing was his inability to exercise even the smallest degree of control over his magnates. The king was trapped between their competing ambitions and his wife's equally fierce determination to do them down.

THE HUNDRED YEARS WAR: THE FINAL PHASE, 1429–53

→ Joan of Arc's campaigns, 1429-30
┅► Joan of Arc's movements in captivity, 1430
➤ Other French campaigns, with details
▨ English losses, (including lands no longer recognizing Henry as King of France), by 1453
☐ Held by Charles VII, 1453
▓ Burgundian-held, 1453
▨ English possessions, 1453
🗡 Revolt, with details

The loss of the final English lands in France may have been played out only slowly (map right). Nonetheless, from the mid-1430s, inspired by Joan of Arc's improbable heroics in 1429, French gains became inexorable. With the final French victory at Castillon in 1453, English territory in France had been reduced to Calais and its immediate hinterland.

1429	1431	1435	1436	1437	1440	1441	1444	1447
Siege of Orléans lifted by Joan of Arc	Henry VI crowned King of France in Paris. Joan of Arc executed	Burgundians ally with Charles VII. Death of English commander in France, the duke of Bedford	Paris recaptured by Charles VII	Henry VI reaches his majority	Eton College founded by Henry VI	King's College, Cambridge, founded by Henry VI	Treaty of Tours signed with Charles VI; Henry VI marries Charles's niece, Margaret of Anjou	Maine returned to French control; Duke of Gloucester, arrested and executed on charges of conspiring to overthrow the king

Eton and King's College

Henry's most admirable qualities were his generosity, his meekness, and his dislike of violence, none of them attributes that would serve a late-medieval king well. He was also passionately attached to the ideal of Christian education. His greatest memorials are Eton College (the King's College of Our Lady of Eton beside Windsor), and King's College, Cambridge (the College Royal of Our Lady and St Nicholas). The former was founded in 1440, when Henry was only 18, the latter in 1441.

The two were intended as interconnected institutions. The 70 scholars at Eton, all of them educated for free, were expected to go on to King's College. Indeed, until the 18th century, King's accepted only Etonians. Both institutions were lavishly funded – King's College had an annual grant of £1,000 – and were intended to be magnificent. In 1448, Henry ordered that the chapel at Eton, still unfinished, be demolished to make way for a larger one.

King's College Chapel, Cambridge

Joan of Arc's impact on the Wars of the Roses was brief but spectacular and played a key role in inspiring the Valois comeback under Charles VI. In 1430, the year after she had broken the English siege of Orléans (left), she was captured by the Burgundians who sold her to the English, who in turn tried her for heresy. She was burned at the stake in Rouen in May 1431.

wringing anguish. Margaret herself proved a further source of friction when she persuaded Henry to hand over Maine to the French crown. The decision not only provoked crisis in England, it did nothing to placate the French. By 1450, the French had retaken Normandy.

Henry's reign effectively disintegrated. Three years later, Gascony was overrun, ending its 300-year rule by England's kings. The loss provoked Henry's first bout of madness. For 18 months, he was plunged into silent melancholia, apparently unaware of his surroundings. In the inevitable power struggle that followed, control see-sawed between the dukes of Somerset and York, both with claims to the throne as descendants of Edward III. By 1455, armed conflict – the Wars of the Roses – had begun (see pp.106–7).

By 1461, Henry, little more than a bemused spectator, had lost his throne to the duke of York's son, Edward IV. He spent the next four years partly in Scotland, latterly wandering aimlessly around northern England until, in 1465, he was captured and imprisoned in the Tower of London. To his evident surprise, in October 1470 he was briefly restored after a falling-out between Edward IV and the Earl of Warwick (hitherto Edward's most important supporter).

Henry's "Readeption" lasted the seven months it took Edward IV to regroup and, in short succession, overwhelm Warwick and Margaret. In May 1471, a prisoner of Edward once more, Henry VI was stabbed to death in the Tower of London.

that in 1437 Henry VI achieved his majority. He showed alarming political naivety from the start, turning over his government to a narrow circle of magnates, chief among them the earl of Suffolk. They in turn excluded all those other magnates who might reasonably have expected a share of power. The seeds of future conflict were being sown.

The five-year truce negotiated with France in 1444, under which Henry married Margaret, daughter of the duke of Anjou, caused further splits: between those determined to continue the war and those seeking peace. Henry's response was hand-

1449	1450	1451	1453	1461	1463	1465	1470	1471
Rouen recaptured by French	Normandy recaptured by French; earl of Suffolk impeached and executed; rebel Jack Cade leads popular revolt	Guyenne recaptured by French	Battle of Castillon: Henry suffers mental collapse (Aug.); son, Prince Edward, born (Oct.)	Edward (son of duke of York), proclaimed King Edward IV. Defeats royalist army at Towton	Margaret flees to France with Prince Edward	Henry VI captured and imprisoned	Henry VI restored; Edward IV flees to Burgundy	Edward IV restored; Henry VI re-imprisoned and executed

THE WARS OF THE ROSES

THE WARS OF THE ROSES PLUNGED ENGLAND INTO A LONG ROUND OF DAMAGING DYNASTIC DISPUTES. KINGSHIP
BECAME A MATTER OF ARMED FORCE RATHER THAN OF LEGITIMACY, AS WELL AS DISTURBINGLY DEPENDENT ON THE
FICKLE LOYALTIES OF A RAPACIOUS, OFTEN VENGEFUL ARISTOCRACY. AT INTERVALS OVER
30 YEARS, ORDERLY GOVERNMENT CAME CLOSE TO COLLAPSE.

T HE WARS OF THE ROSES STEMMED FROM Henry IV's seizure of Richard II's throne in 1399. The problem was not just that a legitimate king, however tyrannical, had been deposed but that his designated heir, the earl of March, had also been bypassed. In purely pragmatic terms, there was much to support Henry IV's action, not least that the earl of March was only seven. In contrast to the inevitable threat of instability that a minority would bring, the worldly, experienced Henry Bolingbroke could at least promise firm, capable government.

In the event, whatever the baronial disturbances of the early part of his reign, Henry's usurpation came to seem increasingly justified. Stability was restored, the more unruly magnates brought under control. The new order was then emphatically consolidated by the dazzling success of his son, Henry V, after 1415. The overthrow of Richard II was beginning to look more like a blip rather than a rupture in English hereditary kingship

Two factors conspired to undermine the new order: the unravelling of English rule in France in the face of a resurgent Valois dynasty; and the personality of Henry V's heir, Henry VI, who even before his majority at the age of 15 in 1437 was showing himself almost uniquely ill-equipped for late-medieval kingship. More specifically, with power concentrated in the hands of a narrow clique of magnates, first the duke of Suffolk, then the duke of Somerset – both actively supported by Henry VI's wife, the fearsomely aggressive Margaret of Anjou – those excluded from government became increasingly embittered

Foremost among them was the duke of York, nephew of the Earl of March whose claims to the throne had been ignored by Henry IV. From 1450, a state only just short of outright warfare existed between York and Somerset, each already with an eye on the throne following Henry and Margaret's failure to produce an heir. In 1452, York went so far as to lead an army against London, though his revolt fizzled out rapidly.

In 1453, however, events swung decisively York's way. The loss of Gascony not only tainted Somerset's government, it tipped the ailing king into madness. York was able to step into the power vacuum and declare himself Protector. From his point of view,

Edmund, Duke of Somerset, is executed at the Battle of Tewkesbury, 1471 (above). *With the death of the Beaufort Duke of Somerset in 1455, his heir, Edmund, had taken every opportunity to destabilize the Yorkists. His motive, first and last, had been revenge. For his part, Edward IV, finally victorious at Tewkesbury, was equally swift to order the execution of Somerset.*

the only drawback was the surprising birth of an heir to Henry and Margaret the previous autumn. There were many, then and now, who doubted the child was Henry's.

The king's partial recovery of his sanity in the spring of 1455 led to York's overthrow and Somerset's restoration. It also made a final trial of strength between them all but inevitable. This duly followed in May when the two clashed at St Albans. Despite the presence of Henry VI at the battle, it was more a matter of two private armies meeting than of a king of England reasserting his authority over a rebellious magnate. As with the whole sorry

1452	1454	1455	1458	1459
Duke of York attempts armed overthrow of duke of Somerset	*Duke of York appointed Protector; arrests duke of Somerset*	*York dismissed, Somerset restored (Feb.). York and Somerset clash at St Albans (May); Somerset killed, York restored as Protector*	*Henry attempts reconciliation of warring parties*	*Margaret defeats York at Ludlow, forcing him to flee to Ireland*

conflict until his death in 1471, Henry VI had become no more than a spectator.

St Albans signalled the formal start of the Wars of the Roses. If more skirmish than battle, it nonetheless saw the death of Somerset and the capture of Henry. Yet though York was afterwards clearly in the ascendant, there was still no question of his overthrowing the king. Few wanted another dynastic upheaval. By the same token, the majority of the previously excluded magnates were content for Henry to remain king now that they were able to share in the fruits of government. It had been the overthrow of Somerset they wanted, not that of the king.

That the war continued – in fact became ever more savage – was partly the result of something approaching a Mafia-style blood-feud that developed between losers and winners after St Albans, and partly the result of the queen's implacable desire to do down York. In 1459, with the support of the Percy earls of Northumberland, Margaret all but destroyed the Yorkists at Ludlow. York fled to Ireland; his son, the earl of March, and the earl of Salisbury with his son, the earl of Warwick, fled to Calais.

The war now entered its most confused and improbable phase, with each side gaining and then losing an apparently decisive advantage in the space of less than a year. In late summer 1460, at Northampton, the Yorkists won an overwhelming victory in which Henry was captured. Though York succeeded in being named Henry's heir, his bid for the throne was rejected by Parliament.

Margaret meanwhile had regrouped at Wakefield. In December, her army destroyed the Yorkists. The duke of York himself was killed. On Margaret's orders, his severed head, wearing a paper crown, was displayed on the gates of York. Hurrying south to press home her advantage, Margaret swept aside a small force under the earl of Warwick at St Albans, recapturing the king at the same time. She got no further, however. London had already welcomed the new duke of York, who had declared himself Edward IV at the beginning of March. Turning north again, she was pursued by Edward and the remnants of Warwick's army. They met at Towton in Yorkshire. Here, Edward wiped out her army.

Whatever the firmness of Edward's rule, the degree of instability engendered by this first phase of the Wars of the Roses – combined with the apparently impregnable position that the Earl of Warwick, the self-styled "kingmaker", had engineered for himself – would always make a renewal of conflict likely. That Margaret herself, now in France and actively supported by Louis XI, was thirsting for revenge almost guaranteed it.

In 1470, the conflict duly began again. Edward IV was forced to flee to Burgundy. Warwick meanwhile declared the witless Henry VI king again. For all that this second phase of the war saw equally extreme swings in each side's fortunes, this time it was swiftly resolved. Supported by the Burgundians, Edward returned to England in March 1471 and in rapid succession inflicted victories over Warwick (who was killed) at Barnet, and over Margaret at Tewkesbury, where Henry VI's son, Prince Edward, was killed.

The final Yorkist victory proved a false dawn. Within 12 years, the dynastic unrest began all over again when Edward IV's brother, Richard, seized the throne, in the process doing to death Edward's sons, Edward V and his brother Richard. Within scarcely more than two years, Richard II himself had been killed by the last of the Lancastrian claimants, Henry Tudor. Even then, there were risks of renewed rebellion.

The years of actual conflict may not have been that many, but the dynastic turmoil that climaxed in the Wars of the Roses destabilized England and its monarchy for close to a century.

Richard Neville, the Earl of Warwick dies at the Battle of Barnet, 1471 (above). *The earl epitomized the power-hungry manoeuvrings of England's senior magnates in the Wars of the Roses. The man who more than anyone was responsible for putting Edward IV on the throne had no hesitation in turning against the king when Edward asserted his authority.*

1460	1461	1470	1471	1483	1485
Royalist army defeated by York at Northampton; Margaret and Henry flee to Scotland; York attempts to persuade Parliament to declare him king (Oct.). Royalist army defeat and kill York at Wakefield (Dec.)	Royalist army defeats earl of Warwick at St Albans but is refused entry to London. New duke of York proclaimed Edward IV (Mar.). Royalist army defeated at Towton	Warwick allies with Margaret, Louis XI and Edward IV's brother; Edward IV flees to Continent; Henry VI restored	Edward IV allies with Burgundians; defeats Warwick at Barnet and Margaret at Tewkesbury, where Prince Edward is killed. Edward IV restored	Death of Edward IV; Richard, duke of Gloucester, seizes throne as Richard III; Edward V and brother, Richard, murdered in Tower of London	Richard III killed by Lancastrian claimant, Henry Tudor, at Bosworth. Henry VII; unites Lancastrians and Yorkists with marriage to daughter of Edward IV, Elizabeth of York

KING EDWARD IV

EDWARD IV 1461–70/1471–83

EDWARD IV DELIBERATELY SET OUT TO MAKE ENGLISH KINGSHIP STRONG AGAIN. IF THE AFTER-SHOCKS OF HIS SEIZURE OF THE THRONE INITIALLY THREATENED HIS RULE, HE APPEARED ULTIMATELY TO TRIUMPH WITH HIS FORCEFUL RESTORATION IN 1471. YET IN THE END, WHATEVER THE SUCCESSES OF HIS REIGN, YORKIST RULE WAS UNDERMINED BY FURTHER DYNASTIC FEUDING.

BORN: April 28 1442, Rouen
ACCEDED: March 4 1461; crowned June 28 1461, Westminster Abbey
DEPOSED: October 3 1470; RESTORED: April 11 1471

Earl of March, Duke of York, Earl of Ulster, Earl of Cambridge, King of England, King of France, Lord of Ireland

Edward IV's charm, like his good looks (above), was legendary. He was blessed with the gift of treating everyone equally. He is said, too, to have had a prodigious memory for names. The king, it was claimed, "was so genial in his greeting that if he ever saw a new arrival at court bewildered at his appearance and royal magnificence, he would give him courage to speak by laying a kindly hand on his shoulder." At any rate in the early part of his reign, this apparently easy-going exterior hid a capable, hard-working administrator.

IN THE FIRST PERIOD OF HIS REIGN, EDWARD IV approved 113 Acts of Attainder, legal measures stripping Lancastrian supporters of their lands, titles and money. In the second period, not a single such act was passed. Most of these former Lancastrian holdings were lavished on Edward's own supporters, above all his cousin Richard Neville, the earl of Warwick.

Warwick, the so-called "kingmaker", ambitious, ruthless and unforgiving, dominated Edward's early reign, mopping up the remaining pockets of Lancastrian resistance and reinforcing his position as easily the most important magnate in the land. Edward himself, however, was no mere tool of Warwick. Tall, vigorous and good-looking, he was a shrewd general and a skilled politician who understood perfectly how to trade on his considerable popularity. A consistent theme of his reign was not merely the boosting of English trade – the support of London's merchants had been crucial to his adoption as king in 1461 – but the restoration of financial stability. Even if most of these measures had to wait until the second half of his reign, Edward's declaration to Parliament in 1467 that he would "live of mine own" was a key statement of intent that the heavy taxation of earlier reigns would be ended.

The king's most obvious failing was that "he thought upon nothing but women and that more than reason would". In 1464, unable to persuade her into bed in any other way, he married Elizabeth Woodville. It provoked a slow falling out with Warwick. The new queen was not only a Lancastrian but she brought numerous family to court. The rewards showered on them inevitably undermined Warwick's own position. As important, the marriage ended Warwick's self-seeking negotiations with Louis XI under which Warwick, in return for lands and titles in France, had been attempting to secure a French alliance by arranging the king's marriage to a French princess.

The growing rift climaxed in 1470 when Warwick – with Edward's brother, the duke of Clarence (with designs of his own on the throne) – allied himself with Louis and his former bitter enemy, Margaret of Anjou. Though temporarily forced to flee to Burgundy, Edward's subsequent return, restoration and defeat of Warwick and Margaret in 1471 signalled an apparently final triumph.

Edward's reforms of government and finance and extension of royal justice were widely welcomed and generally successful. For several years, he was able to rule without once asking Parliament for taxation. In July 1475, a seven-year truce was agreed with France that also brought important financial benefits. Edward had, it is true, initially hoped to launch a conquest of France, assembling an army 10,000 strong and sailing with it to Calais. Once there, the non-appearance of his Burgundian and Breton allies persuaded him to settle for peace instead. However unintended, the benefits were clear. In 1482, a successful invasion of Scotland was launched under Edward's highly competent brother, the duke of Gloucester, which ended with the permanent return to England of Berwick.

By any measure, Edward's clandestine marriage to Elizabeth Woodville (left) was a gross error of judgement. However desirable, the queen was haughty and manipulative. More importantly, her presence generated Warwick's lasting hostility. She also took against Edward's brother, the Duke of Gloucester. The feud that developed led directly to Gloucester's usurpation and the deaths of her sons in the Tower.

1464	1468	1469	1470
Earl of Warwick defeats remaining Lancastrian opposition at Hexham. Edward IV secretly marries Elizabeth Woodville, provoking outrage when news is announced four months later, and ending Warwick's secret negotiations with Louis XI	*Edward pursues rival diplomatic strategy, marrying his sister, Margaret, to duke of Burgundy*	*Warwick provokes risings in Midlands and north; leaves for Calais with duke of Clarence, who marries his daughter Isabel (July); Warwick traps Edward in Nottingham and takes him prisoner; subsequent widespread disorder forces Warwick to release Edward*	*Further uprisings in Wales and east Midlands provoked by Warwick. Warwick and Clarence return to France and make pact with Margaret of Anjou and Louis XI (July). Warwick returns to England (Sept.), forcing Edward to escape to Burgundy (Oct.). Henry VI restored. Warwick and Louis declare war on Burgundy*

EDWARD IV

▨	Yorkist (including Crown holdings/dependencies), c. 1480
→	Edward's campaign, 1461
→	Edward's campaign, 1470
→	Edward's campaign, 1471
→	Important Lancastrian campaign
✕	Lancastrian victory
✕	Yorkist victory

Edward VI won his throne through five years of warfare (map left) and seemed in 1461 to have secured it, confiscating large areas of the country from his erstwhile Lancastrian rivals. Yet dynastic conflict was far from banished; Edward was briefly deposed in 1470 by a resurgent Lancastrian party, whilst shortly after his death the civil war flared up once more.

I have many times seen our neighbours here when they were summoned before the King. When they went, they looked as though they were going to the gallows. When they returned they were in high spirits, saying they did not regret the money they had paid because they had talked with the King, he had welcomed them as though he had always known them and had spoken so many kind words ... he plucked the feathers from the magpies without making them cry out.

Dominic Mancini, Italian visitor
to England, on Edward IV

Edward was a generous and discriminating patron of the arts. He rebuilt Eltham Palace in Kent as well as overseeing major construction at Windsor Castle, including the enlarged St George's Chapel. He also took a keen interest in the new invention of printing, financing the first book printed in England, The Dictes and Sayenges of the Phylosophers, *translated into English by the queen's brother, Lord Rivers, and printed by William Caxton in 1477 (above).*

Yet for some years Edward had been sliding into corpulent self-indulgence. His court, intended to rival those of France and Burgundy, became more elaborate, his gluttony more obsessive. When he unexpectedly died in 1483 at the age of only 40, Edward had "grown fat in his loins". More disturbingly, his Woodville heirs immediately began to agitate against the duke of Gloucester, named Protector in Edward's will. Dynastic conflict was poised to re-erupt.

1471	1472	1475	1477	1478	1482
Edward returns to England, reclaims throne, defeats Warwick and Margaret. Birth of son, Edward.	Brittany, Burgundy and Aragon wooed in attempt to create anti-French coalition.	Attempted invasion of France gives way to seven-year Treaty of Picquigny with Louis XI	Clarence indicted for treason	Clarence executed, reputedly by drowning in butt of Malmsey	Scotland successfully invaded by duke of Gloucester; Berwick returned to England

RICHARD III 1483–85

IN OUSTING EDWARD IV'S HEIR, THE 12-YEAR-OLD EDWARD V, AND SECRETLY MURDERING HIM AND HIS BROTHER, RICHARD III EARNED HIMSELF AN ENDURING REPUTATION AS UNIQUELY EVIL. IN REALITY, HIS ACTIONS WERE ALWAYS RATIONAL AND, BY THE STANDARDS OF THE TIME, NOT NOTABLY TREACHEROUS. HIS TRAGEDY WAS TO BE THE VICTIM HIMSELF OF A FURTHER COUP TWO YEARS LATER.

BORN: October 2 1452
ACCEDED: June 26 1483;
crowned July 6 1483,
Westminster Abbey

Duke of Gloucester, King of England and Lord of Ireland

Richard III's (above) reputation suffered so badly at the hands of the Tudors – whose systematic blackening of his name was a crude attempt to justify their rule – that even today it is generally assumed that the king had a body as warped as his mind was said to have been. The widespread belief that he was a hunchback is without any foundation. In fact, though he was smaller than Edward IV, at five-foot-eight Richard III was considerably taller than average for the time.

BEFORE HIS SEIZURE OF THE throne in 1483, Richard III, then Duke of Gloucester, had consistently shown himself to be his brother Edward IV's most reliable supporter. His devotion to the Yorkist cause was absolute. While their brother, the Duke of Clarence, was conspiring with the Earl of Warwick to overthrow Edward IV in 1470, Richard remained steadfastly loyal, accompanying Edward in his brief Burgundian exile and thereafter serving with distinction at the battles of Barnet and Tewkesbury that regained him his throne.

Richard's reward was marriage to the younger of Warwick's daughters, Anne, automatically making him one of the greatest landowners in England, and giving him responsibility for the administration of northern England. It was a task he carried out with tact, energy and intelligence. In effect, as "Lord of the North" he became king of the whole region in all but name, dispensing "good and impartial justice to all who sought it, were they rich or poor, gentle or simple". Richard's successful, if expensive, campaign against Scotland in 1482 was typical of his all-round competence.

For Richard, service in the north had the added advantage of distancing him from the intrigues of Edward's increasingly dissolute court. He could not completely escape it, however, and it is clear that Richard shared the general Yorkist distrust of Edward's queen, Elizabeth, and her many Woodville relations. Certainly, he seems to have held the queen largely responsible for pressurizing Edward to order Clarence's execution for treason in 1478.

Richard's suspicions of the Woodvilles were justified. Though Richard had been appointed Protector in Edward IV's will during Edward V's minority, the Woodvilles swiftly succeeded in overturning the decision and setting up a Regency Council under their control. For Richard, increasingly convinced that the true Yorkist inheritance was safe only with him, the choice was straightforward: to await an inevitable Woodville-inspired charge of treason or seize the throne himself.

The manner of his usurpation was characteristically decisive. The new king, Edward V, was intercepted

RICHARD III, 1483–5

- 🌿 Rebellion
- → Buckingham's advance, 1483
- ▨ Area reinforced against expected landing by Henry Tudor
- → Henry Tudor's campaign, August 1485
- ⋯ Frontiers, 1485

Richard III's reign was dominated by attempts to shore up his position (map right). The revolt by his former ally, the duke of Buckingham, in 1483 was relatively easily contained, in the process thwarting the attempted landing by the last Lancastrian pretender, Henry Tudor. Within less than two years, however, Henry Tudor mounted a new invasion. Deserted by key allies, Richard III was killed by Henry Tudor in August 1485 at Bosworth.

1469	1470–71	1472	1478	1482
Richard suppresses Welsh rebellion on behalf of Edward IV	*Accompanies Edward IV to Burgundy before assisting in his restoration*	*Charged with responsibility for north of England by Edward IV*	*Duke of Clarence executed for treason*	*Richard leads successful invasion of Scotland; storms Edinburgh and takes Berwick*

> *From this day, these dukes [Gloucester and Buckingham] acted no longer in secret, but openly manifested their intentions. For, having summoned armed men, in fearful and unheard-of numbers, from the north, Wales and all other parts then subject to them, the said Protector Richard assumed the government of the kingdom, with the title King, on the twentieth day of the aforesaid month of June; on the same day, at the Great Hall of Westminster [he] obtruded himself into the marble chair.*
>
> The Croyland Chronicle

en route to London for his coronation and placed in the Tower of London with his younger brother, Richard, duke of York. The queen's brother, Lord Rivers, was summarily executed, as was Richard's former ally, Lord Hastings, who had objected to Richard's plans to oust the new king. However flimsy Richard's legal justification for assuming the throne – that both Edward IV's sons were illegitimate – it was nonetheless accepted by Parliament on June 25. The next day Richard was proclaimed king. The two princes were last seen alive the following month.

Richard's motive in ordering the deaths of his nephews was the obvious one of removing a potential focus of rebellion against him. But with the death of his own son the following year, it also meant that only Richard now stood between Henry Tudor – the sole remaining Lancastrian claimant – and the crown. Once Henry, already supported by Charles VIII of France, allied himself to the Woodvilles, it was clear he would mount a bid for the throne. In August 1485 Henry Tudor defeated Richard at Market Bosworth and became Henry VII.

In attempting to assert the legitimacy of Yorkist rule, Richard III had managed only to perpetuate the lawlessness and treachery generated by the dynastic disputes of the 15th century. Richard III, the last English king to die in battle, was also the last victim of the Wars of the Roses.

What evidence there is suggests that Richard III and his queen, Anne Neville (right), "his most dearly beloved consort", were unusually close. In very striking contrast to Edward IV, Richard seems to have had no mistresses after his marriage, though he had fathered several children before it. Ironically, given the fate of his young nephews, when Richard and Anne's sole child, Prince Edward, died in 1485 at only eight, it was reported that: "You might have seen his father and mother in a state almost bordering on madness by reason of their sudden grief."

Edward V

Edward V was king for two months and 17 days. It was the shortest reign of any king of England. The young Prince Edward was brought up by his uncle, Lord Rivers, at Ludlow. It was while he was being brought from there to London in April 1483 for his coronation, due to take place on June 24, that Richard, professing his loyalty to his new king, effectively arrested him and sent him to the Tower of London. A month later, Edward was joined by his younger brother, the Duke of York, who on Richard's orders had been removed by force from Westminster Abbey where he and his mother had taken sanctuary. There are reports of both children playing in the gardens of the Tower but "day by day [they] began to be seen more rarely behind the bars and windows until at length they ceased to appear altogether."

Though the precise fate of the children has never been established, there can be little doubt that it was Richard III who had them murdered. That said, it is true that their deaths were equally in the interests of Henry Tudor, who was accordingly keen to blame Richard. In 1674, two skeletons, presumed to be those of the princes, were discovered in the Tower. They were reburied in Westminster Abbey. In 1993, tests established they were of approximately the right ages to have been the princes but no definitive identification was possible.

Edward V, as Prince of Wales, with Edward IV and Elizabeth Woodville

1483	1484	1485
Mar: Death of Edward IV, accession of Edward V; Richard is Protector; Apr: With duke of Buckingham, Richard intercepts Edward V en route to London; executes queen's brother, Lord Rivers; May: Edward V installed in Tower of London; June: Edward's brother, the duke of York, removed from sanctuary in Westminster Abbey and joins Edward in Tower; Richard proclaimed king; Sept: Presumed death of Edward V and brother in Tower; Oct: Revolt by duke of Buckingham (intended to coincide with attempted invasion from Brittany by Henry Tudor), crushed; Buckingham executed; Henry turns back	*Death of Richard III's only son, Prince Edward. Henry Tudor flees to France after Richard attempts to seize him in Brittany. Three-year truce agreed with Scotland*	*Mar: Death of Richard's wife, Anne Neville; Aug: Henry Tudor successfully lands in Wales; defeats and kills Richard at Battle of Market Bosworth*

SCOTLAND: FROM BRUCE TO STUART 1329–1625

DAVID II 1329–33/1336–71

EDWARD BALLIOL
1332/1333–34/1335–36

ROBERT II 1371–90

ROBERT III 1390–1406

JAMES I 1406–37

JAMES II 1437–60

JAMES III 1460–88

JAMES IV 1488–1513

JAMES V 1513–42

MARY, QUEEN OF SCOTS 1542–67

JAMES VI 1567–1625

WHATEVER THE SUCCESSES OF ROBERT THE BRUCE (SEE PP.64–5) IN WITHSTANDING THE ATTEMPTED PLANTAGENET CONQUEST OF SCOTLAND AND IN REINVIGORATING SCOTTISH KINGSHIP, HE WAS FOLLOWED BY A SERIES OF INEPT AND WEAK KINGS. BETWEEN THEM, THEY PRESIDED OVER A SCOTLAND THAT, WHEN NOT BEING FURTHER THREATENED BY ENGLAND, WAS TORN APART BY DYNASTIC INSTABILITY, THE AMBITIONS OF ITS LEADING MAGNATES, CIVIL STRIFE AND ECONOMIC BACKWARDNESS. THOSE RULERS WHO SUCCEEDED IN IMPOSING A DEGREE OF CENTRAL CONTROL ALMOST ALWAYS FELL FOUL OF THEIR DISGRUNTLED LEADING SUBJECTS. MOST, HOWEVER, FOUND THEMSELVES NEAR-PERMANENTLY AT THE MERCY OF EVENTS.

Of the 10 Scottish monarchs who followed Robert the Bruce, eight were minors at their accession, including all seven in succession from James I to James VI. Of the remaining two, both came to the throne in their 50s already exhausted. One, Robert II, had become so incapacitated he was widely known as "Auld Blearie". His son, Robert III, who became little more than an invalid after being kicked by a horse, composed his own memorable epitaph: "Here lies the worst of kings and the most miserable of men". He asked to be buried in a dungheap.

Two kings, David II and James I, were imprisoned by the English for 11 and 18 years respectively. David II was also forced to spend most of his childhood and youth in France, Scotland's only reliable ally in the period (see The Auld Alliance, pp.66–7). The long periods of regency government such enforced absences imposed only added to the near endemic instability. In both cases, the enormous ransoms demanded for their release also proved an intolerable burden on the country's slim economic means.

Exposure to the much more sophisticated mechanisms of royal government in England at least had the virtue of demonstrating to David II and James I the kind of strong, centralized government that could be introduced in Scotland. In practise, though David II had some success in asserting his authority, like James II he, too, consistently had to contend with an unruly baronage that resisted all attempts to reduce their own powers. In James I's case this baronial resentment led to his assassination. As an indication of the continuing turbulence, 15 years later James I's successor, James II, personally stabbed to death his most rebellious subject, the Earl of Douglas. It was perhaps a mark of the ill-fortune that dogged Scotland in the period that at 30, having established a measure of control over Scotland, James II himself was killed when a cannon exploded at the siege of Roxburgh.

That said, from the mid-15th century onwards royal authority was very slowly being increased. The reign of James III, while disastrous at its end, saw the Orkneys and Hebrides ceded by Norway and brought under nominal Scottish control. With the exception of Berwick, lost permanently to England in 1482, Scotland had attained its current extent. His successor, James IV, further extended active Scottish rule in the Western and Northern Isles, in 1493 formally ending the 200-year-old semi-independent rule of the Lords of the Isles in the Hebrides. James III and James IV also began to bring Scotland into gradual contact with Renaissance ideals of learning and the arts.

Yet fundamentally it was relations with England that did most to destabilize Scotland and undermine its kings. Edward III, for example, actively attempted to exploit dynastic divisions within Scotland by sponsoring the attempts of John Balliol's son, Edward Balliol, to seize the Scottish throne after the death of Robert the Bruce in 1329. Having proclaimed himself king in 1332, Balliol was deposed three times and restored twice in the space of only three years. In much the same way, 150 years later Edward IV sponsored the efforts of the self-styled Alexander IV to oust his brother, James III.

Similarly, of the nine kings of England between Edward III and Henry VIII, only three did not launch invasions of Scotland. Even during the Wars of the Roses, when England itself was at its most vulnerable, Scotland, by formally allying itself with the losing Lancastrians, managed only to spark bitter internal divisions as well as to invite Yorkist reprisals. Even the most apparently successful and martial Scottish king of the period, James IV, decisively came unstuck against superior English arms, losing his life at the disastrous Battle of Flodden in 1513. The equally crushing English victory over Scotland at Solway Moss in 1542 was followed within a month by the death of the 30-year-old James III, apparently from cholera. As a result, it brought the youngest-ever British monarch to the throne, the week-old Mary, "Queen of Scots".

The catalogue of woe continued. After being ousted from her throne in 1567 at only 24 in yet another power-struggle, Mary spent the last 19 years of her life a prisoner of her English cousin, Elizabeth I. She remains the only Scottish monarch to be executed by the English.

Yet a paradox runs through this sorry tale. The succession of Robert II in 1371 had brought a new dynasty to the Scottish throne, the Stewarts (Mary, Queen of Scots, introduced the later, French spelling of Stuart). The marriage in 1503 of James IV to Henry VII's daughter Margaret under the short-lived Treaty of Perpetual Peace between England and Scotland gave rise to a dynastic alliance of unforeseen but momentous consequences. The failure of Henry VIII's three children to produce a single heir between them meant that with the death of Elizabeth I in 1603, the English crown passed to Margaret Tudor and James IV's great-grandson, James VI. However improbably, the king of Scotland had also legally inherited the throne of England.

DAVID II TO JAMES II 1371–1460

AFTER THE DEATH OF ROBERT THE BRUCE IN 1329, SCOTTISH KINGSHIP WAS PERSISTENTLY UNDERMINED BY DYNASTIC DISPUTES AND INTERNAL WEAKNESS, THE WHOLE AGAINST A BACKGROUND OF RECURRENT ENGLISH DESIGNS ON SCOTLAND. THE REIGNS OF EACH OF THE FIRST FIVE OF BRUCE'S SUCCESSORS WERE DISRUPTED, OFTEN CATASTROPHICALLY. THE SURVIVAL OF AN INDEPENDENT SCOTTISH KINGDOM WAS FREQUENTLY IN THE BALANCE.

James II (above), the only survivor of twins, was disfigured by a prominent scarlet birthmark which covered the left side of his face, giving rise to his nickname 'James of the Fiery Face'. He proved a vigorous ruler, more than able to control the magnates who had destabilized his minority.

The efficient administration implied by Robert II's issuing of his own coinage (right) is at odds with his reign itself. Though he had been an effective regent during his (younger) uncle David II's absences, his reign itself was chaotic and lawless. For the last six years of his rule he was largely senile.

I N 1328, AT THE AGE OF FOUR, ROBERT THE Bruce's son, David, was married to Edward II's seven-year-old daughter Joan. For Robert the Bruce, it marked the symbolic climax to the Treaty of Edinburgh: not only had England been forced to acknowledge the independence of Scotland but the two countries were now dynastically linked. David marked the occasion of his marriage with a different kind of symbolism that more accurately presaged the years to come. Suffering from diarrhoea, the four-year old "David Drip-on-Altar" emptied his bowels during the ceremony.

Three years later, following the revoking of the papal interdict placed on his father, David II became the first Scottish king to be crowned and anointed. It may have been a mark of the growing status of Scottish kingship under Robert the Bruce, but it was no reflection of the reality of Scotland under the new boy-king. In less than a year, David was deposed by Edward Balliol. The resulting dynastic turmoil opened the way for Edward III, who, having reached his majority, lost little time in rejecting the Treaty of Edinburgh. Edward invaded Scotland, inflicting a shattering defeat on David's forces in July 1333. David was forced to France.

Though Edward Balliol effectively gave up his claim to Scotland in 1336, and the English king then turned his attentions to France, David did not feel secure enough to return to Scotland until 1341. Within five years, however, he was an English prisoner, captured at the Battle of Neville's Cross.

To all intents and purposes, Scotland remained subservient to England for the rest of David's reign. Even after his release in 1357, David suggested that Edward III's son Lionel should succeed as King of Scotland if he, David, died childless. In fact, though David never produced an heir, the throne passed to his sister's son, Robert Stewart, Robert II.

The reign of the first two Stewart kings, Robert II and Robert III, marked the low point of Scottish kingship. Both were ailing and infirm when they succeeded. Neither demonstrated any obvious talent for personal rule. Under Robert III, power effectively passed to his younger brother, the duke of Albany, who in 1401 arrested the heir to the throne, his nephew David, and starved him to death. Rousing himself for a final, feeble effort, in 1406 the king arranged for his remaining son and new heir, James, to be sent to France for safe-keeping from his uncle. En route, James I, as he had now become, was captured and for the next 18 years kept prisoner in England. When he at last secured his release in 1424, he returned to a country gripped by lawlessness and ruled by a series of factious magnates. Though his often successful efforts to assert his authority inevitably brought him into conflict with his barons, it was military failure against England that eventually accounted for him. In 1437, a disastrous attempt to take Roxburgh sparked his murder.

The baronial feuding, which was by now endemic, disfigured the minority of his successor, James II. But on reaching his majority in 1449 the new king seemed to have the measure of his subjects. In a campaign of exceptional ruthlessness, in which his most obvious rivals were systematically executed and their lands declared forfeit, he set about restoring his authority. James II himself killed the earl of Douglas, stabbing him in the neck, though more in sudden rage than as a premeditated act. However, despite his efforts, his own death in 1460 and the succession of yet another child-king brought only a further round of instability.

> *But if your Holiness puts too much faith in the tales the English tell and will not give sincere belief to all this, nor refrain from favouring them to our prejudice, then the slaughter of bodies, the perdition of souls, and all the other misfortunes that will follow, inflicted by them on us and by us on them, will, we believe, be surely laid by the Most High to your charge*
>
> The Declaration of Arbroath *1320*

1331	1332	1333	1334	1336	1341	1346	1357	1371	1384	1385	1390
Coronation of David II	Edward Balliol claims throne of Scotland	Edward III crushes Scots at Halidon Hill; restores Edward Balliol	David II forced into exile in France	Edward Balliol renounces claim to Scotland; Robert Stewart (later Robert I) made regent	David II returns from France	Scots crushed at Neville's Cross; David II prisoner of English; Robert Stewart reass-umes regency	David II released; returns to Scotland	Accession of Robert II, first Stewart king	Effective administration passes to Robert II's son John, the earl of Carrick	Scotland raided by Richard II	Accession of Robert III; government passes to his brother, the duke of Albany

By the accession of Robert II, the first Stewart king, in 1371, the country was being destabilised not just by England but by the rival ambitions of a series of Scottish magnates (map left). Foremost among them were the lords of the Isles and the earls of Douglas, both effectively beyond the reach of the enfeebled Scottish crown.

SCOTLAND UNDER THE STEWARTS 1371–1460

→ Scottish campaigns, with date

→ English campaigns, with date

▨ Semi-autonomous lordship of the Isles and earldom of Ross, c. 1410

→ Donald's campaign, 1411

⚑ Held by the Livingstones and allies, 1449

LINDSAY Controlled by earl of Douglas and allies c.1452, (with names of allied families)

⚑ Held by Scottish crown during civil war

▬ Lordships and earldoms annexed to the Crown, 1455

Following his capture at Neville's Cross in 1346, David II became a firm friend of his English gaoler, Edward III (above). He was particularly taken by the chivalric atmosphere of the English court.

DAVID II JUNE 1329–AUG. 1332 (DEPOSED), DEC. 1332–MAR. 1333 (DEPOSED), 1336–FEB. 1371
BORN 1324 SON OF ROBERT THE BRUCE
Aged only five at accession, his minority rule was repeatedly challenged by Edward Balliol, bringing a return of the Balliol–Bruce rivalry that disfigured Scotland in the 1290s. He was exiled in France between 1336 and 1341. Led Scottish army to defeat by England in 1346 at Neville's Cross, where he was captured and held prisoner in England until ransomed in 1357. Thereafter, attempts to raise huge annual ransoms provoked repeated baronial rebellions.

EDWARD BALLIOL AUG. 1332– DEC. 1332 (DEPOSED); MAR. 1333–1334 (DEPOSED); 1335–1336; FORMALLY RESIGNED CLAIM TO THRONE 1357
BORN c.1290
Effectively no more than a tool of Edward III, who

successfully used him to destabilize Scotland. In theory Balliol ceded the whole of southern Scotland to Edward III. If only a footnote in Scottish history, Balliol still contributed to the dynastic and baronial turmoil that damaged his country so persistently.

ROBERT II FEB. 1371–APR. 1390
BORN c.1316
First of the Stewart kings. For long periods, he was an effective and efficient regent of Scotland during David II's absences. But when he came to the throne, he was a spent force and largely delegated control to his son John, Earl of Carrick (later Robert III) and then to his corrupt younger son Robert, Duke of Albany.

ROBERT III APR. 1390–APR. 1406
BORN c.1337
A pawn in his brother Robert's hands almost from the start of his reign. In 1398, his much more alert wife, Annabella, attempted to make their son, David, ruler as Lieutenant of the Realm. He, too,

was unable to resist his uncle, who in 1401 had David killed. Robert III presided over a period of lawlessness and dissolution of royal authority.

JAMES I APR. 1406–FEB. 1437
BORN 1394
Effectively raised in England, where he had been held prisoner since the age of 12. In 1424, at the age of 30, he returned to Scotland determined to reassert royal authority, but he succeeded only in antagonizing his leading magnates. He was murdered by Sir Robert Graham after a failed attempt to retake Roxburgh.

JAMES II FEB. 1437–AUG. 1460
BORN 1430
Acceded at only seven and spent much of his minority the prisoner of warring magnate factions within Scotland. On his majority, he proved forcefully aggressive and could possibly have made an effective king had he not been killed by an exploding cannon during yet another siege of Roxburgh.

1393	1398	1400	1401	1402	1406	1424	1428	1437	1449	1452	1460
Brief attempt by Robert III to regain control of Scottish government	Robert III's heir, David, made Lieutenant of the Realm	Scotland invaded by Henry IV	David murdered by his uncle, the duke of Albany	Scots defeated at Homildon Hill	Duke of Albany Governor of Scotland after capture of James I	Release and coronation of James I	Rebellious clan leaders in Highlands suppressed by James I	James I murdered after failure of siege of Roxburgh; accession of James II	Majority of James II	Earl of Douglas murdered by James II as king gains firmer control of Scotland	Accidental death of James II at siege of Roxburgh; accession of James III

JAMES III TO JAMES V 1461–1542

SCOTLAND'S MONARCHY UNDERWENT A REVIVAL OF SORTS AFTER THE DEATH OF JAMES II. THOUGH
THE SELF-SEEKING AMBITIONS OF THE COUNTRY'S SENIOR MAGNATES CONTINUED TO DISRUPT THE
COUNTRY, AND RELATIONS WITH ENGLAND WERE OFTEN BLOODY, BY THE EARLY 16TH CENTURY THE
AUTHORITY OF SCOTLAND'S KINGS HAD NOTICEABLY INCREASED.

*A double portrait of James
IV and Margaret Tudor
dating from c.1600
(above). Though unforeseen
at the time, the marriage
of Stewart and Tudor in
1503 would have profound
implications for the
kingdoms of Scotland and
England. Exactly 100 years
later, their great-grandson
would rule both.*

THE ACCESSION OF JAMES III IN 1460 AT the age of only eight threatened a return to lawlessness. Though initially protected by his mother, the formidable Mary of Gueldres, her death in 1463 opened the way for a consortium led by Sir Alexander Boyd to mount a bid for power. In 1466, Boyd kidnapped the king and proclaimed himself guardian.

It was not the disaster it might have been. Boyd's prime interest was personal enrichment rather than mastery over Scotland. Further, it was Boyd who in 1468 negotiated the marriage of James III to the daughter of the king of Norway. As a result, with the Norwegians unable to pay the promised dowry, the Northern Isles were ceded to Scotland.

James III has often been written off as a weak king, aloof and enigmatic, whose semi-imperial pretensions found outlets in huge building projects and ill-conceived schemes for grandiose foreign ventures. But the one consistent theme of his reign was a desire for peace with England. It was this, ironically, that proved his undoing.

Though forced by his increasingly disaffected magnates to confront Edward IV in 1482 – when the Scots were routed and Edinburgh stormed – James III persisted in his pro-English stance. By 1488, open rebellion, actively encouraged by James's heir, had broken out. At Sauchieburn, James III was defeated. He was killed as he fled the battlefield.

The accession of his son, the 15-year-old James IV, promised much. He has convincing claims as the most effective of the Stewarts, an able and energetic administrator who suppressed all attempts at his overthrow as well as being a keen patron of the arts and education. Edinburgh and Stirling castles were both extended and the new Palace of Holyroodhouse (Holyrood Palace) begun. In 1507 he also approved the installation of the first printing press in Scotland. His extension of active Scottish rule in the Northern Isles was no less important. Further, the Treaty of Perpetual Peace agreed with England in

*James III being crowned by St Andrew (right). Whatever his personal
failings, James III was never less than conscious of the dignity due to him
as a crowned and anointed king. His lofty self-assessment was starkly at
odds with the growing lawlessness of his reign.*

*James V's (far right) Catholicism made him one of the most eligible
bachelors in Europe. His successive marriages to François I's daughter and
to Mary of Guise, briefly elevated Scotland close to first rank of
European powers.*

> *We will with his [Albany's] presence take our adventure of peace or war as shall please God to send it; assuring
> your grace that … we neither may nor will, at the request of your grace, nor any other prince, consent nor suffer in
> any manner that our said Lord Governor depart furth of this realm during the king of sovereign lord's minority …
> And if, for this cause, we happen to be invaded, what may we do but take God to our good quarrel in defence,
> and do, as our progenitors and forebears have been constrained to do, for the conservation of this realm heretofore.*

Reply of the Scottish Parliament to Henry VIII's demand for the dismissal of the Duke of Albany as Governor of Scotland, 1522

1460	1463	1466	1469	1470	1474	1474	1481	1482	1483	1488	1493
Accession of James III	Peace treaty agreed with Edward IV of England	James III captured by Sir Alexander Boyd, who declares himself guardian	Majority of James III; Alexander Boyd forced into exile	Shetlands and Hebrides ceded to Scotland by Norway	James III seeks active rapprochement with Edward IV	James III dispossesses brothers the duke of Albany and earl of Mar	James III pushed into war with England	Edward IV supports Duke of Albany's bid for throne; English take Berwick	James III expels Alexander	James III overthrown and killed by rebel barons supported by his son and heir at Sauchieburn	John II, last Lord of the Isles, over-thrown. Scottish rule extends over all Northern and Western Isles

Though its own authority was increased with its take over of the Orkneys and Shetlands after 1468 and the annexations of the previously rebel earldom of Ross and lordship of the Isles in 1469 and 1493 respectively, Scottish kingship was still largely in thrall to the England (map right). James IV's efforts to stabilize relations with England could not prevent his death at Flodden in 1513. His heir, James V, was as decisively routed at Solway Moss in 1542.

STEWARTS 1461–1542

	to Scotland from Norway, 1469/72
	Earldom of Ross, annexed by the Crown, 1476
	Lordship of the Isles, annexed by the Crown, 1493
→	*English campaign, (Gloucester and Albany), 1482*
→	*Albany's movements 1482-83*
┈▶	*James III's route in captivity, 1482*
→	*James III's movements to counter his son's revolt*
	Revolt

1502, followed in 1503 by his marriage to Henry VII's daughter, Margaret, promised a new era in Anglo-Scottish relations.

That within 11 years England and Scotland were again at war and James IV had been killed at Flodden was less a consequence of Scottish ambitions than of the increasingly complex three-way power-politics being played out between England, Spain and France, into which Scotland, courtesy of the Auld Alliance, was inevitably sucked. This was the theme that dominated the reign of James V. It was given still greater urgency after 1532 with England's break from Rome: James V, as the ruler of a Catholic Scotland, found himself wooed by Catholic rulers from across Europe. As a result, he was able to negotiate a highly favourable marriage in 1537 with the daughter of François I of France, Madeleine, and a second marriage the following year with Mary of Guise after the early death of Madeleine. He also demanded – and received – greatly increased French military and financial aid.

Whatever this new status, the result for Scotland and its king was familiar. With Henry VIII of England increasingly believing himself surrounded by hostile Catholic powers, war with Scotland re-erupted. In 1542, James V's army was wiped out at Solway Moss. Within a month, James himself was dead, apparently from cholera. His heir, the new monarch, was not only a girl but she was less than a week old.

JAMES III AUG. 1460–JUNE 1488
BORN MAY 1452

Though consistently said to be ineffective, James III presided over a lengthy period of peace and gradually increasing prosperity. He was never popular, however, and signally failed to win the support of his barons. His grasp of administration was slack. In the end, whatever the potential benefits of his policy of peace with England, it ignored the reality of his magnates' desire for renewed war with the traditional enemy.

JAMES IV JUNE 1488–SEP. 1513
BORN MARCH 1473

Scotland's first indisputably Renaissance ruler whose wide interests – in architecture, literature, medicine (he was reputed to be able to pull teeth) and learning – were complemented by intelligent, just and strong rule. He was financially shrewd enough to be able to spend lavishly on his court without ever incurring

debts, and by the time of his death royal revenues had been tripled. Ultimately, though generously supported by France, he had to confront the reality of an always more powerful England.

JAMES V SEP. 1513– DEC. 1542
BORN APRIL 1512

James V has traditionally been dismissed as "the most unpleasant of the Stewarts". It is almost

certainly an unfair judgement. If harsh in his treatment of disloyal barons, he was no more so than many of his predecessors. In addition, his shrewd negotiations in the 1530s with Charles V and François I were a rational response to his strong bargaining position. Nonetheless, his inability to win over his leading subjects contributed significantly to the Scottish defeat at Solway Moss.

MARY, QUEEN OF SCOTS 1542–67

THE IMAGE OF MARY, QUEEN OF SCOTS, AS THE MOST ROMANTIC STEWART RULER ENDURES. QUEEN OF SCOTLAND AT LESS THAN A WEEK OLD, AND QUEEN OF FRANCE AT 16, SHE RETURNED TO SCOTLAND A WIDOW AT ONLY 18. HOWEVER CAPABLE – IF IMPETUOUS – SHE WAS TO FIND HERSELF OVERWHELMED BY THE NEW RELIGIOUS FORCES TEARING UP THE MAP OF EUROPE.

MARY, QUEEN OF SCOTLAND AND FRANCE

BORN: December 8 1542
ACCEDED: December 14 1542; crowned September 9 1543, Stirling Castle
ABDICATED: July 24 1567

Queen of Scotland, Queen Consort of France (July 10 1559 to December 5 1560)

Unquestionably beautiful, Mary (above) was also shrewd and intelligent. Whatever her own Catholic convictions, in Scotland she steered a pragmatic middle course between the Catholic and Protestant camps. At least until 1566, Mary engineered a degree of unity rare to Stewart Scotland. However, she could also be loftily impetuous. Her disastrous marriage to Bothwell in 1567 just months after he had murdered her husband was extraordinarily perverse.

B Y THE TIME OF MARY'S BIRTH, SCOTLAND had been decisively drawn into the wider religious conflict that was destroying established political certainties across Europe. Were Scotland to remain Catholic, its value to the major Catholic powers of Europe – France, Spain and the Papacy above all – in the growing conflict against the heretic Protestant nations of northern Europe was clear. At the age of six, Mary was accordingly sent by her French mother, the implacably Catholic Mary of Guise, to France to be brought up a forthrightly aristocratic champion of the Catholic church.

Mary, "La belle des belles", feted for her beauty and charm, spent the next 13 years in François I's sumptuous courts. Her mother, meanwhile, ruled in Scotland as regent. In 1558, at the age of 15, Mary was married to the dauphin, heir to the French throne. When, in 1559, the dauphin unexpectedly became king of France as François II, Catholic Franco-Scottish dynastic destinies appeared to have been cemented for good: a Catholic king had become king of Scotland. Furthermore, as grand-daughter of Margaret Tudor, wife of James IV, Mary and her husband had legitimate claim on the English throne. For the nervously Protestant court of Elizabeth I, the Queen of Scots had become exceptionally dangerous.

These grand designs were partly thwarted by the sudden death of François II in 1560. In the following year, the undaunted Mary returned to Scotland, which was by then becoming ever more vocally Protestant. Almost from the start, her brief period in Scotland as queen in her own right became a bloodsoaked epic in which baronial power-plays confronted the new realities of the pan-European religious conflict. In the background loomed the great prize that was the throne of England.

As a sinner I am truly conscious of having often offended my Creator. I beg him to forgive me. But as Queen and sovereign I am aware of no fault or offence for which I have to render account to anyone here below.

Mary defending herself against charges of plotting to overthrow Elizabeth I, 1586

The Murder of David Rizzio

T he murder in March 1566 of Mary's Italian secretary, David Rizzio, remains among the most gruesome events of her troubled reign. The motive was that Rizzio was held to be persuading Mary to mount a full-blown counter-Reformation of the kind Mary's Guise relations were currently unleashing on France's Huguenots. To the disaffected Protestant nobles of Scotland, Rizzio's removal was a matter of urgency. The role of the bone-headed but beautiful Henry Darnley (above) in the affair is harder to explain. He seems to have acted purely out of alcohol-fuelled malice, partly having convinced himself that Rizzio and the queen had became lovers. At all events, Darnley and his co-conspirators forced their way into Mary's room at Holyrood Palace and, in front of the pregnant Queen, hacked the terrified Rizzio to pieces. They then threw his corpse down a lavatory.

Mary's revenge was to arrange that Darnley himself be murdered, an act that the Earl of Bothwell, aided by a number of those who had themselves killed Rizzio, was happy to take on. The following February, Darnley's body was found smothered in the grounds of his house outside Edinburgh. The house itself had been blown up. Mary's subsequent and almost immediate marriage to Bothwell remains her single greatest error. In aligning herself with a man known to be a murderer – in spite of his acquittal in a palpably rigged trial – she guaranteed an overwhelming coalition of interests against her. Within two months of her marriage, she was forced to abdicate.

1543	1544–45	1547	1548	1554	1558	1559	1560
Earl of Arran appointed Regent of Scotland. Treaty of Greenwich with England (not ratified) agrees marriage of Mary to Henry VIII's heir, Prince Edward	English invasions of Scotland – Henry VIII's "rough wooing" – attempts to force Scots to implement Treaty of Greenwich	English influence in Scotland increased after victory at Battle of Pinkie	Mary sent to France	Mary appoints her mother, Mary of Guise, Regent in Scotland	Marriage of Mary to François, Dauphin of France	Accession of François II; French influence over Scotland at its height; Scottish Protestants persecuted	Deaths of Mary of Guise (June) and François II (Dec.)

The five-year reign of Mary, Queen of Scots, may have begun brightly but almost from the moment of her bizarre marriage to Bothwell in 1567 it rapidly degenerated. Having escaped to England the following year, she found herself shunted from stronghold to stronghold, increasingly a pawn in the wider conflict between the Catholic and Protestant powers of Europe (map below).

In 1565, Mary was married again (with full Catholic rites) to her cousin, the dashing but dissolute Henry Stewart, Lord Darnley. Scarcely more than a year later, and in front of his now pregnant wife, Darnley murdered Mary's secretary, the hunchback Italian David Rizzio, whom he accused of having an affair with Mary. Eleven months later, Darnley was himself murdered by the Earl of Bothwell. Mary, her wits perhaps disturbed, then married Bothwell. Unsurprisingly, her new marriage provoked outrage on the part of those demanding justice for the murderers of Darnley.

The chaos that inevitably followed saw Mary, now safely delivered of her only child, the future James VI, hounded out of her kingdom. For his part, Bothwell summarily deserted her and fled the country. Mary, forced to abandon

The tragic drama of Mary's life reached its climax with her execution in February 1587 (below). Her refusal to renounce her claim to Elizabeth's throne and fierce defence of Catholicism ensured her status as persecuted martyr. It was a very public performance carried off with complete conviction. Elizabeth, when told of her cousin's death, "… gave herself over to grief putting herself into mourning weeds and shedding abundance of tears".

Abdicated under duress, July 1567; escaped from captivity, May 1568

Married Darnley, 1565

Mary's son crowned as, James VI, July 1567

Mary's secretary Rizzio murdered in her presence, 1566

Darnley murdered, February 1567

BROUGHTY

Married Bothwell, May 1567

STIRLING

LOCHLEVEN

to Roscoff, Brittany as bride to be of the Dauphin, 1548

DUMBARTON

EDINBURGH

LINLITHGOW

Carberry June 1567

Langside 1568

Mary born, 1542

Pinkie 1547

DUNBAR

on the death of husband, Francis II, 1561

Escaped to England, 1568

CARLISLE

NEWCASTLE

BOLTON

Isle of Man

Inconclusive conference on Mary's role in her husband's murder, 1569

YORK

IRELAND

DUBLIN

Involved in Ridolfi conspiracy, 1571

SHEFFIELD

BUXTON

CHATSWORTH

CHESTER

NOTTINGHAM

CHARTLEY

TUTBURY

Involved in Babington conspiracy, 1585

LEICESTER

NORWICH

FOTHERINGAY *Executed, 8 February 1587*

WEXFORD

COVENTRY

WALES

WARWICK

NORTHAMPTON

CAMBRIDGE

WORCESTER

HEREFORD

GLOUCESTER

OXFORD

Sentenced to death for role in Babington conspiracy, 1586

RICHMOND

LONDON

WESTMINSTER

BRISTOL

Parliament recommends execution, 12 November 1586

Conference in 1569 fails to find conclusive evidence for Mary's complicity in murder of Darnley

CALAIS

WINCHESTER

PORTSMOUTH

EXETER

English Channel

Married the Dauphin, 1558; Queen 1559–60

PLYMOUTH

FRANCE

her son (whom she never saw again) and to abdicate in his favour, made her bedraggled way to England.

It is clear that she assumed her royal cousin Elizabeth would restore her to her throne. Elizabeth, however, only too conscious of the threat posed by Mary but reluctant nonetheless to order her death, did what she did best and prevaricated. Over the following 19 years, Mary, increasingly aware that she was a prisoner not a guest, and ever more shrill in her demands that her royal dignity be observed, was moved from stronghold to stronghold. She became involved in a series of improbable plots to overthrow Elizabeth and seize the thrones of England and Scotland. As a focus of Catholic unrest, her execution became inevitable. She died, as she said, "like a true Scottish woman and a true French woman".

1561	1565	1566	1567	1568	1569	1586	1587
Mary returns to Scotland, where she attempts to reconcile Catholic and Protestant interests	*Marriage of Mary to Henry Stewart, Lord Darnley*	*Darnley and others murder Mary's secretary, David Rizzio (Mar.); birth of future James VI (June)*	*Darnley murdered by Earl of Bothwell (Feb.); marriage of Mary and Bothwell (May); Mary forced to abdicate (July) and held prisoner at Lochleven*	*Mary escapes from Lochleven but her small army is immediately overwhelmed; Mary flees to England*	*As prisoner of Elizabeth I, Mary conspires with Duke of Norfolk to overthrow Elizabeth; Norfolk executed*	*Mary implicated in further Catholic plot to oust Elizabeth and convicted of treason*	*Execution of Mary (Feb.)*

ENGLAND AND WALES: THE TUDORS 1485–1603

HENRY VII 1485–1509

HENRY VIII 1509–47

EDWARD VI 1547–53

MARY I 1553–58

ELIZABETH I 1558–1603

ON THE FACE OF IT, HENRY VII'S SEIZURE OF THE THRONE IN 1485 WAS NO MORE THAN ANOTHER ROUND IN THE DYNASTIC TURMOIL THAT PLAGUED 15TH-CENTURY ENGLAND. FOUR KINGS HAD BEEN OVERTURNED (ONE OF THEM TWICE) AND MURDERED. THREE SEPARATE DYNASTIES HAD FORCIBLY INSTALLED THEMSELVES ON THE THRONE. YET HENRY TUDOR'S TAKE-OVER OF POWER NOT ONLY PROVED ENDURING BUT, AT ANY RATE IN RETROSPECT, IT CAN BE SEEN TO HAVE MARKED THE BEGINNING OF A NEW ERA NOT JUST OF ENGLISH, AND LATER BRITISH, MONARCHY BUT, BY EXTENSION, OF ENGLISH AND BRITISH HISTORY AS A WHOLE.

I n part, this was a matter of a return to strong, stable government in place of the chaos of the middle years of the century. This was not something that Henry VII can claim sole credit for. The process was already well underway in Edward IV's reign, though it is certainly true that Henry VII's very much more active style of kingship accelerated it. But as important was a parallel growth in the power of the state itself. This was a largely new development, one of lasting importance.

In essence, England, in common with a number of other west European states, France and Spain pre-eminently, saw a rapid growth in the mechanisms and efficiency of its government. Expanding economies and growing populations meant that larger resources became available to the crown – provided that taxes could be collected efficiently and law and order maintained. The creation of a stable, centralized, bureaucratic government accordingly became a priority.

Henry VII, though otherwise inexperienced in kingship, proved to have precisely the kind of meticulous, calculating mind that made the concentration of this kind of power possible. The crucial consequence, however slowly it unfolded, was that the monarchy's dependence on its leading subjects was reduced. Medieval kings would certainly not have claimed to have enjoyed any less authority than their Tudor counterparts, but their ability to deploy it and to exercise power effectively was unquestionably less. To take only one obvious example, medieval armies had to be raised by the leading magnates, whose troops in effect they were and thus potentially able to be turned against the monarch. From the 16th century onwards, armies and later navies, raised and paid for by the state, were answerable directly to the monarch. In an era of almost perpetual warfare, it was a vitally important difference.

Though Henry VIII had none of his father's administrative talents, he more than made up for it by his eager embrace of the quasi-imperial nature of this new monarchy. However unpredictable and extravagant, he instinctively understood that his power had to be projected absolutely. It was further reinforced after 1534 when, breaking with Rome, Henry made himself Supreme Head of the new Church of England. By any measure the monarchy's personal standing had been enhanced. As a spin-off, with the existing administrative structures unable to cope with the regulation of the Church, new councils and boards had to be created, strengthening central authority further.

In reality, the acquisition of greater royal authority was never a straightforward business. For one thing, the avaricious Henry VII aside, the Tudor monarchs were permanently hedged in by a lack of resources. Growing it may have been but 16th-century England was never as rich as France let alone Spain, the super-power of the age. One obvious consequence was that England's capacity to wage wars was always limited. Henry VII, pragmatic to the last, scarcely even tried to. Henry VIII, by contrast, made repeated efforts. Yet even against Scotland he made patchy progress at best. Only against Wales was he unequivocally successful. Against France, he consistently came off worst. Elizabeth I, by nature highly cautious, adopted an exclusively defensive posture.

But as important, with onset of the Reformation, the Tudors also had to contend with religious conflict. This was a wholly new, even more destabilizing phenomenon, one that transformed the political map of Europe, plunging it into a seemingly endless round of divisive wars. The huge problems it created were complex and multi-layered, giving long-standing international rivalries a new twist. Put most simply, for Spain, France and the Papacy, whatever their own rivalries, the overthrow of Protestant, heretic England became not just a matter of conventional conquest so much as an absolute crusade. In precisely the same way, as the Protestant nature of England took firmer shape, so resisting the Papists, bent as they were on their ungodly subjection of England, became just as much of a necessity.

The manner in which wider European political and religious issues had become so thoroughly intertwined and could spark such bitterness found a ready and inevitably dangerous parallel in England itself. For many, especially in the north, giving up Catholicism was unthinkable. Well into the 17th century, England would be destabilized by religious conflict. The Tudors themselves encapsulated these conflicts. For Henry VIII the adoption of Anglicanism was a matter of state, not of religious conviction: Henry remained a devout Catholic to the end of his life. His heir, Edward, by contrast, espoused a very much more ardent, not to say fanatical Protestantism. His successor, Mary, was an equally committed Catholic, determined to restore the Roman church. In the space of no more than a year, England was wrenched from one religious pole to the other.

It was the particular genius of Elizabeth I to calm these passions. Though England under Elizabeth became unequivocally Protestant, its identity all the more strongly felt, it avoided the worst excesses of religious conflict that disfigured so much of the rest of Europe. However much on the defensive, Elizabethan England saw the birth of an English identity that persists even today.

In the end, the Tudors, for all that they presided over the transformation of English kingship, were the victims of a permanent threat to all dynasties: their failure to provide sufficient heirs. With the death of Elizabeth, the virgin queen, in 1603, the throne passed to the Stuarts. That their realm had been immeasurably strengthened, however, is undoubted.

HENRY VII 1485–1509

HENRY VII'S CLAIM TO THE THRONE WAS THE WEAKEST OF ANY KING OF ENGLAND SINCE WILLIAM THE CONQUEROR. YET HE NOT ONLY ESTABLISHED A NEW DYNASTY, HE LAID THE FOUNDATIONS FOR WHAT WOULD PROVE A NEAR REVOLUTION IN ROYAL GOVERNMENT. ENGLAND UNDER HENRY VII BEGAN THE PROCESS THAT WOULD LEAD A NEW ERA OF ABSOLUTIST MONARCHY.

BORN: January 28 1457
ACCEDED: August 22 1485; crowned Westminster Abbey, October 30 1485

Earl of Richmond (from 1457), King of England and Lord of Ireland

It is doubtful if England has ever had a more naturally astute – or tough-minded – king than Henry VII (above). Yet for all his reputation for avarice, he was a generous patron of the church and of the arts. Yet "serious, sad and full of thoughts", his life, like his court, became increasingly sombre.

THE DEATH OF RICHARD III AT THE BATTLE of Bosworth in August 1485, along with the majority of those magnates who had remained loyal to him, eliminated at a stroke almost all rivals to the new king, Henry VII. It was a significant advantage, no less than had been the murders of the Princes in the Tower by Richard III two years earlier. Of equal importance, Henry now added all the former Yorkist lands to his existing Lancastrian lands. As by far the richest individual in the kingdom, Henry was not only removed from dependence on any one faction, the crown itself was elevated above dynastic squabbling, allowing the restoration of impartial, royal authority. Henry's claim to the throne may have been tenuous but it was effectively unchallenged from the start.

That said, he was consistently at pains to emphasize his legitimacy. His marriage in 1486 to Edward IV's daughter, Elizabeth, just as much as his personal device, the Tudor rose, which combined the red and white roses of York and Lancaster, was deliberately intended to underline the new union of the dynasties. He also permanently stressed his Welsh and thus "British" blood, ensuring for example that his eldest son, symbolically named Arthur, was born at the Anglo-Saxon capital, Winchester. In the event,

the die-hard Yorkist challenges that did emerge were relatively easily contained, including those of the two improbable pretenders Lambert Simnel and Perkin Warbeck (see box).

Perhaps as a result of the insecurity of his upbringing, 14 years of it as a Lancastrian exile in Brittany, Henry remained highly cautious, not to say suspicious, to the end of his reign. Equally, there is no question but that the particular cast of his mind – methodical, painstaking and shrewd – allowed him to reinforce royal authority to an unprecedented degree. His preferred means were financial prudence – he has rightly been described as "the best businessman ever to sit on the throne of England" – and the concentration of government in the hands of a small group of trusted advisors, with Henry unambiguously as its head. This, the King's Council, meeting in the Star Chamber, effectively by-passed Parliament, whose importance in approving new taxation was in any case greatly lessened by Henry's parsimoniousness. At the same, Henry developed a new means of taming his magnates by levying often huge fines for alleged misdemeanours. The king also authorized no less than 138 Acts of Attainder under which the property of those convicted of treason passed to the crown.

The Yorkist Pretenders

Uncertainty over the fate of Edward IV's two young sons, Edward V and Richard, duke of York, both in fact murdered by Richard III, gave rise to bizarre attempts by Yorkist supporters to pass off two transparent impostors as the real heirs to the throne.

The first, Lambert Simnel, son of an Oxford joiner, was recruited by the earl of Lincoln, Edward IV's nephew. He claimed variously that Lambert was the younger of Edward IV's sons then that he was another of Edward IV's nephews, the earl of Warwick. (To Henry VII's evident amusement, the real earl of Warwick, meanwhile, was a prisoner in the Tower.) In 1486, the earl of Lincoln took Lambert to Ireland. There, in May 1487, he was crowned Edward VI. The next month, Lincoln invaded England and was almost immediately defeated. Henry VII took pity on Simnel and gave him a job in the royal kitchens.

Perkin Warbeck's challenge was more sustained but no less absurd. He was a Fleming who spoke no English. Nonetheless, in Ireland after 1491 he claimed first to be the earl of Warwick, then an illegitimate son of Richard III and finally the duke of York. With the support of Edward IV's sister, Margaret of Burgundy, and the Holy Roman Emperor Maximilian I, who saw him as a means to destabilize Henry VII, in October 1494 he was proclaimed Richard IV. He also won the support of James IV of Scotland.

By the time Warbeck had assembled an army of sorts, his insistent, self-important demands had already alienated most of his supporters. Warbeck pressed on, however, landing in Cornwall in 1497 and raising a small army among those already protesting at Henry VII's punitive levels of taxation. Within a month he had been captured. When he tried to escape, he was placed in the Tower with the real earl of Warwick. When, inevitably, they plotted to overthrow Henry VII, the king had them executed.

1471	1483	1485	1486	1487	1492
Henry Tudor forced into exile in Brittany	Attempted invasion of England, in tandem with duke of Buckingham, thwarted; Henry vows to marry Elizabeth of York if he wins crown of England	Successful landing at Milford Haven followed by defeat of Richard III at Bosworth (Aug.); Henry VII's legitimacy recognized by Parliamentary statute (Oct.); King's Council (Star Chamber) formed	Marriage of Henry VII to Elizabeth of York; birth of Prince Arthur. Papal recognition of Henry VII's legitimacy granted	Lambert Simnel and Yorkist supporters routed at Stoke	Brief invasion of northern France

For he began to treat his people with more harshness and severity than had been his custom, in order (as he himself asserted) to ensure that they remained thoroughly and entirely in obedience to him. The people themselves had another explanation for his action, for they considered they were suffering not on account of their own sins but on account of the greed of their monarch. It is not indeed clear whether at the start it was greed; but afterward greed did become apparent.

Polydore Vergil, Anglicae Historia, 1534

Legend:

- Rebellion, with date
- Route of Lambert Simnel's Yorkists supporters
- Lambert Simnel's campaign, following his Dublin crowning as Edward VI
- Resisted Simnel's pretence, 1487
- Perkin Warbeck's movements, with details
- Supported Perkin Warbeck, 1495, with name
- Campaign in support of Perkin Warbeck, 1495
- Rebel campaign, 1497
- Henry's campaigns, with date
- Other English campaigns, with date

Whatever the attempts by the remaining Yorkists, chiefly based in Ireland, to oust Henry VII, in reality Henry's throne was secure (map below). Both the Yorkist pretenders, Lambert Simnel and Perkin Warbeck, the latter half-heartedly supported by James IV of Scotland, could mount only token attempts on Henry's throne. The king's foreign relations were similarly stable. Prudence was the consistent theme of his reign.

For all that theirs was a dynastically arranged marriage, Henry VII and Elizabeth of York developed what seems a genuine affection. When she died, in 1503, Henry "privily departed to a solitary place and would no man should resort unto him". They were buried side by side in the magnificent chapel Henry built at Westminster Abbey. Their tomb effigy (below), by the Florentine sculptor Pietro Torrigiano, is one of the earliest Renaissance works in England.

The same instinctive caution was evident in Henry's foreign policy. Though he conducted one invasion of France, in 1492, it lasted only a day and ended with a handsome pay-off from the French king, Charles VIII. A one-day invasion of Scotland in 1496 was followed the next year by a week-long invasion.

Even more typical were the marriage alliances with Aragon and Castile in 1501, under which Prince Arthur married Catherine of Aragon, and with Scotland in 1502, under which, the following year, Henry's eldest daughter married James IV. In both cases, Henry's aim was to secure important allies against the traditional enemy, France.

Henry VII's secretive, close nature may never have made him a likeable figure. But he was unquestionably among the most effective of England's kings. English kingship was turning a crucial corner.

1496	1497	1499	1501	1502	1503	1508
Brief invasion of Scotland after James IV supports Perkin Warbeck	Further invasion of France. Cornish rising, protesting at high levels of taxation, suppressed. Perkin Warbeck captured after landing in Cornwall	Execution of Perkin Warbeck and earl of Warwick. Richmond Palace begun	Revolt by duke of Suffolk suppressed. Marriage of Prince Arthur to Catherine of Aragon	Treaty of Perpetual Peace between England and Scotland. Death of Prince Arthur	Marriage of Margaret Tudor to James IV of Scotland. Chapel to Henry VI (later Henry VII's chapel), Westminster Abbey, begun	Execution of duke of Suffolk, last Yorkist claimant

HENRY VIII 1509–47

BORN: June 28 1491
ACCEDED: April 21
1509; Westminster
Abbey June 24 1509

*Duke of York, Duke of
Cornwall, Prince of
Wales, Earl of Chester,
King of England and
Ireland*

*By the last years of Henry
VIII's reign, the lithe and
handsome youth had become
bloated ruin, scarcely able
even to walk: he had to be
pushed around Hampton
Court in a specially built cart.
Not even Holbein could
hide the reality of "a gross
and selfish tyrant" (above).*

THE 17-YEAR-OLD HENRY VIII CAME TO THE THRONE AS RULER OF AN INCREASINGLY WEALTHY CATHOLIC COUNTRY. HE DIED THE RULER OF A NEAR-BANKRUPT PROTESTANT COUNTRY WHOSE DECISIVE SPLIT FROM ROME SPARKED RELIGIOUS CONFLICTS THAT PERSISTED FOR DECADES. WHATEVER ITS SUPERFICIAL GLAMOUR, IN THE SHORT TERM AT LEAST HIS REIGN SPAWNED ONLY DIVISION AND ECONOMIC DISLOCATION.

GLAMOROUS AND ACCOMPLISHED, BURSTING with youthful vigour, the new King Henry seemed destined to consolidate his father, Henry VII's, achievements. England was poised to become a power of European repute under a ruler whose dazzling potency would put even the Holy Roman Emperor in the shade. As the Venetian ambassador reported in 1515: "His Majesty is the handsomest potentate I have ever set eyes upon… he is in every respect a most accomplished prince". Yet the fundamental shallowness of Henry's character, in which an insatiable appetite for acclaim sat side by side with a vindictive vaingloriousness, was clear from the start. Within a year of his accession, he had executed his father's two principal tax collectors in an attempt to curry popularity. Of more lasting significance, in the same year he also married Catherine of Aragon, who had previously been married to Henry's elder brother, Arthur, who had died in 1502.

Two themes dominated Henry's reign, both intended to reinforce what the king increasingly came to see as his "imperial" status. The first was foreign conquest, the second church reform. If the latter was essentially a reaction to events, the former was a conscious act of policy from the start.

Casting himself as a reborn Henry V, in 1513 Henry mounted a costly invasion of France, the net result of which was the capture of two towns, Tournai and Thérouanne, and the so-called Battle of the Spurs, in reality little more than a skirmish. Similarly inconclusive campaigns were launched against France in 1522 and 1523 and again in 1542.

But if Henry's fantasies of continental conquest came to nothing, he came much closer to success in Scotland, even if in the end he could no more make himself master of Scotland than could Edward I. In 1513, attempting to exploit Henry's absence in France, James IV of Scotland invaded England. His army was peremptorily annihilated on the Anglo-Scottish border at Flodden by an English force under Thomas Howard, the earl of Surrey. Among the victims, his corpse hauled from under a pile of dead Scots, was James himself.

Encouraged, Henry spent much of his reign attempting to unite the English and Scottish crowns. His efforts climaxed in the 1540s when, after a further crushing defeat of the Scots at Solway Moss in 1542, Henry began what he called his "Rough Wooing", a series of invasions of Scotland in 1544 and 1545 in which Henry attempted to force the Scots to accept his young son, Edward, as the husband-to-be of Mary,

The Field of the Cloth of Gold

Henry VIII's early attempts to reconquer France may have ended in failure but, in 1520, they gave rise to one of the most remarkable spectacles of the period: the Field of the Cloth of Gold. Ostensibly called to confirm peace between England and France, the meeting outside Calais between the 29-year-old Henry and the new king of France, Francis I, was an opportunity for each to demonstrate, to the other as much as to the world, their imposing power. Effectively the whole of England's nobility, probably in excess of 5,000 earls, churchmen and knights, were transported to France. Francis brought even more men. A small city of gaudily decorated tents was erected. As a sign of their fellowship, Henry and Francis hunted, feasted and wrestled together. The promise of England and France alike as world powers in the making had never appeared more convincing. The emptiness at the heart of the spectacle was exposed less than two years later when war between England and France was resumed.

1512	1513	1520	1522	1529	1533	1534
First invasion of France	Second invasion of France; Scots defeated at Flodden by the Earl of Surrey – James IV of Scotland killed	Field of the Cloth of Gold confirms peace with France	War with France and Scotland renewed	Cardinal Wolsey dismissed (died 1530); Thomas More made Chancellor	Catherine of Aragon divorced	Act of Supremacy establishes Church of England

Henry's Wives

CATHERINE OF ARAGON (1485–1536)
MARRIED: Arthur, Prince of Wales, 1501;
Henry VIII, June 1509 (marriage annulled May 1533)
SURVIVING CHILDREN: Mary, b. 1516

ANNE BOLEYN (1501–1536)
MARRIED: Henry VIII, January 1533
(executed May 1536)
SURVIVING CHILDREN: Elizabeth, b. 1536

JANE SEYMOUR (1509–1537)
MARRIED: Henry VIII, May 1536
SURVIVING CHILDREN: Edward, b. 1537

ANNE OF CLEVES (1519–1557)
MARRIED: Henry VIII, January 1540
(marriage annulled June 1540)
SURVIVING CHILDREN: none

CATHERINE HOWARD (1520–1542)
MARRIED: Henry VIII, July 1540
(executed February 1542)
SURVIVING CHILDREN: none

CATHERINE PARR (1512–1548)
MARRIED: Sir Edward Burgh, 1529;
John, Lord Latimer, 1533; Henry VIII, July 1543;
Thomas Seymour, 1547
SURVIVING CHILDREN: none

Henry VIII's Continental ambitions consistently outstripped his means to put them into practise (map right). Early invasions of France achieved almost other than prodigious expenditure. The king's naval campaigns were no more successful. His attempts to subdue Scotland met with similar lack of success. Only in Wales, incorporated with England in 1536, could Henry claim to have to achieved his ambitions.

HENRY VIII AND THE 'IMPERIAL' EXPANSION OF ENGLAND

- England and English-held during reign of Henry VIII
- Transferred to direct English control, 1536
- Annexed to England, 1536
- Under temporary English control, 1514-18
- English campaign, 1512
- English naval campaign, 1513
- Henry VIII's campaign, 1513
- Area of fighting on the Continent, 1543-5
- Rough wooing, from 1544
- English naval campaigns, 1545
- French naval campaigns, 1545
- Revolts

the infant-queen of Scotland. That the Scots, with the active support of France, were able to resist, despite an English army of occupation stationed in Scotland for several years, effectively ended Henry's dynastic ambitions to unite the Scots and English crowns under a future Tudor monarch.

At least on paper, Henry was more successful in making himself master of Ireland, where a half-hearted invasion led Henry to style himself King of Ireland in 1541. In reality, English rule was restricted to the Pale, the area immediately around Dublin. Only in Wales, which was united with England in 1536, was Henry unequivocally successful (see box).

1535	1536	1539	1540	1541	1542	1543
Execution of Thomas More. Dissolution of monasteries launched	*Pilgrimage of Grace. Act of Union integrates Wales with England*	*Act of Six Articles reaffirms primacy of Catholic orthodoxy. English-language Great Bible published*	*Cromwell executed*	*Henry declared "king" of Ireland*	*Scots defeated at Solway Moss*	*Renewed invasion of France; Boulogne captured*

ENGLAND UNDER HENRY VIII, 1509–47

——— Frontier of bishoprics before the Reformation

New diocese created after 1540; frontier between them

Monasteries before the Reformation

- Benedictine and Cluniac
- Cistercian
- Orders of Friars and Carthusians
- Abbots executed by Henry VIII
- Area of Pilgrimage of Grace, 1536
- Main movement of "Pilgrimage of Grace" rebels
- Welsh counties under terms of the Act of Union with England, 1536
- Transferred to England from Wales under the terms of the Act of Union
- Jurisdiction of the Council in the Marches under the terms of the Act of Union
- Jurisdiction of the Council in the North from 1537
- NORWICH Cathedral town

Other than the absorption of Wales in 1536, by far the most striking act of Henry VIII's reign in England was his break from Rome and subsequent take over of the country's monastic foundations (map left). It would lead directly to widespread anti-Reformation movements, notably the Pilgrimage of Grace in the still strongly Catholic north.

By 1527, Henry had convinced himself that Catherine's failure to produce a son was a punishment from God for having married his brother's wife (though she had six children, only one, a girl, Mary, survived). In fact Henry, now in his late 30s, was not merely neurotically anxious to secure an heir but had fallen obsessively in love with the much-younger Anne Boleyn. He instructed his Lord Chancellor, the otherwise supremely able Cardinal Thomas Wolsey, to persuade the pope to approve a divorce.

Even for Wolsey, this was a royal command too far. Infuriated by his Chancellor's failure to give him what he wanted, 1529 Henry stripped Wolsey of his office and condemned him to death.

By 1534, prompted by a new and equally capable Chancellor, Thomas Cromwell, and a new Archbishop of Canterbury, Thomas Cranmer, both enthusiastic supporters of the Reformed church, the necessary legislation that would give birth to the Church of England, with Henry at its Supreme Head, was put in train.

The logical consequence was that the church's properties in England should now also belong to the monarch. From 1536, Cromwell began the "dissolution" of England's monasteries. It was a campaign of systematic vindictiveness in which, in less than four years, charges of laxity and corruption were used to justify the forced dismemberment of every single one of the country's monasteries. 560 were suppressed, yielding the crown more than £200,000. Over 15,000 monks and nuns were displaced.

This gold medal (above) *showing Henry as Supreme Head of the new Church of England, bears the words* **Fidei Defensor** (*Defender of the Faith*). *Ironically, the title was awarded by Pope Leo X to Henry VIII in 1521 for a pamphlet written in 1519 in which Henry defended the Catholic church against Protestant attacks.*

Henry's church reforms, by contrast, were successful from the start, at any rate in his terms. By establishing the Church of England under the 1534 Act of Supremacy, with the monarch its Supreme Head, Henry not only engineered a complete split from papal authority but placed Britain firmly in the north European Protestant camp. As elsewhere in Europe, the religious divide thus created would lead to prolonged and bitter struggles. The consequences were momentous.

Henry's motive was never religious reform. He remained a devout Catholic to the end of his life, profoundly opposed to all attempts to reform Catholic religious practice. Rather, his goal was short-term and expedient: to secure a divorce from his ageing queen, Catherine of Aragon. His solution – that he could exploit religious reforms elsewhere in Europe to make himself his own pope able to authorize his own divorce – was an idea that seems to have dawned only slowly.

In becoming head of the church and acquiring the enormous riches of the country's monastic foundations, Henry had theoretically greatly increased the power of the monarchy. In practice, almost the opposite was the case. To give his claims against the monasteries legitimacy, Henry had been forced to co-opt parliament. The long-term result was that it was parliament's influence that was strengthened rather than the king's. At the same time, Henry's permanent need for money obliged him to sell off most monasteries almost as soon as he acquired them, prompting the greatest change in land ownership since the Norman Conquest. Henry squandered the wealth of the church in a matter of years.

Characteristically, Henry's infatuation with Anne proved short-lived, not least as the only child she had produced was a girl, Elizabeth. In 1536, his queen was beheaded on charges of adultery. (As sign of his clemency, Henry agreed she could be decapitated with a sword

Whilst Henry VII had begun the building of warships, it was under Henry VIII that a large-scale expansion of the navy began, the largest such programme since the time of Alfred the Great. Pictured (**right**) *is the* **Henri Grace à Dieu**, *the largest ship in the fleet. It weighed over 1,000 tons and had 72 guns.*

rather than an axe.) Two weeks later, Henry married Jane Seymour. Though the rigours of childbirth killed her, she was at least able to give the king a son, Edward.

Three further wives followed. The first was Anne of Cleves, in 1540. Young and apparently beautiful, as the sister of the German duke of Cleves she would also provide Henry with an important Protestant ally. But having only seen Holbein's ravishing portrait of his bride-to-be, Henry was appalled to meet a fleshy young woman of, at best, lumbering charm. Their unconsummated marriage ended in divorce after six months. Within three weeks, Henry married the teenage Catherine Howard, who briefly put a spring into his gouty step. Two years later, Henry had her executed for infidelity. His sixth and final wife, the matronly Catherine Parr, the only one of his wives to survive her despotic husband, seems finally to have brought a degree of serenity to his premature old age.

Henry may have owned 55 palaces by his death, but his reign ended as a gross parody of the promise with which it had begun. His wars against Ireland, Scotland and France were effectively bankrupting the kingdom. Simultaneously, a total of only three surviving legitimate children, one boy and two girls, left the succession worryingly uncertain. Above all, the country was wracked by religious turmoil. The legacy of the "most accomplished prince" was chaos and misery.

The Pilgrimage of Grace

The execution of Anne Boleyn in 1536 sparked the most serious civil uprisings since the Peasants Revolt in 1381, the Pilgrimage of Grace. It was not the actual beheading of Anne that caused the protests but the assumption that, with her death, Henry's split with Rome was now no longer necessary and could be reversed. Vast crowds assembled, above all in the Catholic strongholds of the north, demanding the restoration of papal authority. Faced with popular protest on this scale, Henry had no option but to give way. Once the immediate threat was over, however, he exacted a fearsome revenge, instructing the Duke of Norfolk that "you shall cause such dreadful execution to be done upon a good number of every town village and hamlet that have offended as they may be a fearful spectacle to all others hereafter that would practise any like matter". His deception – and cruelty – was entirely in character.

The title page of the Great Bible (**right**), *which was published, in English, in 1539 under the auspices of Thomas Cromwell. Henry distributes the new bible to Cranmer (to the king's right) and Cromwell (to his left) who in turn hand copies to clergy and laity alike.*

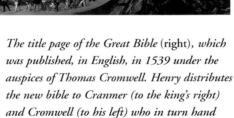

The Act of Union with Wales

In 1536, simply by asserting it as fact – His Highness therefore… established that this said country… of Wales… shall be… incorporated, united and annexed to and with this realm of England… – Henry presided over the absorption of Wales into what became the renamed Kingdom of England and Wales. A series of reforms were enacted, of which the most important was the banning of the Welsh language for all official business and the reorganization of Wales into 13 counties, five of them new. All the counties had the right to be represented by Members of Parliament at the English Parliament in Westminster. At the same time, the border between England and Wales was precisely fixed for the first time and the privileges of the Marcher lords, introduced by William the Conqueror, were ended. Though inevitably the cause of resentment among many Welsh, the Act, at any rate in English terms, achieved exactly what it was intended to: the first step in the creation of an English "empire" in Britain.

EDWARD VI 1547–53

BORN: October 12 1537
ACCEDED: January 28
1547; crowned
Westminster Abbey,
February 20 1547

Duke of Cornwall, King
of England
and Ireland

EDWARD VI'S SIX-YEAR REIGN WAS DOMINATED BY RELIGIOUS CONTROVERSY. HENRY VIII'S BREAK FROM ROME HAD PRESERVED THE FORMS OF CATHOLIC WORSHIP INTACT. UNDER EDWARD, HOWEVER, CHILD THOUGH HE WAS, AN IMPLACABLE PROTESTANTISM WAS EMBRACED. COMBINED WITH ECONOMIC DISLOCATION AND CONTINUING CONFLICT WITH SCOTLAND AND FRANCE, THE RESULTS WERE RARELY LESS THAN TRAUMATIC.

THE PERILS OF A MINORITY WERE EPITOMIZED by Edward VI's reign. However carefully prepared for kingship, including a demanding education that saw him learning Latin and Greek at five, and however specific Henry VIII's provisions for a Council of Regents to prevent power falling into the hands of an individual behind the throne, within weeks of Henry VIII's death, Edward's uncle,

the Earl of Hertford, had effectively seized power. Hertford disbanded the Council of Regents, declared himself Lord Protector and persuaded the young king to make him duke of Somerset.

Precocious or not, the nine-year-old Edward immediately found himself a tool in Somerset's hands. The Protector's goals were twofold: the continuation of Henry VIII's ruinously expensive

Child or not, Edward VI's embrace of Protestantism, though clearly manipulated by Somerset, Cranmer and Warwick, was quite genuine. At 10, he called the Pope "the true son of the Devil, an anti-Christ and an abominable tyrant". His enthusiasm thereafter for the imposition of Protestantism never wavered. Fanaticism of this order in a child was chilling. This portrait (above left) was painted shortly after he became king.

Lady Jane Grey

Though endorsed by Edward VI shortly before his death – indeed, possibly originated by the king – the attempt to proclaim the 15-year-old Lady Jane Grey his legitimate heir was so transparent a ruse that it is hard to see how Edward or Northumberland ever imagined it could work. As Henry VIII's great niece, her claim to the throne was genuine if distant. Nonetheless, both Edward's sisters, Mary and Elizabeth, had clear priority as had been spelled out in Henry VIII's will. Moreover, by marrying his son to her a matter of weeks earlier, Somerset's own motives were almost laughably obvious.

On July 10, three days after Edward's death, Lady Jane Grey was declared queen by the Council. On July 19, she was deposed. In the meantime, support had rapidly grown for Mary, effectively exiled in Hertfordshire. Within days, an army up to 15,000 strong had rallied to her. In the circumstances, there was no hope either for Lady Jane Grey or for her father-in-law, Northumberland, who was almost immediately executed. Lady Jane Grey and her husband were sent to the Tower where, in February 1554, they, too, were executed.

1547	1548	1549
Earl of Hertford abolishes Council of Regents, declares himself Lord Protector and is made Duke of Somerset. Scots defeated at Battle of Pinkie (September), pushing them closer to French. Henry VIII's Act of Six Articles repealed	*Henri II declares war against England, sending 6,000 troops to Scotland and laying siege to Boulogne*	*Act of Uniformity outlaws all Catholic practices; Cranmer's English-language Book of Common Prayer published. Uprising in West Country and East Anglia (Kett's Rebellion). Somerset overthrown*

Tudor propaganda such as this allegory of Edward VI's succession (left), *painted by an unknown artist two years after he became king, leaves little room for doubt as to the legitimacy not just of Edward's succession but of his victory over a corrupt papacy. Edward's own right to rule is confirmed by Henry VIII's deathbed gesture. The new king sits on his throne under the royal arms. The pope is hunched at his feet, crushed by the English text in the bible over his neck: "The word of the Lord endureth for ever". Two monks are sent from the room next to the legend: "feigned holiness". To Edward's left is Somerset, the Lord Protector; to Somerset's left, the Royal Council, Cranmer (in white) among them.*

wars against France and Scotland, chiefly with the aim of implementing the Treaty of Greenwich, under which Edward was to marry Mary, Queen of Scots; and the establishment of an aggressively Protestant church. If the former was pursued with a characteristic combination of vacillation and inefficiency on Somerset's part, the later, relentlessly directed by the Archbishop of Canterbury, Thomas Cranmer, was implemented much more single-mindedly.

Victory over the Scots at the Battle of Pinkie in 1547 succeeded only in driving the Scots closer to France, despite the active Protestant minority within Scotland. By the summer of the following year, the French king had sent 6,000 troops to Scotland, declared war on England and laid siege to Boulogne. Agreement between the Scots and French the same year that Mary should marry the heir to the French throne effectively signalled the collapse of Somerset's foreign policy.

At the same time, Cranmer's reforms were taking shape. As early as July 1547 traditional Catholic forms of worship had been banned. Anything that suggested idolatry – stained glass windows, wall paintings, sculptures, even bell ringing – was outlawed. The measures were given legal force in 1549 with the Act of Uniformity, itself reinforced by the publication of Cranmer's *Book of Common Prayer*. Its use was compulsory.

Combined with a rapidly deteriorating economy, exacerbated by the expense of Somerset's ineffectual military campaigns, the net result was widespread unrest. Uprisings in the Catholic West Country in the summer of 1549 in protest against the *Book of Common Prayer*, which saw Exeter besieged, were paralleled by an even more serious rebellion in East Anglia against land enclosures.

In the resulting turmoil, Somerset, predictably, was overthrown. By 1550, the prime instigator of the coup, the earl of Warwick, had declared himself "Lord President of the Council". The following year he had himself created duke of Northumberland.

Northumberland, no less unprincipled than Somerset had been but considerably more pragmatic, successfully extricated England from its French and Scottish entanglements. He also turned his attention to the

The Lady Mary, my sister, came to me at Westminster where after salutations she was called of my Council into a chamber where it was declared how long I had suffered her [Catholic] mass. She answered that her soul was God's and her face she would not change nor would she dissemble with contrary doings.

Edward VI confronting his sister Mary's refusal to abandon Catholicism, 1549

succession. By 1552, it was clear that Edward, now 14, was dying. With no prospect of his producing an heir and with his legitimate successor, his sister Mary, as avowedly Catholic as Edward was Protestant, it became a matter of real urgency to ensure a Protestant succession. The cynical solution was the nomination of Edward's cousin, Lady Jane Grey, as heir (see box). Northumberland meanwhile took the precaution of marrying his son, Guildford Dudley, to her.

With Edward's death, Lady Jane Grey, like her father, was swept away on a tide of enthusiasm for Mary. It was premature. Her reversal of Edward's religious reforms plunged England into chaos.

1550	1551	1552	1553
Warwick made Lord President of the Council	*Warwick created duke of Northumberland*	*Somerset executed*	*Second edition of Book of Common Prayer published. Forty-two Articles of Religion establish theological principles of Protestant Church of England. Edward names Lady Jane Grey his heir*

BORN: February 18 1516
ACCEDED: July 19 1553;
crowned Westminster
Abbey, October 1 1553
❦ ❦ ❦
*Queen Consort of Spain
January 16 1556 to
November 17 1558,
Queen of England
and Ireland*

MARY I 1553–58

MARY NOT ONLY REVERSED EDWARD VI'S PROTESTANT REFORMS, IN RESTORING PAPAL SUPREMACY SHE REVERSED HER FATHER'S, TOO. FOR MARY, DOCTRINAL PURITY AND POLITICAL EXPEDIENCY HAD BECOME THE SAME. IN SUBSEQUENTLY MARRYING PHILIP II OF SPAIN, SHE CAME CLOSE TO MAKING ENGLAND A PAWN OF CATHOLIC SPAIN. ONLY HER EARLY DEATH SAVED ENGLAND FROM FURTHER RELIGIOUS DIVISION.

I N 1533, MARY, THE ONLY SURVIVING CHILD OF Henry VIII's first wife, Catherine of Aragon, was declared a bastard by Act of Parliament. Princess Mary became plain "The Lady Mary". Henry's divorce from Catherine of Aragon and marriage to Anne Boleyn necessitated wiping the slate clean in every sense. Much as would later happen to Elizabeth after her mother, Anne Boleyn, was executed, Mary became a non-person.

Not surprisingly, though subsequently reconciled with Henry at the prompting of his last wife, Catherine Parr – and, like Elizabeth, restored to her place in the succession – the memory of her mother's fate at Henry's hands remained the dominant motif of her life, confirming the ardent Catholicism under which she had been brought up. Even at the height of her brother, Edward VI's, imposition of militant Protestantism, Mary obstinately refused to tone down her

Any child of Henry VIII's might justifiably feel alienated. In Mary's case, not just excluded from the succession at 14 but legally proclaimed illegitimate, the result was predictable. With her mother shunned by the king and her own status threatened, it is hardly to be wondered at that she grew up suspicious and alarmed. Yet contemporaries consistently described an intelligent, dutiful child, always anxious to please. This portrait (far left) shows Mary at 13.

Catholic observance. She was her father's daughter in more ways than one.

Whatever Mary's clear espousal of the old religion in a country ever more obviously embracing Protestantism, her accession was nonetheless generally welcomed – and not just by those who had remained true to the Catholic church. It was widely assumed that Mary would reinstate Catholic forms of worship while confirming the primacy of the Church of England – in other words, that she would broadly restore the status quo under Henry VIII.

From the outset, Mary disabused them. Almost immediately it became clear that her goal was the full restoration of Catholic supremacy. A series of parliamentary measures were enacted repealing Edward's Protestant legislation. At the same time, Mary announced her intention to marry Philip, son of

> *When they send me orders forbidding me the Mass, I shall expect to suffer as I once suffered during my father's lifetime … I am like a little ignorant girl and I care neither for my goods nor for the World but only for God's service and my conscience.*
>
> *Princess Mary, 1549*

Foxe's Book of Martyrs

*T*he publication in 1563 of John Foxe's Acts and Monuments, *more generally known as* The Book of Martyrs, *confirmed Mary's reputation as a cruel, Catholic fanatic. Above all, it was the book's evocative and explicit woodcuts of Marian Protestant martyrs at the stake that damned her in the by now firmly Protestant national imagination. The book was clearly propaganda. Foxe double-counted some of the victims. He made no mention of the burnings under Henry VIII. Yet its impact was immense, above all that of the 1589 edition, published the year after the Spanish Armada.*

The illustration shows the deaths in February 1556 of the Bishop of London, Nicholas Ridley, and the Bishop of Worcester, Hugh Latimer. "Be of good comfort, Master Ridley, and play the man," Latimer is reputed to have said. "We shall this day light such a candle by God's grace in England as I trust shall never be put out." Watching the scene on the right is the imprisoned Thomas Cranmer, chief architect of Edward VI's Protestant reforms and himself burned five months later.

1533	1544	1553	1554
Mary declared illegitimate after marriage of Henry VIII and Catherine of Aragon declared void	*Mary partly reconciled with Henry VIII after intervention of his sixth wife, Catherine Parr*	*(Aug.) Triumphal entry of Mary to London as queen at head of army 15,000 strong; coronation of Mary (Oct.) makes her first regnant queen of England since Matilda in the 12th century*	*(Jan.) Thomas Wyatt's uprising in protest at Mary's planned marriage to Philip of Spain put down. (Feb.) execution of Lady Jane Grey. England officially reunited with church of Rome and return of Reginald Pole as papal legate (Nov.)*

Charles V of Spain. At 38, and with the succession paramount, the question of Mary's marriage necessarily loomed large. But for Mary to insist on marriage to the son of the most powerful and militantly Catholic ruler in Europe disturbed all but her most ardent supporters. That he was 11 years her junior was scarcely an issue.

Though a nervous compromise was reached whereby Philip would become king consort only – and be excluded from the succession if no heir was produced – resistance to the union was widespread. In January 1554, there was an armed uprising, led by Thomas Wyatt, against London. Though easily suppressed, it was symptomatic of the wider unease.

Mary subsequently not only aligned England with Spain in a disastrous war against France in which Calais, England's last foothold in France – and last link with its Norman, Angevin and Plantagenet kings – was lost, she also engineered the return of Reginald Pole, the papal legate, who in 1556 was appointed Archbishop of Canterbury.

It was under Pole's urging that in February 1555 Mary began what subsequently confirmed her status as the demonized enemy of Protestant England, "Bloody" Mary herself: the burning at the stake of Protestant martyrs. In fact, with heretics being done to death across Europe, there was little unusual in her actions. Nonetheless, the 287 Protestants executed on Mary's orders alarmed even Catholic opinion, fearful at the reaction it would provoke.

In the event, all came to nothing – except in later Protestant propaganda. Mary, increasingly ill, ever more convinced of her Catholic destiny, died childless and embittered only five years after coming to the throne. Her husband had all but abandoned her, her country was on the brink of full acceptance of the heretic Protestant religion. Her failure was painfully total.

When Mary, to the horror of her advisors, decided to marry Philip of Spain (left), the Spanish approached the projected match with a cynical mixture of pragmatism and contempt. A Spanish witness to the wedding wrote: "If she dressed in our fashions, she would not look so old and flabby. It will take a great God to drink this cup." For his part, Philip spent less than a year with his bride, leaving as soon as he decently could for the Netherlands and his mistresses. The tragedy for Mary, who just a year earlier had written to the Spanish ambassador saying that "[I] have never felt that which is called love, nor harboured thoughts of voluptuousness", is that she seems genuinely to have loved Philip. Two false pregnancies only confirmed her sense of loss.

Neither Edward VI's nor Mary's brief reigns saw the kind of long-lasting change that so marked their father's kingship, despite a series of popular rebellions, almost all with a religious component (map left). Importantly, the continuing and draining conflicts with Scotland, that Henry VIII had so energetically pursued were wound up after the execution of the duke of Somerset in 1552. In 1558, the last English possession in France was permanently lost.

EDWARD VI AND MARY I

→	Salisbury's campaign, 1547
///	English-occupied from 1547
→	French attack, 1548
▮	Rebellions, with details
→	Wyatt's campaign, 1554
	Lost under Peace of Boulogne, 1550
⚑	Last English strongholds in Scotland, evacuated under Peace of Boulogne
	Lost, 1558

Marriage of Mary and Philip | *Burnings of Protestants begun* | *Reginald Pole made Archbishop of Canterbury* | *Calais lost to France*

ELIZABETH I 1558–1603

BORN: September 7 1533
ACCEDED: November 17
1558; crowned
Westminster Abbey
January 15 1559

*Queen of England
and Ireland*

*Very unusually for the
period, Elizabeth (above)
was fearsomely well
educated. It showed later
when, as queen, she wrote
all her own speeches, often
producing several drafts in
her exceptionally elegant
handwriting. This portrait
was painted at the request
of her brother Edward VI
when she was 13. She
wrote to him: "For the
face I might well blush to
offer, but for the mind I
shall never be ashamed to
present".*

ELIZABETH I'S REPUTATION BELIES THE UNCERTAINTIES OF HER EARLIER YEARS ON THE THRONE. YET ONCE ESTABLISHED SHE PRESIDED OVER AN INCREASINGLY SELF-CONFIDENT NATION WHOSE SENSE OF AN INEVITABLE PROTESTANT DESTINY BECAME EVER CLEARER. DESPITE HER FAILURE TO MARRY AND ENSURE HER SUCCESSION, SHE CAME TO PERSONIFY HER KINGDOM AS NO MONARCH BEFORE OR SINCE.

WHATEVER THE OUTBURST OF PATRIOTIC fervour that greeted the accession of the 25-year-old Elizabeth in 1558, she was confronted with an immediate political problem. The violent see-sawing between her brother, Edward VI's Protestantism, and her sister, Mary's, equally aggressive Catholicism, had polarized England. If there was a general acceptance that England's destiny was now broadly Protestant, encapsulating this in Parliamentary legislation that would not permanently alienate both extremes called for an unusual degree of tact.

This Elizabeth possessed in abundance. The hallmark of her reign, however occasionally infuriating she could be, was an ability to combine regal authority with an almost infinite capacity to prevaricate, all the while appearing wholly in sympathy with her subjects. That she also enjoyed the support of a number of exceptionally able ministers, William Cecil and Francis Walsingham in the early and middle parts of her reign, Robert Cecil, William's son, at the end of it, underlined a shrewd judgement backed by an intelligent willingness to delegate.

Elizabeth's childhood encapsulated the perils of Reformation England. At less than three, her mother, Anne Boleyn, was beheaded and Elizabeth declared a bastard by Act of Parliament, removing her from the succession. Until her reconciliation with her father, engineered by Catherine Parr in 1544, she was brought up an exile from the court. Her education, however, was exemplary. By her teens, she was fluent in French, Italian, Latin and Greek. "Her mind", wrote her tutor, Roger Ascham, "has no womanly weakness… her memory long keeps what it quickly picks up."

Even in the reign of her younger brother, Edward VI, otherwise almost the only secure period of her youth, she was falsely suspected by the Duke of Somerset, the Lord Protector, of a plot to overthrow him. In the reign of her sister, Mary, she was not only re-declared a bastard, in 1554 she was sent to the Tower for two months on suspicion of involvement in Thomas Wyatt's uprising. Only on Mary's deathbed was Elizabeth reluctantly acknowledged heir by her sister.

Let Tyrants fear; I … have placed my chiefest strength and safeguard in the loyal hearts and goodwill of my subjects. … I know I have the body of a weak and feeble woman, but I have the heart and stomach of a King and a King of England too and think it foul scorn that Parma or Spain or any Prince of Europe should dare to invade the borders of my realm … I myself will be your General, Judge and Rewarder of every one of your virtues in the field. I know already for your forwardness you have deserved rewards and crowns; and we do assure you, on the word of a Prince, they shall be duly paid to you.

Elizabeth I, Tilbury, August 9 1588

Virgin queen or not, there were many who were convinced that Elizabeth and Robert Dudley, the Earl of Leicester, must have been lovers. Elizabeth was to have a number of similar relationships later in her reign, including with Robert Devereux, the Earl of Essex, and the Duke of Alençon (who the queen called "frog"). But none approached that with Leicester for intensity or duration. He was never a serious candidate as king, however. It was widely thought the death of his wife in 1560 after falling down stairs was more than coincidence. Here (left) the queen and Leicester are shown at Kenilworth.

1536	1544	1553	1554	1558
Elizabeth declared illegitimate and removed from succession after execution of Anne Boleyn	*Elizabeth reinstated as royal heir and restored to Henry VIII's court*	*Re-declared illegitimate on succession of Mary*	*Sent to Tower on suspicion of involvement in Thomas Wyatt's uprising against Mary*	*Accession of Elizabeth*

Elizabeth I's foreign policy was conceived in almost entirely defensive terms (map right). Whatever the threats posed by France, Scotland and militantly Catholic Spain, she consistently resisted entangling English forces in wider Continental conflicts, though she was happy to allow privateers such as Drake and Frobisher to mount raids of their own. The defeat of the Armada in 1588 was a triumphant vindication of her stance.

Elizabeth I 1558–1603

- Rebellion
- Northern rebellion; campaign and retreat, 1569
- Subject to English raids, 1570

IRELAND
- "Planted" under Elizabeth, with date
- Principal areas from where English settlers moved to Ireland
- Limit of the Pale, 1596
- O'Neill's campaign, 1601
- Essex's campaign, 1588

- Other English campaigns
- Route of the Armada
- Other Spanish campaign, with date
- "Cautionary towns" English held, from 1585
- Other English occupied towns in the continent, with dates
- Spanish Habsburg possessions
- Approximate extent of English activities in the Netherlands from 1586
- Frontiers, 1600
- Frontier of the Holy Roman Empire, 1600

The Elizabethan period saw the beginnings of a golden age of English seafaring. Elizabethan England could scarcely claim yet to rule the waves, but the seeds of later British maritime domination were being sown. For Elizabeth herself, the advantages were less the country's burgeoning naval strength than the semi-private raiding ventures, mostly directed against Spain, carried out by the likes of Drake (below), Frobisher and Hawkins, pirates in all but name. Their ventures cost the country nothing but guaranteed it a share of the profits.

**Map labels:**
SCOTLAND
North Sea
Lough Swilly 1567
Earl of Tyrone (O'Neill), 1595–1603
1570
1591
Westmoreland/ Catholic earls, 1569
BRANCEPETH DURHAM RICHMOND
LANCASHIRE RIPON SELBY
IRELAND
DUBLIN
CHESHIRE
In revolt against Spanish rule from 1567
NETHERLANDS
AMSTERDAM
Zutphen 1586
LIMERICK
WALES
ENGLAND
BRILL
James Fitzmaurice/ Munster Confederacy, 1569–73 Munster rising, 1579–83
1586
WATERFORD
Essex, 1601
LONDON
FLUSHING RAMMEKENS
Ostend 1601
Nieuport 1600
Gravelines 1588
1586 KINSALE
SOMERSET
DORSET
CALAIS
1601
Frobisher, 1593
John Norrey, 1591
English Channel
DIEPPE 1591–2
LE HAVRE 1562–3
Willoughby, 1590
PARIS
Ivry 1590
Drake/Essex, 1589
Drake, 1587
1588
PAIMPOL
BREST
CROZON
1593
Craon 1592
FRANCE
Religious wars, 1562–98
Bay of Biscay
BORDEAUX
CORUNNA
VIGO
PORTUGAL
SPAIN
PENICHE
John Norrey, 1589
LISBON
Drake, 1587
Essex, 1596
CADIZ

Acts of Supremacy and Uniformity re-instate Protestantism; Elizabeth declared Supreme Governor (not Head) of Church of England	Temporary peace with Scotland (Treaty of Berwick) and France (Treaty of Edinburgh). Irish Act of Uniformity attempts to impose religious settlement on Ireland, in rebellion to 1573	Mary, Queen of Scots, returns to Scotland	Armed assistance unsuccessfully given to French Huguenots	Renewed peace with France (Treaty of Cateau-Cambrésis). Catholic uprising in north of England under earls of Westmoreland and Northumberland	Elizabeth excommunicated by Pope Pius V

continued on next page

continued from previous page

ELIZABETH I, ENGLAND AND THE WORLD

English possessions, 1558

Area of activities of Drake and Hawkins in Americas, 1562–85

Routes of English voyages, with date

→ Jenkinson

→ Frobisher

→ Drake

→ Fitch

→ Gilbert

→ Davis

→ Cavendish

→ Lancaster

→ Raleigh

Other coloured areas represent the approximate extent of English trading companies established in the Elizabethan era, with name and date of establishment

Religious division dominated Elizabeth's reign. It took the form not just of continuing conflict between the still substantial Catholic population in England and the Protestant majority but, more dangerously, coloured almost every aspect of the queen's foreign policy. It also had an immediate impact on the question that was being asked even before her accession: who would she marry?

It was taken for granted, by Elizabeth as much as by her Council, her Parliament, indeed by her country at large, that she would marry as soon as possible in order to secure the succession. For almost 20 years after her accession, an imposing array of possible suitors was put forward, beginning with her sister's husband, Philip II. All were rejected. A foreign marriage, however otherwise apparently suitable, risked dragging England into precisely the kind of damaging foreign entanglements Elizabeth spent most of her reign studiously avoiding; furthermore, whether Protestant or Catholic, a foreign king would alienate the substantial proportion of her subjects professing the other religion.

Yet that Elizabeth rejected domestic candidates, despite a series of credible suitors as well as a number of openly flirtatious dalliances, above all with Robert Dudley, the Earl of Leicester, argues a rather different motivation. In her own mind at least, she increasingly seems to have come to see herself as

married already – to her realm. By the middle years of her reign, the cult of the Virgin Queen had acquired an almost semi-mystical status.

Yet the longer the queen remained unmarried, the greater the risk to the delicately contrived Protestant edifice Cecil was creating on his sovereign's behalf. With the Catholic Mary, Queen of Scots, closest to the throne after Elizabeth, there was a real prospect of a return to the religious turmoil of Edward VI's and Mary's reigns and which Elizabeth's and Cecil's religious settlement of 1559, which officially re-embraced Protestantism while in practice allowing Catholics to retain their faith in private, had been expressly designed to prevent.

As it was, Elizabeth's England was seriously threatened from within on a number of occasions, most seriously in 1569, when an armed Catholic uprising, led by the earls of Westmoreland and Northumberland, swept across northern England. It was eventually savagely repressed. Ireland, too, where Protestantism was shallowly rooted at best, was gripped by Catholic uprisings in 1569–73, in 1579–83 and in 1595–98.

Nonetheless, it was from abroad that the most sustained threats came. At any rate until the abdication of Mary, Queen of Scots in 1567, the prospect of simultaneous war with France and Scotland was never far away. In 1560, Elizabeth had been prevailed

1571	1572	1579–83	1580	1584	1585
Catholic Ridolfi plot leads to execution of duke of Norfolk (1572)	Francis Drake begins raids against Spanish settlements in Americas	Further religious uprisings in Ireland	Return of Francis Drake after first English circumnavigation of globe	Attempted establishment of English colony at Roanoake in Virginia by Walter Raleigh	Armed support for Netherlands against Spain

Elizabethan England may never have been in the first rank of European-based exploration, still largely dominated by Spain, but its maritime and trade links in many parts of the globe were, if tentatively, being extended (map left), a process crucially boosted by Drake's circumnavigation of the globe in 1577–80. Colonization of the New World was less successful. Whatever the declamatory promise of England's New World colony of Virginia, the first settlement there, at Roanoake, was a total failure.

on to send a small force to Scotland in support of the Presbyterians. It was followed two years later by a botched invasion of France in support of the Huguenots. But if by 1569 the combined Franco-Scottish threat had mostly disappeared, it was followed by a much more serious one from Spain.

Religion inevitably formed the principal background to the Anglo-Spanish conflict, not least after Elizabeth's excommunication by Pius V made it a Catholic duty to bring about her overthrow. In riposte, English mariners such as Francis Drake considered themselves at liberty to raid Spanish settlements in the Americas. When a small force was reluctantly sent by Elizabeth to the Netherlands in 1585 and even more so two years later when Drake impudently raided Cadiz, Philip II's plans for revenge coalesced. In the summer of 1588, he launched his great Armada.

Its defeat, in part at the hands of superior English seamanship, in part at the providentially Protestant wind that sprang up, first pinning the Spanish fleet against the Flemish coast, then dispersing it in a gale-wracked epic, sealed Elizabeth's reputation. "Our Gracious Majesty … so inflamed the hearts of her good subjects as I think the weakest person amongst them is able to match the proudest Spaniard that dare land in England," wrote the Earl of Leicester immediately after the Armada.

In fact, she needed all the support she could muster. The final years of her reign, far from being a glorious apotheosis, were among the most difficult. Economic hardship, poor harvests and renewed threats from Spain combined to create an air approaching crisis. Even the queen herself, visibly ageing though still publicly projecting an official image of eternal youth (and virginity), began to attract criticism.

In the event, it was as much her ability to appeal directly to her subjects as her political acumen that saw her through the crisis. In 1601, two years before she died, she memorably asserted to the House of Commons that: "… there is no prince that loves his subjects better, or whose love can countervail our love. There is no jewel, be it never so rich a price, which I set before your jewel: I mean your love". For Englishmen, their destiny – and their loyalty – had never seemed more clear.

Gloriana: the Cult of Elizabeth

From about 1570, Elizabeth's curious hold on her people began to assume almost the status of a cult. She became venerated as no other English ruler has been. It was a role the queen was never less than keen to encourage, one that she played up to with considerable intelligence. Nonetheless, the effect she had on even the most sober could be remarkable. Sir Christopher Hatton, an otherwise undistinguished member of parliament, fell so much in love with his queen he came close to losing his wits. "… Passion overcometh me. I can write no more. Love me for I love you … Ten thousand farewells", he wrote to her.

In similar style, what should have been the queen's greatest betrayal of her people – her failure to marry and provide a secure Protestant succession – was elevated into the cult of the all-wise Virgin Queen in which Elizabeth, in a variety of guises, became the personification of her country. Her accession day, November 17, became a national holiday, greater than all of the Catholic feast days it replaced. Walter Raleigh named his New World colony, Virginia, after the Queen. Edmund Spenser dedicated The Faerie Queen to Elizabeth: "I mean glory in my general intention, but in my particular I conceive the most excellent and glorious person of our sovereign the Queen, and her kingdom in Fairy land", he wrote. Even in death, Elizabeth dazzled her subjects, passing away "as the most resplendent sun setteth at last in a western cloud".

The Armada

By any measure, the Spanish Armada, launched against England by Philip II in May 1588, was the single greatest threat Elizabeth faced, the culmination of years of tension between England and its Catholic enemies. Its purpose was not the invasion of England itself but to ferry Spanish troops from the Netherlands to England where, it was hoped, they would be joined by an uprising of English Catholics.

The Spanish fleet, 130 strong, was defeated less by superior English naval tactics and technology than by the imperatives of geography. The smaller, faster-firing English ships certainly had an edge over the lumbering Spanish galleons, but, as the Spanish knew, they were taking a huge risk. When they finally anchored off Calais, they were immediately vulnerable to English fire ships. As the wind increased from the west, they then had no choice but to head north, hoping to out-sail their pursuers on a huge circuit around Scotland and out into the Atlantic before turning south again for Spain. Around 15,000 Spaniards died against only 100 Englishmen in the abortive invasion. It was indeed a deliverance.

1587	1588	1595	1596	1598	1601
Execution of Mary, Queen of Scots. Cadiz raided by Drake	Attempted Spanish invasion of England – the Armada – thwarted	Irish revolt led by Hugh O'Neill	Further attempted Spanish invasion (and 1597)	English force in Ireland massacred by O'Neill	Execution of earl of Essex after failure of mission to Ireland and attempted coup against Elizabeth

England, Wales, Scotland and Ireland: The Stuarts 1603–1714

James I 1603–25

Charles I 1625–49

Charles II 1660–85

James II 1685–8

William III 1689–1702
(jointly with Mary II 1689–94)

Anne 1702–14

The accession of James VI of Scotland to the throne of England in 1603 represented an unlikely triumph for the principles of hereditary monarchy. the Tudors' apparently triumphant kingship petered out, passing not just to a junior branch of the Tudor family but to the kings of England's most consistent enemy. Even if in reverse and more by accident than design, the dynastic hopes of Edward I as much as of Henry VIII had been brought to fruition. England and Scotland were ruled by a single king.

However, this did not mean the two kingdoms had been united. Indeed, a brief spell under the Commonwealth aside, they would remain quarrelsomely separate legal entities for over 100 years. A common king was not the same as a common kingdom. Vested interests on both sides of the border ensured that dynastic accident did not translate automatically into political union.

Scarcely less of a puzzlement to James was that his own ideal of kingship, precisely worked out and logical though it was to him, had to confront another equally inescapable reality: that of parliamentary prerogative. True, such a concept would have been recognized by almost no one at the start of his reign. Parliament in the early 17th century, whatever its importance in approving taxes, remained almost as much a tool of royal government as it had in the 13th century. But quite early on in his reign, parliament was asserting itself in unprecedented ways. It was a development that continued decisively with the accession of his son, Charles I, in 1625.

Charles I, rigid, dutiful and well meaning, was wholly convinced of his absolute right to govern. Kingship was a sacred duty he took quite literally. It was as clear to Charles as it was to his counterparts elsewhere in Europe that a powerful monarch was essential to the well-being of any realm. The radical choice in early to mid-17th-century Europe called for more, not less royal supremacy. Only this way could complex, expanding states be efficiently governed.

If Charles I had been the King of France, he might well have been proved right. As King of England and Scotland, however, he grossly miscalculated. By the mid-1630s, a new idea was taking shape in England, one that had no parallel elsewhere in Europe. In essence, it held that Parliament as the representative of the people, narrowly defined though they were, enjoyed an authority superior to the king's. Taken to its extreme, it might even mean that Parliament had the right to overthrow a king who disregarded what were increasingly coming to be seen as the ancient, time-honoured "liberties" of the English.

That Parliament was able to assert this new-found authority over Charles I was more the result of Charles's obtuseness, which led him to an almost permanent political tactlessness, than a coherent parliamentary effort to oust the king. Right up to the outbreak of the Civil War in 1642, there was a chance for Charles to come to terms with Parliament. But in insisting not just on his own royal authority but pushing through religious reforms that raised the spectre of a reversion to Catholicism, Charles I cack-handedly succeeded in crystallizing the opposition to him. There may have been nothing inevitable, politically as much as militarily, about his eventual fall, but Charles's refusal to compromise finally proved fatal in every sense.

Yet whatever the more radical ideas circulating about parliamentary supremacy, the execution of the king was still far from a straightforward matter of parliamentary authority overriding that of the monarch. Even after Charles's defeat, a substantial majority in parliament had no thought of executing the king – though what precisely should replace him was far from clear. Rather, it was a hard-core of largely Puritan MPs who engineered the king's trial and execution. In effect, Charles's tyranny was being replaced by a new, parliamentary brand.

And in fact, the 10 years of the Commonwealth ended precisely because the absence of a monarch produced a power vacuum that no amount of immature parliamentary authority could fill. Nor, whatever his own formidable if contradictory talents, could even as imposing a personality as Oliver Cromwell come up with a lasting political settlement. By 1660, support for a restoration of the monarchy had become overwhelming. The turmoil and bitterness of the Civil War had apparently been for nothing. England was back where it started.

Yet in the event, the restoration of the worldly, intelligent Charles II, ready to agree to the kind of compromises that his father had resisted, restored a kind of natural balance to his kingdoms, one his own personal charm went far to ensure. That this was as much a matter of personality as of the institution of monarchy itself was amply demonstrated by the succession of his brother James II, in 1685. Within three years, by insisting not just on his own supreme authority but in attempting to engineer a Catholic restoration, James II, as high-handed as he was obtuse, inadvertently completed the revolution that had been begun in the reign of Charles I. His ignominious overthrow in December 1688 signalled a final, sudden triumph of parliament over royal authority. It was the single most decisive moment in English kingship since Alfred had claimed to rule over all the *Angelcynn*, "the English folk", in the 9th century.

In his place, a dependably Protestant ruler, William of Orange, husband of James II's daughter Mary, was invited in by a coalition of leading magnates acting under the authority of parliamentary sanction. This was a move that went far beyond previous attempts to assert parliamentary authority. The reasoning was clear-cut and logical. As the husband of a Stuart, William upheld the essential principles underpinning the legitimacy of the monarchy. As a Protestant champion, he was similarly guaranteed to uphold England's fundamental destiny, as it seemed to the prime movers in the plot to give the throne to him. Nothing, however, changed the fact that for the first time the succession had become the gift not of God but of Parliament.

JAMES I 1603–25

JAMES I WAS AMONG THE MOST PARADOXICAL OF KINGS. CONVINCED OF HIS ABSOLUTE RIGHT TO RULE, HE WAS FORCED INTO ACCOMMODATIONS WITH PARLIAMENT THAT SAW THE MAJORITY OF HIS INITIATIVES THWARTED. THE MOST INTELLECTUAL OF ENGLAND'S KINGS, HE WAS ALSO AMONG ITS MOST DISSOLUTE. YET HIS REIGN WAS GENERALLY STABLE, HIS INTENTIONS NEARLY ALWAYS HONOURABLE.

KING JAMES VI OF SCOTLAND, JAMES I OF ENGLAND AND IRELAND

BORN: June 19 1566
ACCEDED IN SCOTLAND: July 24 1567; crowned July 29 1567, Stirling
ACCEDED IN ENGLAND AND IRELAND: March 24 1603; crowned July 25 1603, Westminster Abbey

Duke of Rothesay, Duke of Albany, Earl of Ross and Baron Ardmannoch, King of Scotland, England and Ireland

James I's combination of high intelligence, learning, vanity and occasional sloth make him the most unusual of England's kings. His published works, above all The True Law of Free Monarchies *(1598) and* Basilikon Doron *("The Prince's Gift", 1599), make him the only English king with claims to literary stature. Similarly, his attempts to unite England and Scotland were far-sighted, reflecting his "wish above all things … to leave one worship to God: one kingdom, entirely governed: one uniformity of laws". This portrait (above), by Nicholas Hilliard, was painted just after he came to the English throne in 1603.*

WHEN JAMES STUART BECAME KING OF England in 1603, as James VI he had already been king of Scotland for 36 years. Only in the last ten of them had he been able to impose himself on his kingdom. His mother, Mary, Queen of Scots, was forced off her throne when James was only one, shortly after the murder of his father, Lord Darnley. His 16-year minority, which saw the violent deaths of all four Scottish regents against a background of political infighting and religious controversy, was hardly less unstable. In addition, after the execution of Mary in 1587, James's subsequent reign was dogged by uncertainty as to whether he would, as he fervently hoped, succeed the childless Queen Elizabeth in England. Even as Elizabeth was dying in the spring of 1603, he could not be sure of the succession.

As James I of England and Ireland, his prospects were transformed. His new kingdom was substantially richer, his own powers, especially over the church, more extensive. Furthermore, James himself had not just had wide experience of the uncertainties of 16th- and 17th-century monarchy; he was a man of impressive learning with a natural grasp of the imperatives of political moderation, above all in the sensitive matter of religion.

Set against this were English suspicions of a Scottish King of England, and Scottish suspicions that James would abandon his native land for England. In addition, there was the inescapable matter of James's personal oddities. Bulging eyes, a tendency to drool, extravagance and an obvious homosexuality allied to indolence and drunkenness hardly suggested the dignified absolute monarch James professed to be. His

When God hath conjoined then, let no man separate. I am the Husband, and all the whole Isle is my lawful Wife; I am the Head, and it is my Body; I am the Shepherd, and it is my flock: I hope therefore no man will be so unreasonable as to think that I that am a Christian King under the Gospel, should be a Polygamist and husband to two wives; that I being the Head, should have a divided and monstrous Body; or that being the Shepherd to so fair a flock should have my flock parted in two.

James I addressing Parliament on the proposed union of England and Scotland, 1604

James's "sweete boyes"

James I's homosexuality manifested itself in a number of infatuations with younger men. In the early part of his English reign, his favourite was a Scot, Robert Carr, made viscount Rochester in 1611, then earl of Somerset in 1613. Carr's fall two years later was spectacular. His wife, Frances Howard, "that base women", was discovered to have murdered her principal critic, Sir Thomas Overbury, by arranging for a poisoned enema to be administered to him.

George Villiers's (above) hold on the king's affections was even more remarkable. In rapid succession he was made viscount Villiers (1616), earl of Buckingham (1617), marquess of Buckingham (1618) and duke of Buckingham (1623), by which point "Steenie", as James I called him, had become almost an equal partner with the king. Buckingham's outrageous flattery of the king, his "deare dad" was equally extreme. He was stabbed by a madman in 1628.

1582	1583	1586	1587	1589	1591	1592	1596	1599	1600	1603	1604
The "Ruthven Raid": James seized by Lord Gowrie	Majority of James VI	Treaty of Berwick names James as successor to Elizabeth I in England	Execution of Mary, Queen of Scots, prompts only faint protest from James VI	Marries Anne of Denmark	Attempted kidnap of James by earl of Bothwell (and 1592)	Presbyterianism established as official religion in Scotland	James establishes firmer control over church in Scotland	Treatise on kingship, Basilikon Doron, published by James	Attempted kidnap of James by Lord Gowrie	James I named as successor to Elizabeth	Hampton Court Conference attempts religious settlement with Puritans and Catholics; leads to

Escape of
conspiring
northern earls,
1592

S C O T L A N D

1589,
1592

ABERDEEN

Flight of the Earls. O'Neill,
O'Donnell, and 97 other
Irish leaders leave for Rome,
1607. Confiscation of their lands
opens way for plantations.

EDINBURGH

CARLISLE

IRELAND

DUBLIN

YORK

E N G L A N D

CHESTER

NOTTINGHAM

LIMERICK

COVENTRY

NORWICH

WEXFORD

BRISTOL

LONDON

PORTSMOUTH

PLYMOUTH

FRANCE

Though united in a personal union under James, Scotland and England remained distinct kingdoms with their own quite different laws (map left). The king's visionary efforts to unite them foundered on persistent Anglo-Scottish jealousies and misunderstandings. The Plantation of Ireland by Protestant Scots, begun in 1611, reinforced a religious conflict that survives today.

JAMES I AND VI 1603–25

	Ruled by James from 1567
⚑	*Held by the Queen's men during civil war, 1567–73*
⚑	*Held by the King's men during civil war, 1567–73*
→	*James's campaign, with dates*
	Inherited by James I, 1603
	Union proposed by James to parliament, 1606–07 (Plan abandoned)
	"Planted" by James
	"Planted" privately during James's rule

Towards the end of his life, James I had become a shambling, gout-ridden, semi-senile figure (right), made all the more improbable by self-regarding pomposity. Yet his reign was far from a failure. He bequeathed his heir, Charles, a stable and secure if indebted throne. This portrait, by Daniel Mytens, was painted in 1621.

The Gunpowder Plot

Writing to Robert Cecil in March 1603, just before he became king of England, James asserted that he would: "never allow in my conscience that the blood of any man be shed for diversity of opinions in religion". Unfortunately, in the over-heated religious climate of early 17th-century England, this moderation found few supporters.

Anti-Catholic prejudice was raised to new heights in November 1605 with the discovery of the Gunpowder Plot, an attempt to blow up both the Houses of Parliament along with the king and the Prince of Wales. Whether the plot had been encouraged by James's chief minister, Robert Cecil, in the hope of allowing the conspirators to incriminate themselves, or was discovered only at the last minute, remains unknown.

Either way, the predictable effects of the plot's discovery was to scupper all hopes of extending tolerance to Catholics prepared to practise their faith discreetly, and to create an even more rabidly anti-Catholic mood. It also provided a huge boost to James's popularity. Parliament declared November 5 a national holiday, in the process praising James as: "… the most great learned and religious king that ever reigned".

shameless promotion of court favourites, above all George Villiers (made duke of Buckingham in 1623), created great resentment.

Of more lasting importance was a political tactlessness, most obvious when James was haranguing his Parliament even when accepting its right to refuse him new taxes or to pass his laws. This inability to gauge the political temperature was responsible for the failure of James's most cherished project: the union of Scotland and England. After several years of increasingly strained relations with Parliament, all James achieved, by 1607, was the repeal of mutually hostile laws between England and Scotland, and the adoption of a new Anglo-Scots flag for all ships, the "Great Union", or "Union Jack" as it was known after the king's preference for the French form of his own name, Jacques.

If at the end of his reign James found himself reluctantly sucked into the wider European religious conflict that would become the Thirty Years War, for the most part he managed to keep England clear of costly foreign wars. He was also successful after 1611, in beginning the Ulster "Plantation", the settlement of mostly Scottish Presbyterians in Ulster, the most Catholic province of Ireland, in order to stamp on potential Catholic uprisings. Successful in its own terms, it would blight Ireland itself for centuries.

James I scarcely deserved his description, in the memorable phrase of the French king, Henri IV, as "the wisest fool in Christendom". Yet it contains a kernel of truth about a likeable, well-intentioned but faintly absurd figure.

1605	1606	1607	1610	1611	1612	1613	1616	1619	1623
commissioning of English-language King James Bible (1611). Peace reached with Spain	Catholic attempt to blow up James and Parliament – the Gunpowder Plot – foiled	Union Jack introduced	Union of Scotland and England – Instrument of Union – rejected	The "Great Contract", an attempt to reform royal finances rejected by Parliament	Ulster Plantation begun	Death of James's elder son Henry, Prince of Wales	Marriage of James's daughter Elizabeth and Frederick, Elector Palatine	Rise of new court favourite, George Villiers, begins	Palatine Elector accepts throne of Bohemia, provoking war with Spain	Villiers and Charles, Prince of Wales, make disastrous secret visit to Spain attempting to secure new Anglo-Spanish alliance by marriage of Charles to the Infanta

CHARLES I 1625–49

CHARLES I REMAINS THE ONLY KING OF ENGLAND TO HAVE BEEN LEGALLY MURDERED. WHATEVER HIS PERSONAL VIRTUES, CHARLES'S COMBINATION OF AN ALOOF CERTAINTY IN HIS OWN DIVINELY ORDAINED JUDGEMENT AND A WILLINGNESS TO DISSEMBLE MADE HIS PARTICULAR BRAND OF ROYAL GOVERNMENT ALL BUT IMPOSSIBLE IN THE RELIGIOUS AND POLITICAL TURMOIL OF MID-16TH-CENTURY BRITAIN.

BORN: NOVEMBER 19 1600
ACCEDED: March 27 1625; crowned King of England February 2 1626, Westminster Abbey and King of Scotland June 8 1633, Holyrood Abbey

ෙ෨ ෙ෨ ෙ෨ ෙ෨ ෙ෨ ෙ෨

Prince of Wales (1616–25), Duke of Albany, Marquess of Ormonde, Earl of Ross, Baron of Ardmannoch, Duke of York, Duke of Cornwall and Rothesay, Earl of Chester, King of Scotland, England and Ireland

Charles (above) became heir to James I only at 12 with the death of his 18-year-old brother, Henry, who was everything that Charles was not: dashing, glamorous and able. By contrast, the sickly Charles – he didn't walk until he was seven – was hardly expected to live. Even fully grown, Charles was small, only five-foot-four. He also had a stutter that never left him. These were not attributes that lent them-selves to the heroic conception of absolute monarchy to which Charles aspired.

I N 1637, LESS THAN FIVE YEARS BEFORE THE beginning of the Civil War in England, Charles I's throne had never looked more secure. His succession had been unchallenged, his subsequent rule, notwithstanding a series of embarrassing foreign policy reverses, decisive and firm. His finances more-over, in marked contrast to those of the final years of his father's reign, were healthy. The absolutism he professed had apparently been entirely vindicated.

Charles, Henrietta Maria, Prince Charles (the future Charles II) and their eldest daughter, Mary, in the mid-1630s (below). Images such as this immense and sumptuous canvas by Van Dyck portrayed the king at his most majestic, a Baroque prince of European repute gravely presiding over his family as he presided over his kingdoms. In time, the Catholic Henrietta Maria would become almost the dominant influence on Charles, consistently urging him not to give ground to his critics.

Yet the means by which Charles I had arrived at this position were already alienating a substantial body of opinion. For one thing, from 1629 he had dispensed altogether with what he saw as an increasingly unruly Parliament, simply refusing to summon it. Henceforward, or at least until Parliament agreed to behave more reasonably, Charles would govern alone.

Legally, his action was justified – by established convention, Parliament met only at the king's con-venience. Yet such high-handed treatment not only inevitably created resentments, it also circumscribed the king's own freedom of action. Without Parlia-ment, Charles could raise no new taxes. To circumvent this, he adopted a measure of dubious legality at best. In 1634, the long-established tradition of Ship Money, whereby coastal towns were required to provide either ships or, in their place, money to the crown, was extended to cover every town in England.

1623	1625	1626	1627	1628
Abortive secret visit to Spain with Duke of Buckingham to secure marriage of Charles to Infanta of Spain	*Marriage of Charles and Henrietta Maria of France*	*"Forced loans" raised by Charles outside parliamentary scrutiny*	*Failed campaigns to assist French Huguenots led by Duke of Buckingham (to 1629)*	*Assassination of Duke of Buckingham. Petition of Right drawn up by Parliament in attempt to prevent raising of non-parliamentary revenues by Charles*

- Areas affected by 'Bishops' War', 1639
- Scene of Argyll's anti-royalist activities, 1640
- Campaigns of Covenanter forces, 1640
- Royalist raids, with details
- Under temporary Scottish occupation under Ripon treaty 1640
- Revolt, with details
- Attack by Irish Catholics under Phelim O'Neill
- Under Confederate control, 1642
- Charles I's campaigns, 1642
- Eastern and Southern limit of area held by Charles I, January 1643
- Eastern and Southern limit of area held by Charles I, September 1643

The name "English Civil War" does less than justice to the confused three-way conflict that began with the Bishops' War in Aberdeen in February 1639 (map left). If much of the subsequent fighting after 1642 was between royalist and parliamentary forces in England, the Irish and Scottish dimensions to the conflict were crucial. It was consistently at least as much a religious war as one fought to curb unbridled royal power.

[I would know] by what power I am called hither ... I would know by what Authority, I mean, lawful; [for] there are many unlawful Authorities in the world, Thieves and Robbers by the high ways ... Remember I am your King, your lawful King, and what sins you bring upon your heads, and the Judgement of God upon this Land, think well upon it ... before you go further from one sin to a greater

Charles I at his trial, January 1649

That Charles intended the money to strengthen the navy did little to deflect the ensuing protest. There was a growing sense that the king was willing to bypass ancient parliamentary practices, however vaguely defined, and to impose illegal taxes.

At the same time, through his new Archbishop of Canterbury, William Laud, Charles was pushing forward a series of religious reforms that, to many, smacked dangerously of an attempt to reintroduce popery. Given the extreme volatility of religious opinion across the British Isles, and the militant fervour it aroused in all quarters, Charles's appointment in 1633 of William Laud had been provocative at best. Laud, like Charles, was determined to impose a brand of religious uniformity on England and Scotland that, in the eyes of his many

continued on next page

1629	1633	1634	1637	1638
Charles dismisses Parliament and embarks on personal rule (to 1640)	*William Laud appointed Archbishop of Canterbury*	*Ship Money imposed by Charles I, provoking claims of illegal taxation*	*Imposition of Book of Common Prayer in Scotland provokes religious riots*	*Great Covenant drawn up in Scotland in protest against Laud's religious reforms*

The Irish Dimension

By 1640, something like 100,000 Protestant settlers had been introduced into Ireland, the majority of them Scottish Presbyterians, most of whom settled in Ulster. The Catholic Irish – whether the "Old English" descendants of the original Norman settlers or the native Gaels – were dispossessed or forced to the less fertile western extremities of Ireland. The policy sought to prevent a recurrence of the Catholic Irish revolts of the later 16th and early 17th centuries by fusing Ireland culturally with Scotland and England. Especially with the appointment of the hard-nosed Thomas Wentworth, earl of Strafford, as Lord Deputy of Ireland in 1633, it was a success.

Strafford, however, was as tough on the Protestant "New English" and the Scots Presbyterians as he was on the native "Old English". When Parliament engineered his execution in 1641, on the ground that he had been an "evil counsellor" to the king, the Catholic Irish lost what small protection they had enjoyed. The success of the Scots "Covenanter" armies was another cause of Irish Catholic fear, and in October 1641 an uprising began, ostensibly to aid Charles I in his struggle against Parliament and the Covenanters alike.

Much of the planned rebellion never even started, but in Portadown more than 2,000 Protestants were killed. In the heightened political climate of the day, evidence of a renewed popish uprising of this kind was electrifying. Rumours of further massacres abounded. Charles himself was said to have masterminded the revolts and was seeking Spanish help to train an Irish Catholic army to invade England. If the tragedy – as usual – was Ireland's, the political fallout for the king was scarcely less great, and further reinforced Puritan parliamentary opinion to oust him.

The legality of Charles's trial, ordered as it had been by the "Rump" of the Long Parliament, troubled many. In the event, the judges, though hand-picked, divided almost exactly, 68 to 67 – a majority in favour of the king's death of just one. His guilt as a "tyrant, traitor and murderer, a public and implacable enemy to the Commonwealth of England" was announced on January 28. This painting (right) by Edward Bower of Charles at the trial shows the king haggard and drawn but dignified to the last.

continued from
previous page

vociferous Puritan critics, was little better than papism.

Though the political opposition and religious protest provoked by Charles were separate, the two overlapped in crucial respects. Certainly, when the Civil War began, it was the case that there were few Puritans on the king's side just as there were few Laudians, let along Catholics, on the Parliamentary side. But what most united opposition to the king was not just his overbearing sense of divinely appointed self-righteousness – his refusal, once his mind was made up, ever to change it – so much as his use of any means, however low, to put his will into practice. Trust, like compromise, was not an option that Charles I entertained.

At least in retrospect, his reign began its sudden unravelling in 1637, when Laud instructed the Scottish Kirk to use the *Book of Common Prayer*. Within a year, virulent Scottish opposition had hardened in the form of a massive popular protest and petition – the Great Covenant. The following year, a Scottish "Covenanter" army invaded England. Charles's response – to invade Scotland in turn – immediately fell foul of his inability to raise the necessary taxes to finance an army. In April 1640 he was humiliatingly forced to summon a new Parliament in London.

The following 18 months would prove the most remarkable and unpredictable in English kingship. Amid a mood of mounting and apparently unstoppable crisis, the certainties of Tudor and early Stuart monarchy evaporated. Scarcely more than two years later, a bitterly divisive civil war had begun.

The immediate cause was partly parliamentary resentment at the king's abrupt dismissal of his new Parliament less than a month after he had summoned it, partly growing anxiety that, if he could not raise an English army, Charles planned to exploit a Catholic uprising in Ireland to raise a Catholic Irish army, potentially supported by Spain, to repress the

Scots. Even so, when Parliament had to be recalled the following November, the vast majority of its members favoured an accommodation with the king. What they sought was a reaffirmation of Parliament's established place in the government of the country, not the overthrow of the monarchy.

Backtracking rapidly, Charles appeared, in February 1641, to have come to an accommodation with his Parliament, agreeing to a series of measures that significantly reduced his royal prerogative. The king, however, was doing no more than play for

time. Precisely like King John when he signed Magna Carta in 1215, Charles had no intention of honouring his commitments. By the following August he was in Scotland attempting to persuade

1639	1640	1641	1642	1644
First Bishops' War: Charles's weak army easily defeated by Scots	"Short" Parliament dismissed after less than a month. Second Bishops' War (Aug.): Scots occupy Newcastle. "Long" Parliament (meets until 1660) called and insists on dismissal of Laud and execution of Strafford; Ship Money rescinded	Catholic uprising in Ireland. Parliamentary grievances in form of Grand Remonstrance presented to Charles (Dec.)	Attempted arrest of parliamentary critics (Jan.) by Charles turns into embarrassing fiasco. Formal declaration of hostilities by Charles at Nottingham (Aug.); first major battle, at Edgehill (Oct.), inconclusive	Parliamentary victory at Marston Moor, Yorkshire

the Scots to mount a further invasion of England to quell his troublesome English Parliament for good.

His actions had the inevitable result of hardening parliamentary opposition to him in England. In December 1641 he was presented with a "Grand Remonstrance". For the first time, the notion was made explicit that Parliament could dismiss a king who was held to have broken his trust with his people. Charles responded by a botched attempt to arrest the ringleaders, arriving at the House of Commons with an armed troop. By now, almost every convention governing relations between monarch and Parliament had collapsed. The war, when it came, appeared inevitable.

In ways unparalleled before or since, the Civil War divided communities and opinions across England. There were few clear-cut loyalties. Support for the king only rarely meant the same as opposition to Parliament. Likewise, support for Parliament was rarely the same as opposition to the king. For all but the Puritans, convinced of their role as the agents of a benevolently vengeful God, the resulting bloodshed and suffering were all the more unbearably arbitrary.

Charles proved a resilient general, resisting the growing strength – and professionalism – of the parliamentary armies for almost five years. Even after his capture in 1646, he was able to exploit the continuing atmosphere of division and uncertainty dogging the country. Unlike his earlier attempts to control Parliament, Charles now revealed a near masterly talent for playing off one side against another – although always with his own restoration in mind.

That Parliament decided on the king's execution was mainly the result of an enforced takeover of Parliament by the only force that now really counted: the parliamentary "New Model Army", godly, forthright and, above all, victorious. Dominating it was a man who would repudiate completely Charles I's failed brand of absolute monarchy, Oliver Cromwell.

In January 1649 Charles was tried, found guilty and executed. Ironically, it was Parliament, purged of its royalist members, that now seemed to have become the tyrant. In death Charles I found the dignity that his duplicitous kingship had so obviously lacked.

The surrender of Charles I to Scottish troops in May 1646, after his West Country stronghold had been gradually reduced by parliamentary forces, heralded no more than a pause in the conflict. By the summer of 1648 a series of royalist uprisings broke out, the so-called Second Civil War (map left).

THE ENGLISH CIVIL WAR 1644–9

→ Scottish interventions in England on the side of parliament, with date
/// Northern England, effectively lost by the King by July 1644
→ Montrose's campaigns, August-November 1644
→ MacColla's campaign, 1644
\ Theatre of Montrose's activities, December 1644- August 1645
▪▪▶ Montrose's campaign, August-September 1645
▬ Eastern limit of area held by the King in England and Wales at beginning of 1645
/// Lost by the king during 1645
⚑ Isolated royalist outposts in parliamentarian territory
⚑ Isolated parliamentarian outposts in royalist territory
→ Charles's movements June 1645-May 1646
• Places where Charles was held after Scottish withdrawal from England
✺ Risings of the Clubmen, 1644-5
▭ Approximate extent of royalist activity during Second Civil War, May-July 1648
→ Scottish campaign in support of royalists during Second Civil War, July-August 1648

1645	1646	1647	1648	1649
Parliamentary New Model Army formed; royalists routed at Naseby. Laud executed	Charles surrenders to Scots, who come to terms with English parliamentarians; Charles handed over to parliamentarians	Charles comes to terms with Scots, promising to impose Presbyterianism on England	Second phase of Civil War: Scottish invasion of England defeated by Cromwell; remaining royalist resistance crushed. New Model Army purges Parliament of members seeking accommodation with Charles (Dec.), leading to "Rump" Parliament	Charles tried and executed in London (Jan.)

THE COMMONWEALTH 1649–60

THE EXECUTION OF CHARLES I IN 1649 LAUNCHED ENGLAND ON AN EXPERIMENT IN NON-MONARCHICAL GOVERNMENT WITHOUT PARALLEL IN EUROPE. IT WAS DOMINATED BY THE FORBIDDING FIGURE OF OLIVER CROMWELL. IN THE EVENT, EVEN HE WAS UNABLE TO DEVISE A STABLE FORM OF GOVERNMENT THAT RECONCILED PURITAN DEMANDS WITH LIBERTY UNDER THE LAW. BY 1660, THE MONARCHY HAD BEEN RESTORED.

I N MAY 1649, FOUR MONTHS AFTER THE EXECUTION OF Charles I, the Rump Parliament declared the existence of the Commonwealth and Free State of England. The supreme authority of Parliament was confirmed, as was the abolition of the monarchy. The House of Lords was similarly ended along with the Anglican Church and its bishops.

It was under this new and radical constitutional arrangement that, in September, Oliver Cromwell was sent to Ireland at the head of a parliamentary army to suppress the remaining Irish Catholic royalist elements, at least in part as revenge for the massacres of Protestants in 1641, and to bring the country firmly under parliamentary control. His brutal victories, at Drogheda and Wexford, were as complete as those he subsequently inflicted over the Scots at Dunbar in September 1650 and over Charles I's son, the future Charles II, at Worcester the following summer. Whatever royalist discontent still existed, an English Republic, which now in effect extended over the whole of Britain, had become a fact.

Yet despite these successes, soon to be matched by victory over the Dutch in the first of three wars over commercial supremacy (itself the herald of a new age of English commercial and colonial expansion), a lasting political settlement remained elusive. Cromwell's appointment as Commander-in-Chief of the parliamentary army in 1651 confirmed what had been evident even before the death of Charles I: that Cromwell, the outstanding parliamentary general in the Civil War and a man of unflinching Calvinist rectitude – part country squire, part reborn Moses – had become the dominant figure of the age. Now, as leader of the only really coherent political body in the country, the army, his pre-eminence was absolute

Cromwell was practical, decisive and competent, but he was also, first and last, a man of God, wholly certain that any attempt at the "healing and settling" of the nation had to be based on a government guided by religious principle. Indeed, at least since the 1630s religion and politics for Cromwell had become inseparable. "Religion was not first the thing contended for [in the Civil War] but God brought it to that issue at last and at last it proved to be what was most dear to us," he ringingly declared

The Rump Parliament by contrast, at least for Cromwell, had degenerated into a self-serving, worldly body, more interested in lining its own pockets than in dispensing justice. Certainly it was no vehicle for God's will. In April 1653, in a fury of Old Testament rage, Cromwell abolished it, mounting in effect an armed coup, striding up and down the chamber shouting: "You are no parliament. I say you are no parliament…. In the name of God, go."

His motive was honourable. Cromwell genuinely intended to establish a new Parliament, as indeed he did within a matter of months. But his means called into question the very principles for which the Civil War had been fought: the protection of parliamentary independence in the face of Stuart tyranny. In the event, the new Godly assembly, the so-called "Barebones" Parliament, appointed rather than elected, lasted a matter of months before dissolving itself and handing power back to Cromwell.

In December 1653, a new constitution was adopted, the

By 1658, Cromwell was king in all but name. Here, as the "Embleme of England's Distractions" (above) he is shown at his most regal, a just Christian warrior and bringer of peace to all the countries of Britain, crushing underfoot the serpent of error and the whore of Babylon.

Oh, I lived in and loved darkness, and hated the light. I was a chief, the chief of sinners. This is true; I hated godliness, yet God had mercy on me. O the riches of His mercy!

Oliver Cromwell, 1638, on his Christian reawakening

"Instrument of Government". Under it, Cromwell was made Lord Protector, and a Council of State was formed to take on the daily business of government. Parliament, even though now to be elected every three years, would not be allowed to challenge the "fundamentals" of the new constitution, which was extended to include Ireland and Scotland.

It was to prove no more successful a solution than its predecessors. When the new Parliament met, in September 1654, it immediately insisted on its own supremacy. Predictably, Cromwell dissolved it, replacing it in July 1655 with a wholly new system under which the country was divided into 12 regions, each ruled by a major general. If in many ways the high point of righteous Puritan rule – a Swearing and Cursing Act was passed; the penalty for adultery was death – in practice the system proved unworkable. Elections the following year revealed its unpopularity. Puritan representation in the new House of Commons all but disappeared.

By the summer of 1657, yet another constitution had been adopted, the "Humble Petition and Advice". Under an "Ordinance of Union", originally issued by the Council of State in 1654, Ireland and Scotland were formally united with England. At the same time, the House of Lords was revived. The resulting arrangement was so similar to the reformed monarchy the Long Parliament had tried to persuade Charles I to accept in 1641 and in 1647, that the revival of the monarchy itself seemed logical and inevitable. All but the most fervent Puritans had come to realize that stable government under the law and sanctioned by parliamentary authority was impossible without the central figure of a monarch to unite it.

Cromwell declined repeated requests to become that king himself, despite the fact that he was already styled "Your Highness" and had been given Whitehall Palace to live in. This was the result of his unshakeable religious conviction. Cromwell took it as fact that the monarchy could only have been overthrown because God had wanted it. Unless given equally incontrovertible evidence of a divine change of heart, Cromwell was unprepared to disobey his God.

Yet that Cromwell had become king in all but name was clear not just by his naming his son, Richard, to succeed him as Lord Protector, but also by his dissolution of yet another Parliament in the spring of 1658. This came just months after he had extolled it with the assertion: "If there be any higher work which mortals

The most serious charge to be levelled against Cromwell was not that he was a dour, irascible Puritan bigot – in fact he was remarkably liberal in matters of religion – so much as that he was an increasingly despotic figure whose often arbitrary exercise of power was very much more damaging than anything Charles I did. His dissolution of the Rump Parliament in April 1653 (above), a clear violation of Parliament's legally sanctioned independence, was undertaken for no better reason than that Cromwell lost his temper.

Despite its military successes, The Commonwealth struggled to find a lasting political settlement (map below). Crushing victories by Cromwell in Ireland and Scotland were followed in summer 1651 by the defeat of Charles II, accepted as king of Scotland in 1650. Devising a workable form of non-monarchical government, however, was beyond even Cromwell.

THE COMMONWEALTH 1649–60

- Ruled by Charles II as King, 1649: formally incorporated into Commonwealth, 1657–60
- Cromwell's campaigns
- Land reserved for the government or provided for parliamentary army
- Land assigned to the Irish
- Montrose's campaign, 1649–50
- Charles II's campaigns, 1651
- Other movements of Charles II
- Engagement in First Dutch War
- Revolts
- Frontier of administrative units of 1655, with name of Major General
- Monck's advance, 1660

can attain unto in this world, I acknowledge my ignorance of it." In the end, Cromwell's visions of parliamentary liberty and religious zeal proved incompatible.

After his death in September 1658, the unstable British Republic gently collapsed. Richard Cromwell, with none of his father's messianic potency, resigned as Lord Protector after just eight months. By October, chaos threatened. That it was avoided was thanks to George Monck, commander of the parliamentary army in Scotland. Marching his men to London early in 1660, he restored the Long Parliament, which in turn dissolved itself and called for new elections. To no one's surprise, this new "Convention" Parliament immediately voted to restore the monarchy. The wheel had come full circle.

BORN: May 29 1630
ACCEDED IN SCOTLAND:
June 11 1650; crowned
January 1 1651,
Scone Abbey; deposed
September 3 1651;
restored May 29 1660
ACCEDED IN ENGLAND
AND IRELAND: May 29
1660; crowned April 23
1661, Westminster
Abbey

*Duke of Cornwall
and Rothesay,
King of Scotland,
England and Ireland*

CHARLES II 1660–85

CHARLES II WAS THE MOST SUCCESSFUL STUART KING OF ENGLAND. NOT ONLY WAS HIS RESTORATION A TRIUMPHANT VINDICATION OF THE REVIVED PRINCIPLES OF HEREDITARY MONARCHY, HE MANAGED THE FALLOUT FROM THE TUMULTUOUS REPUBLICAN EXPERIMENT WITH EXCEPTIONAL SKILL. NONETHELESS, THE UNDERLYING TENSIONS BETWEEN PARLIAMENTARY AND ROYAL AUTHORITY RESURFACED WITH THE ACCESSION OF CHARLES'S BROTHER, JAMES II, IN 1685.

THE DEFT POLITICAL TOUCH OF CHARLES II was amply demonstrated by his Declaration of Breda in April 1660. With England desperate for a return to legitimate royal government after the inconclusive republican experiments headed by Cromwell, Charles, exiled in Holland, decisively reinforced his position, promising to honour parliamentary liberties and religious freedoms. It

Inconclusive in themselves, the three Anglo-Dutch wars were nonetheless important in the longer term in reinforcing England's emerging naval prowess (map below). The first, fought between 1652 and 1653, was prosecuted with characteristic vigour by Oliver Cromwell. Under Charles II, the conflict flared up twice more, in 1665 to 1667 and in 1672 to 1674. In fact, Anglo-Dutch rivalry was already nearing its end: a shared Protestant destiny would prove more important than mercantile rivalry.

was all that was needed by an England clamouring for a return to legitimate royal rule. In May 1660, both Houses of Parliament voted overwhelmingly for Charles's restoration. He arrived in London on May 29 1660, his 30th birthday, to a triumphant welcome.

The ambiguously worded Declaration of Breda aside, Charles had had to make few compromises to regain his crown. In almost every important sense, he was restored to a throne that was as absolute as his father's. The Godly republican experiments of Cromwell might never have been. That said, in ways that would have seemed unimaginable to Charles I,

The worst that can be said of Charles II (above) is not just that he allowed a sense of drift to settle over his government, reacting to events rather than guiding them, but that his concern to preserve the monarchy led him to align himself too closely with Catholic France, where monarchy and Catholicism seemed to have reached their apogee in Louis XIV. In a country where virulent anti-Catholic feeling was always close to the surface, it would not always prove a prudent course.

CHARLES II 1660–85

✕	*Engagement in Second Dutch War, with details*
	Nominal foe in Second Dutch War
///	*Temporary ally in Second Dutch War*
||||	*Overrun temporarily by Münster during Second Dutch War*
🍃	*Revolt, with details*
///	*Walcheren, to become English under secret Treaty of Dover, 1672*
✕	*Engagement in Third Dutch War, with details*
///	*Ally in Third Dutch War*
→	*French attack on Holland, 1672*
----	*Frontiers, 1664*

BERGEN

Attack on Dutch convoy results in Demark declaring war on the side of the Dutch, 1665

NORWAY
(to Denmark)

Bothwell Brig rebellion, 1679

PERTH

EDINBURGH

Pentland rising, 1666

NEWCASTLE

CARLISLE

IRELAND

YORK

DUBLIN

Landing at Terschelling 'Holmes's Bonfire' 1666

Naval blockade, 1666

Texel 1673

Lowestoft 1665

AMSTERDAM

SHREWSBURY

Southwold Bay 1672

NETHERLANDS

B. OF MÜNSTER

HODDESDON

'St James's' 1666

BRISTOL

LONDON

'Four Day's' 1666

DUNKIRK
Sold to France, 1662

SMALL STATES

PORTSMOUTH

SPANISH NETHERLANDS

PLYMOUTH

Thames Estuary 1667

FRANCE

his son recognized from the start the need to reach an accommodation with Parliament.

Worldly, cynical and shrewd, even if his belief in absolute monarchy was at least the equal of his father's, Charles was always prepared to compromise for the sake of his throne. Also, unlike his unbending father, he had the common touch. For easy charm, Charles II was rivalled only by Edward IV. Like his Plantagenet forebear, Charles was a notorious womanizer, his court a byword for sophisticated and extravagant dalliance.

If his attempts to secure religious freedoms for all his subjects, Presbyterian as much as Catholic, were thwarted by an intolerant Parliament, Charles's inclusive early administrations went far to heal the divisions of the Civil War. Puritans, parliamentarians and royalists alike were drafted in. The wounds of the previous 20 years were successfully bandaged.

Charles's relaxed kingship may have helped set the tone for an increasingly expansive, confident and prosperous Protestant nation, but unresolved issues remained. Religion, inseparable from the question of parliamentary liberty, remained the core issue – as almost always in 17th-century England. Charles's own instincts were clearly in favour of the Catholicism of an increasingly powerful France. In 1670, he agreed a secret treaty with the Catholic Louis XIV of France, promising to help Louis in his wars against the Protestant Dutch in return for a handsome pension. His hands are reported to have shaken visibly when he denied the existence of the treaty to Parliament.

Even more destabilizing to his regime was the attempt, masterminded by the earl of Shaftesbury from 1679, to exclude his brother James, a Catholic, from the succession. Charles saw off the threat with characteristic insouciance and nerve. If nothing else, he could later console himself at his death in 1685 that the principle of hereditary monarchy had been defended. In fact by the time the "Exclusion" crisis had been settled in the king's favour in 1681, a booming economy, leading to increased customs revenues, which accrued to the crown without the

The Great Fire of London

The euphoria of Charles II's restoration was undermined by three calamitous events in the mid-1660s. In 1665, the Great Plague returned to London, carrying off fully one-sixth of its population. In 1667, the Dutch humiliatingly raided the Medway, less than 50 miles from the capital.

Sandwiched between them was an even more terrifying disaster, the Great Fire of London, which broke out early in the morning of September 2 1666, in a baker's shop. The fire burned uncontrolled for four days, destroying 13,000 houses and making 100,000 people homeless. Eighty-eight churches were burned down, including St Paul's Cathedral. "Oh the miserable and calamitous spectacle," wrote John Evelyn. "… all the skie were of a fiery aspect, like the top of a burning Oven, and the light seen above 40 miles round about for many nights." "It made me weep to see it," Samuel Pepys reported. "The churches, houses and all on fire and flaming at once, and a horrid noise the flames made, and the cracking of the houses at their ruin."

Although work on rebuilding the city began almost at once, and the Rebuilding Act of 1667 enacted – for the time – strict building regulations to prevent a similar disaster, the sense that this was a punishment was widespread. For many, it seriously suggested divine wrath that England had turned its back on its Puritan heritage.

need for parliamentary approval, had made the king financially secure. In the last four years of his reign, Charles II was able to govern without once summoning Parliament. However, with no legitimate heir, Charles's throne was poised to pass to James. His reign may have shown that England could not be governed without a monarch, but the exact relationship between monarch and an increasingly assertive Parliament was about to be finally decided.

Essentially an indolent man, Charles II (right) raised pleasure seeking almost to an art form. He took a real and deep interest in the theatre. He established the racecourse at Newmarket. He was the first monarch to have his own yacht, the Royal Escape. His string of mistresses was legendary. As Charles put it, he did not believe "God would damn a man for a little irregular pleasure". Not all his subjects were inclined to take such an indulgent view. The diarist John Evelyn saw the excesses of Charles's court as little short of scandalous, finding in it "a sense of utmost vanity".

JAMES II 1685–88

THE CONSTITUTIONAL CRISES OF THE 17TH CENTURY CAME TO A SUDDEN AND UNEXPECTED CLIMAX IN THE BRIEF REIGN OF JAMES II. DETERMINED TO ALLOW RELIGIOUS TOLERATION, HE SUCCEEDED ONLY IN CONVINCING ALMOST THE WHOLE POLITICAL CLASS THAT HIS REAL GOAL WAS THE RESTORATION OF CATHOLICISM. THE CAREFUL POLITICAL SETTLEMENT OF CHARLES II WAS OVERTURNED IN SCARCELY MORE THAN TWO YEARS.

BORN: October 14 1633
ACCEDED: February 6 1685; crowned April 23 1685, Westminster Abbey; remained King of Ireland until July 1 1690

⚜ ⚜ ⚜ ⚜ ⚜

*Duke of York,
Earl of Ulster,
Duke of Normandy,
King of Scotland,
England and Ireland*

James II (above) was experienced, intelligent and able. Yet he attempted a revolution in English kingship that could never have succeeded. In uniting the entire weight of Britain's political establishment against him, he guaranteed his own overthrow. His last-ditch attempts to regain support were too little and too late. His ignominious flight to France, where he arrived on Christmas Day 1688, ended the slim possibility that unencumbered personal rule could ever be restored in England.

The Birth of James Francis Edward Stuart

The marriage in 1673 of the Duke of York, as he then was, to Maria d'Este, the Catholic daughter of the Duke of Modena, provoked predictable fury in Parliament. On the other hand, those anxious at the possibility of the continuation of a Catholic Stuart dynasty could subsequently take comfort from the fact that of the 10 children born to James and Maria none survived. Assuming (as was the case) that the Duke of York would succeed Charles II, the succession then seemed certain to pass in turn to his two surviving daughters from his marriage to Anne Hyde. These were Mary, now married to William of Orange, and Anne, who in 1683 married the son of the King of Denmark. Like their spouses, both were resolutely Protestant.

The birth of a healthy baby boy, christened James Francis Edward, to James and Mary in June 1688 was one of those dynastic accidents whose consequences were out of all proportion to the event itself. Entirely against the odds, James II seemed to have secured his Catholic succession. Almost immediately, rumours began that the baby had been smuggled into the royal bedchamber. Mary and Anne in particular were convinced that the "warming-pan baby" was an imposter, a foundling passed off as a royal child. Less than a month later, the first overtures were being made to William of Orange to mount an invasion of England and bring James to his senses.

The Queen is brought to bed of a Boy

Reported so

JAMES II HAS BEEN WRITTEN OFF AS A HUMOURless despot, set on the destruction of parliamentary independence and the restoration of unfettered royal supremacy. Further, as a Catholic in an overwhelmingly Protestant nation, he has always aroused suspicions that his real aim was not just the restoration of Catholicism, but to deliver England to the rabidly Catholic France of Louis XIV.

Given the hostility aroused by Charles II's more modest attempts to introduce tolerance for non-Anglicans both in 1662 and 1672, indeed given the hysterical anti-Catholic mood not just of England but of Scotland, too, especially after 1678, it is extraordinary that James II should ever have thought he could engineer a Catholic restoration. Even with a large measure of Tory support at the start of his reign, healthy finances, a strong army, and a continuing desire to avoid conflict in the country at large, no monarch could now hope to rule in defiance of Parliament. This, after all, was why Charles I had lost his throne. It has even been suggested that James's actions were the result of premature senility. What is certain is that they represented the last attempt to introduce a Continental style of absolutism into England. They were a complete failure.

James began his reign prudently, telling the Archbishop of Canterbury that he would "undertake nothing against the religion that is established by law". The strength of his position was also underlined in 1685 by the ease with which two abortive anti-Catholic uprisings – by the Duke of Monmouth in Dorset and the Earl of Argyll in Scotland – were put down. And, as a philanderer at least the equal of his brother, James II seemed an unlikely champion of religious purity.

He received a significant boost the following year when his right to grant a colonel's commission to a Catholic, a man by the name of Hales, was upheld by 11 out of the 12 judges who heard the case. Encouraged, James set about the promotion of Catholics everywhere: the army, the navy, the Privy Council, the universities, the courts and in Parliament.

In 1687, James issued a Declaration of Indulgence allowing open, public worship for all denominations. When seven bishops challenged the king's right to do

The attempt by Charles II's illegitimate son, the Duke of Monmouth, to oust James II fizzled out ignominiously. Though a favoured champion of Protestantism, Monmouth, who had landed at Lyme Regis on June 11 1685 (and was declared king in Taunton nine days afterwards), could muster only the feeblest of forces. In less than a month, he had been defeated at Sedgmoor (below), the last set-piece battle in England, fought on July 5. Ten days later, he was executed at the Tower of London.

→ Monmouth's campaign
▭ Approximate limit of area from where Monmouth's supporters came
→ Government campaign against Monmouth
⇢ Monmouth's attempt to escape
→ Argyll's campaign
⇢ Argyll's attempt to escape
→ Rebel leaders' movements in captivity

The Defeat of the Rebells 2000 Slayn & their Canon taken

The ease with which the anti-Catholic uprisings led by the duke of Monmouth and earl of Argyll (map left) in the early months of James II's reign were put down appeared to suggest that William of Orange's invasion in November 1688 would stand hardly more chance of success (see pp. 150–1).

so, they were arrested for seditious libel. On the face of it, the Declaration was, as has been said, "balanced and reasonable". In late 17th-century England, it was also politically explosive, a clear threat to the Protestant supremacy so painfully established over the last 150 years. Even so, with James now well into his fifties and with no legitimate children, his opponents could still afford wait for what they hoped would be his early death.

The unexpected birth of a son to James in June 1688 transformed the situation, raising the prospect of a further generation of Catholic Stuart monarchy. In response, an unlikely coalition of Whigs and Tories, the "Immortal Seven", issued an invitation to James's son-in-law, the Protestant William of Orange, to restore England to Protes-

Know I am your King. I will be obeyed, and I command you to be gone. Go and admit the Bishop of Oxford, Head, Principal, what do you call it, of the College … I mean President of the College. Let them that refuse it look to it. They shall feel the weight of their sovereign's displeasure

James II to Fellows of Magdalen College, Oxford, after their refusal to accept his appointment of a Catholic as President

tant good sense. His arrival in Torbay on November 5 at the head of 15,000 troops threatened a return to the kind of bloodshed everyone feared. James, however, lost his nerve. He marched his army to Salisbury, panicked, went back to London, and fled to France. In February, Parliament confirmed the joint rule of William and James's daughter, Mary.

1672	1673	1679	1685	1686	1687	1688
Forced to resign as Lord High Admiral under Test Act banning Catholics from public office	Marries (Catholic) Mary of Modena	Sent by Charles II to Brussels to escape anti-Catholic fervour; thereafter appointed Governor of Scotland where begins persecution of Covenanters	As James II, suppresses anti-Catholic invasions by Monmouth and Argyll. Revocation of Edict of Nantes by Louis XIV leads to expulsion of French Huguenots	Begins appointments of Catholics to public offices in England	Declaration of Indulgence extends official religious tolerance to all non-Anglicans	Birth of son, James Stuart (June); invitation to govern England issued to William of Orange (June); William's army lands at Torbay (Nov.); James II flees to France (Dec.)

THE GLORIOUS REVOLUTION 1688–9

HOWEVER UNPLANNED THE CONSEQUENCES, THE OVERTHROW OF JAMES II IN DECEMBER 1688 COMPLETED THE PARLIAMENTARY REVOLUTION THAT HAD BEGUN IN THE REIGN OF CHARLES I. IN RETROSPECT, IT LOOKED INEVITABLE; AT THE TIME, IT WAS ANYTHING BUT. YET, LOOKED FOR OR NOT, A TRANSFORMATION OF ENGLISH KINGSHIP HAD TAKEN PLACE. CONSTITUTIONAL MONARCHY, ANSWERABLE TO PARLIAMENT, HAD BECOME A FACT.

IF THERE WAS ONE POINT THAT THE RESTORATION OF CHARLES II in 1660 had confirmed, it was that hereditary monarchy formed the bedrock of English political life. Even if the precise details of the king's relationship with Parliament had been left vague, few disputed that kingship, allied with a duly constituted Parliament, was fundamental to the political well-being of the nation.

In the prudent hands of Charles II, however much he may have believed in the ultimate supremacy of the monarchy, this led to a largely pragmatic accommodation with Parliament that generally disturbed no one. In the hands of James II, it led to a head-to-head conflict with his leading subjects that resulted directly, if unexpectedly, to his overthrow. The issue was not just absolutism – James's claim to be able to rule without reference to Parliament. Rather, it was religion, specifically the generally held belief that James's attempts to impose religious toleration were a smokescreen for the reimposition of Catholicism on England.

Among England's governing classes (if not always its kings), since at least the rule of Elizabeth I, the belief that the country's destiny was permanently Protestant had become a given. That,

fitfully, Protestantism had come to be also associated with a free Parliament and that, in turn, a Protestant Parliament was seen as the ultimate guarantor of English liberties, themselves dating back to Magna Carta in the 13th century, had become equally entrenched articles of faith. The rule of law, embracing both monarchy and Parliament, had become indistinguishable from Protestantism.

In the circumstances, James II's attempts to force Catholicism on England inevitably provoked great and lasting hostility. That said, there was very little in practical terms that could be done to restrain him. Catholic despot or not, James II was a legitimate king who ultimately could expect to count on the loyalty of the dominant political group in the country in the embryonic world of English political parties – the Tories, staunch defenders of royal supremacy.

So the best that could reasonably be expected was that, like Charles II, James would die young, allowing the Protestant supremacy to be restored with the succession of his daughter, Mary. She was not merely Protestant but was married to Prince William of Orange, leader of the anti-French Protestant coalition in Europe.

Famously, the birth in June 1688 of a son and heir to James

Blown by a fair "Protestant wind", William of Orange's fleet landed at Torbay, 100 years after the Spanish Armada, on the most auspicious day of the English Protestant calendar, November 5 (above). It was an invasion in every sense: 250 ships carrying the cream of the Dutch army. James's response was entirely out of character, suggestive of a mental breakdown. He marched just a portion of his army out of London to meet the Dutch, but got no further than Salisbury. There, as desertions mounted and in a state bordering on panic, he turned round and went back to London, before fleeing to France. Even that was bungled. He was found in Dover and, to the exasperation of William, sent back to London before he finally made his way to Versailles. A French courtier reportedly claimed: "When one listens to him, one understands why he is here."

ended all such hopes, prompting a coalition of Whigs and Tories, the so-called "Immortal Seven", to "invite" William to "rescue the nation and the religion". That they should turn to a Dutchman to protect them from the actions of a legally sanctioned king of England was a startling measure of their desperation.

At this stage, neither William nor the Tories reasonably expected to oust James. William was chiefly concerned to keep England in the Protestant camp, the Tories that James be brought to his senses. Further, any attempt to overthrow the king ran the clear risk of a return to the bloodshed of the Civil War. James was an experienced and able general who could call on an army of 40,000. There was no reason to believe he would not use it.

But when William arrived in England in November, he brought with him an army of invasion 15,000 strong, underlining both the huge risk he was taking and how dramatically the stakes had been raised. Even so, James's position remained formidable. And so it would have stayed had he not unaccountably lost his head and, after a token resistance, made for France and the protection of Louis XIV's court. This was the crucial turning point.

Meeting in January 1689, the "Convention" Parliament gave itself legal status by the simple expedient of asserting it. It then went on to declare that the throne of England was vacant as James's flight amounted to abdication, though in point of fact James had not abdicated and never would. Even now, highly reluctant to overturn the principles of hereditary monarchy, most Tories were unwilling to hand the crown to William and Mary jointly, arguing instead that they should govern as regents until the death of James II. William, his position entirely secure (and his troops patrolling London), refused point-blank, insisting on full and immediate sovereignty. He got it.

But this was monarchy with a difference. Under the Declaration of Rights, formalized at the end of the year as the Bill of Rights, William and Mary became joint rulers not through the hereditary principle, which was deliberately set aside, or even by right of conquest. Rather, it was because Parliament had ordained it. And this ultimate parliamentary supremacy was further strengthened by a series of checks on royal authority, above all that the monarch could not maintain a standing army and that the Crown's finances were to be dependent on Parliament. At the same time, elections, to be held every three years, were to be free, and freedom of speech within Parliament guaranteed.

Neither the Scots nor the Irish were included in these arrangements. For the latter in particular, the "Bloodless Revolution" would turn out to be anything but (see pp. 152–3). The new Protestant parliamentary supremacy also failed to address the longer-term question of the succession should William and Mary have no children. Securing the throne against the claims of James II's son would prove a permanent preoccupation of Parliament in the following decade. But what had happened was momentous enough.

After 1688, limited, legitimate and, above all, Protestant constitutional monarchy became the hallmark of English government as well as England's most distinctive contribution to the evolution of kingship. The path to it – via the Civil War, the execution of Charles I, the short-lived and uncertain Republic under Cromwell, and the Restoration of Charles II – had been circuitous. But what to a later generation of Whig historians was the nirvana of parliamentary supremacy had been reached.

"Whereas the said late King James II having abdicated the government, and the throne being thereby vacant, his Highness the Prince of Orange (whom it hath pleased Almighty God to make the glorious instrument of delivering this kingdom from popery and arbitrary power …". This was the ringing declaration that began the Bill of Rights (left), passed into law on December 16 1689. Among its many provisions was that James II and his descendants were excluded from the throne, as were all Catholics and those married to Catholics. Under the Coronation Oath Act, passed the same year, the sovereign was also obliged to swear to maintain Protestantism.

THE GLORIOUS REVOLUTION, 1688

- Ruled by William as Stadholder from 1672
- Country ruled by James which invited William to become king
- → William's route, 1689
- Rising in support of William, 1689
- → James's movement following William's landing
- Countries which continued to acknowledge James as King, 1688

After his invitation by the "Immortal Seven", Wiliam landed with a Dutch army at Tor Bay on 5 November. Deserted by almost the whole political class, James II lost his nerve and fled for France (map left). At any rate in England, the coup was bloodless.

SCOTLAND
NEWCASTLE
CARLISLE
IRELAND
DUBLIN
YORK
CHESTER
NOTTINGHAM
SHREWSBURY
WALES
CAMBRIDGE
AMSTERDAM
HELLEVOETSLUIS
NETHERLANDS
ENGLAND
BRISTOL
WINDSOR
LONDON
SALISBURY
ROCHESTER
PORTSMOUTH
SPANISH
NETHERLANDS
EXETER
AMBLETEUSE
SMALL STAT
TOR BAY
FRANCE

Ruled jointly with Mary II until December 28 1694

BORN: November 4 1650
ACCEDED: February 13 1689; crowned April 11 1689, Westminster Abbey

⤞⤝ ⤞⤝ ⤞⤝

Prince of Orange and Count of Nassau-Dillenburg, King of England, Scotland and Ireland

Queen Mary II

Ruled jointly with William III

BORN: April 30 1662
ACCEDED: February 13 1689; crowned April 11 1689, Westminster Abbey

⤞⤝ ⤞⤝ ⤞⤝

Queen of England, Scotland and Ireland

WILLIAM III AND MARY II 1689–1702

THE PROCLAMATION OF WILLIAM AND MARY AS JOINT MONARCHS OF ENGLAND MAY HAVE REPRESENTED A TRIUMPH FOR PROTESTANT PARLIAMENTARY SUPREMACY, BUT IT HAD NOT SEEN OFF THE CLAIMS OF JAMES II. FURTHER, THE EXPANSIONIST AIMS OF JAMES'S CHIEF SUPPORTER, LOUIS XIV, REMAINED A PERSISTENT THREAT. CONTENDING WITH BOTH WOULD PROVE THE DOMINANT THEME OF THE JOINT MONARCHY.

William (left) was never a popular figure. To some extent, this was the result of inevitable English distrust of a foreigner – and of the Dutchmen he brought with him to England: as late as 1699, Parliament demanded that he expel his Dutch Blue Guards, a request the king agreed to only reluctantly. But William himself was an unprepossessing figure, short, stooped, withdrawn, and a chronic asthmatic. He had few personal interests other than hunting and gardening; his life was dominated by his single-minded determination to do down Louis XIV.

Sweet-natured, elegant and charming, Mary (below left), five inches (12cm) taller than her husband, was hugely popular and much admired for her efforts to raise the moral tone of the court. Her marriage to William, arranged in the face of her father's bitter opposition, was purely a matter of state dictated by the need for Charles II to strengthen the anti-French alliance. Mary herself reacted unenthusiastically, "weeping all afternoon and the following day". Yet on the whole, though their marriage produced only three stillborn children, William and the dutiful Mary seem to have been well suited. She was only 32 when she died from smallpox in December 1694.

The Tory-dominated House of Lords in particular would have preferred to make Mary sole ruler and preserve the sanctity of the divine right of succession. However, Mary herself refused, partly from guilt at having abandoned her father, James II, and not wishing to appear to have usurped his throne. William, perfectly aware of his unique opportunity to strengthen the anti-French Protestant alliance, was simply adamant that he would accept nothing less than the crown itself, asserting that he would not be "his wife's lackey". The picture (above) shows them on their way to the Banqueting House in February 1689 to accept their joint crowns.

ALTHOUGH WILLIAM AND MARY WERE proclaimed joint monarchs in 1688, in reality "the sole and full exercise of regal power" was vested in William. It was an arrangement that suited both parties. Mary had little interest in government, though she agreed to act as regent during her husband's many absences abroad. For his part, even if his long-term – indeed overriding – interest was the defeat of Louis XIV's aggressively expansionist France, in the short term it was the consolidation of his Scottish and Irish thrones that was William's immediate priority.

Strictly speaking, James VII was still King of Scotland. In practice, however, the Scottish Parliament accepted the new sovereigns with only token objections, deposing James with a Claim Act that was broadly similar to England's Bill of Rights. Resistance remained, however, especially in the Catholic, pro-Stuart Highlands. In July 1689, a small force under Viscount Dundee at Killiecrankie inflicted what might have been a decisive victory over the Williamite troops, had not Dundee himself been killed in the fighting. Without his leadership, the Jacobite cause temporarily collapsed. William still insisted on extracting oaths of loyalty from the clan leaders, a policy that largely backfired with the notorious Glencoe Massacre in February 1692. When the Chief of Glencoe, Alasdair Macdonald, failed to take his oath, it was officially decided to put the Macdonalds to the sword. The resulting scandals severely dented William's popularity.

Ireland saw bloodshed on a far wider scale. As early as March 1689, James II had arrived there with 20,000 French troops. Huge numbers of Catholic Irish joined him. In May, the Irish Parliament formally declared their support for him. In December, the siege of Protestant Londonderry was begun. Six

1670	1672	1677	1685	1688	1689
William of Orange makes first visit to England	*Restoration of William of Orange in Holland*	*Marriage of William of Orange and Mary, daughter of the Duke of York*	*Anglo-Dutch treaty renewed*	*William signals his agreement to invade England in response to invitation by disaffected "Immortal Seven" (Sept.); invasion army lands at Torbay (Nov.)*	*William and Mary accept English throne as joint rulers under the Declaration of Rights. Act of Tolerance allows limited religious toleration. Jacobite uprising in Scotland collapses despite victory at Killiecrankie (July). Troops sent to confront James II in Ireland (Aug.). Grand Coalition formed to confront France (Sept.): King William's War begins (to 1697)*

*Forty years on from Cromwell's brutal reinforcement of
Protestantism in his Irish campaign of 1649–50, William
III's routing of the Catholic Irish and French army
assembled by James II in Ireland just as crucially hardened
the religious divide in Ireland. James II and his French
allies were hardly likely to prove indulgent toward the
Protestants in Ireland, as their 105-day siege of
Londonderry (left) from December 1689 proved. Equally,
William's defeat of James II at the Battle of the Boyne
created a myth of Protestant supremacy that endures today.*

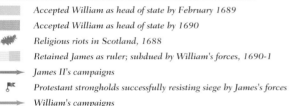

WILLIAM AND MARY 1689–1702

- Accepted William as head of state by February 1689
- Accepted William as head of state by 1690
- Religious riots in Scotland, 1688
- Retained James as ruler; subdued by William's forces, 1690-1
- James II's campaigns
- Protestant strongholds successfully resisting siege by James's forces
- William's campaigns
- Other English campaigns
- French fleet from the Mediterranean, 1690
- Jacobite stronghold successfully resisting siege by William
- Conquered by William's forces, 1691
- Clans largely supporting James
- Area of William's military activities 1692-4
- Frontiers, 1689

*William and Mary's joint
monarchy provoked
widespread conflict in
Scotland and Ireland (map
left). If Scottish opposition
to the joint monarchs was
relatively easily contained,
in Ireland it gave rise to
bitter fighting. William's
resounding defeat of James
II at the Battle of the Boyne
did nothing to reduce
Catholic Irish opposition to
the Protestant monarchs.*

months later, William himself was in Ireland with an army of Danes, Germans, Dutch and English. At the Battle of the Boyne, he led them to a resounding victory. Within three days, James had fled back to France.

Whatever the scale of his Irish victories, for William they were essentially sideshows compared with his real struggle with Louis XIV. By September 1689, the king had formed a Grand Coalition, headed by the Dutch and the English, against Louis. King William's War, as it became known, was inconclusive. The Treaty of Ryswick, which ended it in 1697, really signalled no more than a pause in the hostilities, which duly restarted in 1702. But its consequences for England were substantial. For the first time since Elizabeth I's reign, England was involved in a full-scale Continental conflict. From being a spectator of Continental wars, England was poised to become a major player. Almost as important was the foundation in 1694 of the Bank of England, intended chiefly to facilitate the financing of the war. Its long-term impact on England's burgeoning commerce would be difficult to overstate. Scarcely less important, William's long absences meant that power became further concentrated in Parliament.

William's relationship with Parliament was rarely smooth. He may have owed his position to it but he still resented the limitations it placed on him. Nevertheless, crucially, he always submitted to it – however grudgingly. More than ever it was Parliament in which ultimate authority was vested, something unmistakably underlined in 1701 with the Act of Settlement. Under this, the wholly obscure but reliably Protestant German Hanoverians were named successors to Queen Anne, William's own successor.

1690	1692	1693	1694	1696	1697	1700	1701
James II defeated by William at Battle of the Boyne	Glencoe Massacre. Naval victory over French at La Hogue	French victory over Dutch and English at Neerwinden	Foundation of the Bank of England. Jacobite plot against William foiled. Death of Mary	Further Jacobite plot foiled	Civil List Act strengthens parliamentary control over royal finances	Death of Duke of Gloucester, son of Mary's sister Anne, prompts renewed succession fears	Act of Settlement nominates Hanoverians as legal successors

ANNE 1702–14

PORTLY, SOMEWHAT DOUR, BUT ALWAYS CONSCIENTIOUS, ANNE PRESIDED OVER A NATION EXPANDING MILITARILY AND COMMERCIALLY. HER REIGN ALSO SAW THE GROWTH OF PARTY POLITICS OF A RECOGNIZABLY MODERN KIND. AS IMPORTANT, IN 1707 IT WITNESSED THE FORMAL UNION OF ENGLAND AND SCOTLAND. ANNE WAS THE FIRST MONARCH OF GREAT BRITAIN.

QUEEN ANNE

BORN: February 6 1665
ACCEDED: March 8 1702;
crowned April 23 1702,
Westminster Abbey

Queen of England, Scotland and Ireland; from 1707, Queen of Great Britain and Ireland

An inescapable sense of tragedy surrounds Anne (above). She was haunted by a sense of having betrayed her father, James II, however much she opposed his religious stance. In 1692, she fell out with her sister, Mary, over her continued friendship with Sarah Churchill. Her relations with William, "that Dutch monster", were hardly more cordial. Her celebrated friendship with Sarah Churchill also ended in recrimination. "I believe nobody was ever so used by a friend as I have been since coming to the Crown," wrote Anne in 1710. For her part, Sarah asserted that, "She [Anne] meant well and was no fool; but nobody can maintain that she was wise, nor entertaining in conversation."

A S THE YOUNGER DAUGHTER OF JAMES II, Anne had never had much realistic expectation of becoming queen. Even after the deposition of her father, it was reasonable to assume her sister, Queen Mary, would produce children. It was only the refusal of William to remarry after the death of the childless Mary in 1694 that confirmed Anne as heir. Anne herself would prove no more able to secure her succession. Though marriage to her dull-witted but amiable husband, George, Prince of Denmark, produced 18 pregnancies (one with twins), only one child, William, Duke of Gloucester, survived infancy. His death at the age of 11, reopening the possibility of a Catholic Stuart succession, provoked the Act of Settlement of 1701, which named the elderly Sophia, Dowager Duchess of Hanover, as heir to the English throne.

Scotland, where pro-Stuart sentiments still ran strong, was another matter. In 1703, the Scottish Parliament asserted its obvious right as an independent kingdom to choose its own monarch. With England now fully committed to a major European struggle against Louis XIV, the prospect of a restored Catholic Stuart King of Scotland allying himself with France in a renewed Auld Alliance became alarmingly real. The solution, a formal union of England and Scotland, may not have been popular in Scotland but – backed by implied English threats of something very much less advantageous and accompanied by a huge one-off payment to Scotland – amid considerable Scottish rancour, in 1707 the Kingdom of Great Britain was born.

For England, it was just one part of a rapid consolidation as a major European power. The War of Spanish Succession, which began in 1702 and saw England in another Grand Alliance against France, produced a series of startling English victories over the French, most famously John Churchill's victory at Blenheim in 1704. Furthermore, when the war ended in 1713, Britain had acquired a string of new colonial possessions, Gibraltar among them.

If Anne's reign is generally viewed as a triumphant period of English and then British conquest and imperial expansion, it was also one of tur-

The Success of English Arms

A s late as the reign of James II, England – let alone Scotland – was dismissed as scarcely even a second-rate military power in the wider European world. It was seen as effectively no more than a pensioner of Louis XIV, propped up by the French king's regular handouts to Charles II and James II. Even under William III, when England found itself re-engaged in Continental warfare, its military impact was less than formidable. But the remarkable victories enjoyed by the English in the War of Spanish Succession, above all under the generalship of John Churchill, created Duke of Marlborough in 1702, were of a kind and scale that had not been known since the reign of Henry V in the early 15th century.

The war may have turned into one of colonial conquest, but for England it began principally as a means to prevent Louis XIV's renewed sponsorship of James's II's son, James Stuart, the "Old Pretender." But from at least 1708 onwards, there was a growing tide of Tory opinion in England against the war, not least as a result of its prodigious cost, which by its end in 1713 was £150 million. Nonetheless, Britain's growing military and naval prowess was being unmistakably established.

The Battle of Malplaquet, 1709.

The emergence of England, after 1707 of Great Britain, as a major European power was clearly signalled in Anne's reign (map right). The union of England and Scotland was in itself a significant step, one which would transform Scotland's hitherto secondary position. As important was the startling success of English and British arms in Europe.

ANNE 1702–14

- Great Britain from 1707
- English, later British, dependencies
- → English/British naval activities during the Spanish War of Succession
- → Marlborough's campaign 1704
- Other theatres of English/British campaigns
- Awarded to Britain under Treaty of Utrecht, 1713
- Frontiers, 1702

Charles II memorably said of Anne's husband, George (below), Prince of Denmark: "I have tried him drunk and I have tried him sober, and there is nothing in him." To most only a dolt, to Anne he was "an inestimable treasure". Their greatest sadness was their failure to produce healthy children. Anne had 13 stillborn children and at least one miscarriage. With the death in 1710 of their only surviving child, William, the Protestant Stuart succession ended.

### Map labels

SWEDEN
SCOTLAND
EDINBURGH
Planned landing of James Edward the 'Old Pretender' to foment Jacobite rising failed, 1708
DENMARK–NORWAY
North Sea
IRELAND
MAN
DUBLIN
PRUSSIA
WALES
ENGLAND
LONDON
SAXONY
NETHERLANDS
Oudenarde 1708
DUNKIRK
Malplaquet 1709
Ramillies 1706
SMALL STATES
SPANISH NETHERLANDS
Blenheim 1704
CHANNEL IS.
LORRAINE
English Channel
AUSTRIAN HABSBURG
SWISS CONFEDERATION
FRANCE
SAVOY
Bay of Biscay
GENOA
1702
TOULON
1707
VIGO
Barcelona 1705
SARDINIA (to Spain)
PORTUGAL
MADRID
Brihuega 1710
PORT MAHON
MINORCA Occupied by Britain, 1708
SPAIN
Almanza 1707
Mediterranean Sea
CÁDIZ
MÁLAGA 1704
1702
GIBRALTAR English, 1704
ALGIERS (Ottoman vassal)

---

bulent political division, something with which Anne struggled to come to terms. In many ways it was hardly her fault. Constitutional monarchy of the kind that was rapidly evolving was quite new. The rules could only be made up as everyone went along. If the queen's initial public preference was for a government drawn from all shades of political opinion, her natural instinct was to favour the Tories, still the party of a strong monarchy. However, she was rapidly forced to confront the reality of aggressive Whig political power, which pushed not only for a continuation of what was proving an extremely expensive war, but also for further limits on the Crown prerogatives. In the end, anti-war sentiments in the country at large saw a return in 1710 to a Tory administration, headed by Robert Harley and Henry St John. It was they who secured the Treaty of Utrecht in 1713, which for the time being ended the long struggle against France.

The final years of Anne's reign were blighted by ill-health. The queen was not only in permanent pain, her corpulence was such she could scarcely walk and often had to be moved with pulleys. At her death, her doctor touchingly wrote: "I believe sleep was never more welcome to a weary traveller than death was to her."

Her Majesty was labouring under a fit of the gout, and in extreme pain and agony … Her face, which was red and spotted, was rendered something frightful by her negligent dress, and the foot affected was tied up with a poultice and some nasty bandages … Nature seems inverted when a poor infirm woman becomes one of the rulers of the world.

Sir John Clerk on Queen Anne in 1707

GREAT BRITAIN AND IRELAND: THE HANOVERIANS 1714–1917

GEORGE I 1714–27

GEORGE II 1727–60

GEORGE III 1760–1820

GEORGE IV 1820–30

WILLIAM IV 1830–37

VICTORIA 1837–1901

EDWARD VII 1901–10

IN DECLARING "THE MOST EXCELLENT PRINCESS SOPHIA, ELECTRESS AND DOWAGER DUCHESS OF HANOVER" THE LEGAL HEIR TO THE THRONE OF ENGLAND UNDER THE *ACT OF SETTLEMENT* IN 1701, PARLIAMENT SET ASIDE NO FEWER THAN 57 STUARTS WITH BETTER HEREDITARY CLAIMS. AS A GRANDDAUGHTER OF JAMES I, SOPHIA COULD LAY AT LEAST SOME CLAIM TO THE LINE OF SUCCESSION. BUT THAT AN OTHERWISE OBSCURE GERMAN PRINCESS SHOULD BE SO DRAMATICALLY ACCELERATED TO THE HEAD OF THE QUEUE EMPHATICALLY UNDERLINED, EVEN MORE THAN IN 1689, THAT THE CHOICE OF MONARCH WAS NOW THE GIFT OF PARLIAMENT RATHER THAN A MATTER OF DIVINE-RIGHT HEREDITARY SUCCESSION.

The selection of Sophia as the successor to Queen Anne had been dictated by an absolute imperative in Protestant England: that of preventing a Catholic Stuart succession. Put simply, however far removed from the main line of succession, Sophia and her family were the closest decently Protestant heirs available. Further, unlike many of the Stuarts proper, they were prolific. Sophia herself had six sons.

Barring calamities, the Protestant succession looked guaranteed.

Even the Hanoverians' most obvious drawback – that they were foreigners speaking not a word of English – could be turned to advantage, as it made them dependent on English advisors and thus unlikely to meddle in the affairs of Parliament. It may not be true that under the new arrangement the accession of "a deaf-mute would not have been entirely amiss": the power of the Crown remained formidable. But there is no question that the Hanoverian succession was a decisive step towards a limited constitutional monarchy.

In fact Sophia died first (at the age of 83), albeit only two months before Anne herself. Parliament, however, had already prudently taken care to make Sophia's eldest son, Georg Augustus, an English subject in 1705. Thus with the death of Queen Anne on August 1 1714, the British throne passed to the man immediately proclaimed "George I, King of Great Britain, France and Ireland". However improbably, Britain found itself ruled by a native German dynasty, the Hanoverians. An enforced change of family name aside (under George V in 1917), it persists today. As a mark of this profound German influence, and even as the Hanoverians themselves became more obviously English, every single Hanoverian monarch until Edward VII in 1901 was married to a German.

That said, historically it makes little sense to treat the British monarchy from 1714 to the present as an unbroken whole. The changes in Britain between the accession of George I in 1714 and that of Victoria in 1837 – a period in which Britain was raised from first among equals in Europe to being the world's leading power – were necessarily reflected in the status of its monarchy. For, over this period, the monarchy was transformed from a semi-divinely ordained office, albeit increasingly answerable to Parliament, to a constitutional monarchy of an ever more limited kind.

In much the same way, as Britain became definitively the world's leading power in the long reign of Victoria, so its monarchy underwent a further transformation. As royal prerogative was forced to give way to final parliamentary supremacy – with Victoria, however reluctantly, stepping across the invisible but real line between ruling and reigning – so the monarchy, whatever its importance as symbol of the world's premier state, was increasingly boxed in. To all intents and purposes, by Victoria's death in 1901 constitutional monarchy on a recognizably modern model had come into being.

All of this was very different from the world of the early Hanoverians. George I, irascible, vain and dull, may have been little more than a bad-tempered link between the last of the Stuarts and the emergence of a new, aggressively colonizing Britain. But like his heir, George II, he nonetheless had to contend not just with the reality of a monarchy increasingly answerable to parliamentary party politics but with the after-shocks of the overthrow of James II in 1689. Although they were the most serious, the Jacobite risings in 1715 and 1745 were not the only manifestations of a long-standing Stuart threat to the security of Protestant Hanoverian Britain, albeit one effectively ended with the failure of the 1745 uprising.

If George II could subsequently console himself with having presided over a massive extension of British colonial rule, his successor, George III, who could at least speak English without a German accent, had to confront the equally unmistakable and very much less palatable reality of the loss of Britain's American colonies. It is a measure of Britain's growing standing in the 18th-century world that the monarchy itself, whatever George III's unsuccessful attempts to dictate the composition of his governments, emerged largely unscathed from the American disaster. Ultimately, however, his reign would be blighted by madness, the king reduced to a slobbering ruin, at the mercy of misguided doctors inflicting a series of pointless and humiliating cures.

Even with the Regency and subsequent reign of George IV, unquestionably Britain's most dissolute monarch as well as, when sober, the most talented and artistically minded of the Hanoverians, the monarchy prospered. Britain by now, as confirmed by its defeat of Napoleon, was so clearly a world power that its throne could scarcely fail to reflect its extravagant glory.

Yet a profound change was in the offing. Unwilling or not, Victoria, 18 when she came to the throne in 1837, 81 when she died in 1901, presided over a fundamental redefinition of monarchy. As her actual powers were surrendered and with them any suggestion of an active political role, so her symbolic importance as personification – and hence ultimate guarantor – of the legitimacy and stability of the British state and its empire grew. Accident or not, an entirely new concept of monarch as constitutional symbol had been created.

GEORGE I 1714–27

GEORGE I WAS NEVER A POPULAR KING. BAD-TEMPERED, UNCOUTH AND SPEAKING ONLY THE MOST LIMITED ENGLISH, TO HIS SUBJECTS HE WAS THE BOORISH FOREIGNER PERSONIFIED. HIS ATTEMPTS TO INVOLVE BRITAIN IN HANOVERIAN INTERESTS ALSO DID LITTLE TO ENDEAR HIM TO HIS BRITISH SUBJECTS. BUT HIS BRIEF REIGN SAW THE SUCCESSFUL CONSOLIDATION OF THE PROTESTANT HANOVERIANS AND THE FURTHER REINFORCEMENT OF PARLIAMENTARY GOVERNMENT.

BORN: June 7 1660, Hanover
ACCEDED: August 1 1714; crowned October 20 1714, Westminster Abbey

Duke and Elector of Hanover, King of Great Britain and Ireland

A LMOST THE FIRST ACT OF GEORGE I ON becoming king of Britain in early August 1714 was to declare himself, on his own authority, king of Hanover, a title that would not be recognized elsewhere until 100 years later. He then set off on a leisurely and triumphant progress through Germany, arriving in England only at the very end of September. At 54, he was the oldest ever successor to the English throne.

From the start, he struggled with his new kingdom, finding its customs and habits almost as irksome as the limitations that were imposed on his royal prerogative by Parliament. Whereas in Hanover he had enjoyed almost unlimited power – all expenditure over £13 had to be personally approved by him – in England he found himself constantly thwarted by Parliament. In truth, almost anyone might have struggled to find their feet in the confused, often venomous political climate of early 18th-century Britain. Party politics on the British model were unknown elsewhere. As a non-English speaker, reliant on his son George to translate for him or otherwise forced to speak to his ministers in French, occasionally in Latin, it is hardly to be wondered at if the impatient George I was often out of his depth.

The king's own preference was firmly for the Whigs, a view that helped push a number of Tories into the Jacobite camp, in the process guaranteeing their continued political exclusion, especially with the failure of the Jacobite Rebellion of 1715 (see pp. 160–1). That said, relations between the king and the Whigs were rarely harmonious. Nonetheless, by 1717 George had managed to engineer a more pliant administration – evidence of the still formidable prerogative of the throne – in the process driving the most ambitious and able of the Whigs, Robert Walpole, into the orbit of the Prince of Wales, whose relations with his father, never good, had now broken down almost entirely.

This stand-off was transformed in September 1720 with the spectacular collapse of the South Sea Company, a private venture set up nine years earlier to take over the spiralling National Debt. In 1718 the king had been made governor of the company, so it was with more than just suspicion that the court and government were directly implicated in the greed-driven scandal. Thousands saw their entire investments lost, and the resulting crisis – unquestionably the most serious of George I's reign and actively inflamed by the Jacobites – threatened to bring the Hanoverian dynasty to a sudden end.

George I (above) at least had the virtue of consistency. His most serious failing was his bad temper. In 1694, he discovered his wife, Sophia Dorothea, then 28, was having an affair with a Swedish soldier, Philip von Königsmark. The Swede disappeared, reputedly after George had him hacked to death. For her part, Sophia Dorothea was divorced and incarcerated for life in the Castle of Ahlden. She remained there, forbidden to see her children, until her death 32 years later. It was this treatment of his mother, which shocked Europe, that led to the life-long rift between George and his son, the future George II. At the same time, the king had two publicly acknowledged mistresses. One, Sophia Charlotte, was widely rumoured to be the king's half-sister; in later life she became extremely fat, so much so that she and the king were known as the Elephant and Castle. The other, whom the king was believed to have married in secret, was Ehrengard Melusine von Schulenburg, as thin as her rival was fat. They were described, memorably, as, "old, ugly trulls, such as would not find entertainment in the most hospitable hundreds of old Drury."

The "South Sea Bubble" in September 1720 came close to bringing down the Hanoverians. Though the scheme was not fraudulent when launched, the need to gain political backing for the scheme, essentially by offering stock at artificially low prices to politicians and members of the court, subsequently took it perilously close to illegality. The crisis itself was caused by huge paper profits that rapidly led to a feeding frenzy as others demanded to be let in. Prices were pushed sky high until, as suddenly, they disintegrated, leaving a handful of lucky investors sitting on large fortunes but the vast majority all but wiped out. Hardly surprisingly, there was a widespread demand that someone should be punished, a demand that the more Jacobite Tories were only too keen to encourage. The court's obvious involvement with the scheme made it a natural target. This engraving (right) caricatures the transformation of the "Great South Sea Caterpillar" into a butterfly.

The great South Sea Caterpillar, transform'd into a Bath Butterfly.

1682	1698	1714	1715	1716
Marriage of Georg Augustus to Sophia Dorothea of Celle	Georg Augustus becomes Elector of Hanover	Georg Augustus accedes to British throne as George I. Arrives in London (Sept.)	Jacobite Rebellion (Sept.) suppressed. Discredited Tory administration gives way to Whigs	Tory hopes of rapid return to government thwarted by Septennial Act, under which elections are to be held only every seven years

Hanover, ruled by George since 1697

Great Britain and dependencies, 1714

Added to Hanover, 1715

Frontiers, 1714

Frontier of the Holy Roman Empire, 1714

The accession of the otherwise obscure elector of Hanover as king of Great Britain and Ireland in 1714 was the clearest possible evidence that it was Parliament who made and unmade monarchs now. It was a crucial moment in the history of British kingship (map right).

SWEDEN

N O R W A

D E N M A R K

(to Sweden)

(to Denmark)

AHLDEN

HANOVER

North Sea

GREAT BRITAIN

EDINBURGH

IRELAND

DUBLIN

LONDON

NETHERLANDS

PRUSSIA

PRUSSIA

SAXONY

SMALL STATES

AUSTRIAN NETHERLANDS

English Channel

FRANCE

LORRAINE

BAVARIA

Sir Robert Walpole (above) was the first recognizably modern politician, a master of patronage and a brilliant manipulator of party political advantage. If George I initially resented him for his Whig sympathies, he as soon came to value him for his crisis management after the South Sea Company collapse. George I can hardly be said to have wittingly encouraged the development of party political government, but his willingness to allow Walpole his head after 1720 was crucial to the further consolidation of parliamentary supremacy.

An honest, dull German gentleman, as unfit as unwilling to act the part of a king ... lazy and inactive, even in his pleasures, which were therefore lowly sensual ... England was too big for him.

Lord Chesterfield on George I

An honest blockhead ... our customs and laws were all mysteries to him, which he neither tried to understand, nor was capable of understanding.

Lady Mary Wortley Montagu on George I

Walpole's supreme ability as a political fixer not only calmed the panic, in the process reconciling him with the king (who thereafter came to regard him as indispensable), it also cemented his position as the dominant political figure of the age. With his appointment as First Lord of the Treasury in 1721, he emerged, in effect, as the country's first Prime Minister. A long period of Whig hegemony was begun.

Thoroughly alarmed by the crisis and with Walpole so obviously capable, the king went to ground politically. The last years of his reign were given over to the modest pleasures of his placid court: gardening (at Hampton Court and Kensington Palace preeminently), card playing, horses, and his mistresses. Whenever possible, he also visited Hanover, where it is clear he was most at home and where, in June 1727, he died and was buried.

1717	1720	1721	1722
Near permanent rift between George I and Prince of Wales. Walpole ousted; Tories under Lord Stanhope clear way for George I's anti-Russian alliance with France and Holland	*Collapse of South Sea Company – the "South Sea Bubble" – implicates king and court. George I forced into reconciliation with Walpole and Prince of Wales. Royal Academy of Music established under patronage of George I*	*Walpole made First Lord of the Treasury, effectively Prime Minister*	*Jacobite "Atterbury Plot" foiled*

THE JACOBITE UPRISINGS 1689–1745

WHATEVER THE GROWING POWER OF PROTESTANT BRITAIN, IT WAS PERSISTENTLY THREATENED BY EFFORTS TO ENGINEER A STUART RESTORATION. UNTIL THE MIDDLE OF THE 18TH CENTURY, THERE WERE REPEATED STUART ATTEMPTS, CHIEFLY AIDED BY FRANCE, TO REGAIN WHAT THEY CONSIDERED THEIR LEGITIMATE THRONES IN ENGLAND, SCOTLAND AND IRELAND. THE TWO MOST SUSTAINED CHALLENGES WERE MOUNTED IN 1715 AND 1745.

THE YEARS BETWEEN THE ACCESSION OF WILLIAM III AND Mary II in 1689 and the Hanoverian succession in 1714 were an aggressive statement of intent about the future of Protestant parliamentary government in England. But if England had decisively turned its back on Stuart Catholic absolutism, the Stuarts were no less determined to regain their thrones and to overthrow a constitutional settlement that was considered by the exiled James II to be "contrary to the law of God, nature and the nation". After 1689, the Jacobite cause – from the Latin Jacobus, meaning James – became one of the most persistent and important features of European politics as well as the most serious danger to post-1688 order in England.

Stuart efforts centred on three figures: James II, the ousted king of England and Scotland; then, after James's death in 1701, his son, the "Old Pretender", also called James; and in turn, his son, Charles, the "Young Pretender". Their motives were straightforward and consistent: to return to a throne usurped in 1689. Their supporters, on the other hand, always acted for a more mixed variety of reasons. Consistently the most important, and the major source of funds and men to the Jacobites, was the France of Louis XIV and his successor, Louis XV. Certainly, defending the legitimacy of fellow absolutist Catholic monarchs was a factor that weighed heavily with the French crown. But more important in French eyes was the potential of the Jacobites to destabilize England, which by the early 18th century had emerged as its major European rival. Catholic Spain was a similar if less consistent supporter of the Jacobites; Franco-Spanish rivalry ruled out sustained Spanish support.

In Ireland, other than in the now Protestant north, and in Scotland, above all in the still largely Catholic Highlands, Jacobite support was widespread. If the survival of Catholicism in these areas was the prime factor, anti-English feeling and, for the Scots, loyalty to what was originally a native Scottish dynasty were similarly significant. Indeed by the early 18th century, resentment against England would make Scotland the overwhelming focus of the Jacobite cause. Such resentment was reinforced by the Act of Union in 1707, bitterly objected to by most Scots, and by the Hanoverian succession of George I, "the wee, German laddie", in 1714.

Hardly surprisingly, English Jacobites were much thinner on the ground, though even here growing dislike of the "foreign" dynasties of William and Mary and of the Hanoverians, particularly their pursuit of Continental wars at English expense, gave rise to a growing Jacobite camp. With the Hanoverian succession, the Tories in particular, who had always harboured doubts about the legitimacy of the settlement in 1689, came to see a Stuart restoration as increasingly desirable, if only to offset George I's obvious anti-Tory prejudice.

The first attempts at a Stuart restoration – in Ireland in 1689 and

massively underwritten by Louis XIV – were crushingly defeated by William III at the Battle of the Boyne in 1690 (see pp.153). Remaining Irish resistance was mopped up by John Churchill the following year at Aughrim. The subsequent Treaty of Limerick effectively ended Jacobite ambitions in Ireland, though it also allowed an Irish army – the "Wild Geese", aptly described as a "Jacobite army-in-waiting" – to leave for France. It was this "Irish Brigade" that formed the nucleus of two further French-sponsored attempted Jacobite invasions of England in 1692 and in 1696. Neither came to anything, despite the numbers involved. The former collapsed when the Royal Navy destroyed the French ships assembled for the invasion at La Hogue. The latter, scuppered by a falling out between Louis XIV and English Jacobites, never got further than Calais.

Louis was far from finished. On the death of James II, he provocatively recognized James's son as James III of England and

James Stuart (left), *the soi-disant James III and VIII, was an uninspiring figure, dour, gloomy and dutiful. His loyalty to the Jacobite cause, like his Catholicism, was unquestioned, his capacity to inspire it all but non-existent. During his sole, depressing visit to Scotland in the abortive uprising at the end of 1715, a Jacobite reported: "Our men asked if he could speak." With the failure of the rebellion, he abandoned further attempts to regain his thrones, living in Rome in a state of "pious melancholy". The poet Thomas Gray said of him in 1740 that he had, "… the air and look of an idiot, particularly when he laughs or prays. The first he does not often, the latter continually."*

James VIII of Scotland. In 1708, he sent 18,000 troops to Scotland under the nominal command of James where they were intended to join forces with a Scottish Jacobite army 30,000 strong. In the end, the Scottish Jacobites never materialized while the French, meeting an English fleet, turned back in sight of the Scottish coast.

In December 1715, by contrast, the Old Pretender at least made it on to Scottish soil. It was already too late, however. A planned invasion of the West Country in September had been abandoned almost as soon as it began while a simultaneous Jacobite uprising in northern England was similarly ineffective. Undeterred, the Earl of Mar pressed ahead with the main revolt in Scotland, seizing a series of towns before narrowly avoiding defeat by a much smaller Hanoverian force at Sherriffmuir in November. Thereafter, despite

1689	1690	1691	1692	1696	1697	1701	1702	1707
Scottish Jacobite army under Viscount Dundee defeated by Williamite forces at Killiecrankie	Franco-Irish Jacobite army under James II defeated by William III in Ireland at the Battle of Boyne	Williamite victory over Irish Jacobites at Aughrim followed by Irish political settlement under Treaty of Limerick	Glencoe Massacre. French-sponsored Jacobite invasion halted after English naval victory at La Hogue	Further French-sponsored Jacobite invasion fails to leave France	Treaty of Ryswick signals temporary Anglo-French rapprochement	Death of James II in France; successor recognized by Louis XIV as James III and VIII	War of Spanish Succession: renewed Anglo-French conflict (to 1713) increases Jacobite tension	Act of Union between England and Scots fuels Scottish Jacobite anti-English sentiments

Though lavishly supported by the French, the Jacobite uprising of 1715 (map right) was a complete failure. James Stuart himself, the "Old Pretender", proved a dour, uninspiring figure, incapable of generating either loyalty or enthusiasm for the Stuart cause. His brief stay in Scotland only confirmed the paucity of his military talents.

the belated arrival of James, who spent six increasingly gloomy weeks in Scotland, the uprising fizzled into nothing. But if it was easily suppressed in the end, it had nonetheless caused considerable alarm in England. The reprisals, fully supported by George I, were relentless, just as they would be after 1745.

The Jacobites had suffered a simultaneous set back in 1715 with the death of Louis XIV, for so long the mainstay of the Stuart cause. French championship of the Jacobites increasingly became a matter of lip service. The Stuart court in France, 3,000 strong and maintained entirely at French expense, was turning into an expensive embarrassment to its hosts.

The Spanish subsequently took up the running, in 1719 launching a substantial fleet with weapons for 30,000 Scots Jacobites. It made it only as far as Coruña in northern Spain before being forced back by a gale. Thereafter, despite a minor Jacobite

Where his father was pedestrian, Charles Stuart (shown here, right, at only 12), at least when leading the 1745 Jacobite Rebellion, was dashing and heroic. But if his capacity to inspire loyalty was undoubted, his political and military talents were slim at best, the product of a naivety and optimism that led, in 1746, to the extermination of his army at Culloden. His life thereafter degenerated into indolence and sloth. He was, it was said, "never quite sober".

By the time the Young Pretender had led his hastily raised army south to Derby, the Stuart cause suddenly looked as though it might after all succeed (map right). In the event, isolated and uncertain, the Scots turned back to what, in the spring of 1746, would prove a crushing defeat.

uprising in England in 1722 – the Atterbury Plot – the Jacobite cause languished before reviving briefly and, for a moment gloriously, in 1745. It was the final and, in the end, futile Jacobite flourish.

The 1745 Jacobite Rebellion was led by the youthful, charismatic Young Pretender – Bonnie Prince Charlie – who landed in Scotland in July 1745 with just seven men. Charles's rallying of the clans and subsequent march into England promised much. Panic in London aside, it delivered nothing. By the time Derby had been reached, it was clear that far from outflanking the pursuing Hanoverians Charles had merely isolated himself in enemy territory. Dispirited and increasingly bedraggled, the remnants of his army returned to Scotland. The following year, it was annihilated at Culloden. Five months later, Charles escaped to France.

The Jacobites would not finally abandon their claim to their thrones until the death of Charles's younger brother, the titular Henry IX, in 1807. But after 1745 their cause had become little more than an exercise in nostalgia.

The Jacobite Uprising of 1715

- Anti-Hanoverian riots, 1715
- Movements of the Duke of Ormonde
- Mar's movements and campaign, 1715
- Highlander detachments joining Mar, 1715
- James, the Old Pretender's movements
- Other Jacobite risings
- Other Jacobite campaigns

The Jacobite Uprising of 1745

- Campaigns from France in support of/by Jacobites, with details
- Charles Edward's advance
- Charles Edward's retreat from England and further campaigning in Scotland
- Area strongly supporting Charles Edward
- Hanoverian campaigns, with details

1708	1715	1719	1722	1745	1746	1766	1788
Attempted French-sponsored invasion reaches Scotland but is deterred by English fleet	Major Jacobite uprising in Scotland under Earl of Mar (Sept.); Old Pretender lands Scotland (Dec.) but returns to France after six weeks	Spanish-backed invasion turns back near Coruña	Jacobite Atterbury Plot in England foiled	Young Pretender lands in Scotland (July) and rallies clans; takes Edinburgh (Sept.); Derby reached (early Dec.)	Young Pretender defeated at Culloden (Apr.); escapes to France (Sept.)	Death of Old Pretender; Jacobites declare Charles III titular king of England and Scotland	Death of Young Pretender; succeeded by titular Henry IX (dies 1807)

KING GEORGE II

BORN: October 30
1683, Hanover
ACCEDED: May 28 1727;
crowned October 11
1727, Westminster
Abbey

*Duke and Elector
of Hanover,
Duke and Marquess
of Cambridge,
Earl of
Milford Haven,
Duke of Cornwall
and Rothesay,
Prince of Wales,
Earl of Chester,
King of Great Britain
and Ireland*

GEORGE II 1727–60

GEORGE II'S REIGN BEGAN AGAINST THE BACKGROUND OF WALPOLE'S DISTINCTIVE BRAND OF COMPLACENT POLITICAL STABILITY AND ENDED IN THE BLAZE OF AGGRESSIVE IMPERIAL EXPANSION ENGINEERED BY WILLIAM PITT. COUPLED WITH THE EFFECTIVE ENDING OF THE STUART THREAT AFTER 1745, THE NET RESULT WAS TO CONSOLIDATE NOT JUST THE HANOVERIAN MONARCHY BUT BRITAIN AS A WORLD POWER.

GIVEN THE WIDELY ACKNOWLEDGED TEDIUM of George II's court and the king's prissiness in insisting on the minutiae of its etiquette, it may seem surprising that, as Prince of Wales, the future George II was considered a dashing, fashionable figure, as was his vivacious and intelligent wife, Caroline of Ansbach. Further, though he came to England only when he was 30, he immediately seemed more in tune with his future subjects than his non-English-speaking father.

But the similarities between George II and his father were to prove more striking than the differences. For one thing, soon after his accession in 1727, George II abandoned any thoughts of changing his father's administration. Politically, in the hands of the arch-fixer, Robert Walpole, the first 15 years of George II's reign were largely indistinguishable from the last years of his father's. Though this would later change dramatically, Walpole's competent brand of mild Whiggery seemed unchallengeable.

The pattern was reinforced by George II's relations with his son and heir, Frederick, which

George's son Frederick called his father (left) "an obstinate self-indulgent miserly martinet with an insatiable sexual appetite". In fact, boorish and bad-tempered though he could be and whatever his callous treatment of his son, George was a competent king even if, like his father, he frequently chafed at the restrictions imposed by Parliament and was always ultimately more at home in his native Germany. In the words of Lord Chesterfield: "He might offend but he never deceived." His death, while sitting on his lavatory, was a sordid end to a generally successful reign.

were even worse than his own had been with George I. Unfathomably, both the king and queen loathed their eldest son. Frederick was allowed to come to England, where he was grudgingly made Prince of Wales, only when he was 20, the year after George's accession. The king thereafter went out of his way to alienate his son, who, though foolish, scarcely warranted such sustained bile. "Our first-born," declared George II, "is the greatest ass, the greatest liar, the greatest canaille and the greatest beast in the whole world and we heartily wish he was out of it." His mother was no less vicious. She hoped "the

George II was the last (technically the only) British king to lead his troops in battle. At Dettingen in 1743 at the age of 60 he successfully led a combined British, Dutch, Austrian and Hanoverian force to victory over France (right). In his twenties, serving under the Duke of Marlborough, he had similarly distinguished himself at the Battle of Oudenarde in 1708. His military valour – as well as his obsession with uniforms – was never in doubt.

By far the dominant motif of George II's reign was the foundation of a nascent British empire, achieved very largely at the expense of France, above all in North America and India (map below). As it would continue to be in the 19th century, it was British naval strength that underpinned the country's overseas possessions.

□ ·   *British possessions, with names (those seized during George's rule in Italics)*

▨   *Hanover, 1735*

——   *Principal theatres of the War of Austrian Succession, 1740–48*

——   *Principal theatres of the Seven Years War, 1756–63*

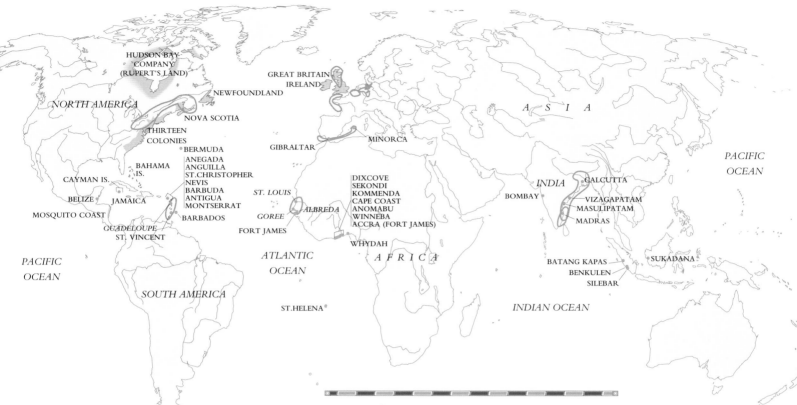

ground would open this moment and sink the monster to the lowest hope of hell." (Caroline, who died in 1737, would not see her wish granted, but George II would: in 1751, at 44, the Prince of Wales died. The king obstinately refused to pay off his debts.)

The predictable result of such animosity was the creation of a rival court and focus of political opposition to the king – exactly as it had happened when George II was Prince of Wales. It was here that a very different political philosophy was formed, aggressively expansionist and determined to confront its most obvious colonial rival, France. Walpole derisively called its champions the "Patriot Boys". Ironically, though it was Frederick who nurtured these new "patriots", it was George II who benefited. With Walpole's fall in 1742, they smartly switched allegiance to the king. In 1740, Walpole had already been forced into the Continental war he had tried so hard to avoid. After his fall, England was almost permanently at war. If this was a more or less conventional European conflict to begin with, from the 1750s it had acquired an entirely new, global dimension.

For a Britain whose Protestant, parliamentary supremacy had been significantly reinforced by the absolute defeat of the 1745 Jacobite rebellion (see pp. 160-161), the subsequent conflict with France after 1756 – the Seven Years War – masterminded

I am sick to death of all this foolish stuff and wish with all my heart that the devil may take all your bishops, and the devil take your Minister, and the devil take your Parliament and the devil take the whole island, provided I can get out and go to Hanover.

George II on England and the English

with implacable determination by William Pitt, was its triumphant vindication. In 1759, the year before the death of the increasingly feeble George, the French were driven from North America and India. The supremacy of Hanoverian Britain had never seemed more apparent.

Almost more than Clive's victories in India, James Wolfe's daring capture of Quebec from France in 1759 dramatically underlined the new military prowess of Britain. The financial cost of the global struggle against France may have been prodigious but the consequences in India and, at any rate for the time being, in North America amply justified them. That Wolfe himself, rather like Nelson at Trafalgar 46 years later, lost his life in the battle (left) only underlined his status as a permanent hero of what was rapidly becoming a British empire.

1745	1746	1751	1756	1757	1759
Jacobite rebellion	*Jacobite defeat at Culloden followed by severe Hanoverian reprisals against Scottish Highlands*	*Death of Frederick, Prince of Wales*	*Seven Years War with France (to 1763). Black Hole of Calcutta*	*Minorca lost to France; William Pitt prime minister. Bengal secured for England by Robert Clive at Battle of Plassey*	*Capture of Quebec by James Wolfe*

GEORGE III 1760–1820

GEORGE III'S REPUTATION AS THE MOST BUFFOONISH OF THE HANOVERIANS HAS PROVED OBSTINATELY HARD TO SHIFT. HIS ATTEMPTS TO REASSERT ROYAL AUTHORITY SPARKED BITTER RESENTMENTS. MORE DAMAGINGLY, HIS REIGN WAS LASTINGLY TAINTED BY THE LOSS OF BRITAIN'S AMERICAN COLONIES. HIS FINAL YEARS ON THE THRONE SAW HIS PATHETIC DESCENT INTO LUNACY.

BORN: May 24 1738
ACCEDED: October 25 1760; crowned September 22 1761, Westminster Abbey; declared unfit to rule February 5 1811

Duke and Elector of Hanover, Duke of Cornwall and Rothesay, Duke of Edinburgh, Marquess of Ely, Earl of Eltham, Viscount of Launceston, Baron of Snowdon, Prince of Wales, Earl of Chester, King of Great Britain and Ireland (from 1801 of the United Kingdom of Great Britain and Ireland)

GEORGE III WAS STRIKINGLY UNLIKE HIS TWO Hanoverian predecessors: kind where they were malicious, moral where they were unscrupulous, religious where they were impious, industrious where they were idle. Further, not only was he born in England – and would never visit Hanover (which he also ruled) – he spoke English with no German accent. As he asserted at his coronation, he "gloried in the name of Briton." There was yet a further, crucial distinction: his determination to restore royal authority in the face of growing parliamentary supremacy.

This was in no sense an attempt to overturn the constitutional settlement of 1689 or to engineer a return to Stuart-style absolutism. George had been carefully schooled in the Protestant, parliamentary tradition and had a passionate attachment to the liberties and laws of his kingdom. And it was

George III (above left) had something of the red-faced, bulging-eyed look of his Hanoverian forebears but he was a far more commanding figure – "… tall and full of dignity" in the words of Horace Walpole. It would not help him in the restoration of his royal authority, however. Further, whatever the magnificence of his projection of power in an official portrait such as this, painted by Alan Ramsay in 1767, George III had a marked preference for simplicity. His court, like his tastes, was frugal, his preference for routine increasingly pronounced. In the circumstances, the behaviour of his heir, the Prince of Wales, an extravagant personality in every sense, predictably caused the upright king enormous sadness and pain.

The turbulent political climate of the 1760s saw open criticism of the king never more aggressively than by John Wilkes, portrayed here (left) by Hogarth, the cap of Liberty propped over his shoulder. As editor of the North Britain, Wilkes led a sustained campaign against the king that saw his arrest in 1763 and the newspaper's suppression. In an earlier period, he would certainly have been executed. In 1768, the radical cause was further advanced by Wilkes when he was barred from taking his seat in Parliament.

precisely these, directed and overseen by him as divinely sanctioned sovereign and implemented by a parliament faithful to his wishes whose consent further legitimized his rule, that George III, in his youthful innocence, saw as his clear duty to reinforce. What else was a monarch for, particularly one as conscientious as George?

In fact, however uncertain the process, by the time George III came to the throne in 1760, the nature of parliamentary authority, and hence the relationship between king and Parliament, was already undergoing a further important change. At least in retrospect, it is clear that the balance of power between Crown and Parliament was continuing to shift in the latter's favour. Parliament, still very much in thrall to the great landed families of the aristocracy, may have been far from democratic in any modern sense. Yet its influence was undeniable. Increasingly, rather than the king appointing ministers who would implement his policies in Parliament, it was the king who found himself having to bow to his ministers' policies as legitimized by Parliament. It was a crucial step in the further evolution of constitutional, parliamentary monarchy. In the circumstances, George III's attempts to reaffirm his royal prerogative would come to seem futile.

In the short term, the stand-off between George III and Parliament manifested itself in a series of short-lived, unstable governments appointed by the increasingly disillusioned king – under the duke of Newcastle, the earl of Bute, Lord Rockingham, William Pitt and the earl of Grafton. It took place, too, against a barrage of criticism of the king that would have been unthinkable in his grandfather's reign. The activities of politicians such as John Wilkes and Charles James Fox raised the political temperature to boiling point.

It was only with the appointment of a new administration under Lord North in 1770 that George III finally seemed to have found a man acceptable to himself and to Parliament. Yet it was North, actively supported by the king, who would engineer the greatest catastrophe of George III's reign: the loss of Britain's American colonies.

The irony was not just that the gains of the Seven

1761	1763	1764	1770	1773
Marriage of George III to Sophia Charlotte of Mecklenburg-Strelitz	*Seven Years War ended by Treaty of Paris, provoking claims of unnecessary concessions to France and Spain. Resignation of Lord Bute, George III's political mentor, sparks frequent turnover of ministers until 1770*	*Attempts to tax American colonies through Sugar Act and Stamp Act (1765), both later repealed*	*Appointment of Lord North brings stability to government*	*Tea Act imposes tax on tea in America leading to Boston Tea Party*

GEORGE III 1760–1820: DOMESTIC DEVELOPMENTS

—— *Approximate extent of food riots, 1766*

—— *Approximate joint extent of republican-influenced Protestant and Catholic revolutionary activity from 1795*

→ *French military activity, with details*

🌿 *Main revolts of United Irishmen and Catholic Defenders, with details*

▨ *French occupation, August–October 1798*

▨ *Self-governing dominions of the British Crown*

▨ *United Kingdom of Great Britin and Ireland, 1 January 1801*

—— *Approximate extent of Luddite revolt, 1811–12*

🌿 *Other revolt revolt/upheaval, with details*

┄┄ *Frontiers, 1820*

We have thought fit, by and with the advice of our Privy Council, to issue our Royal Proclamation, hereby declaring that ... all our Officers ... are obliged to exert their utmost endeavours to suppress such [American] rebellion and to bring the traitors to justice ... that all our subjects of the Realm, and the dominions hereunto belonging, are bound by law to be aiding and assisting in the suppression of such rebellion.

George III, Proclamation of Rebellion, August 1775

Years War, which had apparently seen Britain decisively established (at French expense) as the dominant power in North America, were partly overturned. Rather, it was that George III, self-professed champion of British liberties, would come to be seen by the Americans as set on a despotism and tyranny that the lessons of 1689 had taught all free men to reject. George had no intention of oppressing his American subjects. His goal was to reinforce the kind of natural balance, reinforced by legitimate parliamentary rule, that, at any rate in his eyes, constitutional monarchy demanded. His royal authority could no more countenance revolt in the Thirteen Colonies of British America than it could in Wiltshire.

In throwing the full weight of British military might against the American revolutionaries, George III and Lord North hoped that the overwhelming successes of the Seven Years War would be repeated. It

The surrender at Yorktown in October 1781 of the British army under General Cornwallis (right) was the lowest point of George III's reign. No less than Lord North, the king had been determined to pursue the war in America to the bitter end. The maintenance of legitimate authority made the punishment of the rebelling Americans an imperative. It was a fateful misreading of the mood in America and of the new concept of liberty being developed there. It also ignored the French desire for revenge after their losses in the Seven Years War.

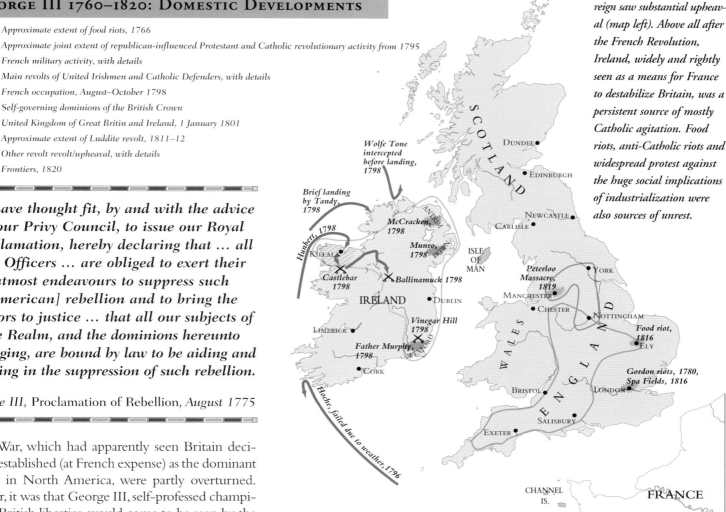

Domestically, George III's reign saw substantial upheaval (map left). Above all after the French Revolution, Ireland, widely and rightly seen as a means for France to destabilize Britain, was a persistent source of mostly Catholic agitation. Food riots, anti-Catholic riots and widespread protest against the huge social implications of industrialization were also sources of unrest.

SCOTLAND

DUNDEE
EDINBURGH
NEWCASTLE
CARLISLE

Wolfe Tone intercepted before landing, 1798

Brief landing by Tandy, 1798

Humbert, 1798

ANTRIM

McCracken, 1798

KILLALA

Munro, 1798

DOWN

ISLE OF MAN

Castlebar 1798 ✕
✕ *Ballinamuck 1798*

IRELAND
DUBLIN

Peterloo Massacre, 1819
MANCHESTER
CHESTER
YORK
NOTTINGHAM

LIMERICK

Vinegar Hill 1798

Food riot, 1816 ELY

Father Murphy, 1798 ✕ WEXFORD

CORK

WALES

BRISTOL
ENGLAND
Gordon riots, 1780, Spa Fields, 1816
LONDON

SALISBURY
EXETER

Hoche: failed due to weather, 1796

CHANNEL IS.

FRANCE

continued on next page

George III – "Farmer" George (right) – *developed a growing fascination for agriculture. In an age when agricultural practices were being revolutionized and outputs dramatically raised, it was a logical interest if not necessarily a very royal one. Nonetheless, the farms he started at Windsor and Richmond, and supervised personally, became enormously successful. Similarly, convalescing in 1789 from his first bout of madness, he embarked on a tour of farms in the West Country. He also wrote pamphlets on agricultural subjects, publishing them under the name Ralph Robinson. There can be little question that had this earnest figure been a country squire rather than the king of Britain, his life would have been immeasurably happier.*

was a disastrous miscalculation. Early British military failure encouraged the defeated powers in the Seven Years War, France pre-eminently, to take their revenge by siding with the Americans. Overstretched and underfunded, Britain found itself hopelessly outmanoeuvred. The surrender at Yorktown in 1781 to a combined French–American army signalled the total collapse of British rule in colonial America.

To his critics, George was now not just a tyrant, he was incompetent. The economic slump that followed only heightened the sense of panic and ruin. But salvation was at hand in the person of William Pitt. Though only in his early twenties, his appointment as prime minister in 1783 transformed both George's reign and British politics. Pitt, cautious where his father had been bold, represented a decisive victory of parliamentary party politics over the power of the Crown. The king was still the single most influential figure in his realm, with formidable powers of patronage, but policy-making was increasingly passing to his ministers. It was a constitutional change of huge significance.

It was reinforced at the end of the decade by the revolution in France. By the early 1790s the French Revolution, particularly once taken over by Napoleon, represented a massive threat to Britain. Whatever its resonant claims to represent liberty, fraternity and equality, at heart it stood for conventional military conquest – and on a larger scale than ever before. Confronting it called for an unprecedented expansion of government in every form: not just a massively expanded army and navy, as well as the taxes to fund them, but a degree of central control quite beyond the conventional means of the Crown. As the actual power of the government expanded, that of the king necessarily contracted.

But George III was far from ready to hand over executive power to his government. As his resistance to Catholic emancipation in 1801 made clear, a move he opposed because it would invalidate his coronation oath to uphold Protestantism, George still saw himself as ultimate ruler in his realm. In addition, British military success against France, on land as much as at sea, had naturally reinforced Britain's – and his – prestige. But that the monarchy was becoming increasingly subject to Parliament – and that Parliament itself was beginning to take on the

The United Kingdom

*T*he success of the American Revolution, coupled with the outbreak of the French Revolution after 1789, led to widespread English anxieties that demands for Irish independence would follow. Limited Irish parliamentary independence had already been granted to Ireland by Lord North in 1782, freeing it from its subservience to the Parliament in London. The painting shows the reformed Irish Parliament in 1780 being addressed by its dominant figure, the Protestant Henry Gratton.

But in the 1790s demands for full Irish independence, above all by the illegal grouping known as the United Irishmen, and a series of abortive French invasions clearly underlined the threat posed by a rebellious Ireland. The response was to incorporate Ireland fully into Britain, which duly happened under the Act of Union, which passed into law on January 1 1801. George III, already king of Ireland, now became king of the United Kingdom of Great Britain and Ireland. At the same time, a curious anomaly was ended when the king formally renounced his titular claim to the throne of France, a claim nominally upheld by every English and later British monarch since Edward III had declared himself the king of France in 1340.

continued from previous page

1783	1788	1789	1793	1798
Treaty of Paris confirms American independence. William Pitt the Younger becomes prime minister	King's first bout of madness	Fall of the Bastille	Britain and France at war (to 1802)	Irish revolt led by United Irishmen suppressed

The Lunacy of George III

Until the autumn of 1788, George III, then 50, had been exceptionally fit. However, in October that year, he began to behave noticeably more strangely, talking more than normal, often incomprehensibly. It was now that the king was claimed to have spoken to an oak tree, taking it for the King of Prussia. Early the following month, he became indisputably insane, talking incessantly and often lewdly, foaming at the mouth, his eyes bloodshot. He also attacked his son, the Prince of Wales. He remained in this state for three months, recovering very much in spite of rather than because of the efforts of his doctors.

Until 1801, his recovery seemed complete but then, and again in 1804, he suffered further bouts of madness. Even so, at least until the end of the decade and despite the inevitable infirmities of increasing old age, the king remained capable. It was in 1810 that he slipped into his final period of madness. This time, there would be no recovery. In February 1811, he was formally declared unfit to rule and the Prince of Wales became Prince Regent. The final years of the king's life were a pathetic parody of his youthful vigour. His hair and beard ever longer and whiter, his sight gone for good, the king, stumbling around Windsor Castle in his dressing gown and subjected to barbaric treatments, became a prisoner of his doctors.

While it was once thought George III's illness was psychological, a reaction to the strain of his reign, above all the loss of America, it is now accepted that he suffered from a hereditary condition called porphyria, essentially a breakdown of the process that produces red pigment in the blood and in which the entire nervous system becomes poisoned. It is almost certain Henry VI in the 15th century had the same condition.

forms of modern party politics that would replace the court as the real focus of political life in Britain – was clear.

But by 1810 George III had been effectively, if unwittingly, removed from this rapidly changing political equation. Earlier bouts of temporary insanity had given way to permanent madness. The debate over monarchical and parliamentary supremacy would continue. But the elderly George III, incarcerated in his straight-jacket, would take no further part in them. In February 1820, the king, mad, ill and old, turned his face to the wall, drew the bedclothes around him and muttered "Tom's a cold". It was a scarcely deserved end to a reign that was never less than well meaning.

GEORGE III 1760–1820: THE GROWTH OF BRITISH POWER

- British possessions, 1760
- Hanover, 1760
- Acquired by Britain during George's rule, with names in Italics
- Lost by Britain during George's rule, (with dates)
- Main theatre of British involvement in the Napoleonic wars

If the Napoleonic Wars necessarily presented the major external threat to Britain in George III's reign, the period also saw a significant expansion of British imperial ambitions (map above). Canada, India, the Cape Colony and New South Wales saw the most important expansions of Britain's overseas interests. By George's death in 1820, Britain had become a world power.

1801	1803	1804	1810	1811	1818
Pitt resigns after George blocks Catholic Emancipation Act, intended to further political reform in Ireland. Ireland then united with Britain to create United Kingdom. George III suffers further bout of madness	Renewed war with revolutionary France (to 1815)	George III suffers third bout of madness	Final madness of George III	George III declared unfit to rule; Prince of Wales created Prince Regent	Death of Queen Charlotte

KING GEORGE IV

GEORGE IV 1820–30

THE HANOVERIANS MAY HAVE BEEN ADMIRED FOR THEIR SENSE OF DUTY BUT THEY WERE NEVER POPULAR. UNDER GEORGE IV THEY BECAME ACTIVELY DISLIKED. RESPECTIVELY PRINCE OF WALES, PRINCE REGENT AND FINALLY KING, GEORGE IV WAS DEBAUCHED, GREEDY AND RECKLESSLY EXTRAVAGANT. YET HE WAS ALSO HIGHLY ABLE. HAD HE TRIED, HE COULD HAVE BEEN A RULER OF DISTINCTION.

BORN: August 12 1762
ACCEDED January 29
1820; crowned July 19
1821, Westminster
Abbey

Duke of Cornwall
and Rothesay,
Earl of Carrick,
Baron Renfrew and
Lord of the Isles, Prince
of Wales,
Earl of Chester,
King of Hanover,
King of the United
Kingdom of Great
Britain and Ireland

If Britain had already established itself as a major colonial power in the reign of George III, under George IV its colonial holdings were significantly expanded, not least in Southeast Asia (map right). In Burma, Singapore and New South Wales, Britain, whatever its rivalries with the Netherlands, established itself as a leading influence.

As a young man, the Prince of Wales was universally praised for his easy charm and elegant figure (left). Even in his early forties, when this portrait by Henry Bone was painted, at least traces of these youthful good looks as "an Adonis of loveliness" remained. Yet as early as 1783 George III had railed against attempts to increase the prince's allowance as "a shameful squandering of public money to gratifying the passions of an ill-advised young man". Given that the of Wales once spent £2,000 on a set of handkerchiefs, the king's outrage is easy to understand. As Prince Regent, despite receiving a much larger allowance, George was forced to ask the Cabinet for £500,000 to pay off his debts. He was turned down.

THOUGH HE WAS MADE PRINCE REGENT IN 1811, after his father's final madness had descended, George IV did not accede to the throne until 1820 when he was 57. But even by 1811 he was a bloated ruin, "the grace of his person … irresistible sweetness of his voice …[and] tenderness of his melodious yet manly voice" long since gone. By 1820 he was well on his way to becoming a virtual recluse at Windsor, what little energy he had left given over to improbable and, at this stage, unrealizable building projects.

Unlike his Hanoverian predecessors as Prince of Wales, George grew up in an atmosphere that was stable and loving. The king in particular was passionately attached to his son. But the new Prince of Wales found the atmosphere at court merely stifling. Even before he was 18, his taste for dissipation was obvious. His rebelliousness against the tedium of his father's dutiful life did more than just encourage him to squander his money on an heroic scale, with debts to match. It also drew him towards the parliamentary opposition, chiefly the charismatic figure of Charles James Fox. To the impotent fury of his father, the prince's London home, Carlton House, became the epicentre of sophisticated raffish society and a clear rival court. The Prince of Wales would later repudiate his championship of

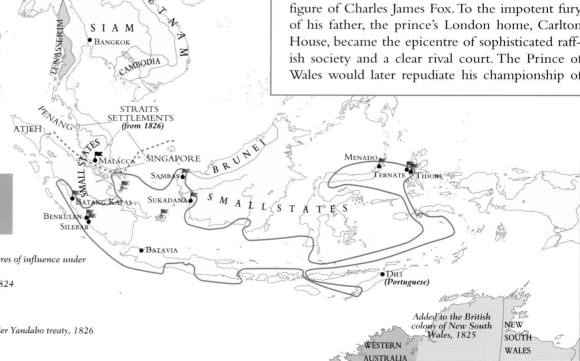

BRITISH INTERESTS IN SOUTHEAST ASIA UNDER GEORGE IV, 1820–30

- British territory, 1820
- - - - Separation of British and Dutch spheres of influence under London Treaty, 1824
- British, transferred to Netherlands, 1824
- Dutch, transferred to Britain, 1824
- Held by the Netherlands, 1824
- Acquired by Britain from Burma under Yandabo treaty, 1826
- Acquired by Britain 1829
- ——— Frontiers, 1830

Added to the British colony of New South Wales, 1825

1781	1783	1784	1785	1786	1787	1788	1795
George III forced to buy back (for £5,000) love letters written by the Prince of Wales to actress Perdita Robinson	First visit of Prince of Wales to Brighton	Prince of Wales meets Maria Fitzherbert	Illegal and secret marriage of Prince of Wales to Maria Fitzherbert	Prince of Wales buys site of what becomes the Brighton Pavilion and begins first of a number of extravagant rebuilding projects	Hoping to get a larger parliamentary allowance, Prince of Wales authorizes Charles James Fox to deny his marriage to Maria Fitzherbert	First madness of George III	Marriage of Prince of Wales to Caroline of Brunswick

The marriage of the Prince of Wales to Caroline of Brunswick (right) was a disaster from the start. Each loathed the other. As soon as decently possible after the birth of their daughter, Charlotte, in 1796, the prince effectively had her sent away, with Caroline spending much of her time in Italy in the company of her chamberlain, Bartolomeo Pergami. Embarrassingly for the new king, Caroline subsequently made an unwelcome return to England, attempting to force her way into Westminster Hall for George's coronation banquet in 1821. In fact, contemporary reports are near unanimous in describing Caroline as fat, dirty and coarse. As daughter of the duke of Brunswick, her credentials as consort were impeccable. It was about all that could be said for her.

There is little doubt that the Prince of Wales never lost his devotion to Maria Fitzherbert (right). Their marriage in 1785 may have been an empty ceremony with no legal weight – certainly it did nothing to prevent the prince taking up with a series of further mistresses – but it was a clear indication of the prince's consistently strong feelings towards her.

Fox's brand of Whiggery. But for many years and with little better reason than mischief, he caused his father and his governments significant political embarrassment. It was not very edifying.

That George was intelligent and charming (when he wanted to be) with an inspired talent for the arts was clear. He presided over a revolution in English taste that remains unique in English and British royal history. That he was self-indulgent is equally clear. With a string of mistresses already to his name, in 1785 in an act of astounding folly he married Maria Fitzherbert, a widow five years his senior and a Roman Catholic. In fact under the Royal Marriages Act of 1772, which forbade the marriage of any member of the royal family under 25 without the sovereign's permission, the marriage was illegal and thus void from the start – though this did not stop Mrs Fitzherbert from regarding herself as the prince's legal wife (or the Pope from provocatively recognizing the marriage).

When in 1795 the prince was eventually obliged to marry legally, both to secure the succession and to receive a larger parliamentary allowance, the chosen candidate was a German cousin, Caroline of Brunswick. It is doubtful if any arranged royal marriage has been more disastrous. The prince's first words on meeting his bride were: "I am not well, pray get me a glass of brandy". A daughter, Charlotte, was born nine months later, and the royal couple thereafter separated.

As king, George was already a spent force. His coronation was magnificent, the visits he subsequently made to Ireland and Scotland, the first by any Hanoverian, scarcely less spectacular. But his interest in the day-to-day business of government was close to non-existent. Occasionally, the raddled king could bestir himself sufficiently to protest his government's actions, notably in 1829 when he threatened to abdicate if the Catholic Emancipation Act was passed. Through his inaction his chief contribution to the evolution of British monarchy was to further the withering of royal authority in the face of parliamentary supremacy.

The Brighton Pavilion

George set fashions all his life. He was a determined and discerning patron of the arts who initiated a number of major rebuilding projects. Though never completed as originally planned, Regent Street and Regent's Park in London are witness to his ability to conceive of town planning on a majestic scale. Similarly, his rebuilding at Windsor Castle, which included the Long Walk and the opulent Waterloo Chamber, transformed the medieval dinginess of the building, creating the building substantially as it is today.

But he is best and most rightly remembered for the Brighton Pavilion (above), without question one of the most remarkable and beautiful buildings in Europe. George did more than just oversee the creation of a sumptuous palace; he set a new taste for seaside life that has continued ever since. Work on the palace proceeded on and off for 35 years. The building today, largely the work of John Nash, was only the last of a number of remodellings. If its domed and minareted exterior is without parallel, its interiors are if anything even more astounding, a staggering example of Regency taste at its most exotically flamboyant. That such an overblown creation should never stray into vulgarity is clear evidence of George's essential good taste. Ironically, by the time the palace was completed in 1822, the king was almost too infirm to visit it.

**A libertine over head and ears in debt and disgrace, a despiser of domestic ties, the companion of demi-reps, a man who has just closed half a century without a single claim on the gratitude of his country or the respect of prosperity.**

Leigh Hunt on the future George IV at 50, in 1812

1796	1811	1815	1817	1820	1821	1822	1829
Birth of Prince of Wales's only legitimate child, Charlotte	Prince of Wales made Prince Regent after onset of final madness of George III	Battle of Waterloo: final defeat of Napoleon. Remodelling of Brighton Pavilion by John Nash begun (to 1822)	Death in childbirth of Prince of Wales's daughter, Charlotte	Accession of Regent as George IV. Attempts to force Parliament to accept Bill of Pains and Penalties to declare void marriage to Caroline of Brunswick	Caroline of Brunswick excluded from George IV's coronation; dies following month	George IV visits Scotland and Ireland	Catholic Emancipation Act passed in face of bitter opposition by George IV

PROJECTIONS OF ROYALTY: *Two*

THE CONSTITUTIONAL BASIS OF BRITAIN'S MONARCHY MAY HAVE BEEN TRANSFORMED BY THE HANOVERIAN SUCCESSION IN 1714, BUT OFFICIAL IMAGES OF ROYALTY SCARCELY CHANGED AT ALL. WINTERHALTER'S 19TH-CENTURY PORTRAITS OF VICTORIA ARE RECOGNIZABLY IN THE SAME TRADITION AS VAN DYCK'S 17TH-CENTURY PORTRAITS OF CHARLES I. BUT THE COURT ITSELF IN THE SAME PERIOD CHANGED DRAMATICALLY.

GIVEN THE RICHNESS OF VAN DYCK'S heroic images of Charles I, as influential elsewhere in Europe as in Britain, it is no surprise that well into the 19th century essentially the same 17th-century pictorial language was being used in official portraits of monarchs and their families. The talents of later court artists may not always have matched those of Van Dyck but their debt to his large-scale, dramatic, heavily idealized images was undoubted.

However, despite this enduring approach to royal portraiture, the public profile of the monarch and his court was changing. Where once the court, with the monarch at its heart, had formed the absolute centre of the nation's political and social being, after 1689 it increasingly became something of a side-show. To a considerable extent, this was a natural reflection of the changed political realities after 1689 and the diminishing of royal power in favour of Parliament. As a result, the court's place as the natural hub of political gossip, intrigue and advancement was gradually taken over: not just by Parliament but by the aristocratic houses in London and elsewhere and, from the early 18th century, the capital's coffee shops and clubs, each with its own political affiliation. The political centre of gravity was shifting irreversibly

Ceiling fresco of William and Mary, The Painted Hall, Greenwich, by James Thornhill. 1700.

This noticeably lower public profile of the court also reflected the tastes and aspirations of the country's new monarchs, above all a marked preference for the domestic over the ceremonial. Where once the monarch had essentially lived in public, increasingly he began to live in private

The trend began with the accession of William III in 1689. Close, secretive and above all a foreigner, he had little taste for the high drama of court life. Partly, too, as a result of his asthma, which made London uncongenial to him, he was always more at home in the relatively modest surroundings of rural Kensington Palace, bought by him and Queen Mary in 1689. Even in the much grander Hampton Court, he and Mary occupied no more than a handful of rooms. But the public projection of the joint Protestant monarchs was a very different matter, nowhere more strikingly demonstrated than on the ceiling frescoes of the Great Hall at Christopher Wren's new Royal Naval Hospital at Greenwich.

The visual language of building and ceiling alike is Baroque, pure and unadulterated. If this was a style that originally, in Rome and later in France, was associated with Catholicism and absolutism, above all at Louis XIV's Versailles, here it is just as emphatically pressed into service on behalf of the Protestant, parliamentary cause. In James Thornhill's great ceiling, William, resplendently enthroned, holds out the cap of liberty to Europe while

Family of George III, by Johann Zoffany, c.1770

trampling tyranny, holding a broken sword, underfoot. The king is no less omniscient than his Stuart forebears but it is tolerance, freedom and prudence he now champions

Neither of the first two Georges made much effort to enhance the majesty of their office. Both took over their palaces if not reluctantly then at least rather like temporary tenants, doing little or nothing to extend or renovate them. Under George II in particular, whether at Windsor or Hampton Court, court life settled into a round of tedious decorum that Charles II for one would have found unrecognizable.

Perhaps not surprisingly under a monarch whose main interest was farming, George III's court was every bit as domestic, almost frugal. His new London home, Buckingham House, bought by him in 1762, was graceful, but it was no Versailles. It was only in the 19th century that most of the alterations that produced today's much grander palace were undertaken. In very much the same spirit, George III's queen, Charlotte, had a marked preference for the still smaller Kew Palace

Nonetheless, whatever their personal tastes, portraits of the king and queen continued to reflect the Baroque image of royalty established in the 17th century. Johann Zoffany, otherwise a brilliant exponent of a new domestic style of portraiture, went so far as to portray the royal family in full 17th-century garb. His portrait of George III, the queen and the first six of their children, painted in the 1770s, is conceived in terms almost indistinguishable from those of his 17th-century predecessors. This is a heroic vision of royalty that would not have disappointed Charles I.

The shining exception to this otherwise persistent Hanoverian preference for domesticity over public ceremony was provided by George IV. As portrayed by Thomas Lawrence in 1822, the king is the epitome of self-conscious, heroic monarchy. Given the painter's unpromising subject matter – an overweight and debauched middle-aged man – Lawrence's achievements in transforming the prince are unmatched. Yet it was even more as a patron of architecture that George IV excelled, both as prince and king. His lavish building projects, at Carlton House, Buckingham Palace, which he had extensively enlarged and rebuilt by John Nash, Windsor Castle, if anything even more substantially transformed, and above all at the Brighton Pavilion testify not just to an exceptional natural taste but to a relentless desire to transform the grandeur of the monarchy's setting. It was a remarkable and enduring legacy which by itself is enough to justify his otherwise indolent reign. Britain's constitutional monarchy may have lost its political power but its majesty was being incomparably enhanced.

To this extent at least the glamorous portraits of the young Victoria and her family by another German painter, Winterhalter, at least reflected a court setting that was now as grand as its official imagery. In fact, no one could mistake Winterhalter for Van Dyke. Just as much a virtuoso and no less concerned to emphasize the iconic status of the royal family, he was equally determined to give Victoria and her family a new human face. His great achievement was to reconcile these two apparent opposites. Winterhalter made Hanoverian domesticity majestic.

King George IV by Thomas Lawrence, 1822

Family of Queen Victoria by Franz Xavier Winterhalter, 1840s

KING WILLIAM IV
BORN: August 21 1765
ACCEDED: June 26 1830;
crowned September 8
1831, Westminster
Abbey

*Duke of Clarence
and St Andrews,
Earl of Munster,
King of the United
Kingdom of Great
Britain and Ireland*

WILLIAM IV 1830–7

FOR MOST OF HIS LIFE WILLIAM IV HAD NO THOUGHT OF BECOMING KING. YET HOWEVER UNLIKELY HIS ROUTE TO THE THRONE, HIS STOP-GAP RULE PROVED SURPRISINGLY SUCCESSFUL. CRUCIALLY, DESPITE THE FURTHER REDUCTION OF ROYAL AUTHORITY UNDER THE REFORM ACT OF 1832, THE MONARCHY ITSELF WAS AT LEAST PARTLY STABILIZED AFTER THE EXCESSES OF GEORGE IV.

For over 20 years, William as Duke of Clarence lived with the comic actress Dorothea Jordan (above), whose real name was Bland, at Bushey Park. Descendants of their ten children (who took the name Fitzclarence) are still alive today. Dorothea's own end was sad. Taking more and more to the bottle, she was abandoned by William in 1811. An attempt to revive her stage career flopped. She died some years later, in France, more or less mad. William seemed largely unconcerned.

At 64, William IV (below) was the oldest monarch to accede to the British throne. His reaction was characteristic. Scarcely able to contain his glee, he took to his carriage and drove through London for hours, doffing his cap and offering lifts to all and sundry. At George's funeral, he talked "incessantly and loudly". He opened his first Privy Council meeting with the question, "Who is Silly Billy now?" Typically, he insisted on a modest coronation, spending on it only a fraction of the £243,000 that George IV had lavished on his ten years earlier. But he became increasingly grumpy as his reign wore on, beginning a bizarre feud with the widowed duchess of Kent, mother of William's niece and heir, Victoria. As he grew older, he came to regard the prospect of the duchess's becoming Regent if he died before Victoria's 18th birthday with undisguised horror. In the event, he lived for just one month after Victoria turned 18.

ON THE DEATH OF GEORGE IV IN 1830, Robert Peel asserted that the monarchy had become so unpopular it could be saved only by a miracle. William IV, George III's third son, seemed an unlikely candidate to perform it. Blunt, forthright and disingenuous, for most of his life he had been widely seen as no more than an irrelevance in British public life. As an obviously minor adjunct to the royal family, "Sailor Bill" was hard to take seriously.

By 1790 and at the age of only 25 he had given up active service in the Navy, which he had joined at 13, for an improbable liaison with an actress, Mrs Jordan. She was several years older than he was and with a marked tendency to run to fat. Nonetheless, for over 20 years she and William lived together, producing a large number of illegitimate children, the Fitzclarences, in what seems to have been a state of cheerful contentment. If William's occasional forays into public life – protesting against attempts to outlaw the slave trade, demanding he be given a new naval command – were typically tactless, they hardly amounted to very much, serving principally to reinforce his reputation as "Silly Billy".

The death of the Prince Regent's only legitimate child, Charlotte, in 1818, changed everything. With the Prince Regent – the future George IV – unlikely to produce a new heir after his estrangement from his wife, Caroline of Brunswick, William was suddenly brought closer to the throne. At 52, he married the 25-year-old Princess Adelaide of Saxe-Coburg-Meiningen with a view to producing legitimate children. Even so, his brother Frederick, the Duke of York, was always more likely to succeed. With Frederick's death in 1827, however, William, however improbably, found himself next in line to the throne.

Whether his head had been turned is hard to say. But it was certainly in character that when his new status was recognized by his appointment to the honorary post of High Admiral of England William insisted on taking a fleet to sea in defiance of orders from the Admiralty. He was humiliatingly forced to resign the position the next year. It did not bode well for his prospects as king.

1779	1789	1790	1791	1811	1816
Enters Navy	*Appointed Rear Admiral*	*Meets Dorothea Jordan; gives up active service in Navy*	*Sets up house with Dorothea Jordan*	*Leaves Dorothea Jordan*	*Death of Dorothea Jordan*

Excitable or not, as King William IV he faced his greatest crisis with equanimity. This was the demand, all the more unstoppable after the electoral defeat of the conservative duke of Wellington as prime minister in 1830, for parliamentary reform. The king's agreement in 1831 to the request for a dissolution of Parliament by his new prime minister, Lord Grey, only six months after the last election to allow Grey to seek a greater mandate for parliamentary reform, was a bold venture into uncharted constitutional waters.

William went even further a year later when he agreed to overcome the resistance of the House of Lords by promising to create new peers sympathetic to Grey's reforms to vote through the necessary legislation. His justification was a blueprint for the role of a constitutional monarch: whatever his personal objection to parliamentary reform, "as sovereign," he declared, "it was his duty to set those prejudices

I trust in God that my life may be spared for nine months longer [and that] no Regency would take place. I should then have the satisfaction of leaving the royal authority to the personal exercise of that Young Lady [Princess Victoria] and not in the hands of a person now near me, who is surrounded by evil advisers and who is herself incompetent to act with propriety in the station in which She would be placed.

William IV, birthday speech, August 21 1836, publicly criticizing Princess Victoria's mother, the Duchess of Kent, in her presence

and feelings aside." However unknowable its consequences, in supporting the Reform Bill William was moving the Crown closer to fully constitutional monarchy. For a king so universally written off as a clownish irrelevance, it was impressive.

The Reform Act of 1832

The Reform Bill of 1832 in no sense produced a democratic Parliament. Nonetheless it was a key step in the process, which continued throughout the century, of making Parliament properly representative of the nation as a whole. Its intention was less to increase the electorate so much as to end the obvious inconsistencies of an electoral system essentially unchanged since the 13th century. Most major manufacturing towns in the north had no MPs at all; Cornwall alone, by contrast, had 42, which was only two less than the whole of Scotland, whose total electorate before 1832 was precisely 4,579.

Needless to say, any proposal to reform Parliament provoked fierce controversy. At one extreme, there were calls for universal male franchise with no property restrictions determining who could vote. At the other, there were those who believed that any change to the electoral system would inevitably result in revolution. In the event, the Reform Act retained a property restriction yet still increased the number of electors by 45 per cent. Even so, this still meant that in England and Wales only 18 per cent of adult

males could vote. The domination of the landed interest in Parliament, especially that of England, remained intact. Nonetheless, lukewarm though it was, the Reform Act was still a change of huge and lasting importance and the direct precursor of further Reform Acts in 1866, 1872 and 1884 (see p. 178–9).

In legitimizing Parliament further, the authority of the monarchy was inevitably reduced. It is little exaggeration to say that by the time of William's death in 1837, royal authority had become little more than a matter of influence, powerful though this could still be. In the circumstances, it is hardly a surprise that William was reluctant to approve the Bill. That, in effect, he had no choice accurately reflects the new forces that the Reform Act symbolized.

Whig — Reform is absolutely necessary to prevent Revolution —

Tory — I do maintain that Reform means nothing else than Revolution.

Liberal — A Lee_tle Reform is wanting but fiddlededee about Revolution.

Radical. — I Say If we dont have a Real Radical Reform we'll have a Revolution

C.J. Grant Delt Sculp

FOUR WEIGHTY AUTHORITIES ON REFORM.

1818	1827	1830	1831	1832	1833
Marries Princess Adelaide Saxe-Coburg-Meiningen	Death of elder brother, Duke of York, makes William heir apparent; William appointed High Admiral of England (resigns 1828)	Succeeds as William IV; collapse of Tory administration under Wellington	Agrees to dissolve Parliament to allow Lord Grey to seek a greater mandate for parliamentary reform	Reform Act passed	Abolition Act abolishes slavery in British Empire; Factory Act prohibits employment of children under nine

VICTORIA 1837–1901

QUEEN VICTORIA
BORN: May 24 1819
ACCEDED: June 20 1837;
crowned June 28 1838,
Westminster Abbey

Queen of the United
Kingdom of Great
Britain and Ireland,
Empress of India
(from 1876)

THE MONARCHY WAS TRANSFORMED MORE UNDER VICTORIA THAN UNDER ANY MONARCH BEFORE OR SINCE. BY HER DEATH, THE LAST VESTIGES OF PERSONAL RULE HAD GONE FOR GOOD, REPLACED BY A NEW, FULLY CONSTITUTIONAL THRONE. IN THE PROCESS, THE MONARCHY ACQUIRED A NEW STATUS. VICTORIA HAD BECOME THE LIVING EMBODIMENT OF HER REALMS.

The Great Exhibition of 1851 (below) was incontrovertibly Prince Albert's crowning achievement. It was conceived and driven through by the prince against formidable opposition as a showcase of imperial arts, sciences and technology. The setting itself, the Crystal Palace, 1,000 feet long, 64 feet high, and built entirely in glass and iron, was as remarkable as many of the exhibits. When it closed in October 1851, six million people had visited it. The opening the previous May was, the queen asserted, "the happiest, proudest day of my life … Albert's dear name is forever immortalized."

WHETHER DISSOLUTE, MAD, BULLYING, eccentric or merely disagreeable, the first five Hanoverian monarchs had done little to endear themselves to their subjects. Each upheld most of their prime duties – maintaining Protestantism, bowing to growing parliamentary supremacy and, by and large, providing for the succession. However unevenly, their reigns also saw a huge increase in British military and naval power. The country's empire and trade increased substantially. As important, Britain was also becoming the world's first industrial power.

However, by the time of the 18-year-old Victoria's accession in 1837, the monarchy was viewed with a mixture of indifference and hostility. Its central place in the life of the nation was not in doubt. But it could hardly claim to be popular. Yet by Victoria's death in 1901, after a 64-year reign that remains the longest of any British monarch, the change in the position of the throne was undeniable. Its popularity was absolute, its status unchallenged.

The changes that swept over Britain in the 19th century – economic, imperial, social, commercial, technological, industrial and political – were so great and their impact so far-reaching that it was inevitable that the monarchy would be affected as much as every other aspect of British life. What these transformations amounted to, however, was

> *When she insists that 2 and 2 make 5, I say that I cannot help thinking they make 4. She replies there may be some truth in what I say, but she knows they make 5. Thereupon I drop the discussion.*
>
> Sir Henry Ponsonby, private secretary to Queen Victoria

always hard to say at the time. Victoria was certainly conscious of her enhanced status as queen of the greatest empire the world had seen. But the extent to which she understood that her own powers had been significantly circumscribed is doubtful. To the very end, she was resolutely conservative, vainly insisting on her royal prerogative, attempting to meddle in government decisions, and implacably opposing anything that smacked of democracy. For fully 15 years after the death of Prince Albert in 1861, and to the bitter frustration of her ministers and advisers, she also effectively withdrew from public life in an extraordinary demonstration of grief. In the process she not only deprived the monarchy of one of its most effective weapons – its visibility – she sparked what briefly threatened to become a widespread republican movement.

Yet it is no accident that, just as much as Elizabeth I in the 16th century, she remains one of the most fêted and celebrated of British monarchs, as well as one of only a handful to have given their name to an era. In Victoria's case, this may have been no more than a happy accident, the longevity of her reign coinciding with an unprecedented expansion of British power. Where Elizabeth I actively ruled, Victoria was not much more than a spectator. But it is equally undeniable that, fitfully or not, as British imperial, industrial and parliamentary supremacy were consolidated, Victoria gradually became the incarnation of Britain and its empire, a fixed point in the lives of millions. The older she became, the more the Queen Empress was venerated. In the end, it was enough merely that she existed.

Victoria's early years on the throne were uncertain. Though her determination to have her own way was

SWEDEN-NORWAY

North Sea

DENMARK

RUSSIAN EMPIRE
*Alfred, 1874
Victoria's grand-daughter married Tsar Nicholas, 1894

*Edward VII, 1863

SCHLESWIG-HOLSTEIN
*Helena, 1866

UNITED

EDINBURGH

DUBLIN

KINGDOM

LONDON

Ernest Augustus, 1837-51

HANOVER

NETHERLANDS

P R U S S I A

*Victoria, 1858;
*Arthur, 1879

POLAND

WALDECK
*Leopold, 1882

BELGIUM
Leopold I, 1831-65

BATTENBURG
*Beatrice, 1885

HESSE-DARMSTADT
*Alice, 1862

SAXONY

COBURG-GOTHA
Ruled by *Alfred from 1893

Wilhelm II, son of *Victoria, emperor of Germany 1888-1918

BAVARIA

A U S T R I A N

Bay of Biscay

F R A N C E

E M P I R E

SWITZERLAND

---

evident from the start, so was her inexperience. Almost immediately, she fell under the spell of her Whig prime minister, Lord Melbourne. That she was gauche was amply demonstrated on his resignation in 1839 when she wilfully refused to agree to the incoming Lord Peel's request that she dismiss those "Ladies of the Bedchamber" with Whig connections. As a result, Peel refused to take office. It was not a trivial matter. As Lord Greville complained, "It is a high trial of our institutions that the caprice of a girl of nineteen can overturn a great ministerial combination."

That similar blunders were later avoided, indeed that Victoria's reign began to take on its decisive shape, was almost entirely owed to her husband, Albert, the Duke of Saxe-Coburg, whom she married in 1840. Albert's influence on Victoria cannot be overstated. High-minded, hard working and intelligent, and with a subtle political instinct, he had an almost-visionary view of a benign, reformed monarchy as a force for absolute moral good. Over the next 20 years, he near

QUEEN VICTORIA: THE DYNASTIC DIMENSION

	United Kingdom and possessions
	Country where an uncle of Victoria was ruler, with details
	Hereditary territories of Prince Albert's family, ruled by Albert's brother Ernest 1844–93, then by Victoria's son Alfred
	Victoria's issue married country's ruler/member of ruling family, with issue's name , date of marriage
⋯⋯	German empire, created 1871, ruled by Victoria's grandson, Wilhelm II
★	Victoria's daughter, son
——	Frontiers, 1861–63

Of Victoria's nine children, only one, Louise, married a Briton . The remaining eight all married members of north European ruling familes, five of them Germans (map above). Among her 38 grandchildren were the German Kaiser, Wilhelm II, and the Russian Tsar, Nicholas II.

Queen Victoria was the first British monarch to be photographed and therefore the first whose likeness can be known with certainty. The photographs of the queen and Prince Albert here (left), with the queen herself holding a photograph of her husband, were taken in 1854.

1848	1851	1854	1855	1857	1861
Balmoral estate bought by Victoria and Albert	Great Exhibition held, London	Crimean War (to 1856)	Palmerstone's first Liberal administration (to 1865)	Indian Mutiny. Albert created Prince Consort	Death of Prince Albert; Victoria begins 15-year mourning, withdraws from public life

No royal consort has been mourned with the single-minded devotion Victoria lavished on the memory of her husband. There was something almost sinister in the passionate intensity of Victoria's grief. It also became increasingly dangerous. What after all was the point of an expensive monarchy if it refused to show itself in public? Here (far right) she poses with her second daughter, Princess Alice, in front of a bust of Albert in a photograph taken in 1862.

single-handedly rewrote the rules governing it. From the self-indulgent shambles of George IV and William IV's reigns, Albert deliberately set out to re-create the British Crown as impartial, moral and above reproach, an arbitrator in the country's political life and a model of responsible behaviour for its people. This was monarchy redrafted on a hugely ambitious scale.

Albert's achievement was all the more remarkable given that Victoria, for all that her devotion to him knew no bounds, initially assumed he had to be kept in the background. So far as she was concerned, he may have been her husband but he was certainly not the monarch. Further, whatever her own German background, as a German himself Albert was necessarily somewhat adrift when he first arrived in England. That he should so successfully have won the confidence not just of the queen but of her ministers, in the process making himself king in all but name, was a triumph of startling proportions.

When he died in 1861, aged only 42, the queen was inconsolable. Yet though she could not have known it, she was little more than a third of the way through her reign. There was nothing forced about the long years of Victoria's mourning for Albert. Her grief was never less than real. But for the queen to

I took his dear left hand which was already cold ... and knelt down by him ... All, all was over. I stood up and kissed his dear heavenly forehead & called out in a bitter and agonizing cry, "Oh! My dear darling!" and then dropped on my knees in mute distracted despair, unable to utter a word or shed a tear! ... Then I laid down on the sofa in the Red Room, & all the gentleman came in and knelt down & kissed my hand, & I said a word to each.

Queen Victoria on the death of
Prince Albert, December 14 1861

The expansion of empire under Victoria (map below) made Britain not just the world's pre-eminent industrial power, at least until the 1870s, but unquestionably its greatest colonial power. If it was in Africa that the greatest expansion of British colonial rule occurred, mostly after 1880, India, whose empress the queen became in 1876, remained the most important colonial possession.

BRITISH COLONIAL EXPANSION UNDER VICTORIA, 1837–1901

- British-held territory, 1837 that remained British by the end of Victoria's rule
- Territory/claim given up during Victoria's rule, (with date)
- Added to British control during Victoria's rule
- Frontiers of British possessions, 1901

CANADA
Dominion, 1867
NEWFOUNDLAND
UNITED KINGDOM
HELIGOLAND *(1890)*
OREGON *(Claim abandoned, 1846)*
BERMUDA
IONIAN IS. *(1863)*
GIBRALTAR
MALTA
CYPRUS
WEIHAI-WEI
KUWAIT
BAHAMA IS.
TURKS AND CAICOS IS.
BAHRAIN
EGYPT *Ottoman dominions under British control*
TRUCIAL OMAN
BRITISH INDIA *Empire, 1876*
BHUTAN
BURMA
HONG KONG
JAMAICA
LEEWARD IS.
BRITISH HONDURAS
KURIA MURIA IS.
GAMBIA
ANGLO-EGYPTIAN SUDAN
ADEN
HADHRAMAUT
ANDAMAN IS.
MOSQUITO COAST *(1860)*
WINDWARD IS.
BARBADOS
TRINIDAD
BRITISH GUIANA
SIERRA LEONE
NORTHERN NIGERIA
BRITISH SOMALILAND
SOCOTRA
LACCADIVE IS.
NICOBAR IS.
BR. NORTH BORNEO
BRUNEI
MALAYA
SARAWAK
GILBERT IS.
OCEAN I.
GOLD COAST
SOUTHERN NIGERIA
UGANDA
BRITISH EAST AFRICA
MALDIVE IS.
CEYLON
SINGAPORE
ELLICE IS.
ASCENSION
NORTH EAST RHODESIA
SEYCHELLES
CHAGOS
SOLOMON IS.
ST. HELENA
NORTH WEST RHODESIA
ZANZIBAR
BRITISH CENTRAL AFRICA
COCOS IS.
BRITISH NEW GUINEA
FIJI
COOK IS.
BECHUANALAND
SOUTH RHODESIA
MAURITIUS
TONGA
PITCAIRN I.
WALVIS BAY
NATAL
BASUTOLAND
AUSTRALIA *Commonwealth, 1901*
NORFOLK I.
CAPE COLONY
TRISTAN DA CUNHA
GOUGH I.
NEW ZEALAND
FALKLAND IS.

Osborne House and Balmoral

Both Victoria and Albert found the formality of Buckingham Palace and Windsor uncongenial. Soon after their marriage they wanted to buy a small, secluded house in the country. Their first choice was the Isle of Wight, remote but still easily reached from London. In 1845 they bought Osborne House, with an estate that eventually amounted to over 2,000 acres, overlooking the Solent near Cowes. The house was torn down and rebuilt as an Italianate villa, largely to the designs of the prince, who also remodelled the grounds. From the start, queen and prince were enchanted. The queen went swimming for the first time; Albert compared the Solent to the Bay of Naples. "Never do I enjoy myself more or more peacefully," wrote the queen. Not everyone was as impressed. The future Edward VII wrote: "Even as a child I was struck by the ugliness of the house." Lord Rosebery said he had never seen an uglier drawing room than at Osborne — until he saw the one at Balmoral. Edward VII gave the house to the nation shortly after coming to the throne.

The Queen and Prince Albert with all nine of their children at Osborne, 1857, the Prince stern, the Queen maternal, the children bored. Bertie, the future Edward VII, is at the extreme right.

Balmoral, "A pretty little Castle in the old Scotch style" in the words of the queen, was originally leased by Victoria and Albert in 1847. The following year, they bought the freehold of the 20,000-acre estate and set about rebuilding the castle, again to Albert's designs, this time in a more or less baronial style. As at Osborne, Albert was also responsible for the interiors, including the famous tartan chair covers, wall-papers, curtains and carpets. For the queen, the castle, like its setting, was "charming … delightful … everything perfection". Others were less taken with it. The most frequent complaint, other than its inaccessibility 700 miles from the capital, was how cold it was. Even when the queen could be prevailed upon to close the windows, the fires were meagre. Tsar Nicholas II said Balmoral was colder than Siberia.

mixture of flattery and guile, above all in agreeing in 1876 to her own pert suggestion that she be restyled Empress of India, Disraeli gradually coaxed the queen out of retirement.

That the queen had come to occupy a core place in the nation's affections was triumphantly underlined in 1887, her Golden Jubilee. Ten years later, they were even more emphatically underlined in her Diamond Jubilee celebrations. Frail and elderly though she was, she had become the central symbol of Britain and its worldwide empire. In ways that have never really changed since, the monarchy had not just found a new stability, it had found a new role.

remove herself so completely from the public gaze was to court disaster. In her own terms, she continued to attend to her responsibilities no less diligently, reading government papers, meeting her ministers, offering advice. Yet whether she realized it or not, her refusal to show herself in public amounted to a dereliction of duty. For her subjects at large it was her public face that mattered, not her private one.

That Victoria was eventually persuaded to return to public life was largely thanks to the second great influence on her life, Benjamin Disraeli. It was Disraeli, twice Victoria's prime minister, who understood better than anyone that, as the constitutional monarch of the world's leading power, the queen had a unique role as the symbol of her nation — but not if she hid herself away. Using an outrageous

Queen Victoria's Golden Jubilee in 1887 was surpassed only by the Diamond Jubilee celebrations ten years later, "this great, this tremendous occasion" in the words of Lady Monkswell. Driving from Buckingham Palace to the service of Thanksgiving at St Paul's in an open landau, the queen was frequently moved to tears. "No one ever, I believe, has met with such an ovation as was given to me, passing through those six miles of streets," the queen later noted. Here (above left), the procession passes the National Gallery.

Despite a variety of increasing infirmities in her old age, above all trouble with her legs, the queen remained vivacious, almost sprightly, virtually to the end (left). But by the autumn of 1900 she was fading visibly, suffering from insomnia and loss of appetite. In the end, she simply faded away, dying at Osborne in January 1901. Not a single one of her subjects under 64 had known any other monarch.

1880	1884	1886	1887	1892	1897	1899
Gladstone's second Liberal administration (to 1885)	Third Reform Act	Gladstone's third Liberal administration	Victoria's Golden Jubilee	Gladstone's fourth Liberal administration (to 1894)	Victoria's Diamond Jubilee	Boer War (to 1902)

THE DEVELOPMENT OF CONSTITUTIONAL MONARCHY TO 1901

SINCE 1689, IT HAD BEEN CLEAR THAT THE AUTHORITY OF THE THRONE HAD BEEN — AND WAS CONTINUING TO BE — REDUCED IN FAVOUR OF PARLIAMENT. BUT IT WAS IN THE BRIEF REIGN OF WILLIAM IV THAT THE KEY MOMENT IN THE TRANSFORMATION THAT WOULD LEAD TO A FULLY CONSTITUTIONAL MONARCHY TOOK PLACE: THE REFORM ACT OF 1832

IN DECEMBER 1834, WILLIAM IV DISMISSED THE WHIG PRIME minister Lord Melbourne, appointing in his place the Conservative Lord Peel. The decision, the king asserted, was "his own immediate and exclusive Act. He removed Ministers whom he considered no longer capable of carrying on the business of the country … and he called to his councils others whom he considered deserving of his confidence." It turned out to be the last time any British monarch would dismiss a government.

In the subsequent general election, called to endorse the king's decision, the Conservatives emerged as the largest single party in the Commons. Still in an overall minority, however, they were effectively powerless, unable to carry the House with them. Nonetheless, Peel struggled on, reluctant to humiliate his sovereign by resigning. But in April 1835, after six defeats in the Commons in as many weeks, he bowed to the inevitable and stepped down. To the clear chagrin of the king, Melbourne was returned to office.

What William IV had discovered so painfully, and what would remain a central fact of life in the reigns of all his successors, was that the Reform Act, passed only two years earlier, had introduced a new and inescapable political reality. Effective power had slipped permanently from the king's grasp. The implications on the still-changing balance of power between the throne and Parliament are hard to overstate.

The Reform Act may have been much less far-reaching than many radicals had wanted but in expanding the franchise, however limited it remained, the Act had an unexpected consequence of huge significance: the development of organized, disciplined political parties. Put most simply, the abolition of rotten or pocket boroughs coupled with the introduction of a larger electorate meant that for the first time politicians had to make a much more coherent appeal to voters if they were to be elected. As was quickly discovered, the most effective way of doing this was through an organized political party. Within a matter of years after 1832, the House of Commons whose members had once been only loosely grouped in factions, themselves frequently fluid, had given way to one dominated by a handful of larger parties following clearly defined goals.

The consequences were twofold. One, the monarch could now no longer hope to strengthen his position by playing off one parliamentary faction against another in pursuit of his or her policies. Two, these new parties were themselves clearly answerable to the electorate rather than to the sovereign. In other words, even if not properly democratic in a modern sense, a fundamentally different political balance was being struck in which ultimate authority was passing to the electorate, restricted though it was.

A parallel development was the rise of what came to be called "responsible government" – that the government was "responsible" for policy in every sense, determining it, executing it and, should it fail, being held to account for it. Again the consequences were twofold. First, that the sovereign's influence on the formation of policy all but disappeared: the sovereign could seek to change government policy if he or she disagreed with it but in the final analysis would always have to bow to it. Second, that even though the government acted in the name of the sovereign, the sovereign could not be blamed for failures of government policy. This would come to be a crucial point.

Constitutional changes of this magnitude were played out very slowly, and many people – at the court and in government alike – had only the vaguest sense of what they actually meant; in extreme cases they were barely aware that they were happening at all. Certainly, when she came to the throne Queen Victoria assumed not just that she was head of state but head of the government, too. That none of these changes was codified – and has never been – added to the general uncertainty, even if this also allowed all sides vital flexibility in adjusting to changing circumstances.

But as Victoria would discover, her estimate of her own powers was quite wrong (though in her idiosyncratic way she frequently continued to insist on them). In effect, the power of the monarchy had now been reduced to no more than influence. But just how extensive this influence was and how it could be deployed best remained largely unknown. As in so many aspects of her reign, the crucial figure in resolving these conundrums was her husband, Prince Albert.

From the start, Albert accepted that the actual power of the throne had been heavily circumscribed. But as he also saw the monarchy as a deeply moral force, he believed that its influence should be as wide as possible. He fervently held that only the monarchy, by virtue of its permanence, could have the best interests of the nation at heart. "Is the sovereign not the natural guardian of the honour of the country?" as he put it. To make its presence felt as strongly as possible, he maintained that the monarchy should be dutiful, conscientious and above all politically neutral.

In fact, in pushing for the widest possible royal influence, neutral or not, Albert was already swimming against the tide. It has been suggested that his early death in 1861 may have prevented a possible later clash between the throne and the government. Within six years of the prince's death, the journalist Walter Bagehot, in his book *The English Constitution*, had produced what remains the classic definition of the constitutional monarchy's influence: the right to be consulted, the right to encourage, and the right to warn.

It can, of course, be objected, as it frequently was, that a throne whose influence had been so severely limited was at risk of becoming no more than a cipher, even that it might wither completely. That this did not happen was the result of an entirely unforeseen series of circumstances that took shape slowly from about 1870. Almost without anyone quite noticing it, what the monarchy had lost in power it gained in prestige.

In part, this was a result of the new respectability Albert had insisted on: the throne had rediscovered its dignity. No less important, it was also a reflection of the country's enhanced imperial status. Most important of all, the throne was increasingly invested with a new role as the essential source of the country's political stability, the ultimate guarantor of the legitimacy and stability of its parliamentary government. As a symbol of Britain and its empire, this recast monarchy proved not just hugely popular but an active source of pride, a focus for the nation's emotions and aspirations. It was, as Gladstone put it in the 1890s, "a subtle, silent yet ... almost entire transformation."

There is a significant irony here. At first sight parliamentary democracy and monarchy look incompatible, the one forward-looking and liberal, the other backward-looking and conservative. Yet whether intended or not it is a fact that parliamentary government as it evolved in 19th-century Britain succeeded in harnessing the ancient institution of hereditary monarchy to its own ends. In the process, it substantially strengthened not just itself but the monarchy. Impartial, benevolent and permanent, the monarchy had come to be seen as a natural partner of Parliament, the fundamental bedrock of the nation's liberties. Accidentally or not, an entirely new conception of monarchy had come into being.

The King [Edward VII] is no longer merely King of Great Britain and Ireland and of a few dependencies whose value consisted in ministering to the wealth and security of Great Britain and Ireland. He is now the greatest constitutional bond uniting together in a single Empire communities of free men separated by half the circumference of the Globe. All the patriotic sentiment which makes such an Empire possible centres in him or centres chiefly in him; and everything which emphasizes his personality to our kinsmen across the seas must be a gain to the Monarchy and the Empire.

Letter to Edward VII from A.J. Balfour, February 1901

EDWARD VII 1901–10

THE BULK OF EDWARD VII'S LIFE WAS LIVED IN THE SHADOW OF HIS MOTHER'S REIGN. ELDERLY AND SOMEWHAT DISSOLUTE WHEN HE CAME TO THE THRONE IN 1901, HIS OWN REIGN TURNED OUT TO BE NOT MERELY CONSCIENTIOUS BUT HIGHLY POPULAR. HIS ATTENTION TO DETAIL MAY NOT HAVE BEEN GREAT BUT HIS SENSE OF MONARCHICAL DIGNITY WAS IMPECCABLE.

BORN: November 9 1841
ACCEDED: January 22 1901; crowned August 9 1902, Westminster Abbey

Duke of Cornwall and Rothesay, Earl of Carrick, Lord of the Isles and Baron Renfrew, Prince of Wales, Earl of Chester, Duke of Saxe-Coburg-Gotha, King of the United Kingdom of Great Britain and Ireland and the British Dominions beyond the Seas, Emperor of India

Perhaps the most striking achievement of Edward VII (above) was to see how the monarchy could be used to project the interests and greater glory of Britain across the world. In effect a roving ambassador for his country, who made numerous state visits overseas, Edward had discovered a new role for the throne. His own considerable personal charm allied to his undeniable natural dignity proved a potent combination.

COMPLAINING OF HER TEENAGE SON, THE Prince of Wales, Queen Victoria wrote: "Poor Bertie! He vexes us much … There is not a particle of reflection, or even attention to anything but dress. Not the slightest interest to learn." At much the same time, his father, Prince Albert, dismissed him with the statement that the prince was "…prone to listlessness and frivolous disputes".

Few children can have been brought up under a more demanding regime than was imposed upon Victoria and Albert's eldest son. To his mother, Edward could never match the "perfection" of his father, Prince Albert. To his father, Edward was a permanent trial. "I have never in my life met such

a thorough and cunning lazybones … It does grieve me when it is my own son." In the circumstances, it is remarkable that Edward turned out to be a perfectly normal young man, albeit with a marked tendency for the kind of high living his parents found so disreputable. As a child, he was known for his violent temper and inability to concentrate. But by his late teens he was described as "the nicest fellow possible" by the dean of his Oxford college.

That said, Prince Edward could do little but wait for his mother's death. His position was hardly enviable. Queen Victoria consistently refused to give him any responsibility, never allowing him to see state papers, restricting him instead to generally undemanding public appearances (including a highly successful visit to Canada and America in 1860).

Both as Prince of Wales and king, Edward VII's taste for the pleasures of high society remained a consistent theme (above). He devoured huge quantities of food (though he was abstemious with alcohol), eating four large meals a day throughout his adult life. He also smoked 12 cigars a day and 20 cigarettes. He had a passion for gambling, shooting, yachting and horse racing (three of his horses won the Derby, another the Grand National). He remained unapologetically non-intellectual to the end of his days.

The Tranby Croft Scandal

It is a curious reflection of the morals of late-Victorian England that while the Prince of Wales's string of mistresses caused no stir, his involvement in the Tranby Croft scandal briefly provoked almost the most serious crisis of his life. It broke in July 1891 when Colonel Sir William Gordon-Cumming began an action for slander over accusations that he had cheated during a game of baccarat, then illegal, at a house party at Tranby Croft in Yorkshire the previous September. The prince, a guest at Tranby Croft, was himself playing in the game.

At the time, it was agreed to hush the matter up provided Gordon-Cumming promised never to play cards again. This he agreed to though vehemently protesting his innocence. The story leaked out, however, prompting Gordon-Cumming's determination to clear his name in public by bringing an action for slander against a number of the other players. Strenuous efforts by the prince to persuade Gordon-Cumming to drop the action came to nothing, and the prince was duly called as a witness.

To the predictable outrage provoked by the news that the prince had been party to an illegal game of cards was added further dismay that, even though he was a Field-Marshal in the army, the prince had not reported Gordon-Cumming to his commanding officer as a cheat.

1854	1860	1861	1863	1864	1870	1871	1887
Prince of Wales makes first of many visits to France	*State visit to Canada and United States*	*Sandringham estate purchased. Girl smuggled into Prince of Wales's tent in Ireland, causes rift with Victoria and Prince Albert. Death of Prince Albert*	*Marriage of Prince of Wales to Princess Alexandra of Denmark*	*Rift between Victoria and Prince of Wales over prince's support for Denmark and over his meeting with Italian nationalist Garibaldi*	*Prince of Wales cited as co-respondent in Mordaunt divorce case*	*Prince of Wales seriously ill with typhoid fever*	*Queen Victoria's Golden Jubilee*

> *I tremble at the thought of only three years and a half before us — when he will be of age and can't hold him except by moral power. I try to shut my eyes to that terrible moment ... Oh! Dear, what would happen if I were to die next winter. It is too awful a contemplation ... His only safety — and the country's — is his implicit reliance in everything, on dearest Papa, that perfection of human beings.*

Queen Victoria on her son, the Prince of Wales, April 1859

After the scandal at the Curragh in Ireland in the summer of 1860, when a girl was smuggled into his tent by fellow army officers, Queen Victoria and Prince Albert were desperate to see the Prince of Wales respectably married as soon as possible. Their choice was the much-sought after Princess Alexandra of Denmark, willowy, attentive and dutiful. Her only handicap was deafness, which grew a great deal worse the older she became. Their first child, Prince Albert Victor, pictured here (above) in 1864 with the beardless Prince and the Princess, was backward and indolent. His death at only 27 greatly grieved his parents but, in making the future George V Edward VII's heir, it almost certainly spared the country a disastrous king.

That he should have thrown himself into what became a life devoted almost exclusively to pleasure – visits to country houses, gargantuan meals, shooting and discreet womanizing (endured with equanimity by his long-suffering Danish wife, Princess Alexandra) – was hardly to be wondered at. He had little else to divert him. If he sailed close to the wind on occasion – in 1870 he was cited in a divorce case; in 1891 he was again dragged into the courts after the Tranby Croft scandal (see box) – his public standing remained high.

When in 1901 and at the age of 59 Edward finally became king, he proved to have not just the kind of common touch his mother had so conspicuously lacked but a kind of fundamental good sense that made him very hard to dislike. Edward VII not only seemed to understand the limitations of constitutional monarchy but to know precisely how to turn them to his advantage. Avuncular and straightforward – to the French he was "the uncle of Europe" – he became the very model of a modern constitutional monarch. His sure-footedness was demonstrated most obviously in 1903 when a visit to France helped pave the way to the Entente Cordiale. Similarly, Anglo-Russian relations were reinforced following the king's visit to the Tsar, Nicholas II, in 1908.

Nonetheless, though it was scarcely his doing, Edward's reign ended in controversy when, in 1909, the House of Lords rejected the Liberal government's radical "People's Budget". The Lords subsequently approved the Budget after a Liberal general election victory in early 1910. But proposals to limit the power of the Lords to veto future government legislation – if necessary by obliging the king to create Liberal peers in sufficient numbers to overcome the Conservative majority in the Lords – provoked a serious constitutional crisis.

In the event, Edward died before the problem could be resolved, leaving his son, George V, to confront it. His timing could hardly be faulted.

There were few changes of note to Britain's empire in Edward VII's reign (map below). The most important were the granting of Dominion status to New Zealand in 1907 and the creation of the Union of South Africa in 1910.

EDWARD VII 1901–10

- British held territory, 1901
- Claim abandoned during Edward's rule
- Added to British control during Edward's rule,
- Union of South Africa, created 1910
- Dominion established during Edward's rule
- Frontiers of British possessions, 1910

KUWAIT
BHUTAN
EGYPT
BAHREIN
Ottoman dominions under British control
TRUCIAL OMAN
HONG KONG
OMAN
ANGLO-EGYPTIAN SUDAN
HADHRAMAUT
KURIA MURIA IS.
ADEN
BRITISH INDIA
BRITISH SOMALILAND
SOCOTRA
LACCADIVE IS.
CEYLON
Considered to be British until 1907. Recognized by boundary agreement as part of Ethiopia
Lado; to Sudan, 1910
BRITISH EAST AFRICA
MALDIVE IS.
From Siam, 1909
BRUNEI
BR. NORTH BORNEO
MALAYA
SARAWAK
SINGAPORE
GILBERT IS.
OCEAN I.
Awarded to Britain by arbitration, 1905
ZANZIBAR
SEYCHELLES
CHAGOS
NORTH EAST RHODESIA
COCOS IS.
PAPUA
SOLOMON IS.
ELLICE IS.
NORTH WEST RHODESIA
NYASALAND
NEW HEBRIDES *Condominium, acquired jointly with France, 1906*
FIJI
SOUTH RHODESIA
MAURITIUS
TONGA
BECHU-ANALAND
Annexed as a result of Boer war, 1902
SWAZILAND
COMMONWEALTH OF AUSTRALIA
NORFOLK I.
UNION OF SOUTH AFRICA 1910
BASUTOLAND
NEW ZEALAND 1907

1891	1892	1897	1900	1901	1903	1904	1908	1909
Tranby Croft scandal	Death of prince's eldest son, Albert	Queen Victoria's Diamond Jubilee	Boer assassination attempt on Prince of Wales in Brussels	Death of Queen Victoria	Order of Merit instituted by Edward VII	Entente Cordiale between Britain and France after successful repairing of Anglo-French relations by Edward VII in 1903	Triple Entente agreed between Britain, France and Russia following successful visit by Edward to the Tsar	Constitutional crisis sparked by House of Lords' rejection of Lloyd George budget

GREAT BRITAIN: THE WINDSORS FROM 1917

GEORGE V 1910–36	GEORGE VI 1936–52
EDWARD VIII 1936	ELIZABETH II 1952–

IN 1917, QUEEN VICTORIA'S GRANDSON AND GEORGE V'S FIRST COUSIN, KAISER WILHELM II OF GERMANY, MADE A JOKE. TOLD THAT GEORGE V HAD CHANGED THE BRITISH ROYAL FAMILY'S NAME FROM SAXE-COBURG-GOTHA TO WINDSOR, HE REMARKED THAT HE WAS LOOKING FORWARD TO SEEING A PRODUCTION OF "THE MERRY WIVES OF SAXE-COBURG-GOTHA".

George V, king of Britain or not, came from a family that was entirely German. Victoria and Albert themselves almost always spoke German to each other and to their children. Both Queen Victoria (whose mother was German) and Edward VII spoke English with slight but unmistakable German accents. (Queen Victoria once complained that her eldest son, later Edward VII, only ever wrote to his then fiancée, Alexandra, in English.) Prince Albert himself was unambiguously German. Further, George V's aunt, the Princess Royal, mother of the Kaiser, had married the Crown Prince of Germany, Wilhelm I, in 1858. George V himself had a German wife, Princess Mary of Teck. However you looked at it, the German pedigree of the Saxe-Coburg-Gothas was impeccable.

Yet with the outbreak of the First World War, this German background, once a source of pride, was becoming more and more embarrassing. As early as October 1914, George's cousin, Prince Louis Battenburg had been forced to resign as First Sea Lord because of presumed German sympathies. As anti-German sentiments mounted during the war, the king bowed to the inevitable. On July 17 1917, it was announced that the family's name would be changed to Windsor. The name itself, suggested by Lord Stamfordham, the king's private secretary, was pure invention. But it was deemed to have a sufficiently British resonance to make it acceptable. At the same time, all the family's "other German degrees, styles, titles, dignatories, honours and appelations" were dropped.

In identifying himself with his people so publicly, George V was acting entirely in character: acknowledging that the German Hanoverians, 200 years after they gained the throne of Britain, were now definitively British; and setting a benchmark for his successors – that duty comes first. The nine-month reign in 1936 of the wayward Edward VIII apart, the hallmarks of the House of Windsor have been precisely the combination of patriotism and duty that George V so conspicuously espoused.

This has always been more than a matter of setting an example. Rather, it reflects that, as constitutional monarchs of a democratic country, the prime, in some senses only, justification for the monarchy has been that it should be above reproach. Only then, properly neutral politically, can it provide the stability that underpins and legitimizes the state.

Even the most hardened republican would be hard pressed to deny that George V and his successors have fulfilled this role with exemplary devotion, the inconvenient example of Edward VIII aside. Further, the stability of the Windsors has found a clear echo in the political stability of Britain as a whole over the same period.

By comparison, elsewhere in Europe the reign of George V alone saw the overthrow of "five emperors, eight kings and 18 more dynasties". The Windsors by contrast have successfully endured two world wars, a series of more or less serious constitutional crises, the shrinking of their realm (with Irish independence) and the almost complete loss of empire.

Further, however stodgy their image, they have proved unusually adaptable. The reign of Elizabeth II has seen changes as sweeping as any that occurred under Queen Victoria. As a result, though her sense of duty may be the equal of her father's and grandfather's (and her constitutional position unchanged), her style of monarchy has become quite different. In place of the "mystique" of George V's reign, which demanded that he be remote, distant and unapproachable, Elizabeth II, though scarcely a populist herself and attacked in the early part of her reign as tweedy and out of touch, has inevitably adopted a more low-key, human approach.

Such informality carries its own dangers. The more visible the monarchy – the more it mingles with the crowd in response to the demands of a less deferent age – the more it risks dissolving the indefinable barrier that separates royal from commoner. By far the most serious danger the throne has faced since about 1985 is that, seen in close-up, their royal "magic" put to one side, the Windsors have not always looked very appealing.

To some extent, this has been the result of an increasingly rampant, sensation-seeking press. Where once the press was fawning in its approach to the royal family, since at least 1990 its coverage of royal affairs has been relentlessly aggressive. If the queen herself has escaped their sights, remaining a model of rectitude and propriety, the rest of her family have come to be viewed as greedy, incompetent, vulgar, or merely eccentric.

They have not always helped their own cause. In stark contrast to the queen and her redoubtable mother – who was clearly the real force behind the potentially shaky throne of George VI – they have married badly. Three of the queen's four children, as well as her sister, Margaret, have been divorced, something that would have been unthinkable even for a minor member of the royal family before the Second World War.

General dissatisfaction with the royal family came to a dramatic head in 1997 with the death of the Princess of Wales, widely seen as the innocent victim of a sustained campaign by the cold-hearted Windsors. The extraordinary displays of public grief for her carried with them an implicit rebuke. In death, the princess had captured the nation's affections in ways the Windsors had not always managed. There was talk that this amounted to the most serious crisis to face the royal family since the abdication of Edward VIII.

But if the future necessarily remains unknowable, it may equally be the case that the relative unpopularity of the royal family after 1980s was little more than a blip. The mourning for the death of the venerable Queen Mother in 2002, followed by unforced national celebrations for the queen's Golden Jubilee celebrations in May 2002, as widespread as they were genuine, may in time come to be seen as much more properly representative of the real standing of the House of Windsor. Duty may yet turn out to be its own reward.

GEORGE V 1910–36

KING GEORGE V
BORN: June 3 1865
ACCEDED: May 6 1910;
crowned June 22 1911,
Westminster Abbey

*Duke of York,
Earl of Inverness
and Baron Killarney,
Duke of Cornwall
and Rothesay,
Prince of Wales
and Earl of Chester,
King of the United
Kingdom of Great
Britain and Northern
Ireland and the British
Dominions beyond the
Seas, Emperor of India*

GEORGE V'S IMAGE AS A BLUFF DISCIPLINARIAN IS AT ODDS WITH THE REALITY OF A SHY MAN WHO STRUGGLED TO COME TO TERMS WITH AN UNLOOKED-FOR ROLE AS KING. HOWEVER STILTED, HIS OBVIOUS DECENCY AND SENSE OF DUTY PRODUCED A REIGN THAT SAW HIS COUNTRY THROUGH A SERIES OF CRISES INCLUDING THE FIRST WORLD WAR.

AS THE SECOND SON OF EDWARD VII, the future George V had never expected to become king. The death in 1892 of George's elder brother, the dissolute Prince Albert, Duke of Clarence, made George heir to his father, the Prince of Wales. George didn't just inherit his new place in the succession from his elder brother, he inherited his fiancée, too. In 1893 he married the formidably upright Princess Mary of Teck, who the year before had been engaged to marry Albert.

By now, George's life had undergone a near complete transformation. George had been destined for the Navy, which he joined in 1877, aged only 12. Over the next 15 years, he served with considerable distinction. It was a period that decisively shaped his outlook and personality. At heart the prince would remain a conscientious and commonsensical naval officer all his life. His extensive travels across the globe also inculcated a fierce pride in Britain's empire, a considerable amount of which he saw at first hand.

Forcibly retired from the Navy on the death of Prince Albert, George now began to be actively groomed for the throne. Established at St James's Palace in London and at York Cottage on the Sandringham estate, his life with Princess Mary rapidly settled into

George V (above, on the right) as Prince of Wales with his first cousin, the Tsar, at Cowes, 1904. The physical resemblance between the two is striking; the political difference immense. Where George would inherit a limited constitutional throne, Nicholas ruled Russia as an unabashed autocrat. As king, George never enjoyed the same close relationship with another first cousin, Kaiser Wilhelm II. George would later write, "I look upon him as the greatest criminal known for having plunged the world into this ghastly war." By 1918, the Tsar had been murdered, the Kaiser forced into exile.

The Prince of Wales, the future George V, with his family in Scotland, 1906 (right). With five sons, the prince had done more than his bit to secure his succession. From left to right, the children are: Mary, created the Princess Royal in 1932; Henry, subsequently duke of Gloucester; George, subsequently duke of Kent; John; Edward, subsequently Edward VIII; and Albert, subsequently George VI. John was an epileptic and died at only 13 in 1919. The Duke of Kent was killed in an air crash in 1942. Despite Edward's VIII's later complaints of the unreasonable discipline imposed by his parents, by late-Victorian standards his parents were generous, almost indulgent.

I may be uninspiring but I'll be damned if I am an alien

*George V replying to H.G. Wells's claim
that his court was "alien and uninspiring"*

1877	1890	1891	1892	1893
Enters Royal Naval College, Dartmouth	Given first command, HMS Thrush	Appointed commander in the Navy	Death of Prince Albert, George's elder brother; Prince George leaves Navy	Marriage of Prince George to Princess Mary of Teck

GEORGE V 1910–36

▨	○	British-held territory, 1910
▨		Brought under British control during George's reign
▨		Acquired by Britain as League of Nations' Mandate after World War I
▢		Lost to another power during George's rule (with date)
▨		Gained independence, with date
⧄		Dominion, with date, if achieved status during George's rule
⚑		Dynasties overthrown in or after World War I
⚐		Revolt with dates
---		Frontier of British Empire possessions and dependencies, 1936

Not only did the British Empire survive the First World War intact, unlike those of Russia, Germany, Austria-Hungary and the Ottomans, it was substantially increased in extent (map above). With the take-over of the former German colony of Tanganyika, Cecil Rhodes's imperial vision of a belt of British territory from the Cape to Suez was briefly attained. The United Kingdom itself was reduced with Irish independence in 1922, Northern Ireland aside.

Despite last-minute efforts to mediate with the Kaiser on the eve of war, George V was in no doubt about the inevitability of war with Germany in August 1914. The king visited the Western Front seven times during the First World War. He also personally distributed 58,000 decorations. He made numerous visits to factories and hospitals in Britain itself. Throughout, his patriotism never flagged. Rightly, as it would be in 1945, it was Buckingham Palace that became the immediate focus of national euphoria with the ending of the war. Here (left), the king with Queen Mary and the Prince of Wales (back left) are seen at Abbeville, France, in 1917.

one of affectionate, domestic and orderly calm. As resolutely non-intellectual as his father, the prince was able to indulge his passion for sport – yachting, golf, and above all shooting (George was generally acknowledged as one of the best shots in the country) – and for his other great hobby, stamp collecting. By his death, his stamp collection was the largest in private hands in the world. Even more important, a clear mark of his level-headed sense of duty, George was consistently faithful to Mary. By the end of his reign, he had become the first British king since Charles I to whom no hint of sexual scandal had been attached. It was in very marked contrast to his Hanoverian forebears.

In equally marked contrast to his father's experience as Prince of Wales, George was given a share in the king's responsibilities: when Edward VII came to the throne in 1901 he allowed the new Prince of Wales to see state papers and invited him to set up his desk beside his own at Buckingham Palace.

1894	1901	1910	1911	1914
Birth of Prince Edward (later Edward VIII)	Death of Queen Victoria. New Prince and Princess of Wales make 231-day visit to Australia, New Zealand and Canada	George V agrees "hypothetical understanding" with Liberal government to end Conservative majority in House of Lords by creating Liberal peers	Coronation of George V followed by visit to India for installation as King-Emperor at Delhi Durbar	Inconclusive Round Table Conference at Buckingham Palace hosted by George V in attempt to resolve Irish Home Rule (July). Germany declares war against Britain (Aug.): the First World War

Typically, though utterly opposed to the means employed by the Trades Unions in calling a General Strike in May 1926, the king was quick to urge Baldwin's government to adopt a conciliatory approach. In the end the government's firm line paid off: the strike was abandoned after only nine days. But it was a foretaste of wider social and economic disruption in the years to come. Here (above), *an armoured car patrols London.*

Two Constitutional Crises

*I*n the early part of his reign, George V faced two serious crises that the rules of the still youthful constitutional monarchy struggled to accommodate. The first was his Liberal government's determination to pass a Parliament Bill restricting the right of the House of Lords to veto legislation passed in the House of Commons. The second was Irish Home Rule. In neither case was George helped by widespread Liberal suspicions of his strongly ingrained Conservative prejudices. In 1908, he had called H.H. Asquith, the Liberal prime minister, "not quite a gentleman". Lloyd George, the Liberal Chancellor of the Exchequer, was "that damned fellow".

In fact, George V was highly conscious of his constitutional responsibilities to be politically neutral and to act in accordance with his ministers' advice. Amid a welter of conflicting advice, in the autumn of 1910 he secretly agreed to create sufficient new Liberal peers, possibly several hundred, to vote through the Parliament Act in the event of a Liberal victory in the subsequent general election. In the event it proved unnecessary. The Lords backed down and passed the Parliament Act. But Asquith's announcement the following summer of the king's agreement provoked fury on George V's part, implying as it did that George could not have been trusted to do his constitutional duty. It was the "dirtiest thing ever done" in the king's view.

Home Rule, threatening outright civil war on the part of loyalist Unionists in Ulster who refused to join a new independent Irish state, proved more intractable still. The king's characteristic response was to act as a mediator, summoning a Round Table Conference at Buckingham Palace in July 1914 to allow all parties to resolve their differences. Good will would never be enough to find a way through a problem that has still not been settled. When eventual Irish independence was granted after the war, it was to the accompaniment of precisely the civil war the king had hoped to avoid. The king's instincts as a conciliator were never less than honourable, however.

When George V came to the throne in 1910, the monarchy had probably never been held in higher regard, a fact that the deliberate magnificence of the new king's coronation and his even more splendid investiture as Emperor of India at the Delhi Durbar the following year were deliberately intended to underline (see p.189). Hindsight has tended to present these years before the First World War as a kind of glorious high summer of certainty and calm. In reality, it was a period of considerable political and military turmoil. The danger was not merely the obvious aggression of Kaiser Wilhelm II's Germany, it was a new political climate that would immediately present the new George V with the two most serious constitutional crises of the 20th century (see box).

Serious as these constitutional threats were, however, they paled in the face of the outbreak of war with Germany and Austria-Hungary in August 1914, which shattered the long period of Victorian and Edwardian peace. The king's response was typical. "I cannot share your hardships," he declared to his soldiers, "but my heart is with you every hour of the day." There is no doubt he meant it. In a gesture of solidarity, he and the queen gave up alcohol for the duration of the conflict, "a great bore" in the king's words but a resolve he stuck to with characteristic phlegm.

The king made a series of visits to his troops on the Western Front as well as to the Grand Fleet. In October 1915, he broke his pelvis badly on the Western Front when he was thrown from a horse, an injury that caused him pain for the rest of life. Only once in the war was a question mark raised over his conduct when, in March 1917, he overruled Lloyd George's decision to allow the deposed Tsar of Russia and his family to come to England. The king's motive was sensible: fear of sparking revolutionary sentiments in Britain. But in effect he was condemning his cousin to death.

The world that emerged after 1918 had been ineradicably changed. British global pre-eminence had decisively given way to American superiority. And while the empire, at least in the short term, remained intact, other changes could not be resisted: the creation of the Irish Free State in 1922; the appointment of the first Labour prime minister, Ramsay MacDonald, in 1924; the social and economic unrest that led to the General Strike in 1926; the formation of a National Government in 1931 to confront the crisis created by the Great Depression. Throughout, the king acted precisely in accordance with his constitutional role, attempting to find common ground and appealing for calm whenever appropriate, never once seeking to go against the wishes of his governments.

1915	1916	1917	1918	1922	1924
George V breaks pelvis during visit to Western Front	Abortive Easter Rising by Irish nationalists, Dublin	George V refuses to allow Tsar Nicholas II and family to come to Britain	German surrender (Nov.): end of First World War	Creation of Irish Free State against background of continuing civil war	Formation of first (minority) Labour government

Ill-health undermined the king's last years. In November 1928 septicaemia had brought him close to death. In early 1936 he fell ill again, with bronchitis. It was now that Queen Mary reputedly suggested he convalesce at Bognor Regis (named in honour of the king after his earlier convalescence there), prompting the celebrated (but apocryphal) comment, "Bugger Bognor." The king and Queen Mary are seen here (left) being driven to church at Balmoral in 1930.

However, he could do nothing to prevent the gradual drift towards full independence of the country's dominions, Australia, New Zealand, Canada and South Africa. To all intents and purposes fully responsible for their own domestic affairs since at least 1914, in 1931 they gained control over their foreign affairs, too. Importantly, the king remained their head of state; indeed the prime relationship between the dominions and Britain became the monarchy rather than Westminster. But however close their remaining ties with Britain, the dominions were now independent. As important, in 1930 George V was forced, much against his better judgement, to agree to the appointment of the first non-British governor general in Australia. That independence would have to be conceded to other parts of the empire, India, above all, was becoming increasingly obvious.

George V's own status throughout the post-war years was unquestioned. Unbending and intimidating though he was, his hold on the affections of the nation was clear. The celebrations to mark the king's Silver Jubilee in 1935 made clear not just the high regard in which the king was held but his great personal popularity. He found it deeply affecting. That said, and declining health aside, his final years were clouded by growing worries over the fitness of his heir, the future Edward VIII, to inherit the throne. Popular and glamorous he may have been; dutiful he wasn't. "After I am dead, the boy will ruin himself in 12 months," said the king. It was an uncannily accurate prophecy.

George V was never a natural innovator but his radio broadcast to the empire at Christmas 1932 (right) began a tradition that endures today. The king may still have been an almost infinitely remote figure to the overwhelming majority of his subjects but never before had such direct contact between king and subjects been possible.

I will not have another war. I will not. The last one was none of my doing and if there is another one and we are threatened with being brought into it, I will go to Trafalgar Square myself and wave a red flag myself rather than allow this country to be brought in.

George V to Lloyd George, 1935

1926	1931	1932	1935
General Strike paralyses Britain (May). Imperial Conference redefines relationship between Britain and its dominions (formalized 1931 in Statute of Westminster creating British Commonwealth of Nations)	*Coalition National Government formed. Sir Isaac Isaacs becomes first Australian-born Governor General of Australia (the monarch's direct representative)*	*George V makes first Christmas radio broadcast to British Empire*	*Silver Jubilee of George V*

THE GROWTH OF ROYAL CEREMONY

THE PAGEANTRY SURROUNDING THE ROYAL FAMILY IS A RELATIVELY RECENT DEVELOPMENT. HOWEVER HISTORIC IT APPEARS, MUCH OF IT WAS DEVELOPED ONLY FROM THE LATE-VICTORIAN PERIOD AS THE NECESSITY OF INVESTING THE NEWLY CONSTITUTIONAL MONARCHY WITH A MUCH MORE VISIBLE PRESENCE AND GRANDEUR BECAME OBVIOUS. FROM THE START, IT HAD A CONSCIOUSLY IMPERIAL DIMENSION.

WRITING IN 1861, LORD SALISBURY complained about the apparent British inability to contrive convincing royal spectacles: "Some nations have a gift for ceremonial ... In England the case is exactly the reverse. We can afford to be more splendid than most nations; but some malignant spell broods over all our most solemn ceremonials, and inserts into them some feature which makes them all ridiculous."

Yet 50 years later, with the coronation of George V in 1911, the British monarchy and spectacle on the grandest of scales had become almost synonymous. No less than 60,000 troops were pressed into service to line the route from Westminster Abbey to Buckingham Palace for George's coronation. They represented not just every branch of Britain's armed forces but large numbers of its imperial forces. There were also special detachments from Germany and Austria as well as from Spain.

The royal families of Europe were present in impressive force. Every ruling European house was represented, as were the Emperor of Japan, the Ottoman Sultan and the Shah of Persia, "... come amongst us to see the descendent of Alfred crowned in the Temple of the Plantagenets" in the words of *The Times*.

The next day, the king journeyed to Portsmouth to review "... the most formidable fleet ever assembled. It was formed in seven columns, each nearly five miles long. The British warships present were 165 – eight Dreadnoughts, twenty-four earlier battleships, four Dreadnought cruisers, sixty-seven destroyers, twelve destroyers' depôt ships, twelve torpedo boats and eight

> *Once more we have to extend our horizon and to regard this ancient Monarchy as the mother of nations and the centre of a world-wide Empire, held together by no bonds of conquest and no assertive central authority, but by some force which none of us can properly name or define, impalpable and intangible as gravity, yet, like that mysterious force, maintaining the system intact while allowing for all the perturbations due to the minor interactions of several parts.*
>
> The Times, *on George V's coronation, June 1911*

Following his coronation in 1937, George VI (above), wife and daughters by his side, were rapturously greeted on the balcony of Buckingham Palace by a huge crowd.

submarines ... His Majesty expressed his marked satisfaction with the review." It was hardly to be wondered at. The express purpose of the coronation had been to underline the might of Britain in all spheres, imperial above all.

The association with monarchy and spectacle on this scale, all of it appearing to draw on earlier tradition, may have been a process that evolved rather than was consciously aimed at. But once it had become clear that a constitutional monarchy was the ideal symbol of the nation and its domains, then for the rulers of the greatest empire the world had ever seen it followed that pomp was its natural accompaniment. Appropriately, it was a process that had begun with Queen Victoria's gradual emergence from her self-imposed seclusion after the death of Prince Albert in 1861. When designated Empress of India in 1876, an "Imperial Assemblage" was held the following year in Delhi. On the site where the Indian Mutiny had been finally suppressed in 1858, 70 Indian princes expressed their loyalty to the Viceroy, the queen's direct representative. As the Viceroy put it: "The further east you go, the greater becomes the importance of a bit of bunting." (It

The highpoint of British imperial pretensions was represented by the Delhi Durbar (above). Iconic and idealistic, George V and Queen Mary personified the seemingly permanent edifice that was British rule in India.

wasn't a flawless success: a number of people were trampled to death after a 101-gun salute stampeded the elephants.)

The discovery of how spectacle could underpin the monarchy, in turn reinforcing the self-esteem of the nation, was substantially enhanced with Queen Victoria's Golden and Diamond Jubilees in 1887 and 1897. However novel most of their forms, both reflected what was widely assumed to be time-honoured tradition; and both were conceived as public spectacles on a deliberately lavish scale. It was also in 1897 that colonial troops were used for the first time – "dusky warriors" as *The Illustrated London News* called them. (The success of the spectacle also inspired A.C. Benson to write the words to *Land of Hope and Glory.*)

George V's coronation had an important follow-up six months later when he and the queen travelled to what had been the Mogul capital of India, Delhi, subsequently proclaimed the new capital of British India, for the Delhi Durbar, a ritual exchange of gifts and loyalties between ruler and ruled. For five days, swelter-

The queen at the Trooping of the Colour in 2001 (above). The ceremony, which has celebrated the sovereign's official birthday since the 17th century, has its origins in the Middle Ages when knights and other nobles carried flags into battle to allow their position to be easily seen in the heat and smoke of conflict. The ceremony today is the annual highpoint of royal pageantry.

The funeral of the Queen Mother in March 2002 was simultaneously moving and uplifting (above). Impeccably organized, it saw the full weight of royal ceremonial deployed at its most commanding. Only the most stony-hearted could fail to have been moved.

ing under the Indian sun, George V and Queen Mary, dressed in their coronation robes, received the submission of India's princes. Even after the king and queen had left, "… tens of thousands of Indians … made obeisance … many kneeling, touching the railings, and prostrating themselves in the dust."

"What lay behind this splendid pageantry, what force was symbolised in the quiet, dignified figure receiving the acclaim of his Indian subjects?" asked *The Times of India*. "Stability … fixity of purpose and continuity of purpose" was its answer. It turned out to be quite wrong. It had been intended that every new British monarch would preside over a similar Durbar: George V was the first and last. His heir, Edward VIII, was not king long enough to be crowned let alone to visit India as its ruler. George VI, was immediately sucked into the European crisis racked up by Hitler. And by the time his successor, Elizabeth II, came to the throne, she was no longer ruler of India. The heyday of imperial pageantry lasted less than 20 years.

Yet in Britain at least, pageantry and the monarchy – for all

that many of its forms were of recent invention – had become inseparable. The coronation of George VI was every bit as gorgeous as that of his father; that of Elizabeth II, in which ancient forms were deliberately exploited to celebrate the country's final emergence from the austerity of the Second World War, almost more so. Further, whether Trooping the Colour or at the State Opening of Parliament, the two annual occasions when the full might of royal pageantry are set out at their most opulent, the monarchy is seen at its most imposing. Notably, the funeral of the Queen Mother in 2002, admittedly planned long in advance, struck exactly the tone of solemnity and cere-monial splendour that Lord Salisbury feared was permanently beyond the throne.

EDWARD VIII 1936

HUGELY POPULAR AS PRINCE OF WALES FOR HIS EASY CHARM, EDWARD VIII – IN A REIGN OF ONLY NINE MONTHS – NONETHELESS SPARKED THE MOST SERIOUS CRISIS TO OVERTAKE THE BRITISH THRONE IN THE 20TH CENTURY. HIS DETERMINATION TO MARRY A TWICE-DIVORCED AMERICAN WAS IMPOSSIBLE TO RECONCILE WITH HIS FAMILY'S – AND HIS NATION'S – EXPECTATIONS OF HIS DUTY.

KING EDWARD VIII

BORN: June 23 1894;
DIED: May 28 1972
ACCEDED: January 20 1936; abdicated December 11 1936.
Never crowned

Duke of Cornwall and Rothesay, Earl of Carrick, Lord of the Isles and Baron Renfrew, Prince of Wales, Earl of Chester, Duke of Windsor (from 1937), King of the United Kingdom of Great Britain and Northern Ireland and the British Dominions beyond the Seas, Emperor of India

HAVING BEEN DISPATCHED ON GOODWILL tours around the world in 1920 and again in 1921, the Prince of Wales returned to Britain enjoying the kind of international celebrity status that was then matched only by the stars of an emerging Hollywood. Always at ease with crowds, he was fêted wherever he went. Young, boyishly good-looking, and (in striking contrast to his parents) informal, he had an obvious common touch.

His affinity with the Jazz Age might conceivably have translated into a genuinely new style of constitutional kingship: accessible, unstuffy and open. But at heart, both as Prince of Wales and, briefly, as king, Edward VIII never had the staying power to follow through his good intentions. Easily bored and enormously rich, he naturally reverted to the pursuit of pleasure that had come so naturally to Edward VII when he was Prince of Wales. This might not have mattered had he married. Instead, a series of more or less long-term relationships with a variety of women, most of them married, followed. As he approached 40, this could no longer be put down to youthful indulgence. Inevitably, relations with his disapproving father deteriorated.

In 1931, he met Wallis Simpson. Elegant and sophisticated, she epitomized the worldly fast life the Prince craved. That she was an American was a drawback but no more. That she had been married twice, however, clearly ruled her out as a possible consort for a man who would one day be Supreme Governor of the Church of England.

Edward's accession in January 1936 was greeted with enthusiasm. Yet from the start, he dismayed his courtiers. Quite apart from his apparent enthusiasm for Hitler, his attention to the business of state was dilatory at best. Pleasure continued to take first place.

The crisis over the king's determination to marry Mrs Simpson was short-lived but decisive. By November 16 1936 he had informed the prime minister, Stanley Baldwin, that he would rather

> *I, Edward the Eighth, of Great Britain, Ireland, and the British Dominions beyond the Seas, King, Emperor of India, do hereby declare my irrevocable determination to renounce the Throne for Myself and for My descendants, and My desire that effect should be given to this Instrument of Abdication immediately. In token thereof I have hereunto set My hand this tenth day of December, nineteen hundred and thirty six, in the presence of the witnesses whose signatures are subscribed.*
>
> *Edward VIII's Instrument of Abdication*

In the summer of 1936, Edward VIII and Mrs Simpson went on a cruise together along the Dalmatian coast in the yacht Nahlin *(right). The holiday provided exactly the opportunity for informal pleasure-seeking the king relished. Other than in Britain, where the press resolutely refused to cover the story almost until the moment of abdication, much of the watching world was shocked by the king's obvious intimacy with Mrs Simpson.*

The marriage of the Duke of Windsor to Mrs Simpson on June 3 1937 at the Château de Condé (right) provided stark confirmation of the couple's pariah status as royal non-persons. Not only did every member of the royal family refuse to attend, including Lord Mountbatten, until then the duke's closest friend, but George VI declared that the new duchess could not be styled Her Royal Highness. The Duke of Windsor never forgave his brother for this deliberate slight.

As Prince of Wales, Edward made a series of extraordinarily successful foreign visits, in which his popularity soared (map right). The majority of these were to countries within the empire, but after his first visit to Germany, in 1912, he developed an admiration for that country which he never lost.

EDWARD VIII'S TRAVELS AS PRINCE OF WALES, 1919–28

- Countries Edward visited during World War 1
- Countries Edward visited that were part of the British Empire
- Other countries of the British Empire
- Other countries visited by Edward
- • Ports of entry and departure

abdicate than give up Mrs Simpson. Less than four weeks later, he did so, passing his throne to his younger brother, the Duke of York, now George VI. Mrs Simpson herself, apparently aware only at the last minute of the constitutional crisis she had provoked, had left the country some days earlier for the south of France. The former Edward VIII was taken by a naval destroyer across the Channel on December 12, and from there he made his way to Austria.

The drama that was Edward VIII and Wallis Simpson was important less for its being a love affair thwarted by a cold-hearted court and government than for the king's inability to see that his privileged position came at a price. King or not, there were absolute limits to what he could get away with. His constitutional position clearly made marriage to a twice-divorced woman impossible, and his failure to recognize this elementary truth reflects no credit on him. Further, Edward VIII's subsequent marriage to Wallis Simpson seems to have been a peculiarly joyless business. In the name of love, the pair found themselves effectively condemned to stick out what to the rest of the world looked like an increasingly gruesome, loveless relationship.

The Constitutional Implications

*T*here was no legal bar to Edward VIII's marrying Mrs Simpson. She was not a Catholic, which would have made the king's marriage to her impossible under the 1701 Act of Settlement. Further, the Royal Marriages Act of 1772 did not apply to the sovereign, only to other members of his family. Rather, the objection to the king's marrying Mrs Simpson was that, as Supreme Governor of the Church of England, which explicitly forbade church marriages to divorcees, the king would invalidate his presumed future coronation oath to uphold the Church. He could have made a civil marriage. He might, technically, have been able to marry Mrs Simpson under the rites of the Church of Scotland, in which he held no formal position. But the obvious shabbiness of such expedients could only have damaged his standing. In short, Mrs Simpson was never a credible candidate as the king's wife and queen.

What has always been extraordinary is that neither the king nor Mrs Simpson seem to have woken up to this central fact until almost the very end. Both seem to have assumed that, as king, Edward VIII could do as he pleased. As his private secretary, Alex Hardinge, damningly put it, the king "appeared to be entirely ignorant of the powers of a constitutional monarch".

In abdicating, Edward at least avoided the constitutional crisis that would have followed if he had remained king and still insisted on marrying Mrs Simpson. It is obviously impossible to know precisely what form such a crisis might have taken. It is certain, however, that in pitting himself against his government, he would have undermined the very basis of constitutional monarchy – its political neutrality. That the king should even have contemplated such a step was something his family could never forgive.

But abdication, however preferable, was no more than the lesser of two evils. In cutting directly against the grain of hereditary monarchy, it inevitably damaged the throne. Further, the king's readiness to jeopardize a sacred duty in pursuit of personal happiness ran entirely counter to the code of duty established by George V.

1936	1937	1940–45	1945
Oct. 20: First meeting of Edward VIII and prime minister, Stanley Baldwin, to discuss Wallis Simpson; Oct. 27: Mrs Simpson granted decree nisi, making her free to remarry in six months; Nov.16: Edward VIII informs Baldwin of his decision to abdicate if he is not allowed to marry Mrs Simpson; Nov. 25: King raises possibility of morganatic marriage to Mrs Simpson; told by Baldwin this would be impossible; Dec. 2: British press breaks self-imposed silence on the affair; Dec. 5: King confirms his intention to abdicate; Dec. 10: Instrument of Abdication signed; Dec. 11: Bill of Abdication passed; throne passes to George VI; Dec. 12: Former Edward VIII leaves England	Edward created Duke of Windsor (Mar.); marries Mrs Simpson in France (June); couple visit Germany and meet Hitler (Oct.)	Duke of Windsor serves as Governor of the Bahamas	Retires to Paris

GEORGE VI 1936–52

IF THERE WAS NEVER A MORE RELUCTANT KING THAN GEORGE VI, THERE WAS CERTAINLY NEVER A MORE DUTIFUL ONE. SUCCEEDING AT A MOMENT OF SUPREME CRISIS FOR THE THRONE AFTER HIS BROTHER'S ABDICATION, GEORGE FORCED HIMSELF TO PERFORM PUBLIC DUTIES THAT A SEVERE STAMMER MADE A TORMENT. HE SET THE NATION A STALWART EXAMPLE IN SELF-SACRIFICE IN THE SECOND WORLD WAR.

BORN: December 14 1895
ACCEDED: December 11 1936; crowned May 12 1937, Westminster Abbey

Duke of York, Earl of Inverness and Baron Killarney, King of the United Kingdom of Great Britain and Northern Ireland and the British Dominions beyond the Seas, Emperor of India (until 1947)

George VI (above), shy, stuttering and uncertain, may not have been cut out to be king but no one could claim he discharged his responsibilities with anything less than fortitude. It is a striking tribute to him that, once free from the shadow of his elder brother, Edward VIII, he set the monarchy back on its feet.

If never exactly hearty, George VI nonetheless had a clear taste for wholesome outdoor life. In 1926, he played in the doubles at Wimbledon (right). He and his partner, Louis Greig, lost 6–1, 6–2, 6–3. More successfully, in 1921 he established the Duke of York's camps, an attempt to introduce working-class city children to the disciplines and rewards of Scouting.

There can be no question that his wife and children provided George VI with an emotional stability he had never known as a child. "We four," as he touchingly called his family, were at the heart of his life. Theirs may have been an incontestably royal existence, but its humanity was never in doubt. This painting (above), showing the royal family at Royal Lodge, Windsor, in 1940, is by James Gunn.

VISITING HIS MOTHER ON DECEMBER 9 1936, two days before Edward VIII's abdication, the future George VI, his completely unlooked-for reign now imminent, "broke down and sobbed like a child". His terror was understandable. Less than a month before, the duke of York, as he then was, had had no idea he was so close to the throne. Not only had he had little or no formal preparation for the task, he was in all respects, save one, scarcely suited for it anyway. Yet it was this one virtue – a refusal to shirk even the most painful duty – that would restore the stability of the throne and make his reign, if not great, then at the very least admirable.

As a child, Prince Albert, as he had been christened, was slow and awkward, prone to illness, bad at his lessons and given to rages. He also developed a stammer that he never lost. With public speaking being a key part of kingship, it was a heavy burden to carry.

Like his father George V, he was destined for the Navy. Unlike him, his career was not distinguished. At Osborne Naval College he was 68th out of 68. Later, at Dartmouth, he came 61st out of 68. Gastritis, appendicitis and seasickness made his naval career stop-start at best, though he was present at the Battle of Jutland in May 1916.

He is of course a fairly reactionary person.

Hugh Gaitskell MP on George VI

Marriage in 1923 to Lady Elizabeth Bowes-Lyon was the making of him. Intelligent and charming, she proved an ideal wife and a permanent support. Their undemanding domestic life, complemented by the births of Princess Elizabeth in 1926 and Princess Margaret in 1930, was contented and settled. That the duke of York was rarely in the public spotlight was, to him, a blessing.

Almost his first act as George VI – a name adopted to emphasize the continuity he hoped his reign would restore – was to sever all links with his brother. For a hesitant man, it was an uncharacteristically

1908	1916	1920	1921	1923	1926	1930	1936
Enters Osborne Naval College	Serves at Battle of Jutland on HMS Collingwood	Created duke of York	Founds Duke of York's camps to enable working-class children to learn Scouting	Marriage to Lady Elizabeth Bowes-Lyon	Birth of Princess Elizabeth, future Elizabeth II	Birth of Princess Margaret	Abdication of Edward VIII; accession of George VI

Map labels:
- DOMINION OF CANADA
- *Former Dominion; left Commonwealth 1949*
- UNITED KINGDOM
- *British occupation zone of Germany, 1949*
- *British sectors of Four Power administered Berlin/Vienna*
- NEWFOUNDLAND *to Canada, 1949*
- IRISH REPUBLIC *1949*
- *Trieste; jointly with US, 1947*
- *British occupation zone of Austria*
- *Rest of former Palestinian mandate to Transjordan (from 1950 Jordan) and Egypt, 1949*
- *Dependency of India, from 1948*
- BERMUDA
- GIBRALTAR
- MALTA
- CYPRUS
- JORDAN *1946*
- KUWAIT
- BAHAMAS. TURKS AND CAICOS IS.
- ISRAEL *1948*
- BHUTAN
- JAMAICA
- LEEWARD IS.
- BARBADOS
- LIBYA *1951*
- EGYPT
- QATAR BAHRAIN TRUCIAL OMAN
- PAKISTAN *1947*
- INDIA *1947*
- BURMA *1948*
- HONG KONG
- BRITISH HONDURAS
- WINDWARD IS.
- TRINIDAD
- BRITISH GUIANA
- GAMBIA
- BRITISH TOGO
- BRITISH CAMEROONS
- NIGERIA
- ERITREA ANGLO-EGYPTIAN SUDAN
- ADEN
- OMAN
- KURIA MURIA IS.
- SOCOTRA
- LACCADIVE IS.
- PAKISTAN
- SIERRA LEONE
- GOLD COAST
- BRITISH SOMALILAND
- SOMALIA *1950*
- MALDIVE IS.
- CEYLON *1948*
- MALAYA
- BRUNEI
- BR. NORTH BORNEO
- SARAWAK
- *British/Australian/New Zealand trusteeship*
- ASCENSION
- UGANDA KENYA
- TANGANYIKA
- SEYCHELLES
- SINGAPORE
- *Australian trusteeship*
- NAURU I.
- OCEAN I.
- GILBERT IS.
- ST. HELENA
- ZANZIBAR
- CHAGOS
- COCOS IS.
- NEW GUINEA
- ELLICE IS.
- WESTERN SAMOA
- PAPUA
- SOLOMON IS.
- NORTH RHODESIA
- NYASALAND
- MAURITIUS
- NEW HEBRIDES *Condominium with France*
- FIJI
- TONGA
- WALVIS BAY
- SOUTH RHODESIA
- COMMONWEALTH OF AUSTRALIA
- *New Zealand trusteeship*
- SOUTHWEST AFRICA *South African trusteeship*
- BECHUANALAND
- SWAZILAND BASUTOLAND
- UNION OF SOUTH AFRICA
- NORFOLK I.
- IS.
- PITCAIRN I.
- TRISTAN DA CUNHA
- GOUGH I.
- NEW ZEALAND
- FALKLAND IS.
- SOUTH GEORGIA

GEORGE VI 1936–52

- British-held, 1936
- Dominion in 1936, independent member of the Commonwealth by 1952
- Administered by a British Empire power (under League of Nations mandate, 1936 or UN trusteeship, 1945
- Independent by 1952, with details
- Under British administration following WWII, with date of termination where applicable
- ——— Frontiers, 1952

Demands for independence, above all in India, proved irresistible. Its loss in 1947 presaged the almost total ending of the British empire (map above). By the end of George VI's reign, Britain's claim to great power status were looking increasingly threadbare, a central fact that well-meaning attempts to promote the Commonwealth in place of the empire could not disguise

The bombing of Buckingham Palace in September 1940 prompted Queen Elizabeth's famous comment: "At last we can look the East End in the face." The king and queen's determination to share their subjects' suffering was almost their most admirable quality. They made hundreds of visits to bombed cities, their sympathy with the suffering of the victims entirely genuine. Here (left), the king and queen inspect the bomb damage at Buckingham Palace.

firm stance, almost certainly instigated by Queen Elizabeth. But as an exercise in damage limitation it was a success. Normal royal business had been restored.

The first years of the king's reign were overshadowed by the threat of war, which George VI was desperate to avoid. It is clear that he was naive – suggesting he send telegrams to Hitler and Mussolini; inviting Neville Chamberlain onto the balcony of Buckingham Palace after the Munich Agreement , but it is even more clear that when war came he did more than just his bit. Uncharismatic he may have been, but the king's determination to stick out the war alongside his subjects, not least his refusal to leave London even at the height of the Blitz, firmly endeared him to the country. At the end of the war, it was wholly appropriate that Buckingham Palace became the focus of wild national rejoicing, a delirious crowd repeatedly calling the king and queen back onto the balcony.

The remaining years of his reign, a successful visit to South Africa in 1947 aside, were darkened by continuing austerity, the break-up of empire, above all Indian independence in 1947, and the king's ill-health. Queen Elizabeth would maintain that the king's death in 1952 at only 56 had been brought on by the strain of kingship. She may have been right. But for George VI there was the consolation of having done his duty.

1938	1939	1940	1945	1947	1948	1951
Royal visit to France cements Anglo-French relations (June); Munich Agreement (Sept.)	*Royal visit to Canada and America cements Anglo-America relations (May–June). German invasion of Poland (Sept.): the Second World War*	*National Government under Winston Churchill (May). Buckingham Palace bombed (Sept.). George Cross and George Medal for civilian gallantry introduced*	*Axis defeat: end of the Second World War. Labour government elected: introduces nationalization and welfare state*	*Indian and Pakistani independence. Royal Family visit South Africa. Marriage of Princess Elizabeth to Duke of Edinburgh*	*Illness forces cancellation of royal visit to New Zealand*	*Conservatives returned under Winston Churchill. King's left lung removed*

QUEEN ELIZABETH II

ELIZABETH II FROM 1952

IN FEBRUARY 2002, ELIZABETH II BECAME ONLY THE FIFTH BRITISH MONARCH TO REIGN FOR OVER 50 YEARS. IF HER REIGN HAS GENERATED CONTROVERSY, IT IS THE INSTITUTION OF MONARCHY ITSELF OR OTHER MEMBERS OF HER FAMILY THAT HAVE COME UNDER ATTACK: THE QUEEN HERSELF, THROUGH HER OBVIOUS CONSCIENTIOUSNESS, HAS SCARCELY PUT A FOOT WRONG.

BORN: April 21 1926
ACCEDED: February 6 1952; crowned June 2 1953, Westminster Abbey

Queen of the United Kingdom of Great Britain and Northern Ireland and of Her Other Realms and Territories and Head of the Commonwealth

The coronation of Elizabeth II in 1953 was widely seen as the moment of Britain's final emergence from the deprivation of the Second World War. The belief in the country's imminent regeneration was palpable. Simultaneously forward-looking yet rooted in tradition, Elizabeth, here (above) photographed in her coronation robes by Cecil Beaton in 1953, was cast as the symbol of a reborn Britain.

QUEEN ELIZABETH CAME TO THE THRONE amid a welter of largely spurious talk about a "new Elizabethan age". With wartime austerity finally behind it, the country, under its young, attractive and obviously capable new queen, was widely expected to embark on a period of confident national pride fully the equal of that under Elizabeth I. In the event, almost the precise opposite happened. Thirty years of seemingly irreversible relative economic and military decline followed. At the same time, in little more than ten years from the mid-1950s, Britain divested itself of what, at Elizabeth's accession, had still been a substantial global empire. Symbolically, in 1958 "Empire Day" was renamed "Commonwealth Day". The former colonies did, it is true, nearly all become members of the British Commonwealth of Nations, with the queen as its head. Almost as rapidly, however, it became clear that the Commonwealth, in the words of a noted historian, was little more than "a marginalized talking-shop with very little political clout".

Over the same period, though its institutions survived largely intact, the country's values were revolutionized. Britain in 1950 was recognizably the same deferent country it had been in 1900; by 1977, the queen's Silver Jubilee, it had become an aggressive, consumer-driven society in which popular culture had emerged as a major force.

The queen can hardly be blamed for being slow to appreciate the significance of the changes taking place around her. Not many others were properly

In 1945, much against her father's wishes, Princess Elizabeth conspicuously supplemented her patriotic duty by joining the Auxiliary Transport Service, the ATS (right). Her service may have lasted only a month, but as a demonstration of the young princess's determination to share her people's burden it was a notable public relations success.

aware of them either. When Lord Altrincham criticized her in 1957 for being out of touch, he aroused a storm of public controversy. But there is no question but that he was right – or that his attitude has since come to be widely shared. Yet finding ways to make the monarchy less remote without sacrificing its essential dignity has proved difficult. In part, and in considerable contrast to her mother, the queen has never had the kind of personality that naturally lends itself to easy public informality. Yet at the same time, it is undeniable that for many people it is precisely the queen's obvious and impeccable formality that is her strongest asset.

Her discharge of her constitutional duties has been flawless. It is a remarkable tribute to her sense of duty that even after 50 years on the throne, and despite inevitable press speculation, she has never once let slip her views on any matter of public policy. However widely it may be assumed that her natural political instincts are to the Right, her conduct towards the four Labour administrations that her reign has seen has been one of complete constitutional propriety, precisely as it has been towards Conservative

I declare before you all that my whole life, whether it be long or short, shall be devoted to your service and the service of our great Imperial family to which we all belong

21st birthday speech by Princess Elizabeth, April 1947

CANADA
UNITED KINGDOM
BERLIN
British sector under Four Power adminstration, 1990
British sector under Four Power adminstration, 1955
VIENNA
British occupation zone of Austria, 1955
Former Trucial Oman, 1971
De facto dependent status ceased, 1971
TURKS AND CAICOS IS.
BERMUDA
BAHAMAS *1973*
BRITISH VIRGIN IS.
JAMAICA *1962*
CAYMAN IS.
ANGUILLA
ANTIGUA-BARBUDA *1981*
DOMINICA *1978*
BARBADOS *1966*
ST. VINCENT *1979*
BELIZE
Former British Honduras, 1981
ST. CHRISTOPHER-NEVIS *1983*
MONTSERRAT
ST. LUCIA *1979*
GRENADA *1974*
TRINIDAD AND TOBAGO *1962*
GUYANA
Former British Guiana, 1966
GIBRALTAR
MALTA *1964*
CYPRUS *1960*
KUWAIT *1961*
BAHRAIN *1971*
QATAR *1971*
UNITED ARAB EMIRATES
Former Gold Coast and British Togo, 1957
GAMBIA *1965*
NIGERIA *1960*
SIERRA LEONE *1961*
ERITREA *1952*
SUDAN *1956*
SOUTH YEMEN
Former Aden, 1967
SOMALIA
Former British Somaliland united with Italian Somalia to form Somalia, 1960
HONG KONG *to China, 1997*
Former Ellice Is., 1978
Former British North Borneo and Sarawak, 1963
Former Gilbert Is., 1979
BRUNEI *1984*
MALDIVES *1965*
MALAYSIA
NAURU *1968 (Aus.)*
KIRIBATI
UGANDA *1962*
KENYA *1963*
TANGANYIKA *1961*
ZANZIBAR *1963*
SEYCHELLES *1976*
BRITISH INDIAN OCEAN TERRITORY
SINGAPORE
Part of Malaysia, 1963-5, 1965
'Malaya', 1957; to Malaysia, 1963
TUVALU
ASCENSION
ST. HELENA
Northern part of former British Cameroons to Nigeria, Southern part to Cameroun, 1961
BOTSWANA
NAMIBIA
ZAMBIA
MALAWI
ZIMB.
SWAZ. *1968*
MAURITIUS *1968*
Former Nyasaland, 1964
PAPUA-NEW GUINEA *1975 (Australia)*
SOLOMON IS. *1978*
VANUATU *1980*
FIJI *1970*
WESTERN SAMOA
AUSTRALIA
TONGA *1970*
PITCAIRN I.
LESOTHO
SOUTH AFRICA
TRISTAN DA CUNHA
GOUGH I.
(Former South-West Africa, administered by South Africa, 1990)
Former Basutoland, 1966
Former Bechuanaland, 1966
Former Southern Rhodesia, unilaterally as Rhodesia, 1965; by agreement, based on majority rule, 1980
Former Northern Rhodesia, 1964
NEW ZEALAND
1962 (New Zealand)
FALKLAND IS.
SOUTH GEORGIA

DECOLONIZATION UNDER ELIZABETH II

- *Under British administration following World War II, with date of termination*
- *Gained independence during the 1950s, with details*
- *Gained independence during the 1960s, with details*
- *Gained independence during the 1970s, with details*
- *Gained independence during the 1980s and '90s, with details*
- *Gained independence from former dominions, with details*
- *British claim for area abandoned to the benefit of Saudi Arabia*
- *British-held territory, 2004*

The dismantling of the British empire was extraordinarily swift and, on the whole, orderly. By the late 1960s, Britain had given up all its African colonies as well as its remaining territories in Southeast Asia (map above). Independence for its remaining island territories, chiefly in the Caribbean, Indian Ocean and Pacific duly followed. The last Crown Colony to be surrendered, in 1997, was Hong Kong.

At only 13, Princess Elizabeth seems to have made up her mind to marry her third cousin, Prince Philip Mountbatten, the impoverished but gallant grandson of George I of Greece. Created Duke of Edinburgh on their wedding day in November 1947, he has proved to be a solid if occasionally unpredictable fixture in the royal family. His reputation for tactlessness pales besides his loyalty to his wife, the Queen. Here (left), the couple pose after announcing their engagement.

administrations. This in itself is a potent argument in favour of constitutional monarchy.

On those rare occasions when the queen has taken a more active part in popularizing her image, the results have been tepid at best. The 1969 BBC documentary, *Royal Family*, purportedly an intimate portrait of the queen and her family, was a very stilted affair. For the most part, therefore, it is other younger members of the family who have taken the lead in generating a new royal image. The results have been generally discouraging.

That said, the marriage of Prince Charles to Lady Diana Spencer in 1981 in a blaze of global publicity did for a time look as though it would genuinely rejuvenate the royal family's fading image. Prince Andrew's marriage to Sarah Ferguson in 1986 briefly sparked a further burst of monarchical fer-

vour. Yet the apparent stuffiness of the Queen would turn out to be very much more appealing than either the extravagance of some younger royals — nowhere more obvious than when they appeared in the 1987 television programme *It's a Royal Knockout* — or Princess Diana's elegant glamour.

Much more important, both marriages ended in divorce, the couples separating in 1992, the queen's *annus horribilis*, the same year in which part of Windsor Castle burned down and Princess Anne was divorced from her first husband, Captain Mark Phillips. It was the beginning of a truly traumatic period for the royal family, the whole played out against a background of intrusive and hypocritical press coverage of a kind that even ten years earlier would have been unimaginable. The separation of Charles and Diana in particular became distinctly

1956	1957	1960	1964	1969	1973
Suez Crisis confirms British imperial military impotence	*Ghana becomes first British African colony to be granted independence*	*Harold Macmillan confirms British decolonization with "Wind of Change" speech. Birth of Prince Andrew*	*Labour government elected under Harold Wilson. Birth of Prince Edward*	*"Royal Family" documentaries broadcast. Investiture of Prince Charles as Prince of Wales*	*Marriage of Princess Anne to Mark Phillips (divorced 1992)*

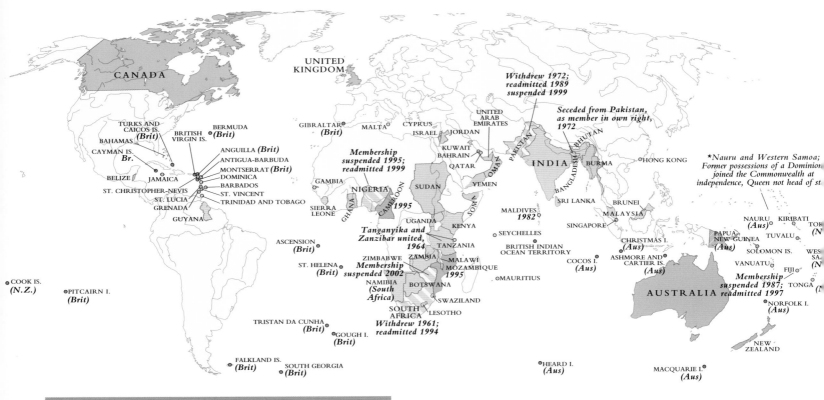

THE DEVELOPMENT OF THE COMMONWEALTH

Joined Commonwealth at independence, Queen head of state

Commonwealth members, Queen not head of state

Former possession of a Dominion, joined the Commonwealth at independence, Queen head of state

Former possession of a Dominion, joined the Commonwealth at independence, Queen not head of state

Joined the Commonwealth, though only a part of the country was a British possession, the Queen is not head of state, with date of joining

Joined the Commonwealth without past connection to British Empire, the Queen is not head of state, with date of joining

Former British possessions that refused to join the Commonwealth

Commonwealth membership suspended, with details

Possession of a Commonwealth member, with details

Her empire may have gone but there is no doubt about the Queen's fervent belief in the benevolence of the Commonwealth, pale substitute though it is for the Empire proper. In this 1995 photograph (below), taken at the bi-annual Commonwealth heads of government meeting, the Queen, Prince Philip by her side, is shown with the leaders of almost 50 Commonwealth countries.

The development of the Commonwealth was not always smooth (map above). Five countries have been suspended or have left, one of them, Pakistan, twice. A number, mostly in the Middle East, have also declined the opportunity to join the organization. Nonetheless, the Queen is recognized as head of the Commonwealth by all 53 member countries and is head of state of 16, Canada, Australia and New Zealand among them.

In the words of one of my more sympathetic correspondents, it has turned out to be my annus horribilis

Elizabeth II, November 1992

sordid, with both sides attempting to manipulate sympathetic press coverage. Diana proved to have a talent for this, successfully blackening the Windsors as cold-hearted, smug and self-absorbed. Charles meanwhile confessed on television to having had an affair with a married woman and Diana admitted to an affair with an army officer. However conscientiously the queen continued to perform her duties, the royal family was being dragged into the kind of disrepute unknown since the Regency.

It came to a head with the death of Princess Diana in Paris in August 1997. Fleeing a pack of pursuing paparazzi in the company of her Egyptian boyfriend, her car crashed in an underground tunnel. The press turned a genuine tragedy into a further attack on the royal family, whipping up a bizarre outpouring of national hysteria masquerading as grief. For the first time, even the queen began to attract direct criticism: that she had not immediately left Balmoral for London; that, when she did return, the royal standard at Buckingham Palace was not flown at half-mast.

In the circumstances, it was hardly surprising if *bien-pensant* views about the desirability of republicanism began to be aired more widely. The monarchy was attacked as reactionary, class ridden, anachronistic, and incompatible with a forward-looking, modernizing Britain. The decision by the Labour government not to replace the royal yacht,

1975	1977	1978	1979	1981	1982	1986
Constitutional crisis provoked when Governor General of Australia dismisses Labour government under Gough Whitlam	*Queen Elizabeth's Silver Jubilee*	*Princess Margaret divorced from Earl of Snowdon*	*Queen's cousin Lord Mountbatten assassinated by IRA*	*Marriage of Prince of Wales to Lady Diana Spencer (divorced 1996)*	*Falklands War*	*Marriage of Prince Andrew (Duke of York) to Sarah Ferguson (divorced 1996)*

Far from the damp squib it was widely feared it would be, the Queen's Golden Jubilee celebrations in the spring of 2002 were a triumphant reaffirmation of Britain's regard for their queen (right). *As the* Guardian *newspaper commented, "The Golden Jubilee may have given those of us who seek a radical change in the way Britain is governed food for thought." On the whole, it was something of an understatement.*

THE UNITED KINGDOM UNDER ELIZABETH II

- Main areas of immigrant settlement
- Worst incidents of Irish republican terrorism since 1969, Home rule suspended 1972, reintroduced 1999
- Returned to Wales, 1974
- England since 1974
- Rejected devolution in 1979 referenda
- Voted for devolution in 1997 referenda
- Rejected devolution in 1997 referenda
- Dependencies of the United Kingdom
- United Kingdom and dependencies, 2002

By far the most important constitutional development in the reign of Elizabeth II has been the move towards the break-up of the United Kingdom (map left). *In Northern Ireland, this has been spearheaded by a terror campaign aimed at the forcible union of the province with the Irish Republic. In Wales and Scotland, the former now with its own Assembly, the latter with its own Parliament, the process has been entirely legal. At the same time, the arrival of immigrants from former British possessions has helped create a multi-racial Britain*

Britannia, on the grounds of cost was typical of this new, sour mood. In 1999, a republican-inspired referendum to replace the queen as head of state in Australia failed by the narrowest of margins.

Yet the monarchy, the queen above all, retains a unique place in the affections of the nation. This was made clear with the death of the Queen Mother in March 2002, only eight weeks after the death of the queen's younger sister, Princess Margaret. It was underlined even more emphatically with the massive popular success of the queen's Golden Jubilee celebrations in May and June 2002. With upwards of a million people thronging central London, all of a sudden it was republicanism that looked out of step. The essential durability of the monarchy had never been more obvious.

1992	1997	1999	2002	2005	2012	2015
Separation of Prince and Princess of Wales and of Duke and Duchess of York. Fire at Windsor Castle. Queen agrees to pay income tax	Royal yacht decommissioned. Death of Princess Diana	Australian referendum votes to retain Queen as head of state	Deaths of Princess Margaret (Feb.) and Queen Mother (Mar.). Elizabeth II's Golden Jubilee celebrations	Marriage of Prince of Wales to Camilla Parker Bowles	Diamond Jubilee celebrations	Queen becomes the longest reigning British monarch

BIBLIOGRAPHY

GENERAL

Brewer's British Royalty, David Williamson, Cassell 1996
Britain's Royal Families: The Complete Genealogy, Alison Weir, Bodley Head 1989
The British Isles – A History of Four Nations, Hugh Kearney CUP 1989
Britons: Forging the Nation 1707–1837, Linda Colley, Yale UP 1992
Complete Guide to the Battlefields of Britain, David Smurthwaite, Webb & Bower, 1984
Conquest, Coexistence and Change: Wales 1063–1415, R.R. Davies, University of Wales Press, 1987
Conquest and Union: Fashioning a British State 1485–1725, ed. S.G. Ellis and S. Barber, Longman 1995
The Historical Atlas of Scotland, ed. P. MacNeill and R. Nicholson, St Andrews 1975
A History of Britain 3000 BC–AD 1603, Simon Schama, BBC 2000
A History of Britain 1603–1776, Simon Schama, BBC 2001
A History of the British Isles, Jeremy Black, Macmillan 1996
A History of Wales, John Davies, Allen Lane 1993
The Isles: A History, Norman Davies, Macmillan 1999
Kings and Queens of Britain, David Williamson, Webb & Bower 1991
Kings and Queens of England, ed. Antonia Fraser, Cassell 2000
The Kings and Queens of Scotland, Caroline Bingham, Weidenfeld and Nicolson 1976
The Mammoth Book of British Kings and Queens, Mike Ashley, Robinson 1998
Modern Ireland 1600–1972, R.F. Foster, Penguin 1988
Monarchs of Scotland, Stewart Ross, Lochar Publishing, 1990
The Monarchy and the Constitution, Vernon Bogdanor, OUP 1995
The Oxford Companion to British History, ed. John Cannon, OUP 1997
The Oxford Companion to Irish History, ed. S.J. Connolly, OUP 1998
The Oxford History of Britain, ed. Kenneth O. Morgan, OUP 1999
The Oxford Illustrated History of the British Monarchy, John Cannon and Ralph Griffiths, OUP 1998, p/b 2000
Oxford, The Kings and Queens of Britain, John Cannon and Anne Hargreaves, OUP 2001
Queens of Britain, Norah Lofts, Hodder & Stoughton, 1977
The Royal Encylopedia, ed. Ronald Allison and Sarah Riddell, Macmillian 1991
Royal Fortune: Tax, Money and the Monarchy, Philip Hall, Bloomsbury 1992
The Saxon and Norman Kings, Christopher Brooke, Batsford 1963
Scotland: The Making of the Kingdom, Archibald Duncan, Oliver and Boyd, 1975
Scotland: A New History, Michael Lynch, Pimlico 1991
Scottish Kings, Gordon Donaldson, Batsford 1967
Uniting the Kingdom? The Making of British History, eds. Alexander Grant and Keith J. Stringer, Routledge 1995

CHAPTER 1: MYTHS AND ORIGINS

The Anglo-Saxon Chronicle, translated and ed. Michael Swanton, Dent 1996
An Atlas of Anglo-Saxon England, David Hill, Basil Blackwell 1981
Anglo-Saxon England, Sir Frank Stenton, OUP 1971
The Anglo-Saxon Landscape: The Kingdom of the Hwicce, Della Hooke, Manchester UP 1985
Boudica, Graham Webster, Batsford 1993
The Celts, ed. Nora Chadwick, Pelican 1971
Celt and Saxon: The Struggle for Britain, Peter Beresford Ellis, Constable 1993
The Earliest English Kings, D.P. Kirby, Unwin Hyman 1991
Early Ireland, M.J. O'Kelly, CUP 1989
Ecclesiastical History of the British People, Bede, ed. D.H. Farmer, Penguin 1990
The English Conquest: Gildas and Britain in the 5th Century, Nicholas J. Higham, Manchester UP 1994
An English Empire: Bede and the Early Saxon Kingdoms, N.J. Higham, Manchester UP 1994
The Formation of England 550–1042, H.P.R. Finberg, Hart-Davis MacGibbon 1974
Gallic Wars, Julius Caesar, translated H.J. Edwards, Harvard UP 1986

Gildas: the Ruin of Britain and Other Documents, ed. Michael Winterbottom, Phillimore 1978
The History of the Kings of Britain, Geoffrey of Monmouth, translated Lewis Thorpe, Penguin 1976
Ireland Before the Vikings, Gearóid Mac Niocaill, Gill and Macmillan 1972
The Kingdom of Northumbria, 350–1100, Nicholas J. Higham, Alan Sutton 1993
King Arthur: Hero and Legend, Richard Barber, Boydell and Brewer 1994
King Arthur: King of Glamorgan and Gwent, A.T. Blackett and Alan Wilson, M.T. Byrd 1981
Kings and Kingship in Early Scotland, Majorie Anderson, Scottish Academic Press 1973
Kings and Queens of Early Britain, Geoffrey Ashe, Methuen 1982
Macbeth, High King of Scotland 1040–57, Peter Berresford Ellis, Frederick Muller 1980
Nennius: British History and the Welsh Annals, John Norris, Phillimore 1980
Northanhymbre Saga: The History of the Anglo-Saxon Kings of Northumbria, John Marsden, Kyle Cathie 1992
The Origins of Anglo-Saxon Kingdoms, ed. Steven Bassett, Leicester UP 1989
Picts, Gaels and Scots, Sally M. Foster, Batsford 1996
Sutton Hoo: Burial Ground of Kings?, Martin Carver, BM Press 1998

CHAPTER 2: PRE-CONQUEST ENGLAND

Alfred the Great: Asser's Life of King Alfred and Other Contemporary Sources, translated S. Keynes and M. Lapidge, Penguin 1983
Alfred the Great: War, Kingship and Culture in Anglo-Saxon England, Richard P. Abels, Longman 1998
The Anglo-Saxons, ed. James Campbell, Penguin 1991
Cnut: the Danes in England in the Early 11th Century, M.K. Lawson, Longman 1993
Edward the Confessor, Frank Barlow, Yale UP 1997
The English Nobility Under Edward the Confessor, Peter A. Clarke, OUP 1994
Harold: the Last Anglo-Saxon King, Ian W. Walker, Sutton 1997
Hastings, Peter P. Wright, Windrush Press and Interlink Publishing 1997
King Alfred the Great, Alfred P. Smyth, OUP 1996
Kings and Vikings, P.H. Sawyer, Methuen 1982
The Life and Times of Alfred the Great, Douglas Woodruff, Weidenfeld and Nicolson 1984
The Oxford Illustrated History of the Vikings, ed. Peter Sawyer, OUP 2000
The Penguin Historical Atlas of the Vikings, John Haywood, Penguin 1995
1066: The Year of the Three Battles, P.F. McLynn, Pimlico 1996
Wessex in the Early Middle Ages, Barbara Yorke, Cassell 1995

CHAPTER 3: ENGLAND: THE NORMANS

Anglo-Norman England 1066–1666, Majorie Chibnall, Blackwell 1986
Conquest and Colonisation: Normans in Britain 1066–1100, Brian Golding, Macmillan 1994
The Death of Anglo-Saxon England, N.J. Higham, Sutton 1998
The Empress Matilda: Queen Consort, Queen Mother and Lady of the English, Marjorie Chibnall, Blackwell 1993
England Under the Norman and Angevin Kings 1075–1225, Robert Bartlett, Clarendon Press 1982
Hereward, Victor Head, Alan Sutton 1995
The Killing of William Rufus, Duncan Grinnell-Milne, David and Charles 1968
Kings and Lords in Conquest England, R. Fleming, CUP 1994
The Norman Conquest: Its Setting and Impact, Dorothy Whitelock, *et al*, Eyre and Spottiswoode 1966
Robert Curthose, C.W. David, Harvard UP 1920
Stephen and Matilda: The Civil War of 1139–53, Jim Bradbury, Alan Sutton 1996
William the Conqueror, D.C. Douglas, Eyre and Spottiswoode 1964
William the Conqueror, David Bates, George Philip 1989
William the Conqueror, David C. Douglas, Yale UP 1999
William Rufus, Frank Barlow, Methuen 1983

CHAPTER 4: SCOTLAND: FROM DUNKELD TO BRUCE

The Anglo-Norman Era in Scottish History, G.W.S. Barrow, OUP 1980

An Antidote to the English: The Auld Alliance 1295–1560, Norman Macdougall, Tuckwell Press 2001
Independence and Nationhood: Scotland 1306–1469, A. Grant, Edinburgh University Press, 1991
The Kingdom of the Isles, R. Andrew McDonald, Tuckwell Press 1997
The Kingless Kingdom: The Scottish Guardianship of 1286–1306, N. Reid, *Scottish Historical Review* lxi 1982
Kingship and Unity: Scotland 1000–1306, G.W.S. Barrow, Edinburgh UP 1989
Medieval Scotland: The Making of an Identity, Bruce Webster, Macmillan 1997
Robert Bruce and the Community of the Realm, G.W.S. Barrow, Eyre and Spottiswoode 1965
Scotland: The Making of the Kingdom, A.A.M. Duncan, Edinburgh UP 1992
Under the Hammer: Edward I and Scotland 1286–1307, Fiona Watson, Tuckwell Press 1998
The Wars of the Bruces: Scotland, England and Ireland, Colm McNamee, Tuckwell Press 1996

CHAPTER 5: ENGLAND: THE ANGEVINS AND PLANTAGENETS

The Angevin Empire, John Gillingham, Holmes and Meier 1984
Angevin England 1154–1258, Richard Mortimer, Blackwell 1996
Angevin Kingship, John E. Jolliffe, A&C Black 1963
The Crowned Lions: the Early Plantagenet Kings, Caroline Bingham, David and Charles 1978
Edward I, Michael Prestwich, Yale UP 1997
Edward II, Caroline Bingham, Weidenfeld and Nicolson 1973
Eleanor of Aquitaine, Alison Weir, Cape 1999
Eleanor of Aquitaine and the Four Kings, A. Kelly, Harvard UP 1950
Eleanor of Aquitaine: Queen and Legend, D.D.R. Owen, Blackwell 1993
England in the Reign of Edward III, Scott L. Waugh, CUP 1991
Henry Plantagenet, Richard Barber, Boydell Press 1972
Henry II, W.L. Warren, Yale UP 1973
The Hollow Crown: A Life of Richard II, Harold F. Hutchison, John Day 1961
King Edward III, M. Packe, Routledge and Keegan Paul 1983
King John, Maurice Ashley, Weidenfeld and Nicolson, 1972
King John, Ralph V. Turner, Longman 1994
King John, W.L. Warren, Eyre Methuen 1998
The Reign of Edward III, W.M. Ormrod, Tempus Publishing 1999
The Reign of Henry III, D.A. Carpenter, Hambledon Press 1996
Richard I, John Gillingham Weidenfeld and Nicolson 1973
Richard II, Nigel Saul, Yale UP 1999
Richard II and the English Nobility, J.A. Tuck, Arnold 1973
The Three Edwards: Wars and State in England 1272–1377, Michael Prestwich, Routledge 1997

CHAPTER 6: ENGLAND: LANCASTER AND YORK

Edward IV, Charles Ross, Eyre Methuen 1974
Henry IV of England, J.L. Kirby, Constable 1970
Henry V, Peter Earle, Weidenfeld and Nicolson 1972
Henry V: The Practice of Kingship, ed. G. Harriss, OUP 1985
Henry V, Christopher Allmand, Yale UP 1993
Lancaster and York, Alison Weir, Cape 1995
The Princes in the Tower, Alison Weir, Bodley Head 1992
The Reign of Henry VI, R.A. Griffiths, Sutton 1998
The Revolt of Owain Glyn Dwr, R.R. Davies, OUP 1995
Richard III, Charles Ross, Methuen 1981
Richard III: A Medieval Kingship, ed. John Gillingham, St Martin's Press 1993
Richard III: A Study of Service, Rosemary Horrox, CUP 1991
This Son of York, Mary Clive, Macmillan 1973
The Wars of the Roses, Charles Ross, Thames and Hudson 1986
The Wars of the Roses, Desmond Seward, Constable 1995

CHAPTER 7: SCOTLAND: FROM BRUCE TO STUART

Court, Kirk and Community: Scotland 1470–1625, Jenny Wormald, Edinburgh UP 1991

David II, M. Penman, Tuckwell Press 2002
The Early Stewart Kings: Robert II and Robert II, S. Boardman, Tuckwell Press 1996
Edward III and the Scots, R. Nicholson, OUP 1965
James I, M. Brown, Tuckwell Press 2000
James II, C. McGladdery, Edinburgh UP 1990
James IV, Norman Macdougall, Tuckwell Press 1997
James V, King of Scots, Caroline Bingham, Collins 1971
James V: The Personal Rule 1528–42, J. Cameron, Tuckwell Press 1998
Mary, Queen of Scots, Antonia Fraser, Weidenfeld and Nicolson 1969
Medieval Scotland: Crown, Lordship and Community, eds. A. Grant and K.J. Stringer, Edinburgh 1993
The Rough Wooings: Mary, Queen of Scots 1542–51, M. Merriman, Tuckwell Press 2000
Scotland: James V to VII, G. Donaldson, Edinburgh UP 1965
Stewart Style 1513–42: Essays on the Court of James V, ed. J. Handley Williams, Tuckwell Press 1996

CHAPTER 8: ENGLAND AND WALES: THE TUDORS
Anne Boleyn, E. Ives, Blackwell 1986
Bloody Mary: A Life of Mary Tudor, Carroly Erickson, Robson Books, 1997
The Cult of Elizabeth: Elizabethan Portraiture and Pageantry, Roy Strong, Pimlico 1999
Edward VI, Jennifer Loach, Yale UP 1999
The Elizabethan Age: The England of Elizabeth, Roy Strong (2 vols.), Macmillan 1955
Elizabeth, David Starkey, Chatto and Windus 2000
Elizabeth I, Jasper Ridley, Constable 1987
Elizabeth I, Anne Somerset, Weidenfeld and Nicolson 1991
Elizabeth the Queen, Alison Weir, Cape 1998
Henry VII: The First Tudor King, Eric N. Simons, Muller 1968
Henry VIII, Jasper Ridley, Constable 1984
Henry VIII, J.J. Scarisbrick, Yale UP 1968
Images of Tudor Kingship, Sydney Anglo, Seaby 1992
Lady Jane Grey, Hester Chapman, Cape 1962
The Later Tudors, England 1547–1603, Pendry Williams, OUP 1995
The Life and Times of Elizabeth I, Neville Williams, Weidenfeld and Nicolson 1972
The Life and Times of Henry VIII, Robert Lacey, Weidenfeld and Nicolson 1972
Mary Tudor, Jasper Ridley, Weidenfeld and Nicolson 1973
The Reign of Henry VIII: Politics, Policy and Piety, Diarmaid MacCulloch, Macmillan Press 1995
The Royal Palaces in Tudor England: Architecture and Court Life 1460–1547, Simon Thurley, Yale UP 1993
The Six Wives of Henry VIII, Alison Weir, Bodley Head 1991
The Tudor Monarchy, John Guy, Arnold 1997

CHAPTER 9: ENGLAND, WALES, SCOTLAND AND IRELAND: THE STUARTS
Absolute Monarchy and the Stuart Constitution, Lenn Burgess, Yale UP 1996
The Army, James II and the Glorious Revolution, J. Childs, Manchester UP 1980
The Causes of the English Civil War, Nora Carlin, Blackwell 1999
Charles II, Christopher Falkus, Weidenfeld and Nicolson 1972
Charles II: King of England, Scotland and Ireland, R. Hutton, Clarendon Press 1989
The Civil Wars Experienced: Britain and Ireland 1638–61, Martyn Bennett, Routledge 2000
Country and Court, England 1658–1714, J.R. Jones, Arnold 1978
Cromwell: Our Chief of Men, Antonia Fraser, Weidenfeld and Nicolson 1973
Cromwell: An Honourable Enemy, Tom Reilly, Brandon 1999
Cromwell in Ireland, J.S. Wheeler, Palgrave 2000
The Fall of the British Monarchies 1637–42, Conrad Russell, Clarendon Press 1990
The Golden Age Restored: The Culture of the Court 1603–42, Graham Parry, Manchester UP 1981
Great Britain's Solomon: James VI and I in his Three Kingdoms, Maurice Lee, Unversity of Illinois Press 1990
The Interregnum: The Quest for Settlement 1646–60, G.E. Aylmer, Macmillan 1972
James I, C. Durston, Routledge 1993

James I by his Contemporaries, R. Ashton, Hutchinson 1969
James II: A Study in Kingship, John Miller, Methuen 1989
King Charles II, Antonia Fraser, Weidenfeld and Nicolson 1979
King or Covenant?, David Stevenson, Tuckwell Press 1996
King James VI and I, D.H. Willson, Cape 1963
The King's Head: Charles I, King and Martyr, Jane Roberts, Royal Collection 1999
The King's War, 1641–47, C.V. Wedgewood, Collins 1958
The Life and Times of Charles I, D.R. Watson, Weidenfeld and Nicolson 1972
The Life and Times of King James, Antonia Fraser, Weidenfeld and Nicolson 1973
The Mental World of the Jacobean Court, ed. Linda Levy Peck, CUP 1991
Monarchy and Revolution: The English State in the 1680s, J.R. Western, Blandford 1972
A Monarchy Transformed, Britain 1603–1714, Mark Kishlansky, Penguin 1996
Oliver Cromwell, Peter Gaunt, Blackwell 1996
The Personal Rule of Charles I, Kevin Sharpe, Yale UP 1992
Queen Anne, Edward Gregg, Ark 1980
The Right to be King: The Succession to the Crown of England 1603–1714, Howard Nenner, Macmillan 1995
The Reign of James VI and I, ed. A.G.R. Smith, Macmillan 1973
The Restoration, R. Hutton, OUP 1985
The Stuarts, J.P. Kenyon, Batsford 1958
The Stuart Age 1603–1714, Barry Coward, Longman 1994
The Trial of Charles I, C.V. Wedgewood, Collins 1964
William III, S. Baxter, London 1966
William III and the Defence of European Liberty, Stephen Baxter, Longman 1996
The World Turned Upside Down, Christopher Hill, Penguin 1978
Writings and Speeches of Oliver Cromwell, ed. W.C. Abbott, Clarendon 1988

CHAPTER 10: GREAT BRITAIN AND IRELAND: THE HANOVERIANS
Albert, Prince Consort, Robert Rhodes James, Hamish Hamilton 1983
Battle for Empire: The Very First World War 1756–63, Tom Pocock, Michael O'Mara 1998
Crucible of War: The Seven Years War and the Fate of Empire in British North America 1754–66, Fred Anderson, Knopf 2000
Edward VII, Christopher Hibbert, Allen Lane 1976
The 18th Century: The Oxford History of the British Empire, Vol. 2, ed. P.J. Marshall, OUP 1998
The English Constitution, Walter Bagehot, 1867
The First Four Georges, J.H. Plumb, Batsford 1956
George I, Elector and King, Ragnald Hatton, Thames and Hudson 1978
George IV, Prince of Wales, Christopher Hibbert, Longmans 1972
George IV, Regent and King, Christopher Hibbert, Longmans 1973
The Jacobite Risings in Britain, 1689–1746, B.P. Lenman, Eyre Methuen 1980
The Jacobites, F. McLynn, Routledge and Keegan Paul 1985
Jacobitism and the '45, ed. M. Lynch, Historical Association for Scotland 1995
The Letters of Queen Victoria, 9 vols, ed. Christopher Benson et al., John Murray 1907, 1928 and 1932
The Life and Times of Edward VII, Keith Middlemas, Weidenfeld and Nicolson 1972
The Life and Times of George III, John Clarke, Weidenfeld and Nicolson 1972
The Life and Times of George IV, Alan Palmer, Weidenfeld and Nicolson 1972
Memoirs of the Reign of George the Third, Horace Walpole, ed. G.F. Russell-Barker, 1894
Queen Victoria's Family, Dulcie Ashdown, Robert Hale 1975
Queen Victoria: a Personal History. Christopher Hibbert, HarperCollins 2000
Robert Walpole and the Nature of Politics in Early 18th-Century Britain, Jeremy Black, Macmillan 1990
Victoria and Albert, Joanna Richardson, Dent 1977

Victoria R.I., Elizabeth Longford, Weidenfeld and Nicolson 1964
Victoria, the Young Queen, Monica Charlot, Blackwell 1991

CHAPTER 11: GREAT BRITAIN: THE WINDSORS
Edward VIII, Frances Donaldson, Weidenfeld and Nicolson 1973
Edward VIII, Philip Zeigler, Collins 1990
Elizabeth, Sarah Bradford, Heinemann 1996
Elizabeth R., Elizabeth Longford, Weidenfeld and Nicolson 1983
George VI, Sarah Bradford, Fontana 1991
George VI, Patrick Howarth, Hutchinson 1987
King George V, Kenneth Rose Weidenfeld and Nicolson 1983
King George V: His Life and Reign, Harold Nicolson, Constable 1952
King George VI: His Life and Reign, Sir John Wheeler-Bennett, Macmillan 1958
A King's Story, HRH the Duke of Windsor, Cassell 1951
Kings, Queens and Courtiers: Intimate Portraits of the Royal House of Windsor from its Foundation to the Present Day, Kenneth Rose, Weidenfeld and Nicolson 1985
Majesty, Robert Lacey, Hutchinson 1977
The Prince of Wales: A Biography, Jonathan Dimbleby, Little, Brown 1994
The Queen, Kenneth Harris, Weidenfeld and Nicolson 1994
The Queen, Ben Pimlott, HarperCollins 1996

INDEX

M

PICTURE CREDITS